Dante's Other World

THE AUTHOR

Bernard Stambler has been teaching English to college students for 18 years. At present he is Associate Professor of Literature at the Juilliard School of Music in New York City.

He has been a Guggenheim Fellow, a historian with the War Department, and the librettist of *Pantaloon*, an opera in three acts which had its world premiere in May 1956. His articles, reviews, and translations have appeared in the major literary magazines.

DANTE'S

OTHER WORLD

THE 'PURGATORIO' AS GUIDE TO

THE 'DIVINE COMEDY'

BERNARD STAMBLER

NEW YORK UNIVERSITY PRESS

Washington Square · New York

1957

Library of Congress catalogue card number: 57-7917
Manufactured in the United States of America

TO A TEACHER, LANE COOPER,
AND A WIFE, ELIZABETH—
OF THEIR CLASSES
MY SINGULARS

Preface

What—apart from his being a 'classic'—impels one to read Dante today? There is a temptation to answer not that he is the greatest of poets but simply that whatever motives there may be for reading poetry are amply fulfilled in the *Divine Comedy*.

But the questioner persists: What can Dante mean to me? Dante himself would have approved the question; the *Comedy* shows a constant, almost nervous concern with the rights and the needs of his reader. We may try to answer this question today by considering one segment of modern readers of the poem and hoping that a discussion of them may extend to others.

T. S. Eliot's 1929 essay on Dante, disclaiming alike possession and depreciation of the 'scholarship' in the field, has introduced a host of readers and, by now, a generation of critics, to the *Divine Comedy*. The quality of this essay, like that of the Dante criticism by Eliot's master Pound, is of inspired enthusiasm leading into poetic dogma and followed by a string of poetic pearls. The isolation of pearls in the *Comedy* is not new; the magnitude and the episodic structure of the poem have exposed it to this kind of fragmentation almost from the beginning, whether the selection has been of philosophical, moral, and theological sentences or of emotional and dramatic episodes.

Two of Eliot's dicta call for attention; not only do they serve as his indirect justification for thus excerpting the poetic beauties of Dante but they have had an effect on critical theory even beyond the study of Dante. The statements are that 'genuine poetry can communicate before it is understood,' and that one who 'can read poetry as poetry' may or must 'suspend both belief and disbelief.' (Has any other single word created more fuzzy criticism than this intransitive 'communicate'?)

There has long been a general and deplorable rift widening, in this country and elsewhere, between the 'scholar' and the 'critic.' It is a rift that antedates Eliot or Pound, and yet both these men have assisted in it as it particularly affects Dante. Possibly the tradition of scholar-critic represented in this country by the line of Lowell-Longfellow-Norton-Grandgent would today satisfy neither scholarship nor criticism; but what when the rift is total, and the scholar finds himself unable to write for a general audience, while the critic no longer makes his half-disparaging and half-extenuating disavowals of scholarship?

A facile dismissal of Eliot's two statements might call them a delayed echo of 'art for art's sake' or refer them directly to his own poetic situation, to an unconscious wish for a less carping and reluctant audience—remember that this essay dates from just after the 'difficult' and 'philosophical' *Waste Land* and before the sequence of the progressively 'easier' plays. Even if this were the true etiology of Eliot's statements, we should still have to examine them for the difference they establish between Dante and the poets or other creative minds of our day.

The *Comedy,* like the *Waste Land,* is difficult to read and, in many spots or aspects, obscure. In the great artist of our day—Eliot, Joyce, Schönberg, Picasso—obscurity is a species of inadvertence: it is the resultant of his highly developed techniques and the expressive substance available to him. A 'truthful' expression of today's realities, as they appear to the eye or mind of poet, composer, or painter, is as likely as not to issue in distorted perspectives, in lacunae, in rebellious negations.

The difficulty and the obscurity of the *Comedy* are not of this kind. Dante did not have, to borrow Yeats' phrase, a quarrel with himself or with the world about him. There were, certainly, things disordered in his world—they provided one of his great motives for writing the *Comedy*—but he had no doubts about the order that needed only to be restored for the right happiness of man on earth. Further he believed, with Plato and with Aquinas, that this order lay in the nature of things and was available for the vision of any man; that the cause of the world's disorder lay in blurred or distorted vision born in and nourished by inept communications, by warped traditions.

Dante's obscurity or difficulty, then, comes from his need to reconstitute a tangled and overgrown path; it is an intended and, so to speak, a pedagogic difficulty. (I am of course not speaking here of such things as the trouble we are put to to identify the names and places that are Dante's exempla.) This difficulty in Dante is inseparable from the complex depth and width of his vision: he may even, he says, for some readers set a dangerous course. In canto 2 of the *Paradise* he warns those who have followed him thus far in the little ships of their minds that they might do well to turn back lest they go dangerously astray if they lose him in this new part of the journey. Yet this is only a challenge held out by a teacher to his followers. Many times in the course of the *Comedy* Dante speaks, in asides to the reader, of the veils that overlie the substance of his poem; but these veils exist only to be lifted, this substance only to be revealed.

What is this path, this vision, this substance? Is it the medieval Catholic dispensation that modern readers can encounter only by employing some portion of Eliot's 'suspension of belief and disbelief'? Perhaps; but I think that the formula needs some careful modification.

Dante is an orthodox medieval Catholic. (This statement is valid, though we shall see some significant qualifications of it in the section on Dante and Theology in Chapter 1.) Orthodox medieval Catholicism, especially of the Aquinian school towards which Dante leaned, comprises a set of beliefs to which few people today could totally subscribe themselves. Must we not, then, suspend belief in our own truths and disbelief in Dante's truths while reading the *Comedy?*

If Dante were a theologian or a philosopher, we should probably have to give assent to Eliot's thesis. But another obligation comes to the reader from the fact that Dante is a poet, and a poet of a certain kind, in whom there is no quarrel between faith and reason. How is this relevant? Such compatibility of faith and reason is of course far from unique in the Middle Ages: it might even be said that the great impulse of later medieval theology, in its encounters with philosophy (i.e., with the logic and the science of Aristotle), was to demonstrate that faith and reason do not teach contradictory things about the world of man and nature—reason only cannot rise to the elements of faith based on revelation.

Reason to a poet, however, is not an exercise in logic or a discursive examination of the physical world—it is a recalling, a blending, and an understanding of experience. Accompanying Dante through the three realms of the *Comedy* does not expose the reader to a cumulative process of conversion—Dante had no thought of a need to convert men to Catholicism—but it does lay before him the orderly substance of Dante's faith in a rational universe. Substance and order: the substance is the totality of human experience gathered by the poet from every field; the order is the structure of his poem. Faith is not susceptible to proof or test; but for Dante this substance and this order make the content of faith understandable —and usable toward the moral aim of his poem, now as then.

This then is the modification of Eliot's statement: a modern reader's relation to the *Comedy* is not to be disjoined from belief and disbelief, but it is better measured on a scale of understanding. It is an understanding of the poet's order that is provided for him in great measure—as it may well have been provided for the medieval reader—by the light that accumulates for him as he continues to read deeply in the poem. Eliot's reservation of belief and disbelief may again have been self-defensive rather than a real issue; few readers of Dante are, I believe, practically troubled by this problem.

It thus becomes all the more pertinent to ask, is this order of Dante's a world-order? Or, to ask the same question in other terms, is Dante a systematic thinker? Eliot, in his 1927 'Shakespeare and the Stoicism of Seneca,' attributes the solidity of Dante's thought to his luck in having been born when an Aquinas had settled the world-order, whereas Shakespeare's lesser luck provided for him only a Seneca and a Montaigne (and Eliot himself had to make do with F. H. Bradley).

Étienne Gilson knows more than Eliot of the differences between Dante and Aquinas, and perhaps (in *Dante the Philosopher*) even exaggerates them; his conclusion, though gently expressed, is also that Dante is not an original or systematic thinker.

We may, nevertheless, take a position midway between the self-conscious extremes of Eliot, poet-critic, and Gilson, philosopher-scholar, and suggest a different verdict. Starting from the lucky advantage of an intellectual and spiritual framework which had already made philosophy agreeable with theology, Dante had still the great task of animating this framework: parts of the skeletal structure had to be adjusted or transposed; and the genius of a poet, developed through an intense awareness of his own art and craft in a preparatory series of earlier works, was needed to give the flesh and life of human experience to these bones. I suggest, that is, that in his power to merge a totality of human feeling, thought, and action with the Aquinian world-order Dante's achievement in the *Comedy* is comparable in depth and originality to the dramatic cosmos of a Shakespeare or a Sophocles or, in another sense, to the achievement of Aquinas himself in blending Aristotelian physics and psychology with Christian faith.

We may now return to the earlier question: What can Dante mean to me, the modern reader of a medieval poem? The answer lies in the combined realms of the poetic and the pedagogic. (For Dante, by the time of the *Comedy*, these two had become one; but we may separate them with the ease used, no doubt, by many of his fourteenth-century readers.) For no modern reader will the pedagogic value be a direct accomplishment of the aim of the poem announced by Dante: 'to remove those living in this life from the state of misery and lead them to the state of felicity.' But how directly, we may wonder, was this aim accomplished for Dante's contemporary readers?

The poetic value is finally to be identified with the opportunity that Dante extends—along with the other master-poets—to go freely and fully into the depths of a widely ranging creative mind. Increasingly, since the Middle Ages, we have separated the psychological from the physical sciences. Social and depth psychologies, psychosomatic medicines—such modern attempts to bridge part of the gap between *psyche* and *physis* are partial echoes of what had been a great organic whole in the mind of Dante. Even when we today, in the 'modern situation,' remember that Socrates, in his search to know himself, went out to speak with other men, though never about himself, we may reach out beyond self-analysis but we rarely go farther than the area of analogies between 'our situation' and that of an Oedipus or a Hamlet—remote situations yet somehow prepared in advance for our analogies.

Dante offers, on the whole, few such easy analogies. And yet, in a sort of self-reversing paradox, he may be found closer to us than Sophocles or Shakespeare. Many of the fundamental questions about the 'situation' of Sophocles, or Shakespeare, or Eliot remain perennial puzzles to us, as they may have been to those writers themselves; such questions for Dante, through his unique inner clarity, are likely after a while to become self-answering in the happily circular fashion already mentioned—through the illumination provided for the reader by his own study of the poet.

In short, the *Comedy* is to be read as is any other poem, but more so. The great and the little, the cosmos and the word—these must both be perceived and, after a time, together. The reader must be constantly alert to the movement of the poem, the movement which might better be called the moment; for time and place, time within a given place in Hell, Purgatory, or Paradise, must be calculated to define the particular quality of event, the particular status or level of truth. Dante, like Plato in his concern for moral education, employs the movement of his poetic form for measured stepwise enlightenment, in the belief that, having learned to cast off one fallacy, a man is the readier to discard others, to see more accurately, to make better generalizations and judgments.

To start this great journey with Dante the reader needs two kinds of guide. One kind he needs recurrently, through many readings: notes, charts, and maps to identify the personal, ethical, historical, and geographical data used by Dante in the building of his poem. Any of a number of well-edited texts or translations will provide this kind of assistance. (It may be a fashion these days to disparage any need of this kind of information, but if we are going to rise superior to the isolated fact we should first know who or what Cacciaguida is so that we may know where and how to rise.)

There is a second kind of guide. He has frequently traveled with Dante, pleasuring as well as profiting. Wishing to share this profit and this pleasure, he locates those vantage points which provide the finest vistas and those tangled intersections where the path is obscured, and then tries to describe the easiest or most direct ways to and beyond these points. Then, when like Virgil he has guided the traveler as far as he himself is permitted to go, he vanishes while the traveler moves upward. This latter kind of guide, employing the resources of modern criticism and scholarship in Dante and in ancillary fields, is what I have tried to be in this book.

BERNARD STAMBLER

Demarest, N. J.
January 1957

Advices and Acknowledgments

The first chapter of this book discusses those aspects of medieval thought and art that need particular elaboration for an understanding of the *Divine Comedy*. It may be well to read through this chapter rapidly and return to it afterwards as needed.

The body of the book is a systematic and detailed analysis of the *Purgatory,* with brief excursions into areas of medieval history, society, and thought as these are needed to clarify a specific passage and the *Comedy* in general. The *Purgatory* was chosen because, of the three canticles, it best exhibits the movement and process of thought that the reader must come to comprehend in the entire poem: the *Inferno,* through the paradoxes of its structure, exhibits part of this process directly and another part in reverse; the *Paradise* enters this process at a height awkward for a beginning.

In the body of this book I have always had the text of the poem close to me; my reader had best do the same. I have addressed myself to the reader who will work mostly or entirely from an English translation. The Huse translation is sufficiently free and colloquial to provide few obstacles to rapid and easy reading; it is, however, almost entirely devoid of the needed explanatory matter and must be supplemented by another text or translation. Grandgent's edition of the text of the *Commedia* (the explanatory material is in English) will admirably fill this need; the Temple Classics edition or the recent translation by Dorothy Sayers, though the notes to both of these are more limited or more biased than the Grandgent, will also be satisfactory. As translations these latter have many virtues, but both are more ponderous reading than the Huse—the Temple through a certain Victorian stiffness, the Sayers through certain stretchings of poetic language imposed perhaps on any translator into an English *terza rima.*

The translations from the *Comedy* are mine, undertaken primarily with an intent to conserve the literal meaning; in so doing I have often found myself close to the Huse translation or to that in the Temple Classics. Other unattributed translations are also mine.

For various kinds of essential help and comfort I should like here to acknowledge my debt to the libraries of Cornell, Brown, Rhode Island State, and Columbia Universities; to Sally and Joseph Cunneen; to Shannock; to Joseph Caulfield; and to my wife Elizabeth.

For the use of copyright material I acknowledge my indebtedness to the Cambridge University Press, the Columbia University Press, the Harvard University Press, and the University of California Press, and to E. P. Dutton & Co.; to the Mediaeval Academy of America and the Editors of *Speculum* for permission to quote from Sir Maurice Bowra's 'Dante and Arnaut Daniel'; to the Oxford University Press for permission to quote from Thomas Gilby's *St. Thomas Aquinas: Philosophical Texts;* to Helmut Hatzfeld and the Editors of *Studies in Philology* for permission to quote from Professor Hatzfeld's 'Art of Dante's Purgatorio'; to Penguin Books for permission to quote from Dorothy Sayers' *Dante: The Divine Comedy. II. Purgatory;* to Sheed and Ward for permission to quote from *The Spirit of Medieval Philosophy* by Étienne Gilson; and to Random House for permission to quote from Étienne Gilson's *History of Christian Philosophy in the Middle Ages* and from the *Basic Writings of St. Thomas Aquinas* by Anton C. Pegis, copyright 1945 by Random House, Inc.

Contents

Dante's Other World

CHAPTER ONE

Environs of the *Commedia*

The Fortunes of the Commedia. The *Commedia* attained high repute within the lifetime of Dante. In 1373, fifty-two years after his death, the city of Florence established a chair for the study of the *Commedia,* the first lecturer being Boccaccio; after the ancient world this was the first such formalized study of a contemporary writer. Before the end of the century similar chairs were set up by Bologna, Pisa, Venice, Piacenza, and Milan. In most of these cities the lectures were delivered in the churches and on feast days, for the convenience of a large popular audience.

An anonymous commentary on the *Inferno* is believed to be of 1320, a year before Dante's death. Before the end of the century there were at least eight commentaries, including those by Dante's sons Jacopo and Pietro and the work known as the *Ottimo Commento,* the 'Best Commentary.' [1] *

Some of Dante's fourteenth-century readers, though Boccaccio does not speak of them with praise, accepted his experience in the *Commedia* as one of literally traversing all three realms of the afterworld and coming at last into the presence of the Trinity. Others saw the work not only as a great poem but also as a polemic tract in the fierce religious and political struggles within Italy. During the fourteenth and fifteenth centuries only Petrarch shared with Dante the laurel wreath for poets other than the great ancients. The two were not rivals: Petrarch's poetry ruled the gentler emotions and the realistic outlook on life; Dante spoke to that time from the higher realms of philosophy and revealed truth.

For the greatest part of the sixteenth, seventeenth, and eighteenth centuries the reputation of Dante remained in abeyance and the *Commedia* itself in neglect. Poets and readers in these centuries

* Notes start on page three hundred and eleven.

preferred the delicate ornateness of Petrarch to the austere power of Dante. Dante's theological preoccupations, and even his spiritual intensity, bored them. His plea for a supranational government ran against the current of the age. At most, during this period the *Commedia* was used as a mine of moral aphorisms—as the Middle Ages itself had mined Virgil, Terence, and Cicero for golden truisms about the life of man.

From the latter part of the eighteenth century on into our own day, the *Commedia* (the adjective 'Divina' was prefixed in the edition of 1555) has been broken into for striking episodes, emotional and spiritual attitudes, or political and theological positions that reflect the tastes or interests of critic or reader.[2] Thus for many readers a handful of passages—Paolo and Francesca, Ulysses, Ugolino—have represented the high, if not the only, spots of the *Commedia.* Little fairer than this to Dante are those who have gone through the *Inferno* with some pleasure and profit and have then bogged down in the *Purgatory;* the number of readers who have done this is nearly equalled by the number of critics and translators who have done the same.

But together these kinds of dismembering the poem, for aspects or for episodes, can lead us into a better way of reading the *Commedia.* Dante's plan for the pilgrim's journey—that he take so many steps in this direction and then stop to speak with this spirit or that—resulted in a structure of episodes that are nearly self-contained. Similarly, the larger division into three canticles produced the sharply distinct tones or climates of opinion of Hell, Purgatory, and Paradise. Understanding the episode, then, in terms of the moral and intellectual tone of its canticle (and of its position, early or late, in that canticle) will start us on the path to a full comprehension of the poem.

Only after the various special and partial ways of reading the *Commedia* are brought together can we have a view of Dante's artistic achievements. Dante's vision of man is one of the noblest ever achieved; it is based on a fervent insistence that men learn—and that men *can* learn—to provide for themselves a world that will enable each man to make the right choices for himself. Dante, as an orthodox Catholic, believes that God's grace is needed for such a full development of man's possibilities—but his vision includes a belief that this grace is extended to every man.[3]

The poetical, as well as the practical, rewards of reading the *Commedia* will come to us after we begin to deal with it entirely on its own terms—in the medieval world, with Dante's conception of the poetic function, and with the *Commedia's* presentation of the relations between one man and another.

This gives the reader a complex task of preparation. He must learn and come to use easily many new ways of comprehending things in the world about him: he had better treat, say, the Ptolemaic system as a new rather than as a discarded way of describing the physical universe—he will have no trouble discarding it whenever he wants to. In a certain sense, however, this complex task is not difficult: the facts and attitudes that Dante believed in and expressed methodically in his poem are easier to come by than are corresponding facts for Sophocles or corresponding attitudes for Shakespeare. This complexity and this clarity are alike founded on the medieval concept of God and His relation to the universe.

Dante's Universe. Dante lived and wrote at a time when the word 'universe' fulfilled its literal meaning with a degree of completeness, clarity, and credibility perhaps never equalled before or since: everything in man, in his governments, and beyond the earth was believed to turn on and be moved by a single central power. God was source and end of every thing and every event. Other ages have believed in God, but not with Dante's degree of explicitness; other ages (including our own) have been explicit about the origin and purpose of things, but not with Dante's simplicity and unity of explanation. Or, in a phrase from Dante's time, only then was the word 'God' simultaneously universal subject and universal predicate. (In the terminology of 'Dionysius the Areopagite,' as expounded by Eriugena, God is beyond all predicates conceivable by the human mind.)

If we can attempt to account for this unique quality of Dante's environment, it would have to be in terms of the six or seven centuries of the Church Fathers in which the highest and best intellectual and emotional efforts of the age were directed upon one question: the nature of God and the qualities of God's relation to man. This period was followed, in the two centuries before Dante, by an equally intense but wider concentration on the meaning of man's place within the physical world created by God. To use other terms: the 'pure' theology of the Church Fathers was now put into a frame agreeable with a body of philosophy derived from the keenest recorded minds of antiquity—Aristotle and somewhat of Plato—as reworked and expanded and put into varied contexts by the great medieval Jewish and Mohammedan philosophers—Maimonides, Algazel, Avicebron, Avicenna, Averroes. In Dante's time there was a nearly perfect balance between intensity of belief in God as the source of everything and extensity of the cosmic, philosophical implications of this belief.

The *Commedia* is difficult reading because we today, regardless of any considerations of religious faith, are not accustomed to practicing a belief like this which is source and touchstone for all questions, whether of ethics, politics, science, aesthetics, or cosmology. We are not accustomed to finding such a belief as the uncompromising basis of a great work of art. We are perhaps not even accustomed to reading long poems. These are, for most of us, considerable barriers to reading and enjoying the *Commedia*. Yet when we have passed beyond these barriers we shall find counterparts of Shakespeare's brilliance of language and detailed poignancy of character, Plato's agile and stimulating dialectic, Goethe's manipulation of cosmic forces and ideas, and even the tightness and emotional power of the greatest lyric poets.

Dante's poem is, as is every other great work of art, an ordering of reality. But 'reality' for Dante embraces everything: it does not have to be divided, as with other ages and writers, into natural, unnatural, and supernatural. Dante's 'reality' comprises everything that is, was, or (so far as he knows) will be. Thus we encounter in his poem, alongside men he fought against or called his friends, men from remotest antiquity, angels, griffons, and giants.[4]

Belief and assertion in poetry are always conditioned by the relevance of what the poet believes, or would like to believe he believes, to his world of experience. For most poets (Sophocles and Shakespeare are two of the noblest examples that might be used here) the will-to-believe conflicts with the wisdom-of-experience in more or less deep measure to produce tensions, ambiguities, doubts, despairs. The world does not order itself in accord with their sense of order—and the cure is usually not at hand.

For Dante too the world was out of joint—but the cure was available to men. It was a cure derived from the nature of the medieval universe and achieved in the *Commedia* through the confluence of experience, theology, art, and cosmology.

The Relation of Dante's Universe to Dante's Poem. The medieval geocentric system, commonly called the Ptolemaic system, was an invaluable concept for one of the great medieval theological paradoxes: the earth was the center of the rotating universe and thus quite expectably could be the scene of the unique drama of the creation of man; but it was also the part of the created universe which was farthest from God Himself (the unmoved mover) and thus quite expectably could foster the fall of man and require the birth of God's only begotten Son.[5]

The Ptolemaic picture of the universe begins closer to experience than does the so-called Copernican (the sun-centered system, as in Aristarchus' hypothesis, was an important part of ancient Greek cosmic theory *). Yet the Ptolemaic system too goes off immediately into unseeable and hypothetical structures: the moon, sun, and planets revolve about the earth—true enough; anyone can see that. But in their revolutions they are carried around embodied in great transparent concentric spheres (echoes of this belief are heard in the 'music of the spheres'); to explain the observable departures from perfect-circle orbits, the Ptolemaic system posited an elaborate set of epicycles, small-circle bulges centered in the circumferences of the large circles. Named outwards from the earth, these spheres

* Pythagoras, who probably introduced the heliocentric belief to Greek astronomy and philosophy, taught publicly that the earth was the center of the universe; to chosen disciples he gave the doctrine that the sun was at the center of the planetary universe and the earth only one of the planets.

are the Moon, Mercury, Venus, the Sun, Mars, Jupiter, Saturn, the Fixed Stars. Beyond the Stars is the sphere of the Primum Mobile, which is set in motion by the Empyrean (the abode of God Himself) and in turn sets all the other spheres revolving. All the spheres make a full revolution every twenty-four hours, with the speed of the Primum Mobile inconceivably greater than that of the inner planets such as Sun and Moon.

The earth itself was divided into two hemispheres: the hemisphere of land, which is the Mediterranean-centered known part of the world, and the unknown, untraveled hemisphere of water. Perhaps Dante's greatest single addition to the traditional system is his placing of Mount Purgatory in the center of the hemisphere of water. (Hell, traditionally, was a great pit or cave within the earth.) Mount Purgatory was diametrically opposite Jerusalem, the center of the known world. The ancient system of the four elements was completed by adding to this water and this earth a circumambient belt of air and, above that, a belt of fire. From the interactions of fire, air, water, and earth came the regular and irregular meteorological phenomena—thunder and lightning, windstorms, rain, etc.—which had such a powerful effect on the human economy but did not prevail above the base of Mount Purgatory.

Charles H. Grandgent (*Discourses on Dante,* pp. 72-3) describes some of the implications of this universe:

> Not without significance is the spherical shape of the earth, and the spherical shape of the entire physical universe, which has the earth as centre or core; for the sphere is the perfect solid figure, even as among plane figures the circle is perfect, having no irregularity and no beginning or end. For that reason the heavenly bodies move in circles or combinations of circles. Modern science has flattened the poles of the earth, has transformed the circular orbits of the planets into ellipses, has opened to bootless discussion the question of the shape of the universe. The medieval world may have been all wrong, but it had a meaning, which has vanished from the world of today.

Dante found most physical details of the Ptolemaic universe well defined in terms of geography, astronomy, and chronography; he also found that the theologians had worked out many of the spiritual implications of a universe so constructed. But much of the detail of this universe was, as we shall see, necessarily of Dante's invention for the purposes of the *Commedia*—detail perhaps implicit in current ideas but not worked out until required by the methodical process of Dante's journey.

Dante's universe finds itself utilized and fulfilled in the *Commedia* with a completeness perhaps not attained by any other poet. Here is an outline of the way Dante's poem employs his universe:

1. PHYSICALLY. The entire physical cosmos, as conceived in the Ptolemaic system (with important modifications by Dante), is methodically traversed by the pilgrim in his journey. The earth's hemisphere of land, though it does not directly appear except perhaps for the opening of the *Inferno,* is amply treated in mentions and memories—almost flashbacks—throughout the poem.

2. ETHICALLY. Every significant vice and virtue conceivable in his day is systematically treated, in an ethical tour parallel with the physical. Apart from the seven great categories treated in each canticle, shadings and combinations express various subtleties of ethical standards.

3. SPIRITUALLY. Perhaps, for our day, the terms 'emotionally' and 'psychologically' must be included here. Every degree of spiritual capability, every kind or shade of emotion, every psychological type or possibility—all these are encountered in the pilgrim's journey, either methodically in a progress parallel with the ethical, or dramatically in the interplay of the pilgrim and his guides with each other and with the spirits they meet. One of the most powerful recurrent effects of the *Commedia* is a spiritual or psychological counterpoint that comes from finding a variety of moods on the same ledge in Hell or the same terrace in Purgatory.

4. HISTORICALLY. Men, women, and events from all periods and places of history known to the medieval world find their places in the poem, as well as all kinds of government and all stations in society.

5. ARTISTICALLY. Not only in direct presentation do concepts of the various medieval arts appear but also in the indirect expressions

possible within Dante's kind of poetry: thus we have, beyond the 'music' of the verse itself, the word-painting or word-sculpture or word-gardening of scenes, a word-architecture of structures and sections, and a kind of word- (or image-) thematizing that falls somewhere between music and dance—all of this more consciously and specifically than with most other poets.

The Making of a Universal Poet. Today the term 'universal' often signifies only that a poet (or composer or painter) has used materials or techniques that still have validity for us. For Dante the term 'universal' is not only a definition of the physical and spiritual cosmos—it is also the term that defines his responsibility as a poet. (Even Virgil, whether as poet or as character in a poem, could accompany Dante for only part of the journey towards universality; few other poets have been interested in such a concept or have had the environment needed to attempt it.)

Dante's concept of the role of poet is discussed, more or less directly, in most of his minor works, but it is embodied in the *Commedia:* the poet, in his own medium and fashion, reproduces (or, perhaps, imitates) the workmanship of God. The poet, like God, must be able to make all things and must be able to bring all things to life, to make them operate, to make everything rational and related—that is, if he has chosen to try to be this certain kind of poet. What is in his mind must acquire external shape, life, and action. There are others who understand and create things, but only this kind of poet must understand and create everything and put this everything into living operation.

Creation is a measure of understanding; with each of his works Dante acquired an increased sense of the purposes and possibilities of creation. His consciously increasing purpose may be seen starting in his early poems as they were interpreted in the *Vita Nuova* and the *Convivio;* a parallel growth, in comparatively abstract and impersonal terms, may be seen in the *De Vulgari Eloquentia* and the *Monarchia.* He saw a greater kind of poetry ahead of him when he promised, in the closing lines of the *Vita Nuova,* to glorify Beatrice as woman had never before been glorified; perhaps he left the *Convivio* incomplete because after accomplishing only a small part of his plan for the work he found himself grown far beyond its needs and purposes. Dante's poetry, from slim beginnings in conventional lyric poetry, grew to undertake in the *Commedia* the whole duty of man as he conceived it for himself—to be a poet in the image of God the Creator.

The poet, however, differs from God in his materials. The poet creates, not from primal matter, nor from pre-existent concepts, nor from nothingness, but from the choices and arrangements he makes from that which exists.

The Poet in a World of Reason and Time. Dante's concern thus grew to be the whole range of human and poetic experience: in a sense, the *Commedia* is a single metaphor for the human capability. The explanation for this might seem to lie in the unique coherence and centricity of the medieval world—a unified world that Dante the poet simply needed to reflect as such. Yet it is doubtful that the Christian Middle Ages were really much more cohesive than other periods of history; increasingly as one becomes acquainted with Dante and his times the notion of Dante as mirror weakens and the notion of Dante as maker strengthens.

That the actions chosen by Dante for depiction in the *Commedia* equal all possible actions depends, then, not so much on the commonality or universality of medieval experience as it does on the medieval idea of the world as rational, an idea worked out by Dante to its farthest reaches as the basis for his poem: whatever is has meaning—*post hoc* is always in the deepest sense, and rightly understood, *propter hoc*. As the device for presenting and operating the universe as rational in his poem, Dante depends on the difference between human perception-in-time and divine spaceless-timeless being; an analogy on a lower level might be the relation between a movie film in transit before the light which gives it life for the audience, and that same film spread out and perceived simultaneously. (This relation between human experience-in-time and divine awareness-of-all reconciles, for example, human free will with God's foreknowledge of what man's choices will be.) [6]

The theologian, like the saint, is likely to be impatient with time: his admonitions, whether to himself or to others, to be patient and long-suffering are only his awareness of the unfortunate necessity of enduring a temporal barrier between oneself and God. The poet rather uses time as the basis, almost the essence, of every poem: the difference between what was at the opening of the poem and what has come to be at the close of the poem constitutes the form and the existence of that poem. Consider Dante (not the poet but the person in the poem) in the degraded uncertainty of the opening of the *Inferno;* then consider him in the exalted knowledge of the close of the *Paradiso.* In these considerations lies the entire *Commedia,* once we realize that the poet who wrote the second of these scenes had the opportunity to revise the first of them. This is a more complex point than it might seem to be: it means, among other things, that Dante is using the device of time deliberately and communicatively, as a necessary device for making his purposes known—as does God Himself. The simultaneity, the timelessness, of his concept (as Dante hints in the closing lines of his poem) employs time in (or as) the process of his poem just as God employs temporal existence as a means of informing mankind.[7]

Why does the movement of Dante's narrative not wander freely back and forth in time and place, as it might in the hands of an ancient poet or a modern novelist? Dante's consecutive journey demonstrates what freedom of choice of form may mean for the poet—free in the sense of being available for use as well as being untrammelled. His freedom to choose this consecutive form comes from the fact (or belief), almost uniquely available in his day, that time and space and causality are one and the same in origin. (Departures of a writer from simple chronology may be reasoned or whimsical: reasoned, if he believes that causality is nonlinear; whimsical, if for him causality is nonessential or nonexistent.) For a relatively simple example: as we travel through the *Inferno* with the poet we come to see that the motivation and environment of evil lies at the end of evil things, as an unholy parody of First and Final Cause.[8] Here, at the end of the *Inferno,* we learn that the chill blasts generated by the motions of Satan's wings (in themselves a parody of that motion which is life and comes from love of God) produce in direct proportion to distance the frozen impotence of evil we have been encountering in Caïna. Only where such a clear and unambiguous statement as this of the origins, qualities, and relations of good and evil is available, is such a form as that of Dante's poem possible for—or imposed upon—the poet. The movement in the *Inferno,* from the least to the greatest sin, is simultaneously a requirement of theology, of poetic form, and of Dante's mission of portraying the fullness of human capabilities.

Dante imitates in the Platonic rather than in the Aristotelian sense: his imitation involves not only specific detail but also something approaching specific, or unique, form. But we must not forget his debt to the theologians and poets who aided him in this very development of freedom of choice. The theologians are those who expounded the medieval Catholicism of a God prior to all purposes and the end of all endeavors. Formally Dante's debt is to those guides he so freely names: above all Virgil and then the Provençal poets and their Italian followers. To the woman-and-love-centered world of the poets of his day Dante added the idea, derived from the Roman poet, of the journey towards universal empire—a journey in which the selfish qualities of personality are progressively discarded while the poetic vision is clarified and enlarged. These two questions—of Dante's guides in theology and in poetry—are most easily discussed separately, but they are not separable problems: Dante's relations to orthodox belief are, for example, greatly affected by his relations not only to Virgil's paganism but to certain Gnostic elements in the poetry of the troubadours and to the Avicennism-Averroism of Guido Cavalcanti. For another sort of example, the teachings of the Neo-Platonists play an important role both in medieval theology and in the poetry of courtly love.

Dante and Theology. The development and the preoccupations of medieval scholasticism and theology; the content and the impact of the quarrel among nominalists, realists, and conceptualists; the subjects of universals, of essence and existence—such questions as these, though central to a study of medieval thought, I shall touch on in this section and in the body of the book only to the extent that they directly provide a context for Dante's thought in the *Commedia*. (Mellone's *Western Christian Thought in the Middle Ages* can serve as an introductory account of the persons and ideas involved in the development of medieval thought; it is enthusiastic while remaining impartial, a rare combination in its field.) We may, however, briefly sketch the growth of medieval Christian thought, a growth that falls into three stages:

1. The Period of the Founders of the Church. The exegetical, moral, and pastoral writings of the Church Fathers came into being during the first six or seven centuries of Christianity; of these the greatest of the Latin Fathers were Jerome, Augustine, Ambrose of Milan, and Gregory the Great. All later Christian theology is firmly tied to the Bible and to this corpus of dogmatic writings.

2. The Period of the Encyclopedists. This perhaps is a tendency rather than a period—a tendency already strong in Boethius and his younger contemporary Cassiodorus in the sixth century and still prominent in the works of Gratian, Peter Lombard, and Thomas Aquinas in the twelfth and thirteenth centuries. Yet there was an essential difference: the masses of facts, decisions, and ideas collected in the twelfth and thirteenth centuries were organized on a clearly practical basis into works called Decretals, Book of Sentences (i.e., judgments or opinions), and Summa, looking forward to serve as codes or works of reference for the legal and theological concerns of the great administrative organism the Church had become. The earlier collectors—from Cassiodorus to Isidore of Seville (died 636), perhaps the greatest of them—are Churchmen looking back nostalgically, almost desperately, to the comparative peace and safety of Christian life while it existed under the protection of the administrative machinery of the Roman Empire. Through the chaos of Europe during the sixth to the tenth centuries such men as Isidore kept alive not only the writings of the Church Fathers (and a great part of pagan literature as well) but the very idea and dream of life under an organized government.

Cassiodorus did much to give the monasteries their important function of being repositories of learning, both secular and theological. His work on secular learning, *Institutiones secularium litterarum* (which had a much wider influence than his *Institutiones divinarum litterarum*), provided a compendium of the 'liberal arts' to be studied for the help they would provide in understanding the Bible and the doctrines of the Church. These liberal arts, in a collection of extracts from earlier writers, Cassiodorus organized in the form that provided the curriculum of learning well into the Renaissance: Grammar, Dialectic, and Rhetoric comprising the Trivium; and Arithmetic, Geometry, Music, and Astronomy comprising the Quadrivium.

Isidore's *Etymologiae* (also called *Origines*) was an attempt to bring together all that could be recovered of ancient learning. For centuries this work remained the most important source of general information. Isidore's *Libri Tres Sententiarum* (Three Books of Sentences) provided a model for later similar collections of the doctrinal opinions of the Church Fathers.

3. The Return of Philosophy. The concepts and methods of Plato and Aristotle had been partially utilized in Christian thought by the earliest Church Fathers, especially from Origen to Augustine and Boethius, and through the recurrent importance of Neo-Platonist doctrines; but, particularly after the sixth century, systematic philosophy played a diminished role in the West. Speaking in necessarily broad terms, we may say that philosophy 'returned' to Western Europe in three stages. The first of these stages began with men like Hrabanus Maurus (died 847), who were not greatly different from the encyclopedists; but Hrabanus adds to his collecting and his classifying a great enthusiasm for the study of Plato. Plato—through the *Timaeus,* the only dialogue available in Latin translation, and through his continuators, the Neo-Platonists—was the center of the ninth-century use of philosophy, a use chiefly to clarify Church doctrine or to combat doubtful or unauthorized teachings. Eriugena (Johannes Scotus) was the most brilliant user of Neo-Platonic thought (chiefly derived from 'Dionysius the Areopagite') in an attempt to establish a philosophical basis for theology.

The stream of Platonism and Neo-Platonism, however, flowed steadily through the later Middle Ages, providing the basis for the doctrine of universals and then for the position of the realists in their quarrel with the nominalists. But always this influence of Plato, though deep, was quieter and less dramatic than the impact of Aristotle, an impact which must be seen under two stages—the first of the turmoil of discovery from the end of the eleventh century, and the second of assimilation, chiefly at the hands of Albertus Magnus and his follower Aquinas.

Some portion of Aristotle's thought—especially the logical treatises brought together under the title of *Organon*—had been part of the equipment of Christian theologians from the earliest centuries. No doubt a greater portion of the Aristotelian corpus could have been quietly assimilated into Christian thought during the eleventh century had it not been for two factors in the current situation, each complex in itself and further complicated by the interaction of the two: the fact that Aristotle's works now came into Western Europe by way of Arabic translations and commentaries; and the fact that the Church of Rome was acquiring a political role more clearly articulated than ever before—a role that, for example, made the Church the leader in the European Crusades against the Arabs. These so-to-speak historical accidents played a part in transforming into a struggle what might otherwise have been a quiet rapprochement between Christian theology and the ancillary aspects of ancient philosophy. (The moderating tendencies of such men as Adelard of Bath and John of Salisbury, though mostly fruitless, indicate the possibilities of such a quiet settlement even in the middle of the contentious twelfth century.)

Certain aspects of the situation of the twelfth century are essential to our understanding of Dante: the increasing significance of the Papacy as the center of a theocratic government; the incorporation of Aristotle into medieval thought, chiefly through the work of Aquinas; the great heresies of the twelfth and thirteenth centuries; and the central tenets of medieval orthodox belief. These subjects I shall discuss in turn.

Augustine, distinguishing between the City of Man and the City of God, found human society at best a poor substitute and preparation for God's. The world, however, forced itself increasingly on the attention of churchmen from the time of Charlemagne on. Gelasius I, in the doctrine of the two swords uttered in 494, had formulated a theory of parallelism of Pope and Emperor: each had his sphere and each was to remain in his sphere. The chaos into which Western Europe was thrown during the subsequent three centuries had made violation of this doctrine as frequent and as meaningless as any attempt to uphold it. The thoughtful work of Adrian I and Charlemagne in reconstituting the Holy Roman Empire had an indirect and undesired effect in intensifying the secular powers and ambitions of the Church and thus leading to the bitter papal-imperial struggles of the subsequent five hundred years; a more important effect, however, was the increasing responsibility the Church now felt towards the total life of man on earth—within her ken now came not only man's spiritual duties but all that had been embraced in the ancient philosophies and more.

It has been said that while early medieval thought lived on the mysteries of the ways of God to man, the twelfth century inaugurates the period when Christian reason tried to discover the ways of man to God. In the sense that the ways of man to God are concerned with all aspects of his earthly life, this change in thought, occurring with dramatic clarity in the twelfth century, had been slowly building up in the revival of learning that began to spread over Western Europe in the latter half of the eleventh century. Two great works were early products of this new temper of the Church: the *Decretum* or *Decretals* of Gratian and the *Liber Sententiarum* of Peter the Lombard, both issued around 1150. The *Decretals,* the greatest of canon law texts, reflected the Church's developed need for an expanded machinery of government and provided a basis for further expansion of ecclesiastical concerns. Peter Lombard's *Book of Sentences* was a compilation of texts from the Church Fathers, particularly Augustine. The *Book of Sentences* was to be the basic text in theology for four hundred years.

But the crest of this revival of learning was achieved with the gradual discovery of the whole body of Aristotle's works. Philip

Hughes, in *A Popular History of the Church,* p. 122, describes this discovery, which began about the middle of the twelfth century:

We can hardly realise the effect, on the two generations that now first saw it, of the gradual unfolding of all that the genius of Aristotle had accomplished. Here was an encyclopaedia of human knowledge, wide and detailed observation of life in all its forms, description, analysis, and coordination. The physical universe, man, man's life of thought, the nature of things, the causes of things, the first cause of all, man's end and the ideals of human conduct, all this was systematically set out in Aristotle. It seemed as complete a guide to life as Christianity claimed to be and it was purely rational. How did all this new knowledge square with the traditional faith? Were Catholics to ignore it? Could they ignore it? And if not, could they continue to be Catholics and to hold to it?

Aristotle alone would have been a difficult morsel for Christianity to digest but, particularly at the beginning of this period, he rarely came alone. What the early thirteenth-century theologian had to deal with was generally a Latin translation of an Arabic translation of a Syriac translation of the original.

The Arabs—Avicenna, Algazel, Averroes—and the Jews—Avicebron and Moses Maimonides—during the eleventh and twelfth centuries reclaimed much of Aristotle for the West by means of their translations and commentaries. But the shape in which they forwarded Aristotle into the Christian West was strongly mixed with Neo-Platonism and overlaid with the theological or mystical preoccupations of both Mohammedan and Jew.

The various bans on the study of Aristotle (by the University of Paris in 1210 and by Pope Gregory IX in 1230) indicate the early official reactions to this mass of confusing wisdom; the inefficacy of these bans demonstrates both the attractive power of this study and the decentralized quality of Church rule. Assimilation of Aristotle by scholars and churchmen continued through the thirteenth century until, in the work of Albert the Great, Bonaventure, and Aquinas, a Christian Aristotle evolved who has been at the core of Catholic philosophy ever since.

It is a commonplace to say that the accomplishment of Aquinas was to reconcile Aristotle with Christian doctrine; it is necessary to understand this statement accurately. First we may take Aquinas' distinction between philosophy and theology, to see why such reconciliation is necessary. The philosopher, acting as metaphysician, is able to attain to some knowledge of God through reflective reason; but adequate knowledge of God can be based only on revelation. This distinction is between different ways of arriving at truths rather than between different objects of enquiry; it is a distinction based on the work of Aquinas' teacher, Albert the Great, demonstrating that though reason and faith are distinct, reason is to be considered supreme in its own realm (though we must never forget, particularly for Aquinas and Dante, the mystical foundation of reason itself).

The tone of Aquinas' writings is almost never one of compromise—it is rather of clarification or even of correction. The very form in which he casts his greatest work, the *Summa Theologiae,* requires presentation of a proposition or question, consideration of existent or possible objections to it, firm statement of the truth about it which must be believed, and refutation of each objection. In this form Aristotle, contemporary and former theologians, even occasionally Augustine himself—any authority, in fact, excepting Holy Writ—may be presented as being in error on a given point. Gilson well describes this purpose of Aquinas (*History of Christian Philosophy in the Middle Ages*, pp. 364-5):

His intention was not to make theology still more learned than Albert the Great had already made it. It was first to eliminate from it all learning irrelevant to the exposition and intellection of the saving truth, then to integrate in theology the relevant learning even if, in order to do so, it was necessary to reform certain commonly held positions and to reinterpret certain philosophical principles. Insofar as Christian faith itself was concerned, Thomas Aquinas never intended to touch it. The magnificent elaboration of Christian dogma left by Augustine to his successors was likewise taken up by Thomas Aquinas and integrated by him in his new synthesis. On the contrary, always with a pious respect for his great predecessor, yet fearlessly, Thomas felt free to reinterpret and, wherever it was necessary, to replace with a truer philosophy the purely philosophical elements integrated by Augustine in his own theological synthesis. His reason for doing so was simple. Philosophy is not necessary for human salvation; it is not even necessary for theology to resort to philosophy, but, if it does, the philosophy it uses should be the true philosophy. When a theologian has good reasons to think that Augustine did not make use of the best possible philosophy, he should not hesitate to change it.

. . . the philosophical reformation achieved by Thomas Aquinas is a moment in the history of theology before being one in the history of metaphysics. Secondly, even on the level of pure philosophy, his doctrine cannot be understood as a further stage in the progressive discovery of Aristotle by the Latins. Thomism was not the upshot of a better understanding of Aristotle. It did not come out of Aristotelianism by way of evolution, but of revolution. Thomas uses the language of Aristotle everywhere to make the Philosopher say that there is only one God, the pure Act of Being, Creator of the world, infinite and omnipotent, a providence for all that which is, intimately present to every one of his creatures, especially to men, every one of whom is endowed with a personally immortal soul naturally able to survive the death of its body. The best way to make Aristotle say so many things he never said was not to show that, had he understood himself better than he did, he could have said them.

Struggles within the Church to define and eliminate heresies had been a large part of her history from the beginning; the twelfth and thirteenth centuries mark a new era in this too. In earlier centuries each triumph of orthodoxy had to start *de novo* in the next battle; now, in the great apparatus of the *Decretals,* the *Sentences* of Peter Lombard, and the specified triumphs of Christian Aristotle over Avicebron-Aristotle and Averroes-Aristotle, as well as in the clearer might of the Church, there was for the first time a mechanism of categorical and enforceable decisions about what was orthodox and what was not. Many of the twelfth- and thirteenth-century heresies, often anticlerical, were put down by the force as well as the logic of the Church. Such was the fate of the three which had the greatest growth: that of Peter of Bruys, who called for the abolition of all organized religion and denounced the Mass as a vain and theatrical show; that of Waldo, merchant of Lyons, whose Waldensians practiced and then preached total poverty; that of Provence, whose Albigensians also preached a simplist return to primitive Christianity and were exterminated in a crusade which destroyed the society in which the troubadours had flourished. The heresy of Joachim of Flora, though it never reached the magnitude of these, must be mentioned here for its connection with the *Commedia,* since we encounter Joachim in the *Paradiso* among the great doctors.

The essentials of orthodox belief were embodied in Church organization, manifested and related to daily life by means of the sacraments. What these essentials were in Dante's time may be briefly stated.

Man, in the person of Adam, by the exercise of his free will had disobeyed God and fallen. This original sin by Adam stained the origin of every human being thereafter; but God, in His love of man, extends His grace [9] to all men, as a bridge by which any man, by the exercise of his free will, may regain salvation. Of God's grace the greatest manifestation, and that which serves as token of His grace in all other respects, was the offering of Christ to life and to violent death—Christ Son of God and Son of Man. The Trinity, the Mystical Body, the Communion of Saints, the Pope as inheritor of Peter's mantle, the one Church—in these beliefs was centered the practice of medieval Catholicism.

The definition of man's soul is Platonic, coming by way of Plotinus to Augustine: man is a soul that uses a body. (This is not a contemning of the body: 'soul' includes a respect for natural things.) The concept of free will is variously stated; it is complicated by an overlapping, often a confusion, among *liberum arbitrium, libera voluntas,* and *libertas. Liberum arbitrium,* 'free choice,' is man's liberty to decide, by exercise of his reason, between what is good and what is evil. *Libera voluntas,* 'free will,' is his power to accede to or to turn away from a judgment based on reason. Both of these are man's power to do what he pleases without being under the sway of a higher power. *Libertas,* 'liberty,' must be defined on a somewhat different basis: it is man's power to preserve the rectitude of his will by choosing the one right thing made available to him by full exercise of his reason. (These are, roughly, the definitions of Albert the Great; other theologians may have varied one or another but the distinctions remain approximately as here given.)

What is Dante's relation to this development and condition of theology? One possible answer is to say that he was a faithful disciple of Aquinas: as the universal doctor beckons, so the poet marches. By and large this is true, but we shall encounter a number of great differences between Aquinas and Dante. Or we might answer that Dante was in the midst of the theological warfare of his times; but it is often difficult to pin him down to one side or another, or even to decide how his theological position is to be determined. Or we might answer with some scholars (including many churchmen), who, finding dubious or unorthodox elements in the *Commedia,* have gone to the other extreme and found Dante contaminated and dominated by one or more or half a dozen major heresies, particularly Pelagianism [10] or Averroism or Joachism.[11] Instead of trying to pin a label on Dante—whether it be Thomist or Averroist, or Joachist, or cryptomember of the Cathari or the Patarini or the esoteric Fedeli d'Amore—we might rather try to define Dante's theology in terms of particulars, at least insofar as they pertain to the *Purgatory.*

The central tenets of orthodoxy Dante uses as the inspiration and foundation of his poem: Trinity-in-Unity, the creation and fall of man, grace and sin and redemption, God's continued love of man as expressed in the Incarnation to recall and redeem man from his fall into sin, man's continued will to be redeemed, a single visible Church and the communion of saints—these and other beliefs and practices of the Church Dante uses in his poem with all the force and conviction at the command of a poet.[12]

More significant than these elements of dogma in establishing the areas of perfect agreement between Dante and the Church of his time is the fundamental idea of the nature of man. A concept of man as drawn towards the good—that is, towards God—by an innate drive of the will is implicit in most medieval theologians and explicit in, for instance, the writings of Thomas Aquinas. Not only man's will but also his intelligence and powers of reason drive him in the same direction. Evil, then, in impulse, decision, or act, is a species of blindness or shortsightedness or a looking in the wrong direction.[13]

An emotional or passionate impulse to do evil is a misuse of emotion and passion. If one deliberately chooses to do evil, he is at best belying or denying his own powers of reason. He is, ultimately, conditioning his own freedom of choice, or free will, by limiting the area of choice to the wrong only, instead of embracing the entire available area of wrong plus right choices.

With this view of man Dante is in perfect accord. The plan and form of the *Comedy* is based on it. Much of his powerful pictorial imagery is derived from this connection between sin and blindness, sin and a willful restriction of the vista or the light available. Thus, in the *Purgatory,* the proud execute and purge their sin by looking only at the ground, the envious by having their eyelids sewn together, the angry by being in a cloud of dense smoke.

Dante's greatest differences with the Church are on the practical fringe of theology, in the realm of the secular activities or ambitions of the papacy and of others of the higher clergy. Although the Church found theological sanction for this activity Dante saw in it the greatest single cause of the turmoil and misery of Italy: for not only was the Church thereby obstructing what he saw as the God-ordained secular function of the Empire but she was acting as the great model instead of acting as the great reproacher in the blind and ruinous race for material things. The *Purgatory* culminates in the great pageant in the Earthly Paradise, a pageant that presents with the cogency of revealed truth a plea for true division of the guidance of the world between Pope and Emperor.

The physical scheme of Dante's poem demanded that he be factual and precise in areas where the Church could remain suggestive and symbolic. An example of this lies in the definition of the location and function of Purgatory. While the Church and Dante agreed that the function of Purgatory was divided between Satisfaction (i.e., punishment for sin to 'make up' to God what had been denied Him by the sin) and Purification (as preparation for

Paradise), the two differed in respect to the relative weight of each. Aquinas, for example, stated (though perhaps with little enthusiasm or conviction) that Purgatory adjoined Hell in the bowels of the earth; the punishments in the two regions were of the same kind, were equally severe, and differed only in that there was a time limit set for the purgatorial punishments. For Dante not only is the punitive element in Purgatory far less important than the establishment of the virtue corrective of a particular sin, but the entire process takes place on a mountain reaching higher towards the heavens than any other earthly thing. (The location and function of the Earthly Paradise are also Dantean extensions of orthodoxy.)

In short, Dante's 'theology' is what theology must be for even a religious poet: part accepted teaching, part personal experience, and part poetical need. We must reject both extreme statements: 'Dante is an open or covert heretic' is no truer than 'Dante sums up and mirrors the orthodox thought and faith of the Middle Ages.' Details of Dante's creed will be brought forward in succeeding chapters of this work as they become relevant to his poetic mission; here let me describe only the fundamental connection between faith and poetics for Dante.

First, from Dr. Moore:

> Religion to Dante was not an escape from the miseries of life; it was, above all, a powerful principle by means of which reality could be modified, and the world transformed from violence to goodness.

For the theologian, particularly before Aquinas, earthly things were at best symbols of what the afterlife would provide: the symbol is here, the reality symbolized is there. 'Alles Vergängliche ist nur ein Gleichnis.'

But for Dante, the poet using symbols (and the other materials and tools of his craft) is akin to (or is a vital metaphor for) God creating creature. As the poet's symbols approach uniqueness (which is not newness but perfect suitability to context) so does his creativity come to resemble God's, and his creation come to life. It is probable that no one has come so close as Dante to fulfilling this concept of poet. The reason for this must again be sought in the relation he was able to employ between experienced reality and revealed supernatural: the relation is, in a word, that there is no division between them. Consider two otherwise comparable poets—Homer and Goethe.

For Homer, the relation between God and man is essentially whimsical; mostly divine whim but occasionally human whim (as Achilles' or Cassandra's) determines the course of events. For Goethe, the Christian God becomes either a supremely detached manipulator of man, as in the *Prolog im Himmel* (here outdoing even Him of the *Book of Job*), or, in most of the rest of the poem, a dark and supernal being (not easily to be distinguished from the Devil) to be tempted and attempted by human sentiment or incantation. For Dante, there is rather at every point definite means, middle, intercession between man and God.

Christ is of course similarly available as intercessor for every Christian poet, if He is function as well as fact. Christ as function (as Dante uses Him throughout the *Commedia* though almost never explicitly) is a true Jacob's ladder for the poet: methodically, step by step, with emotion and never without precise realness, with process and with demonstration, the pilgrim comes into the very presence of God.

In using his system of guides to bring him into the presence of God, rather than using Christ only and throughout, Dante was extending a practice of his age, which, conscious of a great gap between man and Christ, used wholly human Mary to intercede with her Son, and then used personal, regional, or occupational saints to intercede with Mary. Thus starting with Virgil, superior to the pilgrim-Dante in certain realms of experience although inferior in certain realms of awareness, the poet-Dante can move continuously upward, absorbing and clarifying mysteries as he progresses: cantation replaces incantation. His poetry presents not magic—which is always incomplete communication—but the movement of thought come alive. For all his outmoded scientific beliefs Dante confronts his readers with fewer awkward or come-now! moments than any other major poet; with Dante there need be little suspension either of belief or of disbelief—the *Commedia* presents, as it progresses, whatever of system-of-belief is needed to comprehend it. Everything is understandable in terms of its place in the poem; nothing in the poem can be properly understood except in these terms. For Dante the methodical progress possible with this relation between man and God becomes the structural backbone of the *Commedia.*

The history and the current, then, of medieval theology provided for Dante the concepts of a systematic, steadily reasoned body of thought—a reasonable universe which exhibited and proved the reasonableness of God. Such a methodical approach to God Dante might have encountered in a number of works but above all in the *Summa contra Gentiles* and the *Summa Theologiae* of Aquinas. The method of the pilgrim's movement in the *Commedia,* however, whether downward in the *Inferno* or upward in the other two canticles, is not always steady and unremittingly logical: at times he jumps or soars, or is carried while asleep and dreaming. The authority, so to speak, for this kind of progress is to be found in another kind of theologian, the mystic who soars or leaps to God by movements he cannot always trace or understand. One meets in these writers—Bernard of Clairvaux, Richard of St. Victor, and many others—an occasional sentence that seems to contain the essence of the *Commedia.* Such is that line formerly attributed to St. Francis of Assisi but now thought to be by his follower Jacopone da Todi—*'Ordina quest' Amore, O tu che m'ami'*—(Set Love in order, O thou that lovest me). At each such sentence one is tempted to exclaim, 'Here, and here only, are the words that inspired Dante to undertake his great task!'

Of course, what we are here encountering is the other great component of the medieval idea of God: not only is the universe reasonable and comprehensible because it and our minds are alike creations of God's, but there is also between Creator and created, depending on and issuing from the very act of creation, an unbreakable bond of love. Love—whether bond, spark, or attractive power—moves from Creator to created and from created to Creator in all possible variants of clarity and directness. Love perverted, mismeasured, or misdirected is sin, ignorance, error. Love from God too great or too glorious for man to comprehend requires intermediaries

—Christ, Mary, the saints, guides—and eyes shielded from the sun until strengthened by growth in understanding and capacity.

This concept of love, in its nearly infinite ramifications, is the possession and the light of medieval poets as well as theologians.

The Philosophy and Poetry of Love. The structure of Dante's concept of love becomes self-evident as we progress through the *Commedia;* to trace the origins of that concept with any degree of precision takes us through and out of literature, philosophy, and theology into such remote coigns as physiology and embryology (Dante himself takes us into Aristotelian and medieval ideas of these two sciences in canto 25 of the *Purgatory*). We shall follow only the path that leads directly into the *Commedia.*

Our starting place might be the *Symposium* and the *Phaedrus.* In these dialogues Plato, while drawing great distinctions between the carnal lower levels of love and the higher aesthetic and spiritual levels, posits a continuum between the lowest and the highest kinds of love: those whose love is fleshly, concerned with satisfaction and increase, may yet be guided to the summits of love for the ideally beautiful and good. The breadth and nobility of Plato's concept found few echoes in ancient poetry, whether Greek or Latin. Only in the Neo-Platonists (e.g., Plotinus in Book 5 of the *Third Ennead*) and in such works as Cicero's *De Amicitia* and Boethius' *Consolation of Philosophy* were significant portions of the Platonic idea developed (Dante tells us in *Convivio* 2.2 that he had read both Cicero and Boethius).

The Neo-Platonists—the term is a label rather than a description—introduced a new suprarational principle into Western thought in their union of mysticism and ethics, perhaps achieving the highest ethical mood of pagan antiquity. The Neo-Platonic doctrine, of the falling-away of the soul from the Supreme Source of Being and of the path by which the soul might regain union with the Supreme Source, enriched Christian doctrine and literature. Augustine, in Book 7 of the *Confessions,* tells how deeply the Neo-Platonist teachings had affected him.

Neo-Platonism came to medieval Europe by two streams, which

joined after the eleventh century—the Graeco-Roman and the Jewish-Arabian (the latter of these I discuss later).

From the time of Plotinus, the founder of the school in Rome in the third century, to Proclus, the great encyclopedist of the school in Athens in the fifth century, the Neo-Platonists provided schooling for many of the Church Fathers; Hilary of Poitiers and Saint Augustine had been Neo-Platonists before their conversion to Christianity. To Augustine, Plato and Plotinus were the philosophers who came closest to Christianity; Augustine's quotation of words and ideas from the Neo-Platonists started a long tradition of using Neo-Platonic terms to explain Christian doctrine. Macrobius and Boethius played a similar but somewhat lesser role in the Latin tradition of Neo-Platonism.

Equally important with Augustine in this tradition were the treatises of 'Dionysius the Areopagite.' 'Dionysius,' who professed to be Saint Paul's Athenian convert mentioned in *Acts* 17.34, was probably a Christian Platonist living in Constantinople toward the end of the fifth century. The teachings of 'Dionysius' were popularized and spread after the middle of the ninth century by John Scotus Eriugena.

An encyclopedic treatment of ancient ideas of love is found in the Latin poets of the Middle Ages. Some of these poets wrote also on the political order—often, as did Dante, in combination with love themes. At least one of these poets known to Dante, Alan of Lille, in the latter half of the twelfth century wrote, in *Anticlaudianus de Antirufino,* a poem of epic dimensions describing a moral and spiritual journey through the cosmos.[14]

The greatest medieval literary tradition of love developed among the French poets, especially in Provence from the early part of the twelfth century. The Provençal poets (many of them political as well as amatory poets) devised many of the elaborate forms and conventions of love poetry that survived in European verse even beyond the Renaissance.

The origins of the Provençal poetic theory of love (often called 'noble love' or 'courtly love') and of the troubadour poetry that embodied this theory are still uncertain. A great body of the poetry survives, as do one or two theoretical treatises, but these works have not provided definite answers about their sources or about their place in the society of eleventh- and twelfth-century France.

Manuel Lapa (cited by Denomy), in his *Liçoes de Literatura Portuguesa, Epoca Medieval,* pp. 24-66, groups the theories about the source of courtly love under five main headings: ballad, liturgical, classical Latin, medieval Latin, and Arabic. C. S. Lewis, in the *Allegory of Love,* says:

> It is certain that the efforts of scholars have so far failed to find an origin for the content of Provençal love poetry. Celtic, Byzantine, and even Arabic influence have been suspected; but it has not been made clear that these, if granted, could account for the results we see. A more promising theory attempts to trace the whole thing to Ovid; [15] but this view . . . finds itself faced with the fatal difficulty that the evidence points to a much stronger Ovidian influence in the north of France than in the south. Something can be extracted from a study of the social conditions in which the new poetry arose, but not so much as we might hope.
>
> . . . some part of the mystery remains inviolate . . .

If one were inclined to argue against the scholarly insistence that everything worth reading must have been at least influenced by a source, one might find in the circumstances of twelfth-century Provence a sufficiently unusual combination of data to make a new kind of poetry understandable: Provence, *the* Provincia of the Roman Empire; a Sargasso-Sea-like center of eddy currents during two millennia of Phoenician, Greek, Roman, Celtic, Germanic, and Arabic religion, commerce, and cross-conquests; involved in half a dozen extremes of economic ups and downs over the past few centuries—now poverty-stricken and now the funnel of eastern Mediterranean trade into Western Europe; with a climate and temper of living that even near our own day produces a Mistral or attracts a Van Gogh.

But it may be better to examine one or two of the possible sources. The elevation of the lady to a place above any man, the treatment of love as half mystical and half physically tormenting, the frequent casting of love into a political context—all this, in verse and music of elaborate beauty, constitutes troubadour poetry. The mysticism of love and the elevation of the lady find counterparts in the ideals of chivalry (the origins of which are almost equally obscure).[16] Similar ideas are to be found in the twelfth century in such disparate things as the *chansons de geste,* the letters of Héloise and Abelard, and the mystical poems of Adam of St. Victor. The theory of 'courtly love' * as the incentive and occasion for most troubadour poetry provided a likely source combining the chivalric tourney with the even stricter ceremoniousness of the law court. But the nineteenth-century hypothesis of the courts of love is now mostly discredited: few if any of the troubadour poems were written within such a context. (Even the phrase 'courtly love'—*amour courtois*—is fairly recent and may have been first used by Gaston Paris in 1883.)

The mysticism and courtliness of troubadour love, of chivalric ways, and possibly even of feudalism itself may owe a great deal to the Arabs in Spain. Here, from the time of their conquest in the latter part of the eighth century, the Arabs had imported and developed the culture of the eastern Mediterranean—gems of thought and art abruptly cut off from Catholic Europe in the spread of Islam. Yet there were periods in the history of Islamic Spain when the rulers not only allowed Jews and Catholics economic and scholarly freedom—especially in the great city of Toledo—but encouraged a certain amount of commerce with their neighbors in Toulouse and Provence. We have already spoken of the free translation of Aristotle and his Arabic commentators into Latin (and Spanish): there was equally free passage of Arabic poetry and Arabic music across the border into southern France. And, as we shall see, the philosophy and the poetry were not to be separated: a powerful Aristotelian and Averroistic thread comes into the troubadour poetry, is specifically stated by Andreas Capellanus in *The*

* This theory would have had the poems written as prosecution and defense of poet or lady on a given point of the love-code; the poems to be heard and adjudged in annual or semiannual courts of love.

Art of Love, and undergoes intense development among the Italian poets, particularly in Cavalcanti and probably in Dante.*

This interweaving of poetry and philosophy accounts for a certain seriousness and fullness in the mysticism of the Provençal poetry. Even more definitely it gives the poets a greater use of the techniques and vocabulary of introspection: the poet-lover had always examined his feelings with care but never, before Avicenna and Averroes (and, later, Bonaventure and Aquinas), had he had such a rich and precise psychological vocabulary for naming all the parts and transformations of those feelings. Dante was later to say, in defining the *dolce stil nuovo:* 'When Love inspires me I take note, and write down what he dictates within me.'

Love as conceived by the troubadours, called also *fin' amors* and *bon amors,* is love that is pure, good, and true—*fina, bona, veraia.* The virtues prized by the troubadour poets are *cortesia, proeza, mesura, pretz, valors, jovens*—terms technically elaborated far beyond their simple meanings of 'courtliness, prowess, measure, worth, valor, and youth.' 'Noble love,' later called *amor purus* by Andreas Capellanus, is a desire to contemplate the beauty of the beloved and to effect a union of the minds and hearts of the lovers. Yet it is love that is not without physical desire; rather it is sensual and carnal in approving and encouraging the sight and touch of the beloved's nudity—it comprised 'all,' says Denomy, 'that provokes and fans desire,' 'a love that yearned for and, at times, was rewarded by the solace of every delight of the beloved except the physical possession of her by intercourse' (this last act, according to Andreas, transforms pure love to mixed love).

'Noble love,' however, probably had little of its origin in *caritas,* Christian love, spiritual or physical; as little is it either moral or immoral by the values of medieval Christianity. Rather does 'noble love' seem to have had a development parallel with Christianity (with the Neo-Platonic and Arabic elements particularly signif-

* It might be mentioned here that the lighter, more playful and dallying aspects of the troubadour poetry find few echoes in Italy until the time of Petrarch: is it perhaps something Teutonic in the blood or tastes or environment of most of the Italian poets from Sordello and Lentino through Dante that makes them favor the serious and the psychological ingredients of the Provençal poetry?

icant) and to have entered a Christian world in the Middle Ages, a world in which it had, to begin with among the troubadours, a specious compatibility by way of its common vocabulary with medieval Christian philosophy and in which it attained various degrees of assimilation among the poets of Italy and of northern France, perhaps coming to a nearly perfect rapprochement with Christianity in the *dolce stil nuovo* and above all in the *Commedia*.

We must have some knowledge, then, of medieval terminology and theories in that branch of philosophy which might today be called psychology. Here, as in much of medieval philosophy, the modern reader may be troubled for a while by certain terms—words like 'sensitive,' 'animal,' 'virtue,' 'estimation,' 'common sense,' that he has always known but that now seem to be used in incomprehensible ways. Perhaps the best way to comprehend these terms, which through their very differences supply much insight into the medieval mind, is to plunge into a synopsis of the Aristotelian psychology as it relates to love and follow it with some of the Arabic modifications that particularly influenced medieval poets and philosophers. We must remember throughout that soul ('psyche,' as in 'psychology') is a term with meanings beyond as well as including the spiritual aspects of man: it may perhaps be paraphrased as 'the totality of the reactions of any living being.' Thus the vegetative soul is the reactive principle in plant life (as well as being the lowest level of the soul in animals and man), the animal or sensitive soul is the reactive principle of animals (as well as being the middle level of the human soul), while only man tops off these lower forms of the soul with the rational soul. Much of what follows may have a sound of abstracted unreality, yet a little meditation on the terms and relationships of this psychology will often transform it into a remarkably apt counterpart of contemporary psychological theories.

The virtues which are the natural powers of the soul are divided according to whether they pertain to the rational, the sensitive (animal), or the vegetative soul. The powers of the rational and sensitive souls are further divided depending on whether they are apprehensive or motive powers (no such distinction applies to the vegetative soul—its sole powers are those which nourish the body and make it grow and generate): if the apprehended form is apprehended as good (= desirable), the appetite is moved towards it. In the rational soul the apprehensive power (or virtue) is the intellect, the motive power (or virtue) is the will. The appetite, which pursues what seems good, is the motive power of the sensitive soul. The apprehensive powers of the sensitive soul are either interior or exterior: the interior powers are the fantasy, estimation, memory, and common sense; the exterior powers are the five bodily senses—sight, hearing, touch, taste, and smell.

Love comes from the sensitive appetite, according to Avicenna and Cavalcanti. (This may also be put in negative statements: Love is not a moral or intellectual virtue; it is not a motion of the rational appetite). Consequently love is located in the heart, which is the seat of the sensitive appetite.

Since, as Aristotle says, the sensitive appetite is not regulated by reason but rather runs away from it, love may at times actively oppose the reason. Love, when becoming an excessive passion, will impede the reason, prevent sound judgment, and find beauty and goodness in a lady who is known to be far from beauty or goodness. Love, at its extreme of intense passion, may impede the operation of the *virtus vitalis* (the 'life-force') and so produce death in the lover.

This explanation of love, chiefly based on the physical psychology of Aristotle, provides little room for the ennobling qualities of courtly love. For these ennobling, almost idealizing, possibilities of love we must follow the medieval poets and scholastics by turning to the Arabic philosophers.

Avicenna's *Treatise on Love* (translated by Emil L. Fachenheim in *Mediaeval Studies* VII, 208-28) is one of a number of Arabic treatises that combined Neo-Platonic values with Aristotelian categories. Love, in the Arabic systems of philosophy, stemmed from the very nature of God ('First Source'): 'With the First lies the form of love and It is loved *per se,* lovable *per se* even if no being loved It.' Love for the First leads the 'created intelligences' (the 'Second') to perfection. Love for the First also leads human beings to their attainable limits of perfection and brings them to a certain level of community with the immaterial created intelligences of the various heavens (approximately equal to angels).

Love, according to Avicenna, is of two kinds: natural love and spontaneous or voluntary love. A stone falling to its resting place exemplifies natural love, as does the incessant attraction between the nutritive faculty and food. Voluntary love sets up a hierarchy of values, even among animals. A donkey, led by natural love and its nutritive faculty, may be crunching barley; yet when he sees a wolf approaching he will flee, knowing that the impending harm far outweighs the benefits of eating.

Consequently, even on the animal level (and remember that love is a faculty of the sensitive or animal soul), love is associated with some amount of reason and free will. Further, the reason, for its own purposes, may make use of certain of the interior faculties, notably the imagination; the imagination thereby is increased in strength and energy by this leaning of the virtue of reason on it. Such an increase may have bad effects—when the imagination, thus puffed up, aspires to the functions of reason in areas of contemplation and judgment.

More important than this is the ennoblement of love that may result from this contact with reason. Reason may thus impose on the appetitive sexual faculty (the simplest form of love) something other than its essential aim of pleasure. This something is the preservation of the species, whereby the animal faculty of love is imitating the creative act of the First Source. In thus coming close to the First Source, the soul is brought into contact with ideas of unity and harmony higher even than those in nature. Hence come the qualities of love available to man only, although the faculty of love, being part of the animal soul, is shared with animals and even has appetitive counterparts among vegetative forms of life.

Such are the philosophical and mystical theories of Aristotle and his Arabian commentators and completers. Some of this scientific lore could have been available to the earliest troubadours: Avicenna, who came after two hundred and fifty years of Arabic mystical philosophy, died 1037 and William of Poitiers, the first of the known troubadours, lived from 1071 to 1127. The love poets of the generation before Dante unquestionably knew and used these scientific theories.

Without negating the importance of the chivalric and Arabic influences, certain scholars have tried to find the essence of troubadour poetry in a heretical religion—a religion compelled to speak covertly.* Denis de Rougemont, in *Love in the Western World,*[17] makes a good statement of this case. 'In this book,' says Father D'Arcy (*The Mind and Heart of Love,* p. 34), 'De Rougemont dares what Lewis [in the *Allegory of Love*] refrained from doing: he tries to explain why the love of the romantics is so different from . . . Christian love.' There are two loves which fight for man's soul, Eros and Agape. Agape is there for all to see in the teachings of Christianity; Eros, strange and wild, must conceal itself when in a Christian world and go disguised under symbols.

De Rougemont himself says (*op. cit.,* p. 74):

> One great historical event stands out in the Provençal twelfth century. Simultaneously with the rise of the poetry of *domnei* [the lady as lord] and in the same provinces and among the same classes there also arose a great heresy. Historians have declared that the Catharist religion was as powerful a menace to the Church as Arianism had been earlier.

The Catharists drew their heretical beliefs from Gnosticism: God is pure love, but the world was created by the power of evil. Man is a fallen angel imprisoned in matter. Christ merely put on the appearance of a man to show men the way back to the light: the Catharists therefore rejected the Incarnation and the Eucharist—the sacrament of the Last Supper in which the Incarnation is expressed. This condemnation of the flesh, a Gnostic and Manichean doctrine, when held as religious theory leads as often to extreme indulgence of the body as to mortification of it: both, says de Rougemont, are expressions of a death wish. And (p. 70):

* Most recent discussions of courtly love have agreed that it was a glorification of something that could not be freely and overtly expressed: whether this something being glorified was heresy or adultery or a *tertium quid* is still a question.

The cultivation of passionate love began in Europe as a reaction to Christianity (and in particular to its doctrine of marriage) by people whose spirit, whether naturally or by inheritance, was still pagan.

Father D'Arcy adequately deals with the historical and ethical likelihood of de Rougemont's thesis; he does not entirely dismiss it but finds it, as we may, an extreme statement of a real ingredient of troubadour poetry.

We may now consider the troubadour poets and poems.

The great patrons of the *art de trobar* (also named, in 1290 when it was in decline, the art of *gai saber* by the Académie of Toulouse) were the Counts of Provence and of Toulouse; Richard Coeur de Lion, Count of Poitou before he became King of England; the Lords of Montpelier, of Aragon, and of Castille. In Italy a number of small feudal lords favored the art and found many poets ready to compose either in Provençal or in one of the Italian dialects. In the flowering period of the *art de trobar,* the Italian cities or communes, fiercely proud of their democratic institutions, disdained this poetry that celebrated feudal and chivalric ways.

The troubadour might be a great lord, as was one of the earliest, William of Poitiers, Duke of Aquitaine; or he might be little better than a wandering minstrel—like Bernart of Ventadorn, son of a stoker at the castle of Ventadorn. The greatest of the troubadours were professional poets whose political and poetical fortunes rose and fell together—Giraut de Bornelh, Arnaut de Maruelh, Arnaut Daniel, Bertran de Born, and Bernart de Ventadorn.

They wrote *canzons, aubes, serenas, pastorelas*. When these were intended to be sung, they were called *chantar* or *chantaret;* when accompanied by dance, *balada* or *dansa*. *Tenzons* were debates or quarrels, sometimes between two poets on a subject assigned by a lord or lady. *Sirventes,* in praise or blame of some personage, were written by the poet in his capacity of *sirvent,* a word cognate with our 'servant' but meaning the knight or soldier who accompanied his lord when in search of adventure and glory. The *planh,* or plaint, was one of the most eloquent. In form all of these were elaborate in rhyme and meter.

We may look at the troubadours' verse in some stanzas from a *canso* (or *chanson*) by Bernart de Ventadorn (as translated by Mott):

It is no wonder if I sing
Better than all who know that art,
For love most strongly rules my heart;
Him I obey in everything.
Body and heart and mind and thought
And strength to him I consecrate;
He draws me with a force so great,
I look on all but love as naught.

Life without love—what is it worth?
The man whose heart is never fed
With love's sweet food, indeed is dead;
He's but a cumbrance on the earth.
Lord, may thy hatred never move
So fierce against me that I may
Survive a month, a single day
And have no heart to sing for love.

. . .

It is indeed my firm belief
That, when I see my lady near,
I tremble visibly with fear,
As in the wind a quivering leaf;
My weakness before Love is such,
A child would have more sense than I.
And one who thus must conquered lie
A lady ought to pity much.

. . .

Sweet is the wound that Love doth give;
He smites my heart, and smites again;
I die a hundred times with pain,
A hundred times with joy re-live.

So sweet those ills, they have surpassed
All other benefits combined;
And since the ills so good I find,
How good the recompense at last!

Arnaut Daniel appears on the terrace of the lustful in Purgatory, possibly because of the frequent libidinousness of his verse. Yet such a poem as this of his would explain Dante's high respect for him (translated by Bowra): *

I only, who endure excess of pain,
Know of a heart that too much love subdues.
My love for her, unshaken and complete,
Has never turned aside nor looked elsewhere
Since the first sight of her inflamed my mind.
When I am far from her, my speech upsprings;
When she is near, my rushing thought denies it.

I'm blind to others, deaf to their refrain;
For her alone I listen, look, and muse.
No flattering, false praises I repeat;
My heart wants her more than my words declare.
On fields, dales, plains and hills I shall not find
United in one being all such things.
Her worth's from God, who guides and glorifies it.

[*3 stanzas omitted*]

In dance and joust I'll not delight again,
For nothing can my heart with joy suffuse
Compared with her. No one in gossip prate
Shall noise abroad what secret wealth we share.
Is that too much? My faith, no:—she's too kind.
But if, my lady, this my utterance stings,
Out with the tongue and voice that would devise it!

* Sir Maurice Bowra, 'Dante and Arnaut Daniel,' *Speculum,* XXVII, 459-74.

I pray you may not think my song unkind,
But if my music your approval brings,
Arnaut cares not who praise or who despise it!

A theory of love which we shall soon examine is apparent in a poem by Hugh Brunet, also known as de Rhodez (this is my prose translation):

A sweet commotion moves my heart which turns me to amorous desire;
it promises me love but will bring me pain.
too well did Love, who is a courteous spirit,
know how to strike me with his lance:
Love, who lets himself be seen only by appearances (semblans),
and who gently darts from eye to eye,
and from eye to heart and thence to thought.

Much the same is a stanza by Folquet de Marseilles (also my prose translation):

I am so pleased with amorous thoughts,
which have come to take up their abode in my heart,
that no other thought can there find a place:
no other is sweet or pleasing to me.

Perhaps the fullest embodiment of noble love is to be found in the first part (that by Guillaume de Lorris) of the *Roman de la Rose.* More accessible, if less connected with a real tradition of poetry, is the theoretical treatise (c.1174-82) by Andreas Capellanus. The idealized, the elegant, and the practical aspects of the courtly tradition of love are all summarized in his three books *De Amore.* Andreas, who was chaplain to Marie de France, thus states the intent of his work:

And so we must first see what love may be, and whence it may be called love, and what may be the effect of love, and between whom love can exist; how love may be acquired, retained, augmented, diminished, terminated; what the qualities are of mutual love, and what the mutual obligations when one of the lovers has ceased to love.

Andreas defines love as 'a certain innate passion proceeding from the sight and immoderate thought of the beauty of the other sex.' Sight (*visio*) and thought (*cogitatio*) were the centers of this doctrine of love. *Cogitatio* is transferred into Italian either as *pensiero* ('thinking' or 'thought') or as *immaginazione* (the 'image-making faculty,' or 'imagination'): love is conceived not as a function of the intellect but as a function of what the Middle Ages called the *vis cogitativa.*[18] This cogitative power is one of the interior senses, akin to fantasy or imagination. The process of love according to Andreas' concept is then somewhat as follows: the lover, stimulated by an impression of his beloved entering through his power of sight, constructs an interior world of images or fantasies and then, with the use of his cogitative faculty, creates an objective view of his beloved that may be notably different from the external reality, places this object upon a pedestal, surrounds it with a luminous aureole, and adores it as a divinity. The question had been stated by Plotinus: Is love a god or a demon, or a passion of the mind—or all these together? In medieval terms the question became: Does the image evolved by the *vis cogitativa* of the lover bear a valid or a lying relation to the actuality of the beloved? [19]

Dante philosophically discusses the significance of sight (*visio*) and of *cogitatio* in the *Vita Nuova* and the *Convivio;* in the *Purgatory* the dream of the Siren, the dream of Leah and Rachel, the meeting with Matelda, and the unveiling of Beatrice not only ring a number of changes on this concept of love but provide a history and a resolution of the great paradox of idealized love. Dante's series of examples in the *Purgatory* indicates, stepwise, a growth from a concept of love based on false and harmful images through a higher notion embodied in the *dolce stil nuovo* (the poetic school of Dante as a lyric poet) to the crowning idea held only by the mature Dante—an idea of the absolute identity of the external object of love with the highest reaches of the image-making faculty of the lover: the highest soarings of masculine imag matched (or even surpassed) by the reality of God-end ininity.

To understand this development in the poetry of Dant go back to look at the earlier course of Italian love poet

The poetry of the Provençal troubadours [20] spread into Italy, northern France, Christian Spain, and even into Germany and England. The first stage in this diffusion was direct: as early as the middle of the twelfth century Provençal poets were singing their songs at various Italian courts; the first Italian imitators are using the Provençal language in 1180 (Dante finds it necessary to argue against this in his *De Vulgari Eloquentia*).

Sordello, the greatest of these, wrote lyric poems with the same theme that Guinizelli and the others were to pick up: love enters through the eyes when sight is pleased. Sordello's *Ensenhamen* is a didactic work on the manner and conduct of a courtier and lover.

By the second quarter of the thirteenth century, at the splendid court of Frederick II in Sicily, a notable school of poetry in the vernacular had developed, with Giacomino Pugliese, Iacopo Mostacci, Pier delle Vigne, and Giacomo da Lentino as its best-known figures—all of them military or legal personages first and poets second. These poets are sometimes called the Sicilian school; actually of the three greatest only Lentino was a Sicilian—Mostacci was a Tuscan and Pier delle Vigne a Neapolitan. Further, these men, at court and at their various duties, spent as much time out of Sicily as in it. What held them together was their duty to Frederick. The school, then, is better named the Frederician.

Three of these poets engaged in a debate on the subject of love: Mostacci, falconer to Frederick; Pier delle Vigne, ill-fated chancellor to Frederick (we meet him in canto 13 of the *Inferno*),[21] and Lentino, known as the Notary. The Notary, who may have invented the sonnet, is thought to have been the leader of the group; Mostacci opens the debate with a questioning poem: [22]

> *Erstwhile, as I was stirring up my wit,*
> *Expecting to divert myself withal,*

A doubt assailed me and refused to quit:
For help against it now on you I call.
All poets say that love has might, for it
Compels the stoutest hearts to yield and fall;
But this I am not willing to admit,
Since love was never seen *by great or small.*
Well do I know there is an amorous hour
Which seems to be the offspring of delight;
And people say this hour and love are one.
Now, as I cannot comprehend this power,
I summon you to judge the case aright:
Conclude the matter that is thus begun.

The first reply is by Pier delle Vigne:

Since love cannot be seen by mortal eyes,
And has no body, as a monarch ought,
Many there be so mad (who would be wise)
That they believe this sovereign love is naught.
But inasmuch as love so hidden lies
And lords it o'er the victims he has caught,
He merits more of worshipful surprise
Than if he showed himself to those who sought.
We see not how the magnet draws the steel,
But draw it does, and steel must needs obey,
Although the power is no corporeal thing.
And this example bids me humble kneel
Before the majesty of love, and pray
That men may yet believe in love, their king.

And then the Notary replies:

Love's a desire begotten in the heart
By sweet abundance of the joyous mood.
The eyes, far more than any other part,
First waken love; the heart then gives it food.

Sometimes, indeed, it happens that love's dart
Pricks one whose eyes his mistress ne'er have wooed;
But that fierce love that makes us sting and smart
Springs from the eyes: let this be understood!
Firstly the eyes must picture to the heart
The form of everything on which they rest,
Just as it is, regardless of its worth.
The heart, receiving what the eyes impart,
Desires the thing whose image suits it best:
And this is love, which dominates the earth.

A brief analysis of these sonnets will relate them to the technical terminology mentioned a moment ago.

Mostacci opens with his wish to break the circle of accustomed phrases and conventional imagery and to widen poetic horizons by means of philosophical reflections. He doubts the personification of love in the usual form of a knight, tyrant over the heart; but he agrees that there does seem to be an hour, a stage, in life in which the heart is readily moved by youth and beauty. Mostacci, that is, moves from a traditional literary conceit to an observed fact of human behavior and asks: Are the conceit and the fact the same?

The first reply is nearly a step backward. Pier delle Vigne reconstructs Love as a seigneurial lord, a king: his invisibility is but a greater indication of his power and of the worshipful respect in which he must be held. The only forward-moving part of Pier's reply is the analogy drawn from science, the analogy with a magnet: magnetic force is similarly invisible, but there can be no doubt of its existence or of its compulsive power.

Lentino's reply embraces, or implies, most of the body of current scientific doctrine relating to love. The heart, according to Aristotle, is not only the first organ to be formed in embryonic development but also the seat of all the virtues; the heart diffuses its exalted spirit by the subtlest vessels to all parts and limbs of the body and gives them thereby their power to function. The eyes, as we have already seen, first awaken love; but it is the heart (and no lesser organ or function) that gives it food. This species of nutriment (which had been fully discussed not only by Aristotle but by Galen and Avicenna as well) is none other than the *immoderata cogitatio* or *cogitatio plenaria* of Andreas Capellanus, described as essential to the life of the amorous passion. The objective imagination, initiated by the power of sight, presents images within us as though in full physical reality; then the interior work of the heart, namely the imagination, gives life to the most pleasing of these images and thus excites amorous desire. Without this element of fancy, this image-building element which is the fountain of love poetry, love would not be born.

Lentino's reply incorporates an answer to a special problem: Can love be aroused by an image that does not enter by means of sight? The Notary permits the possibility of such a supersensible stimulus to love (as in some of the Platonic or teleological conceits of the Provençal poets) but has a low opinion of the force or fierceness of a love so begun.

With the death of Frederick in 1250 and the disruption of his court the school came to an end, although Frederick's son, King Enzo of Sardinia, himself an accomplished poet, made a worthy attempt to continue its ideals after he was sent into exile in Bologna. The successor of the Frederician was the Tuscan school.

The Tuscans preferred to follow the Provençals directly, preferably in their latest and most recondite moods. For Guittone d'Arezzo, Chiaro Davanzati, and Bonagiunta Orbiciani of Lucca, poetry was primarily a metrical and rhetorical exercise, the more complex and abstruse the better.[23] Guido Guinizelli, in the great university town of Bologna, became the prime leader in a new school opposing these early Tuscans. Out of the Bolognese environment of academic industry, scholastic philosophy, and notable devotion to the Virgin Mary, Guinizelli developed a new theory of love in his canzone *Al cor gentil ripara sempre Amore,* a poem that Dante refers to again and again. Because of its importance this canzone merits quotation in full (as translated by Rossetti):

Within the gentle heart Love shelters him,
As birds within the green shade of the grove.

Before the gentle heart, in Nature's scheme,
Love was not, nor the gentle heart ere Love.
For with the sun, at once,
So sprang the light immediately; nor was
Its birth before the sun's.
And Love hath his effect in gentleness
Of very self; even as
Within the middle fire the heat's excess.

The fire of Love comes to the gentle heart
Like as its virtue to a precious stone;
To which no star its influence can impart
Till it is made a pure thing by the sun;
For when the sun hath smit
From out its essence that which there was vile,
The star endoweth it.
And so the heart created by God's breath
Pure, true, and clean from guile,
A woman, like a star, enamoureth.

The sun strikes full upon the mud all day;
It remains vile, nor the sun's worth is less.
'By race I am gentle,' the proud man doth say:
He is the mud, the sun is gentleness.
Let no man predicate
That aught the name of gentleness should have,
Even in a king's estate,
Except the heart there be a gentle man's.
The star-beam lights the wave.—
Heaven holds the star and the star's radiance.

God, in the understanding of high Heaven,
Burns more than in our sight the living sun;
There to behold His Face unveil'd is given;
And Heaven, whose will is homage paid to One,
Fulfils the things which live

In God, from the beginning excellent.
So should my lady give
That truth which in her eyes is glorified,
On which her heart is bent,
To me whose service waiteth at her side.

My lady, God shall ask, 'What dared'st thou?'
(When my soul stands with all her acts review'd);
'Thou passed'st Heaven, into My sight, as now,
To make Me of vain love similitude.
To Me doth praise belong,
And to the Queen of all the realm of grace
Who endeth fraud and wrong.
Then may I plead: 'As though from Thee he came,
Love wore an angel's face:
Lord, if I loved her, count it not my shame.'

This poem is a treasury, among other things, of science that is no longer science and has to be taught anew to the modern reader. We have already been introduced to the qualities and functions of the heart; just as the center of a flame is the hottest part of the flame (at least in medieval belief), so the heart—at the center of the human body—burns with the quintessential degree of all the vital activities. (The gentle heart is of the gentle man, who is not necessarily of gentle or noble birth: this poem is one of the many sturdy examples of bourgeois poetry during the Middle Ages.)

One of the systems of similitudes or linkages that the Middle Ages firmly held to was that which endowed precious stones with specific virtues and powers, under the suzerainty of a given star or planet. When the stone was taken from out of the deadening earth it received its characteristic power after being exposed to its governing star—but first the earthly impurities had to be burned out of it by the purifying light of the sun. These scientific concepts of heart, fire, sun, star, earth, precious stone are promulgated in the first two stanzas of Guinizelli's canzone; the rest of the poem combines, recombines, and resolves them in terms of the beloved woman, who at the end is made a heavenly being—only slightly inferior to the Virgin Mary herself, Queen of all the realm of grace.

To appreciate the weight and force of this poem we must, then, properly estimate not only the amorous and theological elements of it but the scientific as well; the poem is an ensemble of all that would carry conviction, self-evident proof, to the medieval mind.

The involved compactness of Guinizelli's style did not meet with general favor. One of the objectors was Bonagiunta of Lucca, the poet to whom Dante explains his *dolce stil nuovo,* his 'sweet new style,' in canto 24 of the *Purgatory*. In a pair of sonnets Bonagiunta debates with Guinizelli, whom Dante was to call 'my father and the father of all my betters who ever wrote sweet rhymes of love.' Bonagiunta says: [24]

Since you have found a novel way to write
And changed the laws of our sweet amorous lays,
Both form and matter, turning black to white,
Hoping thereby to win consummate praise,
I liken you unto a torch at night
Which sheds a flickering gleam o'er murky ways,
But shines no longer when the orb of light
Kindles the world with all-surpassing blaze.
Such subtle wit was never seen before:
Your language is so hard to understand
That not a reader can decipher it.
Although Bologna may beget such lore,
It seems preposterous in any land
To furnish poems forth from learned wit.

And Guinizelli replies:

The wise man runs not here and there at will,
But stops and thinks, and measures in his mind;
And, having thought, he holds his thought until
The truth assures him he has not been blind.
Let us beware lest pride our bosom fill;

Let us consider our degree and kind.
Mad is the man who thinks the world sees ill
And he alone is fit the truth to find.
All sorts of curious birds fly to and fro,
Diverse in speed, unlike in temperament,
And each conducts itself in its own wise.
God made a varied universe, and so
Created understandings different—
Which ought to make us slow to criticize.

Guinizelli's concept of love is clearly presented in his sonnets and canzoni. The demonstration, almost the essence, of love is pure contemplation of the beauty of the beloved. Feminine beauty, as Guinizelli thinks of it, is the outer gleam of an interior beauty of soul: this beauty reveals itself not only in harmony of lineaments, but also in chaste and decorous actions, in a gentle way of speaking, and above all in a flashing eye. And this beauty is also, if not essentially at least in tendency, a moral beauty, which purifies and transfigures that which had formerly been defined by Capellanus as a passion closely connected with the sexual instinct. Amorous desire, according to Guinizelli, is born of a need for aesthetic contemplation and finds full satisfaction for the noble soul of the lover in fully yielding in obedience to the gentle inclination of the beautiful lady. If the enamoured one obtains any recompense for his service and feels that his heart beats in unison with that of the lady, he may feel himself fully blissful and indeed equivalent to those celestial intelligences whose beatitude consists in yielding in obedience to God, each in his proper sphere and distance from God, and in contemplating the divine essence without the veil of the images of sense. The adored lady, then, without ceasing to be considered as a real woman, becomes a symbol of the celestial intelligences, i.e., the angels; allegiance to the lady becomes a species of religious cult. Guinizelli reconciles amatory desire and service with the theological doctrine that love is a desire for something eternally and infinitely better than ourselves.

This doctrine of love-in-poetry is considered the beginning of the sweet new style, the *dolce stil nuovo*. Perhaps this term, coined by Dante himself, is better applied to the group of Florentine poets, a generation later, who further developed the innovations of Guinizelli. The elder leader of this group was Guido Cavalcanti; in addition to Dante the group included Lapo Gianni, Cino da Pistoia, and others.

Beyond question the greatest work of Cavalcanti is to be found in his canzone *Donna mi prega,* but his ideas are more compactly presented in the sonnet *Chi é questa che vien ch' ogn' uom la mira:*

Who is she coming, whom all gaze upon,
Who makes the air all tremulous with light,
And at whose side is Love himself? that none
Dare speak, but each man's sighs are infinite.
Ah me! how she looks round from left to right,
Let Love discourse: I may not speak thereon.
Lady she seems of such high benison
As makes all others graceless in men's sight.
The honor which is hers cannot be said;
To whom are subject all things virtuous,
While all things beauteous own her deity.
Ne'er was the mind of man so nobly led
Nor yet was such redemption granted us
That we should ever know her perfectly.

Before discussing the *dolce stil nuovo* I might give samples of other representatives of this school. First a sonnet by Cino da Pistoia (the fact that Death is feminine in Italian and is so personified in the translation adds a fillip to the quality of the lady):

This fairest lady, who, as well as I wot,
Found entrance by her beauty to my soul,
Pierced through mine eyes my heart, which erst was whole,
Sorely, yet makes as though she knew it not;
Nay, turns upon me now, to anger wrought,

Dealing me harshness for my pain's best dole,
And is so changed by her own wrath's control,
That I go thence, in my distracted thought
Content to die; and, mourning, cry abroad
On Death, as upon one afar from me;
But Death makes answer from within my heart.
Then, hearing her so hard at hand to be,
I do commend my spirit unto God;
Saying to her too, 'Ease and peace thou art.'

Dante himself may be represented at this period by a sonnet from the *Vita Nuova:*

Love and the gentle heart are one same thing,
Even as the wise man in his ditty saith:
Each, of itself, would be such life in death
As rational soul bereft of reasoning.
'Tis Nature makes them when she loves: a king
Love is, whose palace where he sojourneth
Is called the Heart; there draws he quiet breath
At first, with brief or longer slumbering.
Then beauty seen in virtuous womankind
Will make the eyes desire, and through the heart
Send the desiring of the eyes again;
Where often it abides so long enshrin'd
That Love at length out of his sleep will start.
And woman feel the same for worthy men.

Finally, the greater part of a ballata (or ballad) by Lapo Gianni:

Ballad, since Love himself hath fashioned thee
Within my mind where he doth make abode,
Hie thee to her who through mine eyes bestow'd
Her blessing on my heart, which stays with me.

. . .

. . . when, at last thine amorous discourse
Shall have possessed her spirit with that fear
Of thoughtful recollection which in love
Comes first,—then say thou that my heart implores
Only without an end to honour her,
Till by God's will my living soul remove:
That I take counsel oftentimes with Love;
For he first made my hope thus strong and rife,
Through whom my heart, my mind, and all my life,
Are given in bondage to her signiory.

Then shalt thou find the blessed refuge girt
I' the circle of her arms, where pity and grace
Have sojourn, with all human excellence:
Then shalt thou feel her gentleness exert
Its rule (unless, alack! she deem thee base):
Then shalt thou know her sweet intelligence;
Then shalt thou see—O marvel most intense!—
What thing the beauty of the angels is,
And what are the miraculous harmonies
Whereon Love rears the heights of sovereignty.

Move, Ballad, so that none take note of thee
Until thou set thy footsteps in Love's road.
Having arrived, speak with thy visage bow'd,
And bring no false doubt back, or jealousy.

In these examples from the *dolce stil nuovo* we may again note the process of the formation of love: entering through the eye, the image of the lady is nourished in the heart. Each of these poets adds significant adornments to this basic theme. Cino equates this entrance through his eyes with a dagger thrust into his heart, a dagger twisted by the lady as she lists: at the end of the sonnet we find that Death has also by this means taken up residence in his heart. Cavalcanti and Lapo Gianni add poetry as the final link in the chain eye-heart-love: the poem celebrating the process issues, so to speak, automatically as the fruit of the process. (Dante defines the secret of the *dolce stil nuovo* in much this way in speaking with Bonagiunta in canto 24 of the *Purgatorio.*)

Cavalcanti and Lapo elevate the beloved woman to something like angelic status. For Cavalcanti she is deity over all beautiful things; even redemption by Christ has not elevated man high enough to enable him to know her perfectly. (That this is only part of Cavalcanti's idea of love we shall soon see.) Lapo, after describing his lady as endowed with all human excellence, elevates her by analogy: by knowing her, he says, one may comprehend the beauty of the angels, the music of the heavenly spheres, and yet more.

Dante's analogies, or equations, for the lady and love are more complex—and strike deeper—than any of these. In the octave of his sonnet Dante uses Guinizelli's formula of the identity between love and the gentle heart, but even here he adds life, death, nature, and reason to the conventional equation. In the sestet Dante adds at least two important statements which, in comparison with the metaphysical qualities of the *dolce stil nuovo,* might well be called realistic, or even practical. His first innovation is the recognition that love has stages, lapses, hibernations—even periods in which the spiritual desire developed in the heart is fed back to the eyes and is there transformed, temporarily, into a physical desire (via the eyes) more powerful than the initial stimulus had been. Dante's second innovation comes in the final line of his sonnet: here women are brought down from their unrealistic (and patronized) pedestal; more accurately perhaps, virtuous men join virtuous (or worthy) women on the pedestal.

This latter innovation of Dante's is developed in the *Commedia;* it might almost be said to *be* the *Commedia,* in its perfect harmonizing of realistic life, science and philosophy, and theology. If the *dolce stil nuovo* is a school of metaphysical poetry (and in almost every way this name is apt), Dante was able to move from metaphysical to realistic poetry—and yet carry the realistic to a higher and more complex plane than the purely metaphysical. (This thesis about Dante's growth as a poet is presented through the last three or four chapters of this book.) [25]

Another aspect of these samples from the *dolce stil* deserves mention. This is the quality of suffering, of melancholy, or even of morbidity that appears in Cino's sonnet and in a great many other poems of this school; Dante himself in the poems dealing with the Lady Pietra has some notable examples in this vein. Historically this is one of the most important themes of medieval love poetry: coming down through Petrarch it becomes the favorite theme of the Renaissance sonneteers (and has its ancestor in the *odi et amo,* 'I hate while I love,' of the Roman lyric poets).

Cavalcanti's *Donna mi prega* is perhaps the most profound analysis of this love-morbidity in terms of the then current philosophy and science. The locus of love, according to Cavalcanti's *réchauffé* of Aristotle in this poem, is the same part of the soul that contains the memory; here love resides also with the faculties of imagination and fancy. Love is a passion of the soul and an appetite (or desire) of the heart.

But love also has a species of visibility: just as a diaphanous body is made luminous by light so is love formed from a darkness concealed in us by a malign influence from Mars. (On this detail Dante and one or two others dissented, holding that it was a benign influence from Venus.) It is this malign influence that generates the amorous passion in a sensitive soul and thereby produces an obscuring of the faculty of reason.

Love then, according to *Donna mi prega,* is not a power or faculty of the soul but rather a quality or accident that springs from that portion or power of the soul which is concerned with the perfection and beauty of the body—that portion of the soul technically called the sensitive. This last point is concerned with the Avicennian doctrine that the sensitive and not the intellective soul is concerned with the perfecting of the human body: hence love rises from the sensitive and not from the intellective soul. From this Avicennian doctrine, which conceives of love as a passion of the sensible (or sensual) appetite, and therefore a passion which hinders the powers of reason, Cavalcanti was led into a pessimistic morality of love which darkens most of his lyric poetry.[26]

From this pessimism Dante was almost entirely free, except during the brief period of his Pietra poems. The *Commedia* is a poem of the triumph and joy coming from the poet's ability to identify the highest degree of love with the highest exercise of reason. The pessimism of the Pietra poems may well be the faltering and backsliding for which Beatrice delivers her tremendous reproaches of Dante in the closing cantos of the *Purgatory*. (There may even be a relevant pun on Pietra-pietra-impietrato at *Purg.* 33.74.) What spared, or redeemed, Dante from this pessimism has already been suggested in the comments on the last line of his sonnet quoted just above. Dante made abstractions, personifications, and allegories in exactly the same modes as did his contemporaries, but he remains uniquely real among them.

To comprehend this uniqueness we must know something of the medieval habits of allegory, symbol, and the like.

The Fourfold Meaning of the Commedia. The setting within which we must understand medieval allegory and symbolism is a system of multiple meanings of a text.[27] Dante, in his letter to Can Grande, written to dedicate the *Paradise,* defines and illustrates this system and applies it to the *Commedia* (trans. by Wicksteed in the Temple Classics):

. . . be it known that the sense of this work is not simple, but on the contrary it may be called polysemous, that is to say, 'of more senses than one'; for it is one sense which we get through the letter, and another which we get through the thing the letter signifies; and the first is called literal, but the second allegorical or mystic. And this mode of treatment, for its better manifestation, may be considered in this verse: 'When Israel came out of Egypt, and the house of Jacob from a people of strange speech, Judaea became his sanctification, Israel his power.' For if we inspect the letter alone the departure of the children of Israel from Egypt in the time of Moses is presented to us; if the allegory, our redemption wrought by Christ; if the moral sense, the conversion of the soul from the grief and the departure of the holy soul from the slavery of this corruption to the liberty of eternal glory is presented to us. And although these mystic senses have each their special denominations, they may all in general be called allegorical, since they differ from the literal and historical; for allegory is derived from *alleon,* in Greek, which means the same as the Latin *alienum* or *diversum.*

When we understand this we see clearly that the *subject* round which the alternative senses play must be twofold. And we must therefore consider the subject of this work as literally understood, and then its subject as allegorically intended. The subject of the whole work, then, taken in the literal sense only, is 'the state of souls after death,' without qualification, for the whole progress of the work hinges on it and about it. Whereas if the work be taken allegorically, the subject is 'man, as by good or ill deserts, in the exercise of the freedom of his choice, he becomes liable to rewarding or punishing justice.'

The origin of this system of double (and then fourfold) interpretation lies in the ancient (probably prehistoric) belief in two worlds: one intellectual and invisible; the other material and visible. Bonaventure, in the thirteenth century, echoed this ancient belief: [28]

. . . duplex est liber, unus scilicet scriptus intus, qui est Dei aeterna ars et sapientia, et alius scriptus foris, scilicet mundus sensibilis.

. . . the book [of the world] is double, that is to say, one is written within, which is the eternal art and wisdom of God; and the other is written without, that is to say, the world of sense.

The search for a double meaning was probably first applied to texts to find an acceptable sense in which ancient myths and legends could be taken; in Greece this process had begun at least as early as the sixth century B.C. From religious criticism to literary criticism was a simple step; Homer became the center of an extensive body of symbolic and allegorical interpretation. Among the Roman poets this method of interpretation was especially applied to Ovid and Virgil.

From the early centuries of the Christian era the commentaries on Virgil were greatly responsible for his reputation as the sum of all worldly knowledge and thus at least indirectly responsible for Dante's choice of him as guide through the Inferno and Purgatory. The greatest of these commentaries was that of the fourth-century rhetorician, Servius Honoratus, who explained the text of Virgil from the points of view of linguistics, history, mythology, and rhetoric. In Book 6 of the *Aeneid,* when Aeneas and the Sybil are about to leave the lower world, Anchises lets them out through one of the two gates of sleep. One of these gates is of horn, through which true shades make their departure; the other is of ivory, for the false shades. This is Servius' comment:

> In this place Virgil has followed Homer. But with this difference, that Homer says dreams go out through both doors, while Virgil distinguishes *true shades,* by which he means true *dreams,* and the meaning is expressed poetically. For he wishes it to be understood that all he has said is false. And physiologically there is this interpretation: by the *horny door* are meant the eyes, which are of horny color, and harder than other members, for they do not feel the cold (as Cicero also says in his books *On the Nature of the Gods*); but by the *ivory door* is meant the mouth, so called from the teeth. And we know that the things we say may be false, but the things we see are certainly true.

It was his *Fourth Eclogue* that brought Virgil into direct contact with the process of Christian allegorizing. In this poem, congratulating his friend Pollio on the birth of a son, Virgil begins:

> *The mighty sequence of time is renewed from its very foundations.*
> *The virgin returneth to earth, and the golden ages of Saturn.*
> *A child like to none before descends from the summit of heaven.*

Virgil is here probably echoing a virgin-birth prophecy in one of the mystery religions imported from the eastern Mediterranean and flourishing in Rome at this time. But the early Middle Ages found in these lines a prophecy, however unconscious, of the coming of Christ: for Virgil, uniquely among the pagans, the veil of the Christian future had momentarily been lifted. (Dante has Statius say that it was these lines that converted him to Christianity.)

This Christianized interpretation of pagan poems was necessarily of infrequent application, but a Christian interpretation of the Old Testament could be, and became, total, within what may be called an economy of conviction. As the Greeks of the fifth century B.C. had derived rationalistic truths for their own day from the mythical and mystical writings of their ancestors, so did the medieval scholars and theologians find the entire Old Testament a set of incomplete doctrines and premonitory events which attained their completeness and realization only with the beginning of the Christian dispensation.

This mode of interpretation had already begun among the Jews themselves during the time when Jerusalem was under Roman domination, in order to find among the older documents of their Testament some hopeful prophecy for their troubled present; Philo of Alexandria devised the most important of these, an elaborate allegorical explanation of the Pentateuch.[29] The most ingenious practitioner of these techniques was neither Jew nor Christian: Porphyry, a third-century disciple of Plotinus, exercised his ingenuity on those Greek philosophical writings that could be bent to mystical ends.

Origen, a Christian contemporary of Porphyry, developed and practiced a threefold interpretation of the Old Testament—a double allegorical significance hid beneath the literal meaning. A century later St. Augustine developed a system of allegorical linkages between the Old and the New Testaments; this established a pairing of the two Testaments as shadow and substance, or anticipation and fulfilment, that was destined to have a long and important history as the very foundation of Biblical exegesis in the Middle Ages. In compliance with this system, Hrabanus Maurus at the beginning of the ninth century, explained the symbolic sense of Exodus and compiled an alphabetical dictionary of the allegories of the Bible. In the twelfth century Hugo of St. Victor, in his *Mystic Noah's Ark,* discussed the Ark as a symbol of the Church and of the people of God; he also worked out an allegorical interpretation of the entire universe. In the thirteenth century Thomas Aquinas systematized the entire technique in discussions of the scope and method of allegorical explanation.

Two different techniques were used interchangeably in these explanations. In one, concrete things were taken as symbols of concepts: for instance, the four letters of the name 'Adam' indicate that his descendants shall inhabit the four corners of the earth and that the elect shall be gathered from the four winds. In the other method, real persons and events of the Old Testament were understood as foreshadowing those of the New: * Joshua and Samson both prefigure Jesus; the episodes of Joshua's and Samson's careers, while literally and historically true, stand for episodes in Jesus' activity. St. Paul had suggested a correspondence between Adam and Christ; the Middle Ages worked out the details of this correspondence, often terming Christ the Second Adam.[30]

But these were only the beginnings of the immense series of correspondences worked out by medieval scholars in their labors of demonstrating the great scheme of the coherent and rational universe. Grandgent thus summarizes these labors, which aimed at reducing the seemingly chaotic universe to the smallest possible number of simple principles:

> Medieval scholars . . . carried the mystic method into their study of biology, mineralogy, and arithmetic, and even extended its application to secular history. The strange significance of numbers, particularly those down to sixteen, was discussed by St. Augustine, St. Isidore, Rabanus Maurus, Hugo of St. Victor, and many others; Dante, in the *New Life,* has a word to say on the subject, telling why the number nine is persistently and mysteriously attached to incidents in the life of Beatrice. The symbolism of beast lore goes back to a Greek allegorized treatise on natural history called the *Physiologus* . . . , which was used by Origen and seems to have been known, in some form, to St. Ambrose, St. Augustine, and St. Jerome. . . . Here is a small specimen of its manner: the lion, to escape from hunters, obliterates its track with its tail; this signifies that God became man secretly, to deceive the devil.

The summation of these techniques, and probably the immediate progenitor of Dante's form of the doctrine, is Aquinas' exposition of the four kinds of interpretation:[31]

* St. Bernard (*On Consideration* 2, 8) extends this series of correspondences to a definition of the Pope:

> Who are you? The chief priest, the Sovereign Pontiff. You are the prince of bishops, the head of the Apostles; in priority you are Abel, in government Noah; as a patriarch you are Abraham, in order Melchizedek, in rank Aaron, in power Peter; in virtue of your anointing you are Christ.

The nature of man requireth that he attain unto the things of the intellect through the things of the senses, inasmuch as our knowledge hath its beginning in the senses. It was therefore most fitting that the Holy Writ should transmit to us spiritual things under bodily images. . . . Revelation is in no wise altered by the corporeal figures wherewith it is clothed. . . . Beneath these emblems it keepeth all its truth; for it lifteth up the inspired authors, and thereby also them that read, beyond the images even to the idea of the things of the intellect. That which in one passage is presented metaphorically, the Writ expoundeth elsewhere openly, literally, without veil or figure. . . . The author of the Holy Writ, God, may give a meaning not only to locutions, but to things themselves. Thus, even as in the books of men words signify things, likewise in the divine books do the very things exprest by words signify other things. The first signification, according to which words denote things, is the first sense, the historical or literal; and the second signification, whereby the things exprest by words designate other things, is the spiritual sense, which taketh for granted the literal sense and reposeth upon it. The spiritual sense is subdivided into three other senses, in this wise: the ancient law is, as St. Paul declareth . . . , the token of the new law; the new law itself, according to the Areopagite, prefigureth the glory of the future world; moreover it giveth us in the acts of our divine Leader a pattern and rule for our own behavior. Now the things of the old law signifying the things of the new is the allegorical sense; the acts of the divine model representing what we must do is the moral sense; finally, the institutions of the present symbolizing future glory is the anagogical sense. Inasmuch as the literal sense is the one with which the author of any writing is principally concerned; and inasmuch as the Author of the Scriptures embraceth all things at once in his intelligence, why should not the same sacred letter . . . contain several senses founded on the literal? . . . The multiplicity of senses in the Writ produceth neither obscurity nor ambiguity; for these senses are multiple . . . not because the words have several meanings, but because the things exprest by the words are themselves the expression of other things. Therefore is there no confusion in the sacred books: all the senses rest upon one, namely, the literal, which alone hath the privilege of furnishing arguments to science; for none are derived . . . from the allegorical sense. . . . The literal sense can contain no error.

We have in this statement a number of concepts of immense importance for understanding Dante: not only the four senses in which a text is to be understood, but a number of ideas which I have treated or shall treat elsewhere in this chapter—God as Author, and the similitude between divine and human poet; the importance of the natural world as the literal text of God's creation; the relation between literal and historical meanings; the infallible importance of the literal meaning; the relation between multiple meanings and obscurity or ambiguity; the simultaneity of God's kind of knowledge, and the relation of this to human perception-in-time.

The four senses, as catalogued by Thomas, were schoolboy commonplaces of the period, imbibed with every lesson in grammar or rhetoric. To keep them straight the young pupil had a mnemonic:

> Littera gesta docet,
> Quid credas allegoria,
> Moralis quid agas,
> Quo tendas anagogia.
>
> The letter teaches deeds [*or,* what has happened],
> Allegory (teaches) what you should believe,
> The moral (meaning) what you should do,
> The anagoge (shows) whither you are headed.

Above all we must remember that both allegorical and literal are knowable, though in different ways: the world is the intelligible enclosed in the sensible.

The Literal and the Allegorical. Knowing about these techniques of fourfold interpretation prepares us only to ask the proper questions: How much of what is involved in the account by Aquinas mattered to Dante, and in what ways? How are these techniques to be applied to reading the *Commedia?* What is the exact status or description of the literal meaning? What is the relation between the literal meaning and the others? Is there anything in today's modes of reading that is comparable to the fourfold method?

Today's readers have been introduced to the critical vocabulary of 'identification,' 'projection,' 'universalization,' and to critics who read in terms of ambiguities and ambivalences, or in terms of

Freudian and other systems of levels of intention and meaning, or of grammars and rhetorics of motive. While none of these modern systems of reading has either the precision or the spiritual aim of the medieval method, we may perhaps point out one or two important connections.

Both medieval and modern systems of reading insist that there is more to the text than appears on the surface of it, and the reader is obliged to use his reason or his ingenuity or his intelligence to discover what it is that lies above or below the surface, since the covert meaning may be more significant than the overt.[32]

But this is only an initial, and temporary, similarity between medieval and modern readings. The medieval was uncompromisingly based on the belief that a world created by God must be rational and meaningful; the twofold (or fourfold) interpretation of a text was the necessary exercise of human intelligence to clarify the rational relevance of every phenomenon or action to First and Final Cause whenever this relation was obscured or obscure. Modern manifold reading is likely to aim in a direction opposite to this. Empson's ambiguities or the Freudian critic's levels of consciousness usually demonstrate the complexities or the murkinesses that lie beneath a simple surface. (This opposition just described is not absolute: many modern techniques of reading aim at a kind of rational clarification that is close to the medieval; the *Commedia* contains many intentional ambiguities of statement under a clear surface.)

A more important connection between medieval and modern techniques is their common aim not merely to make a text comprehensible but precisely to make it comprehensible in terms of contemporary importance. To borrow a phrase from current jargon: both medieval and modern interpreters are concerned with bringing the reader into the picture—'history and fiction include you too.' (This is the same thing Eliot expressed in the line he borrowed from Baudelaire: 'Hypocrite lecteur!—mon semblable,—mon frère!') Whether ancient, pagan history or the Old Testament is being anagogically interpreted in terms of Christian doctrinal aspiration toward God, or *Hamlet* is being analyzed in terms of Oedipal fixations, the interpreter is trying to make a literary or historical event intelligible in terms that he believes are of vital importance to the current reader.* This kind of criticism, then—if there is any other kind—falls into place as a great species of euhemerization. When a critic bases his approach to a text on preoccupations that prove temporary, his work becomes only a curiosity to later generations; if he has the good fortune to choose a long-lived human preoccupation, his work may live along with the text or even longer (as Aristotle's *Poetics* has outlived most of the plays it is based on).

What is Dante's relation to the fourfold method (and to other such conventions of his day) and to what extent must we try to comprehend the *Commedia* in these four ways? Dante exhibits, it seems to me, something approaching impatience when he deals with the fourfold method in the passage, quoted earlier, from the epistle to Can Grande. He first speaks of it as twofold, then gives the traditional four but says they really are two (since the term 'allegorical' covers all those other than the literal), and finally in speaking of the 'subject' of his poem returns to the twofold significance. Dante's impatience—if it is there—amounts to his saying that of course his poem is subject to the traditional fourfold reading, but that these allegorical meanings, whether three or one or six, are there when they need to be and will be perceived by the reader when they are there: understand the two general senses of the poem and with no new efforts you will understand any additional allegories.

Dante is here of course speaking to his contemporary reader, who would read allegorically almost as a matter of course—and who would have in his head much of the information about people, places, and events needed for the easy practice of allegorical reading, information that today must be acquired by note or rote.

* The Middle Ages came to be sharply conscious of a difference as well as a connection between the literal and the figurative meanings of a statement. In recent centuries the difference has become increasingly blurred; writers and readers alike are prone to confuse metaphorical observation with direct. The average man, Middletown, John Bull, the Bureau of Labor Statistics' cost-of-living index—that these are various kinds of allegorical figures rather than simple abstractions is often inadequately considered whether in casual conversation or in great economic and political decisions.

We may have to consider another part of Dante's attitude to contemporary allegory, especially when it turned into allegoresis—a frenzy for finding allegory everywhere. Allegory—as Dante knew he was writing it in the *Commedia*—was not something tacked on or willfully worked in: it was a deeply felt and inevitable extension of his direct and realistic expression.[33] This could not always be said of allegorical writing or reading in his time; the medieval commentators on Holy Writ (and on the patristic commentators on Holy Writ) often turned this method of reading into a mechanical science. Thus Dante must have known, and may well have been disturbed by, the commonplace that 'Job in his trials is Jesus crucified.' This was part of the pattern that insisted that Old Testament events were important only as they prefigured episodes in the life of Christ. But what of Job? A patterned theologian might well have had his eyes shut to everything but the parallel of suffering in God's cause; a poet would have to see those essential circumstances of the story of Job which violate the spirit and the purpose of the passion of Christ: the purposelessness of Job's suffering (or, worse, the tyrannical assuredness of Jehovah, who, like Bacchus in the *Frogs,* says 'Beat my servant all you like and see whether you can make me change my story'); the absence of any meaningful parallel in the Christ story to the financial center of the history of Job; worst of all, the callousness which makes Job suffer through the killing of his wife and children—as though they were merely counters like land and wheat and cattle.

This analogy between Christ and Job, like much more of Biblical exegesis, may well have seemed to Dante to be forced from the outside upon unreceptive material. It would be a pity to do the same kind of thing to Dante himself, and yet the history of Dante-reading abounds with things of the same sort. Luckily such things are outside our present concerns, but we might mention an example, survivor of that early Renaissance allegoresis which was far less artistically sensitive than was that of the Middle Ages. In two recent American translations of Dante, Virgil is rigidly identified as Human Reason ('Virgil' and 'Reason' are used interchangeably), and everything that he does or that is done to him is interpreted under this guise. This is the activity of one who is afraid that unless he forearms himself against allegory it will say boo to him around the next corner.

Dante's allegories grow from the literal sense of his poem; they grow where they are needed—they are absent, or nearly absent, as the need diminishes.[34] This is not poetic inconsistency, unless it be inconsistency to a not-Dante's plan; Dante's is rather a writing about multifaceted things, of which one or six facets or three may be reflecting light under the given circumstances. Virgil, for example, is a great pagan poet in the *Commedia;* he is a man familiar with some parts of the terrain through which he guides the pilgrim (and notably unfamiliar with others); in his career he is venerable and widely experienced; his sympathies are broad and warm; he had had some inklings of a truth greater than any his experience could give him; he is a highly reasonable and intelligent man, almost (though never completely) to the point of being a symbol of Reason. Any number or proportion of these qualities of Virgil may be relevant to any of his appearances in the *Commedia:* this is Dante's method of allegory.

But what *is* this literal sense of Dante's poem? Dante tells us in the *Convivio* that two kinds of allegory were recognized, each with its characteristic kind of literal sense: in the allegory of theologians the literal sense expressed what had happened; in the allegory of poets the literal sense expressed what was likely to happen or to have happened. The theologians, in weaving their allegorical web from the Testaments or comparable material, had precise and clear fact to start from. The poets of the time, presenting their works for allegorical exposition, created a literal level of meaning that was *una bella menzogna*—a beautiful fiction. *Menzogna* is a strong word—it means 'lie,' or 'deception'—but this is the word chosen by Dante to describe the literal sense in the allegory of poets.

The argument that Dante in the *Commedia* is writing the allegory of theologians is most cogently presented by Charles S. Singleton. His reasoning is tight and interwoven, but I believe that the following quotations do not misrepresent it. After saying that the literal sense 'will point beyond itself' and that the allegorical import consists in 'God's justice,' Professor Singleton continues:[35]

> . . . the literal sense is to be taken as the first and literal sense of Holy Scripture is taken, namely as an historical sense. . . . But the kind of allegory to which the example from Scriptures given in the Letter to Can Grande points is not an allegory of 'this for that,' but an allegory of 'this and that' . . .
>
> If, then, the allegory of the *Divine Comedy* is the allegory of theologians, if it is an allegory of 'this and that,' if its allegory may be seen in terms of a first meaning which is *in verbis* and of another which is *in facto,* what is the main outline of its allegorical structure?
>
> In the simplest and briefest statement it is this: the journey to God of a man through three realms of the world beyond this life is what is given by the literal meaning. It points to the event. The event is that journey to God through the world beyond. 'Littera *gesta* docet.' The words of the poem have their first meaning in signifying that event, just as the verse of Psalms had its first meaning in signifying the historical event of the Exodus. . . .
>
> I . . . suggest that Dante abandoned the *Convivio* because he came to see that in choosing to build this work according to the allegory of poets, he had ventured down a false way; that he came to realize that a poet could not be a poet of rectitude and work with an allegory whose first meaning was a disembodied fiction.

One could quibble about some of the terms used by Singleton: 'the literal will point beyond itself'; does it not always? 'It points to the event' is perhaps even more disingenuous. Why 'disembodied fiction'? Is every fiction 'disembodied'? Or is it that the fiction of Dante's *canzoni* were unusually or uncharacteristically 'disembodied'? May a poet of rectitude—say, Sophocles, or Shakespeare, or Milton—never work with a fiction?

But these quibbles would not destroy the force of Professor Singleton's argument; and the point is one on which depends much that must be said about the *Commedia.* To take only a corollary instance, one that depends on the assumption that the *Commedia* is written in the allegory of the theologians: many critics have been extensively exercised by the questions of where Cato will spend eternity, and of how Virgil will act and feel after he has left the

Earthly Paradise and returned to spend eternity in Limbo. These exercises may be a great tribute to the demiurgic truth of Dante, or they may be misapplied theological ingenuity; but if they divert the critic's (or the reader's) attention from the thoughts and feelings aroused by Cato and Virgil within the poem to other thoughts about an unwritten sequel to the poem, such exercises may even be mischievous.[36]

Two general approaches may be taken in trying to deny that Dante is writing the allegory of theologians in the *Commedia,* and in trying at the same time to see what kind of allegory he *is* writing: a practical, external approach, and an approach based on internal evidence from the *Commedia* itself. Remember how much of Singleton's case is based on Dante's abandonment of the *Convivio*—like the dog that significantly *didn't* bark in *The Hound of the Baskervilles.*

In practical terms, then, it is the *journey proper* that I believe to be a fiction. No soul after death makes such a journey: a soul bound for Hell travels thither and then remains in his appointed place; a soul bound for Purgatory and then Paradise does not touch Hell on his journey. Even those pre-Christian elect who awaited Christ's coming in Limbo probably did not go through Hell on their way to the Empyrean (and certainly did not undergo the purgatorial process); their case could not be relevant to the pilgrim's.

Is the *Commedia* a factual account of an actual journey performed by the poet in the flesh (remember how often the flesh of the pilgrim provokes comment or question as he proceeds)? Or is the poem a faithful and quasi-actual account of a dream or vision that Dante experienced? We must consider both of these.

Could Dante have dreamed the journey? Possibly, though he nowhere implies this possibility, and, from the evidence of the dreams in the *Vita Nuova* and the *Purgatory,* he seems to have considered dreams to be quite a different order of reality from that he was portraying in the *Commedia.*

Dante may actually have made the journey through divine intervention. Can we—or could Dante's contemporaries—accept this possibility? When Boccaccio speaks of the belief that Dante *had* made the journey, he attributes this belief to the uneducated; the notion is even less palatable today. Dante did not speak with Virgil and Cacciaguida in the sense in which he spoke with Gemma Donati and Can Grande della Scala. What is more important, he did not think he had. Dante could, even as we, recognize a difference between Aeneas and Virgil, and probably also a difference between Aeneas the historical personage (which of course he was for Dante) and Aeneas the character in a poem—just as he could recognize the difference between the historical Virgil and the Virgil for whom he himself invented actions and words.

Here we may take the next step in our argument. Ancient history, ancient myth, revelation, recent history, fantasy (as described in canto 17 of the *Purgatory*), the poet's invention—all these categories could be subsumed (and the differences among them ignored) under the single head of true and significant exemplar. All of these could merge into the literal level of his poem if Dante could only show by his use and arrangement of them that they were significant and convincing conveyors of his meaning. The literal perhaps consists in the arrangement, in form-to-convey-meaning; the sum of literal and allegorical is the number of ways in which Dante wants the *Commedia* to be credible.

In any case, the *journey* of the poem is contrived: it is a fiction in the sense of something made or put together rather than being something pre-existent or supplied, as history or an actual journey would be. Singleton considers this point when he speaks of the 'possibility of such a journey even in this life.' Of course; even a fiction may be (or must be) possible—but wasn't Dante concerned with the purposes and the results of such a journey rather than with the improbable possibility of it?

Let us turn to another approach to the question of the literal sense. Professor Singleton, in the passage I quoted, spoke of the likelihood that Dante ceased working on the *Convivio* because he realized that he had 'ventured down a false way.' I agree with this hypothesis but should prefer it thus reworded: Dante abandoned the *Convivio* when, and because, he had derived all possible benefit and growth from the kind of thinking represented in the plan of the treatise. The *Convivio* is in itself a re-vision of the state or level of Dante's insight represented in the *canzoni* around which the treatise is written—just as the *canzoni* themselves may represent an advance over the *Vita Nuova,* and the proses of the *Vita Nuova* may in turn represent an advance beyond, or a more inclusive vision of, the poems of that work. In other words Dante's growth as a poet is both incremental and abrupt (one might borrow the terms 'gradual' and 'saltatory' from Gestalt psychology to express this growth and a similar double progress through the *Purgatory*).

It is unquestionable that in the *Commedia,* in the final stage of Dante's development, he is a different kind of poet from his contemporaries and even from what he himself had been in his earlier works—different in terms of insight and scope as well as of control over his medium. This is not a mysterious difference, nor was it a secret from Dante: the qualities of it, and even the stages of it, are a clear and major concern of the last third of the *Purgatory.*

Professor Singleton describes the difference between the early Dante and the latest Dante in terms of a change from poet-allegorist to theologian-allegorist. (If we remember the differences between Dante's picture of Purgatory and the orthodox view we should at least have to consider him as a revisionary theologian.) A 'message' (or more than one) is, on the word of Dante himself, the major aim of the *Commedia.* The formal development of the *Purgatory* (as traced in the body of this book) leads up to the announcement of that message (or that part of it proper to this canticle); the message itself is signalled by the dramatic change of guides and by the tremendous fanfare of the pageant in the Earthly Paradise. The pageant, as we shall see, transfers the mode of the poem to a different level—if not of simple symbolism then of an altered relation between symbol and allegory; after this comes the direct message about the needed separation of earthly powers. At best, then, there are two kinds or two levels of 'message' within the *Purgatory:* in the first twenty-eight cantos the message based on the literal—which looks like allegory of poets; and then the message which is the literal—which looks like allegory of theologians.

Helen Dunbar (*op. cit.*, p. 64, n. 130) some time ago disposed of this hypothesis—that Dante is writing allegory of theologians—by stating 'the fact that Scriptural allegory must center in Christ'; this is attractively simple but easily disproved. This does not mean that we, or Dante, must therefore retreat to the allegory of poets. We may at least consider another possibility, a third kind of allegory.

This third kind (shall we call it 'allegory of Dante'?) might be defined as one in which the literal sense is consciously a fiction, but a fiction about things believed to be essentially as therein presented—a belief based on all the faith, hope, and intelligence of the poet. It is a fiction because the events and conversations, the choices of guides and exemplars, the astronomical, topographical, and chronological details—all these are the conscious contribution of the poet, to be weighed and manipulated by him for the best performance of his convictions. It is a fiction because the *journey* had not happened and probably would never happen. It is a fiction also because only for the sake of a seriously purposive and new poetic structure would Dante have tampered with the fabric of orthodoxy.*

True, this 'allegory of Dante' is not greatly different from Singleton's idea, which tacitly modifies the pure allegory of theologi-

* Perhaps a few details may be added about this kind of fiction.

On the basis of what Dante has to say about the Epicureans in the *Inferno* we are on safe ground in asserting his firm belief in an afterlife and an afterworld.

The afterworld is a permanent place except for the slow movements or modulations within Purgatory. The pilgrim makes, through this realm (which in this special sense is a static realm), a transient journey like those one makes in daily life (or like that which Leopold Bloom makes in *Ulysses*).

However, since this is poetic creation and not personal revelation, this depiction of the afterworld presents, or represents, conditions of daily, actual life. This is one sense in which the *Comedy* is a fiction. It is a corollary fiction that the daily life Dante has seen may be poetically transmuted into the permanent afterworld—although presumably the distance between fiction and fact may diminish as the fiction rises above his direct experiences and becomes a mosaic of the wisdom and experience of all times and places.

ans; it is a certain kind of synthesis of the original two kinds of allegory. But as a concept this spares Dante the shilly-shallying or the finger-crossing that the critic must perform if he treats the literal sense of the *Commedia* as historical. As a practical tool this 'allegory of Dante' recognizes the difference in kind between the *Commedia* and the work of other poets, and the difference in form and aim between the *Commedia* and Dante's earlier poetry. It also recognizes the self-conscious saltatory developments indicated throughout his writings: in the promise in the *Vita Nuova* to celebrate Beatrice hereafter in poetry as woman had never been celebrated before, in the abandonment of the *Convivio,* in the conversation with Bonagiunta, and above all in the attention focused in the last third of the *Purgatory* on the guided transformations of the pilgrim to higher and yet higher ideas of the nature and mission of poetry.

The distinction between the two kinds of allegory had been described in the *Convivio,* which, you remember, Dante abandoned before a third of it was done. In the *Epistle to Can Grande,* presumably written after the *Commedia* was completed, no such distinction is mentioned. True, the example Dante cites, 'When Israel came out of Egypt,' is subject to theological interpretation, but it is cited primarily as a simple and self-contained example to demonstrate the mechanics of allegorical exposition. (Additionally, of course, the substance of this example is a theological parallel to the poetic theme of the *Commedia.*) But every other statement in the *Epistle* that bears on the question of the allegorical quality of the poem adds up overpoweringly to the conclusion that Dante conceived of the *Commedia* as contrived in substance (rather than historical or revealed) and practical and moral (rather than theological) in aim (Wicksteed's translation):

> The form or method of treatment is poetic, fictive, descriptive, digressive, transumptive; and likewise proceeding by definition, division, proof, refutation, and setting forth of examples. . . .
>
> The end of the whole and of the part may be manifold, to wit, the proximate and the ultimate, but dropping all subtle investigation, we

may say briefly that the end of the whole and of the part is to remove those living in this life from the state of misery and lead them to the state of felicity.

But the *branch of philosophy* which regulates the work in its whole and in its parts, is morals or ethics, because the whole was undertaken not for speculation but for practical results. For albeit in some parts or passages it is handled in the way of speculation, this is not for the sake of speculation, but for the sake of practical results; because, as the Philosopher says in the second *Metaphysicorum,* 'practical men sometimes speculate on things in their relative and temporal bearings.'

These, then, premised, we must approach the exposition of the letter, after the fashion of a kind of prelibation; but we must announce in advance that the exposition of the letter is nought else than the development of the form of the work . . .

The very title *Comedy,* as Dante discusses it, can be thought of only in connection with antique fictions in comedy and tragedy.

The literal sense, then, of the *Commedia* is a fiction designed for a practical purpose.[37] 'The state of souls after death' is, in the details of structure and arrangement, the poet's imagined fiction—a fiction based on, or developed from, revelation and faith. The form, import, and impact of this fiction are concerned with 'man, as by good or ill deserts, in the exercise of the freedom of his choice, he becomes liable to rewarding or punishing justice.' Dante at this point (paragraph 8) in the *Epistle* and later, at paragraphs 11 and 15, where he returns to this idea, does not say whether the justice of God he is concerned with is being demonstrated on earth or in the afterworld. The implications, especially of paragraph 15, might lead us to argue for justice-on-earth—until we realize that within the world of the *Commedia* this is an immaterial or nonexistent distinction:

15. The *end* of the whole and of the part may be manifold, to wit, the proximate and the ultimate, but dropping all subtle investigations, we may say briefly that the end of the whole and of the part is to remove those living in this life from the state of misery and lead them to the state of felicity.

Allegory, Symbol, Analogy, Image. These four terms, which at best admit no sharp boundaries between one and the next, are likely to take a reader, by way of a simple confusion of terminology, into a morass of miscomprehension. Let us at least have an understanding about these four.

'Image' and 'analogy' are comparatively easy to deal with, since the meaning of these terms is bound to remain broad, or even vague, no matter how we try to pin them down.

'Image' is today a catchall term to include metaphor and simile plus many more of the figures of speech of classical rhetoric. In the terminology of some critics, 'image' comes to embrace 'concept' and 'idea,' or it is used to denote that which the image-making faculty, the imagination, assembles or creates. For others, 'image' comes to signify all physical actuality, as the term is applied to the means used by God to make immaterial reality sensible to man.

I shall generally use 'image' in its simplest sense, for a figure of speech most like metaphor. In dealing with, say, the bow-and-arrow imagery that Dante uses recurrently in the *Purgatory* to express ideas and feelings of tautness, of aim at a target, of being bent in concentration, and the like, we shall be primarily concerned with the relationships among images. No image (whether new or repeated) is discrete and separable: each is related to, and variable within, its context. For many of Dante's images—light, the bow-and-arrow, thirst, the little boat, the net—the most important part of this context may be the image's own history: that is, the second or the eighth time an image is used it means something increasingly more than it had meant the first time. It comes to have not only the accumulated force of familiarity but also a wider or deeper applicability from the variety of contexts, including association with other images, in which it has been presented.

'Image' shades into 'analogy' when the latter word is used in its theological-poetical sense. Analogy is a means of communicating the difficult by means of the comparatively simple; at its theological limit analogy is a device for expressing by means of sensible things that which is essentially inexpressible. In this sense the created universe is an analogy employed by God to communicate, or reveal, his purposes to man. If the universe seems to be imperfect it may be so because human sense is rarely adequate for the immensity of the communication.[38]

Just as God uses the physical, temporal universe to convey to man, by analogy, the existence and the meaning of His universe, so does Dante the poet use narrative-in-time and detailed sense-experience to communicate to the reader *his* universe, a universe which the poet alone could comprehend simultaneously (in all its purposes) as well as sequentially. Analogy is always imperfect, always a compromise—perhaps a compromise required by the limitations of the material or of the audience rather than by those of the creative artist.

'Allegory' and 'symbol'[39] are the prime means used by a poet like Dante to convey his analogy, or analogies. 'Allegory' and 'symbol' nearly, but inaccurately, correspond with the devices I mentioned just above: 'allegory' with 'narrative-in-time,' and 'symbol' with 'detailed sense-experience.' Before attempting to explain these definitions let us look at a few witnesses. C. R. Post makes a simple distinction:

Allegory starts with an idea and creates an imaginary object as its exponent. If one starts with an actual object and from it receives the suggestion of an idea, one is a symbolist.

We shall see allegory built around real objects, or persons, and such creatures of fantasy as griffons used as symbols; but we need not discard Post's distinction.

Dunbar:

When all objects and all deeds in the physical universe are habitually considered as manifestations of and veils for a deeper reality, then any scripture must be symbolic in a double sense. The words signify certain acts or objects, these acts and objects themselves signify another reality. . . .

In [Jesus] was defined the very function of symbolism itself, as uniting eternally the infinite meaning and its finite expression. . . .

The medieval allegorical method is a series of interlocking symbols of multiplex and mutually essential significations, no one of which can be understood apart from the whole. It is an initiation into the unknown with a very definite basis in the known.

and Hatzfeld (in *Dante—Seine Weltanschauung,* pp. 23-4):

> In a world thus conceived as the creation and projection of God, with the eyes of men turned ever towards redemption and the eternal life-after-death, it was quite expectable that the entire world of nature be conceived, almost perceived, in symbolic terms. 'Alles Vergängliche ist nur ein Gleichnis.' Plants, trees, and stones are present only to remind men of the otherworldly truths of salvation. The redness of actual flowers recalls the red wounds of Christ; the whiteness of lilies recalls chastity and aspiring purity of heart; the grapevine recalls Christ Himself, Who said: 'I am the vine and ye are the grapes'; the appletree is a lasting reminder of the curse of original sin. The lamb is the ancient sacrificial animal; the pelican, thought to nourish its young with its own blood, is a symbol of Christ. The dove is a reminder of the Holy Ghost; the dragon, the snake, and the bear were images of the devil. Among precious stones, the green emerald betokened hope for forgiveness of sin, the topaz industriousness, and the gleaming red carbuncle was the token of love.

A symbolic thing, then, is presented for, or exists for, the sake of the thing symbolized. As a poetic symbol, or as a symbol used in any other art, its behavior is different from that of the real thing it would be if it were not acting as a symbol. In other words, we do not look for the fullness of a leopard's behavior in a leopard symbolizing Christ. Nor are we troubled by the living actions of a nonliving or contrived or synthetic thing—the Flag, John Bull, the unicorn. The reality of a symbol exists on the level of the thing symbolized.

Symbols, rich as they may come to be in associations, exist on the single level of a simple equation, of the type a = b: Flag = United States, or, at most, all tigers = Christ. Allegory, which conveys its meaning by a pattern unfolding in time, tries to relate itself to all similar patterns, then and now and in the future, here and elsewhere. Allegory (or allegorical interpretation of a text) is a device for trying to cancel or neutralize time; to bring past, present, and future into a clear and meaningful harmony; to make past events or personages relate to present interests or problems by means of statements or implications about the future. Allegory is man's effort to see as does God, Who 'embraceth all things at once in his intelligence.' Symbols are the counters in this process.

An allegory may, very often does, use symbolic figures. An allegorical painting is such, rather than symbolic, because 'it tells a story.' Allegory may use its own figures, as well as making use of symbolic figures: they are more varied, more alive and responsive, in going from one context to the next. By comparison, symbols are inflexible and tend rather to alter the environment than to be altered in response. As a symbol starts to react with, to adapt itself to, a living environment, it starts to become part of allegory or to become an allegorical figure.

The difference, then, between allegory and symbol may be stark and grand, or it may verge on splitting cumin seeds or bending a hair this way or that. The danger lies not in definition but in use of these terms: typically in a tendency to seize upon and name a figure as symbolic and then treat that figure as constant throughout, say, a long poem. If this is truly a symbolic figure, well and good; if it is an allegorical figure, such a reader will be blind to most of the subtle life of that poem. It were far better to throw out both these terms than to incur the damage of this last instance. In poetry—as in life—it is often better to defer judgment indefinitely than to leap into it prematurely.

Symbol is a tool, a device for expressing a difficult, complex, or even ineffable concept in concrete and even pictorial terms. Symbol is perhaps essentially of the graphic arts, whether it is God, a painter, a sculptor, or a poet who is providing the depiction. Symbol may be private-associational, as it tended to be among the French Symbolist poets of the nineteenth century; or it may bestride nations and centuries, as did many symbols of medieval Christianity. An allegorical figure may be—in Dante, almost invariably is—a person presented realistically or naturalistically who becomes allegorical only as his behavior or fate is seen to be exemplary. No poet can arbitrarily make allegory; every symbolic figure was originally created arbitrarily.

Allegory is interlocking and contextual, and on the basis of a whole work rather than of separate sections. Symbol tends to be episodic: in different sections of a work there may be more than one symbol representing the same thing. Symbol, finally, may be compared with image: an image is two tangential circles while a symbol is concentric. An image retains its own meaning while lending itself to a function; it is a bow-and-arrow that is related to other things in its own character while it serves to describe a taut mind focusing on a problem. A symbolic tiger merges most of its tigerishness with the thing being symbolized, or, more accurately, it abandons most of its tigerishness.

In the *Commedia* much damage has been wrought in connection with the interpretation of Virgil, Matelda, and Beatrice. A symbolic figure, whether or not based on conventional or traditional symbol, tends to exhibit a one-to-one relationship to the thing symbolized. In the *Commedia* the candle-lights, the chariot, the harlot are symbols of this kind; initially there may be difficulty in pinning the symbol down to a definite identification, but once pinned there it is and remains. Virgil is clearly of a different order of reality from the lights and the chariot: Virgil equated with Human Reason is either much too large for the garment or rattles around within it.[40] And Matelda. Francesco d'Ovidio, opening his discussion of Matelda, presents a list of what she has been found to symbolize:

> . . . chi vuole sia *la vita attiva,* chi *l'amore alla Chiesa,* chi *la grazia preveniente e cooperante,* chi *l'abito di buona elezione,* chi *il principio monarchico,* chi *la filosofia riconciliata con la teologia,* chi *la docilita,* chi *l'arte che nasce dal sapere,* chi *il prete perfetto,* chi *la carita operosa,* chi *la vita cattolica,* chi *la dottrina cristiana,* chi *la vera via del Paradiso,* chi *la mistica pratica,* chi *l'innocenza,* chi *la natura umana perfetta e felice,* chi *la felicita terrena* . . .

Matelda, then, has been identified as: the Active Life, Love of the Church, Prevenient and Cooperant Grace, the Habit of Good Election, the Principle of Monarchy, Philosophy Reconciled with Theology, Docility, Art Born in Wisdom, the Perfect Priest, Operant

Love, the Catholic Life, Christian Doctrine, the True Path into Paradise, Practical Mysticism, Innocence, Human Nature Perfected and in a State of Felicity, Terrene Felicity.

Much more to the point of dealing with one of Dante's characters is the approach of Geoffrey L. Bickersteth:

> Among the qualities of Virgil's poetic character . . . two, by common consent, are outstanding and impart their own peculiar tone to all the rest. The one is a human tenderness of heart, the other a gentle, brooding, wistful melancholy of mind. . . .
>
> In the *Comedy* Dante not only dramatises him, but raises him from being nearly pathetic as he is in the Aeneid, to the dignity of a tragic hero. . . . All the Roman qualities are there—*humanitas, virtus, pietas, gravitas, simplicitas* and so on—: this is unquestionably the very Virgil whom his own poetry has revealed to us and no other.

The conclusion of this is somewhat debatable, but unquestionably Bickersteth's way of opening an interpretation of Virgil will produce more poetic iron and gold than will looking for a symbol of human reason in everything that Virgil does or says.

For Dante's age, which had imbibed symbolic and allegorical in terpretation with every lesson in grammar or rhetoric, the techniques were as simple, unconscious, and precise as are today the techniques of a skillful motorist in his constant but mostly unconscious adjustments to fine details of road, weather, and traffic conditions. Through all these the motorist keeps to his path with little feeling of strain—or of pride in accomplishment. Put the thirteenth-century scholar behind the wheel of a Cadillac, and there you have some sort of equivalent for the modern reader dealing with allegory. He can learn the techniques, of course; he will certainly improve as he goes along; but he is always likely to run it off the road.

The modern interpreter of allegory can soon learn to see and identify the similarities or similitudes which are the basis of allegory and symbolism, but he is likely to ignore the details which may qualify the allegory or shift the symbol to quite a new realm. Building an allegory (or, at the other end, building an allegorical interpretation) is like building a boat; the material must be suitable and malleable to the form but, above all, the structure, when completed, must be seaworthy—not necessarily absolutely watertight but reasonably so and certainly navigable. If not, what you have when you are finished is either not a good boat or else something quite other—a tub, perhaps, or a barn.

If Virgil is identified as Human Reason, and then two-fifths or three-fifths of his actions are found to be either bad-reasonable or non-reasonable, that makes a pretty discouraging picture of human reason or else makes Dante guilty of sloppy symbolism. We might better discard the equation entirely and look for something else.

In their own way both symbolism and allegory are precise techniques. In the last cantos of the *Purgatory* we meet a griffon, a creature that is eagle fore and lion aft—a creature never seen on land or in the air. Yet, as we shall see, when a poet uses a familiar symbolic hybrid of this kind, or creates one of his own, the proportions and relations between the parts of this creature and the meaning of the ensemble must all be precisely definable in terms of what is being symbolized. Allegorical interpretation of the *Comedy,* as I have tried to perform it in the body of this book, is not a matter of following behind one or two symbolic interpretations and hoping to come out straight: it is rather a process of understanding and experiencing the developing form and feeling of the poem as it moves toward accomplishing its aim of educating its readers to a state of felicity.

The Form of the Commedia. The process of understanding the *Commedia* is involved with the technique of its poetic form. Details of identification and description, of points of theology and philosophy—these may be easily brought under control; what remains is to trace the life, or lives, that come into being as we move through the poem.

The form of the *Commedia* is the resolution of all that Dante had to work with to achieve his aims: the concept that the universe was orderly, rational, and in one sense earth-centered (the earth was at the same time farthest from God); the belief that human intelligence properly aimed and directed could comprehend the workings of this universe; the conviction that human free will and divine justice dovetailed perfectly in determining the quality and destiny of each man; a well-established and subtle technique of poetic creation and interpretation designed to communicate all these ideas from poet to reader.

The movement of the *Commedia* is from the condition of being lost in a dark wood to the condition of contemplating the Triune God and comprehending the meaning of His universe. This progress, from nearly total ignorance to nearly total knowledge, is stepwise, by means of recurrent revelations and ever higher and wider syntheses of understanding.

These syntheses are perceptions, or recognitions, of an identity of things that had previously seemed disparate and disjunct. Some of these syntheses are built up by the process and movement of the *Commedia;* others are from the current stock of philosophical or theological beliefs.

This first kind of synthesis need not detain us here, since much of the body of this work is concerned with tracing the growth of a number of these purely Dantean syntheses—for example, the evolution of Dante's ideas of the nature and purpose of poetry. I might however briefly describe here two concepts needed as tools in tracing these growths: 'the competition of ideas' and 'dramatic situation.'

When, in the journey of the pilgrim through the afterworld, two notions about the same thing have been brought up, the better explanation displaces the worse, as in the dialectic of Plato: in the *Purgatory* the question of human free will is explored and answered at least four times, with each later explanation more satisfactory than the previous one. But we must also realize, as is again true of Plato's dialectic as well, that the later answer does not destroy its predecessor—rather it embraces the earlier one and would be neither clear nor substantial without it. This process of intellectual advance in both Dante and Plato is based on faith—faith in order and process and truth; and another kind of faith, faith in the germ of truth even in the most nearly ignorant mind.

Related to the competition of ideas is a notion of dramatic situation. This is the simple principle according to which most of us speak and by which most of us understand what is said to us. It is not only what is said that is to be considered, but also who said it to whom, where, under what circumstances, and why. Learning not to quote (or understand) out of context is the first lesson towards this notion; a later lesson will take us to an understanding of what Virgil, a pagan, says on the various levels of Christian Purgatory.

The syntheses that I described as the common property of Dante's age are the great unspoken truisms that are often the most difficult concepts for a later age to pin down. I have already given some examples of these in discussing the rational universe of the Middle Ages; I might here give one or two other examples for their particular pertinence to the form of the *Commedia.*

Justice, history, and time are involved with each other in a synthesis of this kind. Divine justice (which human justice tries to copy) is the path laid out by divine reason for the highest fruition of mankind. For God it is not necessary to distinguish between fruition (or punishment or reward) in this life and fruition in life eternal; man distinguishes. History, or—to attempt a divine prerogative and make time stand still—the present state of things, is what man has chosen to do within or against these paths of justice; more precisely, the state of things at any moment represents what certain men have chosen and what they are able to compel other men to live by.

The order of God is always there, to be seen as the yardstick by which all may be measured—for justice appears in time. Not only in divine retribution or reward (for this may be delayed or invisible) but in the events and actuality of life can justice be seen as the criterion. Time is one or more species of cause. In the simplest sense this appears in the punishments of the *Inferno:* the glutton or the simonist not only will (according to the beliefs of Dante's time) be thus punished eternally in Hell; but even his present life (according to Dante) is of this kind, and not when considered *sub specie aeternitatis* but simply when measured against the total richness that that life might have had without the absorption by such or such an unbalancing monomania.

In a somewhat different way we see this principle of justice appear in the *Purgatory*. Not as states of punishment (for these are infernal) but as corrective propaedeutics, we see justice using means for straightening those crooked who have seen themselves against the straight yardstick and wish themselves to be straight. In one sense the *Purgatory* is a methodical account of the ways in which error may be perceived and the corrective exercise devised for it—not only for the individual but for the role of society as well.

How are we to relate this synthesis of time and justice to the *Commedia?* We must first acquire a sense of the difference between Dante the poet and Dante the pilgrim, the character in the poem. For Dante the pilgrim, experiences occur in time: he learns, his mind is cleansed or expanded as he goes. Yet Dante the poet knows whither all this is tending. Not until canto 17 of the *Purgatory* (the center of the *Commedia*) does Dante the pilgrim learn of the concept of love which determines the structure of the universe; yet Dante the poet had been utilizing this structural concept from the opening of the poem. Dante the pilgrim knows as man knows: sequentially, by perceiving and conceiving in time. Dante the poet knows as God knows: simultaneously, by conceiving all at once the substance and the structure of his creation. The events of the *Commedia* constitute a journey—time conceived humanly; these same events comprise a vision—time conceived divinely. Perhaps the swoon into which Dante falls at the close of the *Paradiso* is the one from which he wakens at the opening of the *Inferno*. The whole of the *Commedia* is a process explaining how the poet came to be able to write the first line of it.[41]

Dante's journey, in one sense, takes place through himself, through the world of man as he has come to comprehend it. Fergusson has called the *Purgatory* a drama of the mind. The phrase is apt but it is also a dangerous paradox; because of the central creative role of Dante's personality, the *Commedia* tends to be antidramatic in a number of ways: it is lyrical and unritualistic for Dante the pilgrim, and it is systematic and rational for Dante the poet. (We might connect this with the fourfold interpretation of the poem: the literal and the anagogic senses move dramatically with the pilgrim; the moral and allegorical are parts of great patterns which remain spread out and in the same place, like panels of a mural, even after the poetic witness has moved on to the next scene.)

There is, as I have said, a prime element of circularity in the structure of the *Commedia:* the swoon at the end of the poem may be connected with the one at the opening of the poem—at least in the sense that from the final swoon the poet returns to earth to narrate what he can recall (and he recalls everything) of the journey that begins with the first swoon. From this point there are many consequences, but I wish to draw out for consideration only one—one connected with the dramatic qualities of the poem and with the notion of 'dramatic situation.'

The dramatic quality of Dante's poem lies in the keen and perfect awareness given to him by his plan of what everything in his work is leading to—a plan which removes the pitfalls of ill-placed or ill-timed episodes, of misplaced revelations of intent, or of ill-drawn or incomprehensible characters that another author might fall into in his earnestness to get a serious thing expressed.

Any other author has to work hard, and often awkwardly, to inform his readers of the outer circumstances and inner qualities of his characters. Think of how much of this labor is automatically done for Dante by the postulates of his poem. (Think for example of the multitude of miscomprehensions of the dramatic structure and meaning of two such masterpieces as the *Oedipus Rex* and the *Hamlet;* a reader must be perverse or petulant before he can go nearly so far astray as this after reading the *Commedia.*)

Dante's plan is based on a steady—never rushed or premature, rarely even premonitory—increase of understanding as he progresses to the eternal source of all understanding. His progress is what the Gestalt psychologists call a combination of gradual and saltatory development: it is steady and unremitting, but within the steadiness there occur sudden leaps of insight and of development, as though consciousness lagged behind the fact of development and had to be forced to jump to keep up. These leaps of insight are approximately what it has become the fashion, after Joyce, to call epiphanies.

Even the physical course of Dante's progress shows this combination of gradual and saltatory development: for the most part he plugs ahead steadily on foot in the first two canticles; but the passage to a lower level in Hell, to a higher ledge in Purgatory, or to a more transcendent heaven in Paradise is always accomplished by a sudden, even startling, device—he jumps or leaps, he is carried in someone's arms or on someone's back, he is transported in a boat, or—a most interesting process—he clambers arduously through a cleft in a cliff. I shall, at the appropriate point, discuss the particular relevance of each of these methods of development or progress.

These stages in development (or in insight into the situation and into the characters inhabiting that situation) take place in episodes marked off by a unity that is psychological and intellectual rather than only physical. In the *Commedia,* the episode is an unhurried development embracing (not necessarily at the end) an epiphany. The episode or scene, in this sense, is rarely confined within Dante's external unit, the canto: there is, so to speak, almost regularly, canto-enjambement.

The word 'dramatic,' like the words associated with 'tragedy' and 'comedy,' has been used as a metaphor for so long that we need to be reminded that it is a metaphor whenever it is used to describe something not written for the stage. 'Dramatic,' then, means a notable—either by plan or by accident—developing and reacting of one or more persons within a definite situation. Let us ignore the 'drama' of a fight between two wasps or of a tense political or international situation and we still have the fact that dramatic qualities are possibly to be found—and I believe they are always to be found—in any well-constructed short story or lyric poem (generally only a single dramatic development is utilizable in either of these forms) or in any novel or long narrative poem (these forms require many dramatic episodes, generally with some cumulative effect as in a play).

Dante's poem is closest in form to the epos, of which he had many medieval models in addition to Virgil's. But when we think of these models we must also think of the many essential ways in which Dante's poem has nothing to do—for example—with the nationalistic, or at least heroic, qualities of the epic poem. Three literary forms that, historically, have nothing to do with the *Commedia,* may be helpful in coming to grips with it.

The first of these is the short story. In Dante's time there were in circulation great numbers of tales of the kind, for example, that Boccaccio collected a generation or two later for the *Decameron*. These stories may even have provided for Dante models of brief realistic narrative. Most of the episodes of which the *Commedia* is built have qualities resembling those of a well-developed medieval tale—stark, simple, realistic development of a vital moral relationship.

Next is the lyric poem. From those of his own day—and especially from those that he himself had written—Dante could learn a better pacing and keener balancing of materials—in content as well as in sound—than the contemporary tale could have provided. The lyric poem of the time—canzone, sonnette, ballate—aimed chiefly at an intense but ordered expression of emotion: this too is obviously an essential part of Dante's *Commedia*.

The third literary form needs to be subdivided, since here we are right against the fact that Dante's form is unique in the *Commedia*. It is a long narrative with a single hero: for this we might first suggest the Alexandrian and medieval romances, especially the French romance of chivalry. But few of these have the intense concentration on the personality of the hero that we find in the *Commedia;* perhaps a closer analogue then would be the picaresque romance, the Renaissance descendant of the medieval romance. This brings us closer, since the medieval romance has a quality we don't want here: the greatness of the hero is always institutionalized—we must always remember his noble birth or the fact of his being a knight as the surrounding cause of his greatness. The picaresque hero—like the pilgrim in Dante's poem—creates his greatness and convinces us of it as he proceeds on his travels; if you like, you can probably say that Dante's pilgrim is the first great bourgeois, self-made hero in fiction. This brings us to the final point. The picaresque hero is usually no better than he has to be; he is always treated by his author with a great degree of detachment, usually even of irony. Of this there is nothing in the *Commedia*. And so, for my final analogue—and always remembering that we are trying to clarify the greater by referring to the lesser—I might suggest the most important segment of the modern novel, in turn a descendant of—more properly a reversion to—the picaresque romance. I mean the novel in which the hero is a thinly disguised, or not at all disguised, replica of the author, starting with the *Bildungsroman* of the German Romanticists. A novel in which the prime concern of the writer is the situation that confronts himself—perhaps leaving Kafka and Virginia Woolf to the side as too frenetic in their self-concern; a little more regretfully leaving James Joyce to the side, chiefly because he strove too hard to be an analogue to Dante: we can then—not forgetting that the differences are greater than the illuminating similarities—find some help in understanding the total plan of Dante's work by seeing some connections with the intent of Proust and of Thomas Mann, the latter especially in the *Magic Mountain*.

The Inferno. The impelling drive within the *Commedia* is the will to make the most and the highest of what man can do: to exercise that true freedom of the will which arrives only when one is in full awareness of the range of choices and possibilities. For Dante this establishes a certain kind of dichotomy: a nearly endless range of inferior and hence wrong choices (mistaken *liberum abitrium*) is set against the one right choice dictated by thoroughly enlightened self-interest (true *libertas*). (Today this notion may provoke raised hackles, but when were there ever two perfectly equal possibilities unless the issue were indifferent?) The direction of movement within the *Commedia* is ideally based, then, on an increasingly higher ambit of choices. Or, to use other terms: each free choice made consonant with reason increases the possible exercise of liberty.

The fundamental paradoxes of the *Inferno* are contained within the fact that it is an inverted cone: a cone should rather point and direct the mind and body to something ever higher and finer. The spread-outness of the opening of the cone portrays a deceptively wide area of choice: it is wide only in its provision of a multitude of wrong choices. As one descends inside the cone of the Inferno there is, in the unremitting constrictiveness of the place, an inversion, almost a parody, of the refinement of free will, to contrast with the progressive clarification of liberty as one climbs the cone of Purgatory.

It is this essential quality of inversion throughout the *Inferno* that makes the seeming clarity and directness of this canticle turn out for most readers to be a dead-end passage. It is more than a metaphor that as the travelers come to the end of Inferno proper they must reverse themselves with great difficulty and then climb through half the world's thickness before any light or free movement is possible: the pilgrim must be reversed, or converted to a new mode of progress before he can continue his journey in a straight line.

Parallel with the downward movement towards the frozen impotence of Satan there is, inevitably for the reader, a growing comprehension of the materials and ideas of the *Inferno*. The paradox of this canticle may, then, be thus stated: while the form of the *Commedia* (including this canticle) is based on a constant progress in understanding, the movement through Hell is towards the maximum perversity of reason—almost one might say to the nadir of stupidity. The moral sense of this paradox is only too clear: there is a growing towards stupidity and impotence that many men can confuse with a growing towards intelligence and control—no man is born truly stupid; he must work for it.

The *Inferno,* then, is an organization of the disorganized. Medieval ideas about Hell and Aristotelian ethics provided only a start towards this organization. Dante had to alter the contours of this Hell and give direction to this ethics to make them fit into his plan.

The implications of this plan are presented in the opening lines of the poem.

Nel mezzo del cammin di nostra vita
mi ritrovai per una selva oscura,
che la diritta via era smarrita.

In the middle of the road of our life
I came to myself in a dark wood
where the straight way was lost.

To be able to recognize the middle of this road, one must also know the beginning and the end of it. The road, a means of transition between two things, is life; since it is 'our' life, one man's experience can parallel, or at least communicate with, another's.

Here is the plan. One man who knows, or can learn, enough about the ways of life to distinguish between right and wrong ways, who knows the terminus of the ways, who knows that time is of the human essence in arriving at the right destination—such a man, by making and describing a full journey, can help mankind to see and want the right path.

We may call the *selva oscura* an image of 'the intellectual, moral and political ruin of mankind, the state of revolt from God.' Or we may begin our reading of the *Commedia* a little more like poets: before 'meaning' these things the *selva oscura* is itself. It is a dark and tangled woods of indefinable location (*oscura* is 'obscure' as well as 'dark'). It is a place in which—if one has suddenly come to his senses and found himself there—primitive fears are born and nurtured. Like most thoroughly terrifying things the *selva oscura* is so because it is a good thing turned inside out, inverted. A forest can be warm with broken brightness, cherishing and nourishing; such a forest we do not meet, however, until we have made the methodical journey down to the very bottom of things, reversed ourselves, and then made the climb to the top of Mount Purgatory. After that, there is a different kind of journey and a different concept of the soul as we move through Paradise.

The first third of the journey I shall characterize only briefly, in terms of the kind of thing one should catch in a rapid reading of the *Inferno*. The best approach to a good comprehension of the

Commedia is, I believe, through an intensive reading of the *Purgatory,* the canticle which is closest to common human experiences and interests, which is without the perverted and shabby grandiloquence of the *Inferno* or the subtle theological preoccupations of the *Paradiso.*

The melodramatic episodes of the *Inferno* are generally the first things to attract a reader's eye—the meetings with Francesca and Paolo, Pier delle Vigne, Brunetto Latini, the monster Geryon, Farinata, Ulysses, Ugolino. The meetings—variously touching, revolting, terrifying—are arranged in an absolute triumph over the technical difficulty of constantly increasing the reader's horror and repulsion as he descends, while keeping a steady increment of verbal beauty and of the warmth of the relationship between Virgil and the pilgrim Dante.

The character of Virgil is perhaps the most fully developed of all in this canticle. Alongside the recurrently helpless and pettish pilgrim, Virgil shines steadily in his resourcefulness and consideration. He knows the geography, both physical and moral, of the region, as at 4.31 sqq., 8.55-7, 8.73-5; although, as at 9.7-9, he shows that he too, though quick-witted, may need help. Like the great poet that he is, he has a good sense of timing—not the desire of his pupil, as at 3.70-8, but the properties of the situation, at 3.121-9, determine when he utters a piece of information.

In contrast to this calm clarity of Virgil, stands such a noisy puzzle as that of the 'pape Satan aleppe' of 7.1. Are these words Hebrew or French? Or some language spoken, in the disjunct individualism of Hell, only by Plutus? The mention of Michael, who had defeated his master, is enough to collapse the wind-egg of impotent Plutus; and yet the sails (resembling the wings of Satan), the wolf of greed (which we have met at the opening of the *Inferno* and shall meet again in the middle of the *Purgatory*)—these send our mind back and forth until, perhaps, we too shall, like Virgil who (7.3) 'knew all,' come to understand the thwarted command in 'pape Satan aleppe.'

More important than verbal cross references are the episodes in Hell that are parallel with, or parodies of, episodes in the later canticles. At 10.100 we learn that the souls in Hell know the future but not the present. This is a sinful parody of the purgatorial virtue of hope. Just as hope at Judgment Day will come to an end with the virtuous all ensconced in Paradise, so will this hellish foreknowledge (and in fact all knowledge in Hell) come to an end at the same event (10.106-8). Both sin and the virtue of hope, then, are partly a not-living in the present, but sin thereby stores up eternal blankness of the present for itself while hope leads to an eternal present of bliss. Virgil, congenial to this part of Hell, rounds off the little episode by himself making a false prophecy at 10.130-2.

A sad parallel is that between canto 19 of *Inferno* and the closing cantos of *Purgatory*. In the infernal chasm of the simonists, who in their greed made Church offices things of commerce, there is talk of Boniface VIII, of Constantine's donation, of the Evangelist, of the whore that commits fornication with kings: all these reappear in the great pageant of the Earthly Paradise, to resolve the theme of the corruption of the Church by secular power and greed.

The hypocrites in Hell and the proud in Purgatory are, partly, punished in the same way, by being forced to bend their heads to the ground. Here we may see the difference between the two realms. Hypocrisy *is* the action of bending lower than one should; pride *needs* the action of bending low as a corrective.

Hell contains those who have willfully chosen an evil way and live eternally—whether in this life or the next—in the context and consequence of that choice. In Purgatory we find those who, having sinned, offer themselves to the extended hand of God for correction and redemption. In Hell spirits are punished for sins committed; in Purgatory spirits are cleansed of the vices, the sources of specific sins. In the terms we shall see established in Purgatory, the whole of the *Inferno* is one great check on vice—an unmitigated and progressive horror story of the iniquities and miseries to which a man may commit himself through the blindness of his choices of conduct.[42]

From the oppressive climate of the pain that man creates for himself, from the abysses and torments of evil, the pilgrim finally clambers to the surface of the unexplored hemisphere of the earth.

CHAPTER TWO

Scene and Person

[CANTOS 1 AND 2]

To run over better waters now hoists sail
the little ship of my talent,
which leaves behind it a sea so cruel.

And I shall sing of that second realm
where the human spirit is purged
and becomes worthy of mounting to Heaven.

These opening lines of the *Purgatory* provide the imagery, the mood, and the purpose which will dominate the canticle.

The purpose of Purgatory is to cleanse the spirit not only of sin but also of any tendency or need to sin; such a need, for Dante, can be based only on defective vision, vision which is incapable of seeing all that is available to men and hence provides inadequate material for full choice. The cleansing, then, and the becoming worthy of Paradise are separable activities, although they must be performed together: as the negative element of the tendency to err is removed by pain and understanding, so the positive awareness of the better path is instilled—both parts of the process requiring the incessant comprehension and willed cooperation of the penitent.

The mood is one of lightness and freedom, after the murkiness and frozen confinement of the regions of Hell the travelers have just left.[1] The contrast is expressed in parallel lines of the two canticles; here, in the fourth line, the poet promises to 'sing of the second realm,' while in the fourth line of the *Inferno* he exclaims over 'how hard a thing it is to tell' of the wild and rough wood.

The imagery of the 'better waters' and the 'cruel sea' also expresses this contrast. Even more important is our introduction to the water imagery of the *Purgatory:* an imagery perhaps always with the idea of baptism as the root concept, nowhere directly expressed, except perhaps in the dipping of the pilgrim into the stream of the Earthly Paradise in canto 32, but adumbrated everywhere from the washing of the *fomes,* the stains, of evil from the pilgrim's face in canto 1, through the river-imagery that plays so powerful and ambivalent a part in the canticle.

The imagery of these six lines also recapitulates the mode of progress through all three realms. The tossing uncertainty of Hell is in the 'cruel sea'; travel in Purgatory is not only over better waters but is aided by something beyond the labor of the individual—the wind that fills the sail is certainly in many ways like the grace that comes from God; [2] movement in Heaven, as we see in the first canto of the *Paradise,* is accomplished simply by having become the kind of soul able to rise to God with no expenditure of effort.

The nightmarish horrors of Hell are done with, but three or four trailing reminders impose themselves on the mind of the poet before he accustoms himself to the new life here. The wretched magpies, who like the souls in Hell 'despaired of pardon,' had challenged the authoritative way of song. Dante may in this reference be casting a disparaging glance back at his own poetry in the *Inferno,* the 'dead poetry' of line 8: in the pied black-and-white of the birds there may be an image of the double light he there had to follow, the white of poetry and the black of evil. The 'dead air' that had afflicted both his eyes and his lungs (in lines 17-8) attacked the two vital organs of a poet—the eyes by which he sees and the lungs by which he sings. Perhaps, too, we have here a hint that no more than eyes and lungs are needed for infernal poetry; a heart and more will be needed from now on.

Such an analysis as this of these opening lines may seem to overemphasize the concerns of a poet. After all, the pilgrim has an aspect of everyman; is this not overburdening everyman with poetic baggage? Perhaps so; but Dante, like a skillful dramatist, is concerned at the beginning of an action with making the qualities and the drives of his characters unmistakably clear; subtlety of action and description can come later. And Dante knew that the pilgrim could not represent man without first being a specific man. The pilgrim makes his long journey, looking at things, asking about things, with the specific interests of a poet; we shall see as we proceed that the system of guides for the pilgrim, a system that is one of the main formal supports of the poem, is based on the pilgrim's growth as a poet.

The image of the ship, now able to hoist sail and course over better waters, takes on direct poignancy from a moment of autobiography in the *Convivio*. Dante says (*Con.* I.3.21, trans. Wicksteed):

> Since it was the pleasure of the citizens of the most beauteous and the most famous daughter of Rome, Florence, to cast me forth from her sweet bosom (wherein I was born, and nurtured until the culmination of my life, wherein with their good leave I long with all my heart to repose my wearied mind and end the time which is granted me), through well nigh all the regions whereto this tongue extends, a wanderer, almost a beggar, have I paced, revealing, against my will, the wound of fortune, which is often wont to be unjustly imputed to him who is wounded. Verily have I been a ship without sail and without helm, drifted upon divers ports and straits and shores by the dry wind that grievous poverty exhales.

(We must also remember Dante's words here about Florence if we are to appreciate the deep bitterness of the invective against that city at the end of *Purgatory* 6 and elsewhere in the *Comedy*.)

But we are never permitted to forget that Dante is a certain kind of poet. Any poet may stumble, even downwards, as the pilgrim does in the Inferno; he may run and climb, as in Purgatory; he may soar, as in Paradise. Only Dante and one or two others are able consistently to refer rate or kind of motion to an idea at the very heart of their work. To understand the significance of the pilgrim's speed and freedom of motion after the arduous exit from Inferno we need only recall the meaning of motion in Dante's universe: from the whirling speed of the Primum Mobile (that part of the created universe which is closest spiritually and physically to God Himself) the rate of motion diminishes as we move downward till we come to the one still point of the created universe, Satan's midriff, at the center of the earth. Satan's ability to freeze and immobilize the things within his control is the evil parody of God's power of setting things in motion. This metaphorical equation that Dante makes between motion and good is more than a source of metaphor for the poet: it is one of the structural movements (like the equations light is good, darkness is evil) used consistently and cumulatively by the poet to lead the pilgrim with increasing force and clarity to God Himself, the source alike of all good, all light, all motion.[3]

The pilgrim's first meeting with a spirit in Purgatory is magnificently marked by the new feeling he has in this realm. He sees a solitary old man whose appearance inspires 'as much reverence as any son owes to a father.' These are strong terms in which to describe a stranger; only the warmth and trust instilled in the pilgrim by his new environment could call forth such feelings. But lest we make too much of this new thing the poet immediately reminds us that the process of purification is only begun.[4] The stranger speaks sternly, almost menacingly; Virgil replies placatingly and with an odd mixture of ineptness and effectiveness.

This old man worthy of so much reverence is Cato—a pagan, a suicide, a rebel against that very Caesar who is established by the final canto of the *Inferno* as the secular (or at least political) counterpart of Christ. Then why has Cato been chosen to fill so important and reverend a post as that of guardian to Purgatory?[5] The most obvious explanation is that his suicide (in terms of his pagan code not a sin but a virtue) demonstrated the highest possible insistence on personal and political freedom—the same freedoms that constitute two of the main goals in the ascent of the mountain and the same insistence that Dante uncompromisingly manifested in his own life in the terms of his Christian society.[6] The rebellion against Caesar, far from adulterating his virtue, actually brings it to the highest pagan peak: Caesar is the near-founder of the Roman Empire which in the divine plan is to be the birthplace of Christ. Brutus and Cassius sinned against a lord and benefactor in rebelling against Caesar; not so Cato. A rebel against the established

Empire or an assassin of Caesar when he was at the point of establishing it would merit the severest punishment, but Cato's rebellion was against a Caesar engaged in tearing down an established state of things.

Restating this point in terms of time may also be profitable. Christ's so-to-speak endorsement of the Roman Empire is indicated by his choosing to be born under and within its power, but the endorsement is confirmed by the fact that the date of His birth and the date of the birth of the Empire so closely coincide.[7] The magnitude of Cato's act of freedom is proved to be the greatest possible of its kind by the same reasoning: it took place at the last possible moment. After the establishment of the Empire such an act would have been disobedience of the divine order and not the *summum bonum* within a pagan order.

Surely Dante could have found a Christian act of freedom as great as Cato's. Why does he try to fit a pagan into Purgatory?[8] But Purgatory, we must remember, is a region not merely of hope of Paradise. Every Christian spirit who gains access to Purgatory has the certainty of attaining Paradise; what kind of eternal guardian would such a spirit make? The guardian *must* be a pagan, a pagan endowed with the highest possible development (for a pagan) of the love of freedom which is the love of God, but still a pagan with no hope of ever attaining the grace and bliss which are the only complete fulfillments of that love of freedom.[9] Finally, to keep our theological details straight, Cato guards the approaches to Purgatory—he is not within the entrance undergoing the purgatorial process.

We have just had an example, in this discussion of Cato, of the kind of thinking—or thinking-and-feeling—which I believe lay at the heart of Dante's writing the *Commedia* and must come to lie at the heart of our reading of it, whatever our convictions about the world today may be. It is a thinking-and-feeling that, as Dante tells us again and again, justice is the cause of everything in the universe; on earth, it is the justice of God as it interacts with the free will of men. Whatever happens, happens at the right time, in the right place, in the right way, and to the right persons. Whatever happens has only one explanation; this explanation may (rather, always does) have many facets, or senses, or levels, but all these are only different significations of the same thing. What I have just said of the fundamental importance of this method of interpretation may suggest that it is rather difficult and complex to handle; it is, particularly because it seems to involve a completely foreordained, predestined course of history and to peck away at, if not to destroy, human free will. I do not wish to continue discussing this point here in the early stages of our journey; we shall be better prepared for it (and there will be a more appropriate occasion for it) when we reach the middle of the *Purgatory*. Let us now only remember the free will and free action displayed by Cato—and Dante's placing Cato in the highest possible fixed position for a pagan.

But we have not finished with Cato. The successive scenes or segments of the pilgrim's journey may be likened to panels through which he passes—panels in which, accompanied by Virgil or another of his guides, he stops to learn what this place is, who is here, and why. From what we have already said it should be clear that these panels are not *tableaux morts* or even *tableaux vivants:* rather are they dramatic scenes in which a master poet is devoting all his creative consciousness to the subtle ways in which individualities are affected by the qualities of the environment in terms of time, place, circumstances, and companions.[10]

Some of these details we have already mentioned for the meeting with Cato. The pilgrim's thankfulness, hope, pleasure in sight and smell, warmth of spirit, and awkwardness—these we have spoken of. We have spoken of Virgil's will to placate Cato; as he continues he becomes so verbose and repetitive as to make us suspect that he too is ill-at-ease in this new situation, in this introduction to a realm he had never expected to visit.[11] He performs his function here, true enough; he makes the requisite explanations to the guardian. Yet he shows his ignorance of the place (that is, of the criteria of its thoughts and feelings) by making an unnecessary and fruitless appeal to Cato on the basis of conjugal emotions; actually this is a greater ignorance-of-the-place than he displays anywhere else in the *Purgatory*—this is clearly his introduction to a new frame of reference. Cato himself we have seen to be a stern and conscientious performer of his duty. Like an old and efficient watch-dog he has come to have a sense of ownership of his charge: these are *his* cliffs that he is guarding. He has—and we must see that this is confirmation and not denial of his love of freedom, for it is freedom within law—an emphatic sense of law, so emphatic that he is prepared to grumble at any change of law, even if this change has been made by Heaven. Yet his existence here is poorer than that of many another old watchdog: there is no love in it, no charity, no sense of anything beyond the requirements of his function.

Here then, in this meeting of the three men (and notice how much more fitting it is to call them men rather than souls or spirits) we have a scene which for richness of psychological detail and for warmth and fullness of emotion would satisfy the creative standards of the most ambitious novelist or dramatist. But let us recall how Dante has accomplished this richness and fullness. Part, but only part of Dante's expression, has been accomplished by what these men say to each other. Another part, and that the more important, came from the reader's understanding of what this place is, what its demands and possibilities are. These latter things are, of course, indispensable tools of every poet or novelist or dramatist, but only in the plan of Dante's poem can such parts of the writer's task be made so cumulatively clear and forceful.

This point is worth restating since it is the basis not so much of understanding as of enjoying the entire poem. The narrative basis of Dante's poem in certain ways is akin to that used in such forms as the novel or play; in all of these there is a succession of scenes in which the traits of men are displayed within a situation which has physical, ethical, spiritual, and intellectual qualities. Also, in all of these forms, each successive scene has meaning and affects through our accumulated acquaintance with these characters; their words and actions come alive because we see them change to meet new circumstances or—where this is the author's point—we see them remain unchanged in spite of new circumstances. This is, more precisely and more fully than with any other author, the basis on which the *Commedia* lives and grows. The scene we have been looking at has meaning—and we know what the meaning is—because each of the three men has, so to speak, a history for us as well as a moment of appearance. The history of Dante the pilgrim and Virgil the guide consists mostly of what their experiences within the poem have been; any knowledge we might have had of their existence outside the poem is greatly overweighed by what we have seen of their life in the poem up to this point. Our acquaintance with Cato receives a strong impetus from his history outside the poem, at least in the way in which his history must have affected Dante the poet.* These three men meet and interact in clear and decisive terms within a scene (or at a time in the journey—in Dante's plan this means almost the same thing) that ethically and physically is crystal clear in its relations to the three men. We know who and what they are; we know what the significance of their meeting place is, to a rare degree of clarity: we then experience, with an equally rare immediacy of impact, the unfolding of significant aspects of man's relation to man within the City of Man and the City of God.

* * * * *

Within this technique of narrative Dante's timing is worth noting. He has many scenes to visit and many persons to meet, but there is time to pluck the fruits as well as plant the tree—time to present the development as well as the exposition of a scene and of the ideas and feelings associated with it.

Canto 2 opens with one of Dante's methodical reminders of the passage of time, but there is more than mechanical method in the rehearsal of the beautiful color changes in the development of the dawn from white to rosy to orange. Speed and light and freedom, themes presented in the first canto, are developed in the oncoming boatload of souls propelled by the angel's wings. The homeliness of much of Dante's imagery has been noted: along with his images from the arts and crafts, there are metaphors from daily happen-

*It obviously makes little difference whether Dante is using accurate or inaccurate history, whether he is deliberately or inadvertently distorting a historical fact. In any case, the history he *means* is clear.

ings of the farm, the countryside, the hearth. But there is also in Dante a quality, akin to this homeliness, which is another of his structural secrets: in Dante's writing the supernatural happens naturally because of the realism of his preparations.

Let us examine the scene at hand. The pilgrim and Virgil have clambered through an underground passage and have come out on a reedy seashore. They have spoken with someone who lives there and have gained a notion of the meaning of the place. They have not yet become used to the freshness and sweetness, so welcome after the murky noisomeness of Hell; they know where they have to go next but, in one of the many little comments to remind us of the double quality of the narrative,[12] they are like persons thinking of the path ahead and moving in spirit while lingering in body. Here, in this mood, enjoying the sparkling seascape though still a little mazed, they see—what more natural?—a boat coming towards them over the water. In such a context the method of propulsion—angel's wings—of this boat becomes only one more of the rich—and almost natural—details of a realistically portrayed event. It is an important detail, certainly, but not much more important than the detail of these travelers, for all the urgency of their mission, lingering to watch a boat land its passengers.

The naturalness of detail continues. The crowd disembarking look around at the scene new to them and, seeing two men already there, ask the way to the mountain. Not only is this an understandable mistake of theirs but we can also understand why their proper guide, Cato, is not there at the moment. This fussy old watchman has been thrown completely out of sorts this morning by something quite contrary to regulations: two visitors have come by the land path from Hell which is supposed never to be used, and one of them is still alive! It is fortunate for us, though, that his sense of rightness has been outraged since, while he is away wandering sulkily somewhere, we have one of the most touching meetings in the entire *Commedia*—a meeting that Cato would certainly have interrupted had he been there.

The spirits have noticed by the pilgrim's breathing that he is still alive (although their own growing pale on this occasion seems an equal anomaly),* but such is the feeling of the place that they are not frightened or in any way repelled by this; instead they crowd around him expectantly and eagerly—Dante conveys their sure expectancy of hearing a welcome explanation through his cheering image of the messenger bearing an olive branch. Their warm interest in this man who is alive—as though life had held few terrors for them—is a different order of interest from that generally shown in Dante's liveness by the spirits in the *Inferno*.

One of these spirits steps forward to embrace the pilgrim and so much affection does he show that the pilgrim, without recognizing him and with the same immediacy of emotion he had shown towards Cato, is moved to reciprocate. Thrice he tries to embrace the spirit and thrice his arms, meeting nothing but empty air, come back upon themselves. Not until then does he recognize his old friend Casella, the musician. Casella, agreeing to stop for a while and speak, says that he does so because he is so moved by his love for the pilgrim, a love no less now than that he had felt in his mortal body. (This compulsive power of love, a borrowing from the theory of courtly love, reminds us of Francesca da Rimini when she told us of love which exempts no loved one from loving; we shall meet the development of this idea in cantos 16-18.)

Then the pilgrim begs his friend to soothe his weariness with one of the songs of love which had always had this effect. Casella, with almost heavenly sweetness and consideration, complies by singing his own setting of one of Dante's poems, 'Love that in my mind converses with me.' The delight of this singing captures the pilgrim, Virgil, and the spirits so that they seem aware of nothing else. Only the return of grumbling duteous Cato breaks up this handsome alfresco concert.[13] All but Cato then depart for the beginning of the ascent, but their hearts are still with the singing—they move like men who go without knowing where. The warmth and beauty of this scene remain also with us as we accompany the travelers.

* Their growing pale is explained later by what Statius has to say of the soul's 'body' at canto 25.85-108.

CHAPTER THREE

Guides, Ideas, and Representations

[CANTOS 3 AND 4]

As Virgil and the pilgrim, at the beginning of canto 3, continue on their way, Virgil is still troubled by Cato's reproach and by self-reproach for having dawdled when he, at least, should have known better; even his walk takes some time to regain its wonted and needed dignity.[1] He has, to speak plain, been delinquent in his function as guide on coming into this new realm.[2]

Now follows, in the first half of this canto, a curious and important passage: curious for the setting of quiet fun within which an important philosophical statement is made. Virgil presents what is generally assumed to be Dante's definitive verdict on the limits of human reason: man, says Virgil, must realize that some questions remain beyond his powers, for if his reason had been able to follow the infinite path of one substance in three persons, Christ would not have had to be born. Most curious, perhaps, is why such a statement should be made by pagan Virgil.

We have two related questions to concern us here: one, the question of the various guides or companions that escort the pilgrim on his way; two, the question of how abstract ideas are presented in this kind of poem—a poem that is not explicitly theological or philosophical as is, e.g., Prudentius' *Psychomachia* or Lucretius' *De Rerum Natura,* but has some qualities in common with epic or narrative poetry, others in common with dramatic poetry, and in more ways resembles only itself.

The question of the pilgrim's guides—their quality, meaning, and function—is of pervasive importance in the *Commedia.* Except for the opening moment and the concluding moment of the poem, the pilgrim is never without one or more guides. The movement of the entire poem may be described in terms of the guides chosen to help the pilgrim on his way from the desperate lostness of his situation at the beginning of the *Inferno,* to the direct vision of the one substance in three persons at the conclusion of the *Paradiso.* The quality of Virgil's guidance—and of the other guides employed in the *Purgatory*—will grow clear from the various contexts in which we shall see the travelers as they move up the mountain; for the present let us consider only why Dante may have used his guides for so prominent a function and then consider some of the reasons for employing Virgil for so great a part of the journey.

The obvious reason for the device of the guides is, so to speak, mechanical. Recall how much of the event and substance of the poem is presented via the conversation, or even the mere being together, of the travelers and then think of the amount of misguided ingenuity that a poet would have had to expend in finding variegated substitutes for this device. But there is a more profound reason. The idea of man's need for guidance, for teaching, for being shown right from wrong directions, is at the very heart of Dante's belief—whether we take 'belief' in a philosophical or poetic or religious sense. Every man needs this guidance and gets it in various forms at different stages of his life. The development of the idea of guidance was, I believe, one of Dante's chief purposes in writing his poem (as it is one of my chief aims in writing this book).

Meanwhile, we shall have gone a great way in comprehending Dante when we see that these two reasons, which I have given separately, are but special statements of the same thing. Man in all his aspects (whether on his path to God or in his writing a complex poem) is based on his relations to others—this is a more subtle, more flexible, and more profound concept for Dante than was Aristotle's concept of man as social animal: for Aristotle, man's purpose is the smoothly functioning state; Dante's purpose goes far beyond that. An earlier statement of his creed is found in the *Convivio* (I.1.58): '. . . inasmuch as every man is naturally friendly to every man, and every friend is grieved by the defect of his friend . . .'

Whether the guides in the poem are real, symbolic, or allegorical does not permit of a simple answer.[3] To answer that they are all three is not so much an evasion as it is a way of approaching the varied intentions of Dante in his poem. Each guide is real, in the same double sense as the pilgrim himself: he has an objective realness (knowable by others outside the poem) and a fictional realism (of circumstantial, literal detail invented by, and controlled by, the poet). Next—and this is the most difficult and dangerous mode of interpretation—every person in the poem has a symbolic character insofar as he (or any other real person in or out of a poem) may be found consistently representing a given human or abstract quality or combination of qualities.

Establishing the symbolic identity of the important persons in the *Commedia*—where this can be distinguished from analysis of the allegory [4]—has been a major occupation of Dante scholars for half a millennium. Most often it has been—as with the Bible and Shakespeare—an exercise in political, social, or theological special pleading, with each interpreter finding Dante a staunch supporter of the interpreter's favorite cause. Thus we are as likely to find Dante a Lutheran as a member of the Carbonari. But these eccentric identifications do not excuse us from the obligation to look into the symbolism of the persons in the *Commedia*—both at this point in our reading and as we continue to read in the poem.

In the most frequent pattern of identifications the pilgrim represents Everyman; Beatrice, Theology (or Heavenly Wisdom, or Revelation); and Virgil, Reason or Worldly Wisdom—that is, Virgil's symbolic quality is equated with his function in the poem of guiding Everyman as far, or as high, as wisdom and experience of the world can carry one without the increment (or basis) of revelation. We may use this interpretation of Virgil to test the meaning and value of these symbolic identifications.

In the first place what were the qualities that Virgil had—or could be endowed with—that made Dante choose him for this function in the poem? By Dante's time Virgil had already had a spacious development beyond his factual life in pre-Christian Rome. Through his *Fourth* (later called the *Messianic*) *Eclogue,* which announced or echoed a prophecy of the birth of a savior, Virgil came to have in the course of the Middle Ages a role of soothsayer and magician.

His writings took on a function analogous to that of Holy Writ: in a species of fortune telling, or problem analysis, called Virgilian lots, a man with a practical problem could find a solution by opening his Virgil at random and putting his finger blindly on one of its verses—just as he could find spiritual guidance by using a Bible in the same way.[5]

For Dante there are more practical, as well as more wholesome, virtues to be found in Virgil. In the techniques of poetry, particularly in the problems of organizing a poem on the epic scale, Dante could hardly find a better model or guide than the *Aeneid*. That Virgil's great poem included a visit to the underworld, dealt with men and women in the tribulations and triumphs of their earthly lives, and utilized gods and goddesses as dramatis personae—this traversal of the three realms of the universe was as important as the fact that Virgil was the official celebrant of the foundation of that Roman Empire which played so large a part in Dante's political and religious thought. Above all perhaps were the gentility (in the special sense of the *cor gentil* of the *dolce stil nuovo*) and sensitivity with which Virgil wrote about relationships between men and men or men and women.

These are some of the reasons for using Virgil as the pilgrim's guide for nearly two-thirds of the journey. We must also see what constitutes the duty (or qualification) of a guide and then consider how satisfactory or useful is the symbolic identification of Virgil as Human Reason. Reason, thus limited, would seem to be the power to think through a question to its proper conclusion in choice of action in the areas, for example, of poetics, or politics, or geography—any question for which the human mind alone, uninspired by grace, is adequate. (Whether, in Dante's system of thought, there can be such an isolable question is a problem we shall have to put to one side for the present.) Remembering, however, that Virgil guides the pilgrim through the completely Christian realm of Purgatory, and even into the Earthly Paradise, we may have to modify this definition of worldly reason—or else to modify our notion of what constitutes a guide.[6]

The two cantos we have looked at have made it difficult to consider Virgil a qualified guide, or to equate him with Human Reason. Why should Reason choose such an awkward, obsequious, and erroneous way of approaching Cato? Why does Reason pause, is it reasonable that Reason should pause, to dally with the others in listening to Casella's song? We shall soon encounter more serious instances in which Virgil fails to apply to the task of guiding the pilgrim the kind of reasoning needed in this realm, but already it seems impossible to make 'reason' the motive or explanation of everything Virgil says or does. In short, the symbolic equation of Virgil with Reason is too narrow to cope with the dramatic role Dante has given him; Virgil needs the more flexible, more human characterization we are beginning to see. This more flexible role is precisely Dante's kind of allegory.

Let us now return to the opening of canto 3. Both men have been abashed by the remonstrances of Cato; Virgil's embarrassment is greater than the pilgrim's because his responsibility should have been greater. The pilgrim is sensitively aware of this and to show his continued trust in his guide—we might say, to restore face to him—he hurries to manifest his dependence on Virgil: first in the almost exaggerated thought, 'How could I have gone on without him?' and then in the action of being startled when he thinks he has been deserted. This action (at line 19) of turning to reassure himself that Virgil is still there is literally one of being scared by his own shadow; it is the action of a dependent child and as such is perfectly, or instinctively, calculated to restore the rather gruff tone which seems to be Virgil's preference in dealing with the pilgrim. Virgil's response, while he has barely recovered from his feelings of embarrassment, wonderfully shows his dramatic character—impatient with his own faults, but even more impatient with the weaknesses of others: 'Why do you still distrust? Do you not know that I am here to guide you?' *

* In this line the poet is not only showing a mood of affectionate irony toward Virgil—a mood we shall continue to meet; he is also giving the reader a telltale by which to judge the authority of Virgil's forthcoming statement.

And then, from Virgil:

> *'Mad is he who hopes that our reason*
> *can encompass the infinite way*
> *that holds one substance in three persons.*
>
> *Be content, o human race, with the* quia:
> *for if you had been able to see all,*
> *Mary would not have needed to give birth.'*

The immediate environment for Virgil's discourse on the *quia* [7] is, then, the slight unease he is suffering from, an unease that makes his reproach of another's slight stupidity excessively high flown. Yet this little discourse is the first step in a succession of important statements about the nature of the human soul. As is often true in the plan of the *Commedia,* this first step is of value only in indicating a general direction of travel.

Virgil's discourse is based on a tripartite argument: (1) there is a qualitative difference between the pilgrim's body and Virgil's; (2) Virgil does not know the cause of this difference; (3) therefore it is presumptuous for the pilgrim (or any other man) to seek to know this cause. We might immediately label Virgil's argument a defective syllogism, but let us wait for that. (We must wait until chapter 11, in the discussion of Statius' speech at canto 25.31-108, to learn the nature of 'bodies like Virgil's'—and also to go beyond the limitations of Virgil's *quia.*)

The discourse was provoked by the pilgrim's noticing not the difference in the two bodies but the difference in the thing that each body effected—in other words, the *quia.* There had been no occasion in the *Inferno* to notice this difference, since there had been no sun to produce the effect of the shadow.

The pilgrim's possession of a material body is repeatedly noted throughout the poem, but rarely is the significance of this body so nearly made explicit. Here is a place where, in Dante's words, 'the veil grows thin.' (The veil imagery in the *Purgatory* culminates in the dropping of Beatrice' veil in the Earthly Paradise.) Among the immaterial spirits of all three regions—those whose bodies are of a different species from his—the pilgrim travels like another order of being: as different from those about him as, say, Christ in the flesh was different from those among whom He chose to live. The Harrowing of Hell by Christ was a favored medieval subject for paintings and discussions; a point often discussed was whether or not Christ was in the flesh when He travelled through the Inferno to choose His companions for the return to Paradise.

Let us add up these things. We have seen Virgil failing in his duty as guide and feeling a proper shame for this; in the apparatus of the poem it is necessary that Virgil regain his self-importance—the poet quickly gives him a chance to do this; then comes the statement from Virgil that man must be content to know effects and never to know causes. Rather than accept this statement as a convention or staple of Dante's belief let us—at least for the moment—see it as having some connection with Virgil's dramatic qualities in the poem. This would mean that what he says at this point is being possibly modified by these considerations: (1) Virgil's confidence in his power to know cause and effect has been shaken by the Casella-Cato episode; (2) the others he names as having unquietable desires to know—Aristotle and Plato and many others—are the pagan philosophers in Limbo; (3) to 'compass that infinitude which one substance in three persons fills' is an excellent description of Dante's methodical aim in writing the *Commedia;* whether or not he has achieved that aim depends on whether we believe his words at *Paradiso* 33.112-20; (4) the final point—and this explains the difference between Plato, Aristotle, and Virgil on the one hand and Dante on the other—is that Mary *did* give birth. There were two possible ways in which mankind, then, could have attained the full heavenly understanding that comes from unthwarted love: (a) by not falling, but inhabiting the Earthly Paradise until the time for translation to the Heavenly Paradise; (b) by falling, and then by experiencing the Incarnation and the slow, tortuous climb back to redemption by the aid of grace; (a) did not happen, but (b) is history.[8]

This important statement about reason, Dante the poet does not leave without underlining: we must see that it is a statement about reason before the birth of Christ and the different thing that reason is after the birth of Christ. The poet will not abandon this point until he is sure he has made it clear.

Immediately, then, after the discourse of Virgil the two travelers continue their journey—a journey upwards. They are stopped by a cliff so steep that the nimblest legs would here be useless. 'Now who knows on which side the cliff slopes so that it can be climbed by someone who goes without wings?' These are the words of Virgil, especially aware at this moment that he does not possess wings. But while he holds his face low and thinks within his mind about the way, Dante does the simple thing: he looks up and sees on top of the escarpment a crowd of souls who may be able to give them the answer. Dante underscores his point:

> *'Lift,' said I, 'your eyes, my master:*
> *behold there someone who will give advice,*
> *if of yourself you may have none.'*

This section is rounded off with a final touch of delicate comedy when Virgil replies to this 'with a happy look,' and says:

> *'Let us go there, for they come slowly;*
> *and strengthen your hope, my sweet son.'*

Virgil pathetically aware that he does not have wings; Virgil trying to climb a mountain by looking at the ground and thinking within his mind—this Virgil might make one of the company of abstracted scholars parodied in Gulliver's voyage to Laputa. The pilgrim looking straight at the problem; the pilgrim having the simple courage and intelligence to lift his eyes and look up—this, it seems to me, is a portrait of what Dante means by Christian reason. (The final clincher to this point we shall see at the beginning of the next canto.)

The slow-moving spirits whom the pilgrim saw above the precipice are in sharp contrast to the eager souls who had disembarked from the angel's boat. These—the first of four groups we shall meet in Antepurgatory—are the spirits of those who died while under the ban of excommunication but who (at least in Dante's decision) repented at the last moment.

Antepurgatory is reserved for those not yet ready to undergo the labors and the pains of purgation; here, removed from any temptation to sin, they may slowly prepare themselves, above all in strength of will, for the ascent of the mountain. Slow motion, lack of energy, languidness—this is the tone of Antepurgatory. Yet we must note two things: first, the differences between the various flaws of spirit to be found among those working out their time in Antepurgatory and the specific sin of sloth purged on the fourth terrace of the mountain; second, that while a great part of Antepurgatory is scoriac and precipitous it has, e.g., in the vale of princes, pleasances of quiet beauty not matched until we reach the Earthly Paradise at the crest of the mountain. The beauty of Antepurgatory, however, is essentially different from that of the Earthly Paradise. Here, as in the Casella song or the songs at the beginning of canto 8 interrupted by the serpent, there is no time or occasion for any resolved action of enjoyment—in a sense the beauty of Antepurgatory is meaningless. By comparison even with the pain and labor of the penitential terraces, there is more aesthetic enjoyment, e.g., of the sculptures on the terrace of the proud than is available for the souls outside the gate of Purgatory.

In Antepurgatory we shall meet four groups of souls waiting to begin the toils and rewards of purgation: they are almost literally killing time here to atone for their dawdling on earth, dawdling that wounded and nearly killed the time within which they could set themselves on the right path.

The first group is that of the excommunicates (in cantos 3 and 4). These wander about the base of the mountain for a period thirty times the length of their earthly contumacy. While among them the pilgrim converses with Manfred.

The others comprise three groups of the late-repentant—those who were indolent towards repentance for most of their lives, those who died unshriven, and those who were preoccupied with other things during their lives. The indolent, whom we meet at the end of canto 4, are held in Antepurgatory for a period equal to that of their delay in seeking conversion; here the pilgrim chats with Belacqua. Among the unshriven, who are held for a period equal to their earthly lives (canto 5 to 7.63), we have notable meetings with Buonconte, La Pia, and Sordello. The preoccupied (canto 7.64 to the end of canto 8) seem to be exclusively those who held high posts in the secular government of men; here, still accompanied by Sordello, we meet Judge Nino Visconti and Conrad Malaspina.

The meeting with the excommunicates is considered one of the great set pieces of the *Commedia*—especially admired for the elaborate simile of the sheep (lines 79-87). No doubt this simile is a good example of Dante's faculty of close observation, but we must also see that in their quality of being sheep without a leader (except for one of themselves) they represent the status of excommunication.

The spirit with whom the pilgrim here speaks [9] is that of Manfred, pictured in the terms of a mythic sun-god:

> *golden-haired was he and handsome and of noble aspect;*
> *but a cut had cleft one of his eyebrows.*

The gentleness and hopefulness of Manfred's discourse are in contrast with the grandeur and fierceness of most of his known life.[10] Dante herein gives another example of the malleability of historical facts for the purposes of his poem. Even in the last-minute repentance of Manfred, Dante is following not history (the circumstances of Manfred's death obviously make this impossible) but the requirements of his own dramatic plan: this plan is also his sourcebook for the details of the deaths of Paolo and Francesca, of Ugolino, of Ulysses, of Guido of Montefeltro and of his son Buonconte—in short, of the best-known episodes in the *Commedia.*

We might note Manfred's habit of wearing green (the color, again, of the mythic sun-god, as well as that of the theological virtue of hope), which Dante perhaps almost punningly refers to in the river Verde, 'green' (line 131). More important is Dante's choice of so notable a sinner as the spokesman for the excommunicates, as though to emphasize equally the poet's right to invent last-minute repentances and his belief that, in spite of the most deadly ban of the Church,

> *. . . infinite goodness has such great arms*
> *that it takes in all who turn to it.*

In the first twelve lines of the next canto, Dante utilizes the experience he has just been through (the talk with Virgil about how to climb the mountain and then the conversation with the spirit of Manfred) to refute the philosophical error that man has more than one soul. This error is specifically pagan and particularly associated, in Dante's time, with Plato and Aristotle[11]—the very philosophers Virgil had mentioned a short while back with the air of saying 'If there is any problem that these philosophers can't solve, well, it's not to be solved on earth!'

There is a tiny touch of mischief in the recall of 'wings,' but mostly there is the sweetness of Dante's hope and trust in the lines with which he tells how he and Virgil finally are led to the break in the cliff which permits them to start the climb of the mountain: as he follows Virgil up the path he comments that even so arduous a mountain as Bismantove may be climbed to its summit

> *with feet alone: but here one must fly,*
>
> *I mean with the swift wings and with the plumes*
> *of great desire, behind that leader,*
> *who gave me hope and was a light to me.*

The canto closes with an episode which, with fitting casualness in this region, introduces one of the main ideas of the poem—the idea of free will, of free election of destiny. Here, in a setting of sunstruck pastoral, comes a rejoinder to Virgil's slightly pompous pronouncement that rest from weariness will come at the end of climbing this mountain:* from one of a number of spirits sitting in the shade of a great rock, 'as a man through laziness settles himself to rest,' come the words, 'Perhaps you will first have need to sit down.'† This is Belacqua, who, even when he turns his head to look at the travelers, does not lift his gaze higher than his thigh. The pilgrim, recognizing him, asks whether he is waiting for an escort, or whether he has merely resumed his accustomed ways. 'What's the use of ascending?' asks Belacqua; 'the angel of God that sits at the gate would not let me pass . . .' (When we meet this angel he seems rather to be standing, but Belacqua can project his own laziness even upon an angel of God. Even the way he finishes his sour-grapes statement—'would not let me pass to the torments'—may indicate the source of his laziness on earth: he can as yet see only the unpleasantness and not the rewards of what the future holds for him.)

Belacqua is in Antepurgatory, among the indolent who died a natural death, spending a period equal to his indolence before proceeding to the next step; this is what he has so clearly chosen that the pilgrim asks whether he has resumed his accustomed ways. This is one of the simplest demonstrations of what we shall meet throughout Purgatory: the spirits are more than reconciled to their lot—they are comfortable within it because it is what they have chosen for themselves. Even when the indolent way they have chosen keeps them so long from Paradise they are content, as those undergoing purgation are almost fiercely and hurriedly happy in the pain of the penance they are undergoing.

* He characteristically insists on keeping this little prophecy vague, as he concludes his statement with: 'No more shall I answer, and this I know for the truth.'

† Belacqua is of course understating what is to happen. Three times before reaching the summit the pilgrims lie down to rest, even to sleep, and the pilgrim Dante to dream three notable dreams.

CHAPTER FOUR

Manicheism, Nature Myth, and Politics

[CANTOS 5 AND 6]

Dante's plan ordinarily keeps him at a great distance from the cruder or simpler forms of medieval superstition, but in the episode of Buonconte da Montefeltro (Dante's meeting with the father, Guido da Montefeltro, is one of the more striking episodes of the *Inferno*) we have an amazing piece of folklore, with resemblances not only to the medieval fable but also to the classical metamorphosis tale and even the nature myth of primitive culture.

Buonconte is a sad case, seeking pity anywhere it may be: neither his wife nor anyone else, he says, cares for him, so that even among these souls who came in just under the wire—by being repentant at the last possible moment—he must hang his head.[1] At this admission, and remembering not only the evil but also the magnanimity and popularity of his father, we can understand and feel a bit sorry for the kind of life the son's must have been. But it is his death that he is interested in, and we can expect such a self-tearful character as this to spare us none of the bloody details. He had received his death wound in the battle of Campaldino[2] but fled so far from the field that his burial place was not known until he now tells his story. With his throat cut he managed to flee as far as the mouth of the Archiano, where it empties into the Arno (we may even find some parallel between the blood flowing from his throat, thus bringing his life to its end, and the equivalent things happening to the little stream: this is the method of nature myth and metamorphosis).* There, already blind, he uttered

* Dante's rivers seem always to be connected with great emotional outbursts. This one, as we shall see, leads us directly into the great political invective at the end of canto 6. In canto 14 a natural history of Tuscan evil is given in terms of the course of the Arno (see also canto 13.88-90). The immediate clue to this river

his last word, which was the name of Mary; he fell, and only his flesh remained. (Note, that of the four instances we have met in the *Purgatory* telling how salvation was achieved, every one has specified Mary as the means.) When the angel of God took his spirit

> *. . . one from Hell*
> *cried: 'O you from Heaven, why do you rob me?*
>
> *You carry from here the eternal part of this man*
> *for one little tear that takes him from me;*
> *but I shall deal otherwise with the other part'* [i.e., his body].

After this testimony—even from a devil—of the efficacy of last-minute repentance (in God's scale of time, if repentance can come even with the last breath it is because the potentiality and material for it have always been there) we have a definition, perhaps not entirely orthodox, of the powers granted to the forces of evil: the devil

> *Joined that evil will, which seeks only evil,*
> *with intelligence, and moved the mist and the wind*
> *through that power which his nature gave him.*

The aim and effect of the devil's machinations are to increase the vaporization of water over a wide area, so that this vapor, rising and then condensing when it has attained the cold upper levels of air, may fall as rain in such quantities that the level of both Arno and Archiano is raised sufficiently to sweep the body of Buonconte into the Archiano and down the Arno, where it is finally covered over with river sediment.

This story of Buonconte's may be the unexaggerated truth, or it

question is of course in the twin rivers of the Earthly Paradise as sources not only of the stagnant rivers of Hell but also of the major rivers of earth: there results a great complex of ideas of purgation and metamorphosis not unlike (and possibly the source of) James Joyce's use of rivers and sea in *Finnegans Wake*.

may be the grandiose fantasy of an unloved child and unwanted man; in either case it bears many resemblances to the supernatural tampering with the forces of nature that we find in ritualistic tales, with a surly medieval devil thrown in for good measure.[3] Nor should we ignore the political inception of this entire episode, which sets in motion the forces of earth, air, and water: it was in a battle with the Florentine Guelfs that Buonconte, a Ghibelline, received his death wound. The tale of Buonconte serves as a darkly suggestive overture to the political *opera seria* we are going to have in the two succeeding cantos.

In between we have the tiny, but intensely delicate and touching episode of La Pia. It serves to remind us that, in the midst of the violent deeds of man and nature that we have just encountered, there can still be a woman remembering a pathetic detail: before her husband slew her he had wedded her *con la sua gemma,* 'with that gem of his.' And who can say to Dante:

> '. . . *when thou shalt return to the world,*
> *and have rested from thy long journey* . . .
>
> *Remember me, who am La Pia;*
> *Siena made me,* [the] *Maremma undid me.*'

It is with a mind still shaken by the story of Buonconte and a heart still touched by the gentleness of La Pia (although in her self-dramatizing she is not unlike Buonconte) that we come to the opening of canto 6, to meet with one of those opening images of Dante's that seem almost shockingly inappropriate to the place: this is an image of the winner and the loser in a game of dice (another, at the opening of canto 9, has to do with the concubine of Tithonus rising in the morning from the arms of her lover). But the dice game fits the subject which is beginning to haunt the poet: the fortunes of the game, or of war, and the adulatory crowds that flock around the winner. (The word translated 'dice' is *zara,* a game played with three dice—for Faith, Hope, and Charity?)

Two themes more must be introduced before we are ready for the great set piece which constitutes most of this canto. The first of these—on the efficacy of prayer [4]—has a minor interest in developing the complex relationship between the pilgrim and Virgil. The pilgrim recalls a passage of the *Aeneid* which denies that prayer may change a decree of Heaven; if this is true why have so many of the spirits they have met in Purgatory asked for the prayers of those on earth? Virgil, for all of the poet's kindness towards him, bumbles through an answer: 'yes, that's what I said, but that was true only in my pagan existence and is not true now; besides, for a final answer to questions like this you'd better wait until you see Beatrice.' At the name of Beatrice the pilgrim's weariness vanishes, and he urges Virgil to hurry, evidently thinking to see her before nightfall. Virgil must check his hopes by telling him that the sun will return before he will climb far enough to see her (*Purg.* 6.55-7). It turns out, as another of Virgil's bad guesses, that the sun returns not once but three times before the pilgrim sees Beatrice.

But what this answer about prayer had taken away from Virgil's dignity is completely restored by what follows: they meet a spirit, the poet Sordello, who is proud and disdainful and like a lion until he learns that this is a Mantuan. He then embraces his fellow-townsman as an equal; let us anticipate here what Dante so effectively delays: there is a long digression (though a brief interval of time) until at the opening of the next canto Sordello learns that this Mantuan is Virgil—he then kneels to embrace Virgil's knees, 'where the inferior lays hold.'

Seemingly this meeting of the two Mantuans serves as the immediate pretext for the famous invective against Italy that follows. But remember how we have been prepared for this: in the bloody internecine battle at Campaldino which disturbed Heaven and earth; in the image of the fawning adulators around the successful gambler; and in the picture of Sordello, a contemptuous lion transformed to a warm friend merely by the presence of a fellow-townsman; even the little touch of La Pia—in all these we have had the bloody structure of reality built up alongside the warmth of gentleness and friendship, which are equally real but not ever present in society in the same measure. The transformation of Sordello may be even deeper than this. It is almost certain that Dante knew that Sordello fought against Italy as a mercenary soldier under Charles of Anjou —Charles and the House of Anjou representing for Dante the type of usurpation and oppression in the recent history of Italy. It is perhaps Sordello's entrance into Purgatory that has so cleansed him of his sins against his country and made him so pointedly ardent a lover of her. (Perhaps the chief reason for choosing Sordello for his function at this point, however, is the knowledge of kings and princes displayed in Sordello's famous poem, the 'Lament for Blacatz': this, on Dante's principle of experience-as-a-guide, might have suggested that Sordello be used as the guide through the Valley of Princes.)

The invective piece itself is a massive formal structure, with a tremendous range of moods and tones. But one simple theme dominates the piece: when Italy was united under an emperor she was the mistress of provinces; now, a ship without a pilot in a great storm, she is a hostelry of woe—'those living in you do not remain without war.' To proceed we need a summary, however brief, of the state of Italy in Dante's time and of his intense convictions on the causes and cures for the situation.

Holy Roman Emperor warred against King of France for hegemony over Italy; the Pope played one against the other while furthering his private ambitions; the powerful cities—Florence, Milan, Rome—fought against each other while calling Emperor or King or Pope to assist them; one political party in a city, to further its cause, betrayed the other party to one or another of the external enemies of the city; often this civil war divided a family within itself.

The terms 'Guelf' and 'Ghibelline' (originally from the rival German families of Welf and Weiblingen) came to be ascribed to the contending parties in northern Italy and elsewhere. The Guelfs (fundamentally the party of the Pope) and the Ghibellines (the party of the Emperor) served as rallying points (verbal or actual) for the struggles on all possible levels.* Typically the noblemen, from feudal tradition or inheritance and often from Teutonic ancestry, were allied with the Ghibelline party, while the middle-class city dwellers were generally Guelfs out of antipathy to the nobles and out of a vaguely nationalistic espousal of the Italian side in the quarrel. We may use this simplified version of the struggle in Italy only if we remember that the issues were much more complex than a simple struggle for ascendancy between Pope and Emperor, and if we remember that men (including Dante) and cities (including Florence) often shifted allegiance from one party name to another without actually shifting allegiance to the causes they were willing to fight and die for: the name, in a given arrangement of forces, might mean nothing more than a better or a worse way of arriving at the desired goal.

Dante, for whom the attainment of international peace under the Holy Roman Emperor was the *summum bonum* of secular life, in his *Monarchy* had little trouble, in his view of things, in identifying the villains who had made the Emperor impotent and had kept alive the warfare and domestic slaughter: the various secular monarchs who contested the political hegemony of the Emperor; the various powerful cities who put their selfish commercial aims above that of universal peace; and—probably most of all—the higher clergy and the papacy itself, which could have put an end to these struggles but, in refusing to do so, was refusing to comply with the separation of powers and functions that should prevail between the provinces of Caesar and of Christ. This latter separation Dante thought—with many others—had been ordained by God in the act of Christ's being born within the newly established Roman Empire. Only the Empire, so Dante felt with great intensity, could bring peace to Italy and to Europe. The great pageant of the Earthly Paradise, the culminating dramatic episode of the *Purgatory,* makes

* Gabriel Harvey, in his notes to Spenser's *Shepherd's Calendar,* exhibits one of the many vagaries of Renaissance scholarship when he finds the origin of 'elf' and 'goblin' in the impact this struggle made on the popular mind: thus a mother, to frighten-quiet her child, would say, 'If the Guelfs don't get you the Ghibellines will!'

this same point; it is the episode Beatrice insists that the pilgrim understand and then communicate to those on earth.

The invective passage of canto 6 (lines 76-151) reflects this agonized chaos of the Italian political structure; it is spoken as a great aside by the poet himself, as though forced from him in spite of the long suspension it entails of the dramatic role of the pilgrim. The imagery is confused—intentionally so, we may be sure, since this confusion is one of the greatest sources of the power of this passage. In the first three lines we have Italy described as a slave, as a hostelry of woe, as a ship without a pilot in a great storm, as mistress no longer of provinces but of a brothel. Others follow: Italy is a beast that needs the proper spur, saddle, and bridle, a beast that must be controlled by the proper rider. Finally, Florence is a sick woman who cannot find rest on her bed * and, by tossing about, tries to allay her pain. We see that a good deal of the language and imagery is straight from the *Inferno,* almost as though there must be for our pilgrim, before he enters the gate of Purgatory to be purged of the human catalogue of evil tendencies, a separate and private purgation of the vindictiveness aroused in him by thoughts of the political situation in his beloved city and country. These images which remind us so strongly of the Inferno are not only terms such as 'hostelry of woe' and 'brothel' but the explicit recall, in 'one gnaws the other,' of Ugolino and his compound treachery and suffering (*Inferno,* canto 32.124 to 33.78).

Dante blames the clergy, who should be devout and permit the Emperor to enforce the Justinian Code; but he equally blames the titular Emperor, Albert of Hapsburg, for letting his greed for things in Germany persuade him to abandon control over the empire. This section comes to its climax when the poet asks Albert to behold widowed Rome weeping, 'My Caesar, why do you not accompany me?'—with echoes not only of Jeremiah and widowed Jerusalem but perhaps also of those words of Christ on the cross: 'My Lord, why hast thou abandoned me?' It is as though Dante were mak-

* The word here translated 'bed' is *'piume'*—'feathers,' or 'down'—a word we frequently meet in the *Purgatory* in connection with wings, especially angels' wings.

ing the plight of Rome a secular equivalent to the grief of Christ, with faith indestructible but at this moment shaken.

The latter half of the diatribe, now directed entirely against his native Florence, is marked by a powerfully consistent use of the rhetorical device of irony. Yet the personal connection is stronger than ever: those attributes for which he gives Florence this high-praise-in-reverse are those through which he himself had suffered pain, shame, and exile. This personally motivated irony now clarifies and intensifies the closing image of the canto: Florence is not only ill but ill with the greater willfulness and also the greater suffering of a woman; her only effort to allay her pain is the violent and useless, even deleterious, exertion of tossing her limbs every which way.

CHAPTER FIVE

The Idea and Plan of Purgation

[CANTOS 7-10.111]

The opening of canto 7 points up the conscious narrative art of Dante. We can come to understand the emotional and structural justification for the outpouring of bitterness against those responsible for the dire state of affairs in Italy; but it was undeniably a digression, and the poet must now restore the movement of the pilgrim's progress. As on a stage, the chief actor has stepped forward to deliver a passionate soliloquy while the other two continue their conversation unheard; when the soliloquy is over, the spotlight widens to embrace all three. Like any good dramatist, however, Dante is doing more than creating a new scene when the old one is done: the very abruptness of this change permits him, with no fuss over transitions, to return to a mood more appropriate to this time and place, to return immediately to the dignified warmth of the greetings between Sordello and Virgil. Note, too, how quickly this new scene rises to its own climax when Sordello learns that it is not merely a Mantuan but Virgil himself that he is greeting.

And every segment in a well-constructed narrative must also look forward. The section now beginning will have its full climax two cantos later, at the gate to Purgatory, after the pilgrim and the reader have been fully prepared to make that great step upward.

The first step in this preparation is the identification of Virgil. Sordello's question about the nature of Virgil's home in Hell produces a description of Limbo as the home of those who practiced the pagan virtues but were not endowed with the three Christian virtues. These three virtues will continue to be an important theme in the progress to the gate: they are, in a sense, the very three steps of the entrance. They have, even before this, been negatively foreshadowed in the three barren dice at the opening of canto 4 and in the thrice vain attempt of the pilgrim to embrace his friend Casella in canto 2.

Like the meeting with Casella, this one with Sordello is warm and unreserved. As the pilgrims climb the mountain there will be other such notably friendly meetings—with Statius, with Guinizelli—almost invariably with fellow poets.

After Virgil reminds us that he is a stranger to this region and must ask the Christian Sordello for guidance to the area 'where Purgatory has its right beginning' we learn an important law of the mountain—when night falls no further ascent is possible. The obvious explanation of this is the unwisdom of proceeding without the light of God as symbolized in, or transmitted by, the sun. (There is paronomasial play, at this point and others, on *sol,* 'sun,' and *solo,* 'only'—God, the Only One.) But it is at least equally important to see here a provision for the well-being of the penitent—respite after toil and pain, respite that the souls in Paradise do not need and that the souls in Hell do not get.

Sordello then leads his companions into the Valley of Princes, where they will spend the evening and night. The valley, where spirits beat their breasts for the great deeds they left undone, is brilliant in its colorful beauty and sweet in its mixture of a thousand scents. Withal it is as narrow and fettered as the flowery garden of the Earthly Paradise is wide and free.

This self-contradictory beauty of the valley is the key to its quality. These princes were great ones in their day, but few made great imprints on history. The explanation for this (which is the basis on which they are here) is that their negligence in spiritual duties is not to be described simply as a theological error: by being small-minded, by neglecting *any* part of their obligations (a magnified error among these worldly great) they did not see or take full advantage of their secular opportunities for good.

Here, although their purgation has not begun, they indicate by their actions that they are close to the entry gate. In amity and devoutness they sit singing hymns, in pairs comprising sworn enemies on earth but now preparing each other for the labors ahead.

Sordello takes the occasion for a little homily on a theme that occurs frequently in the *Comedy*—the theme of degeneration from father to son. Sordello explains this decay by saying that God takes this means of insuring that men must continue to pray to Him if they wish to become good—they cannot acquire virtue simply by being born to a good father. This is a naive explanation but it contains a strong center of agreement with Dante's concept of individual free choice of conduct. Later in the *Purgatory* we find Guido del Duca (canto 14) attributing this kind of degeneration to greed; Marco Lombardo (canto 16) says that the Church by its worldly ambitions confuses the condition of leadership in both secular and spiritual worlds, and is consequently to blame for the moral decay from one generation to the next. In canto 8 of *Paradise* a broader answer is provided by Charles Martel for this same question: God, requiring a diversified social order (since only He is perfect and uniform), has celestial influences overrule the tendency of heredity to repeat itself.

The coming of the three travelers into the valley had been marked by the compline hymn, *Salve Regina,* a vesper song of exiles from their eternal home. Now, at the opening of canto 8, one of the spirits sings another evening hymn, *Te lucis ante.* As though in immediate response, two angels come from on high; their coming is preceded by another reference to the veil of truth:

> *Here, o reader, sharpen well your eyes to the truth,*
> *for the veil is surely now so thin*
> *that it is certainly easy to pass within.*

Dante, in warning us that the veil (of illusion or of allegory) is here transparent, may here be insisting that his readers be aware of his own double role in the poem: he is not only the pilgrim learning and growing by the difficult means of experience, but he is also the poet who has established these very difficulties in the path of his characters and knows of the solution that lies ahead.*

* As in other places where Dante uses the veil-imagery in this way he probably indicates that the direct literal sense of the poem is here separated by only a thin veil from the concealed allegorical sense—more narrowly, that allegorical figures

The allegory of the two angels seems to devolve on their coming with blazing swords, like the angel appointed to keep the fallen Adam and Eve out of Eden; but these swords have their points broken off, to mark their difference from the guardian of the lost Eden and to indicate that there is no real threat of danger here. Their raiment and feathers are green, the color of hope; but their faces are too bright to be looked at. As in Plato's myth of the cave, the pilgrim traveling towards the source of all light must be slowly trained for direct sight of even such secondary sources or mirrors of light as angels and the sun. We shall continue to meet this phenomenon of excessive brightness in the *Purgatory,* culminating in the great illuminants of the Earthly Paradise.

The fulfillment of the angelic guards comes in their dismissal of the serpent, an evil creature that slides through the beautiful grass and flowers, preening himself—either to match the beauty of the place or to dissimulate his intentions. To underline the point of the serpent, Dante tells us that it is 'perhaps like the one that gave Eve the bitter food.' We must be reminded of the goal of purgation: not only is the Garden of Eden at the top of the mountain but the end of the purgatorial process is the restoration of the innocence of man before the Fall.*

The snake provokes so little commotion that the spirit who had come to stare did not take his eyes off the pilgrim all through the snake's attack. This spirit, Conrad Malaspina, of a great Tuscan

are being used directly and literally. If this is so, we have a datum to apply to the problem (discussed in chapter 1) of the kind of allegory Dante was using in the *Comedy.*

A related device, though not using the veil-imagery, is the direct address to the reader as used for example at 9.70-2:

> *Reader, you see how well I elevate*
> *my subject; therefore do not marvel*
> *if I sustain it with greater art.*

* Even this snake is not left unconnected with the political concerns that provide so thick a context in these early cantos (and again in the pageantry of the Earthly Paradise). This snake has come into the Valley of Princes only eighteen lines after the bitter words of Judge Nino about 'the viper that is the insignia of the Milanese.' Nino is bitter not only that his wife has remarried but that she, the widow of a militant Guelf, has married a Ghibelline.

family, was a worthy son of a worthy father and of a greater grandfather; his words here are a significant statement about the motive power which carries the spirits (as well as the pilgrim) through the arduous ascent of the mountain (and on into Paradise). This motive power is a union between the guiding light which emanates from God and the free will of the individual person: Dante's image is of illuminating grace which may find in human free will a responsive spirit as food for its flame. Conrad, we see, is capable like Virgil of imperfect theology: while his analogy of the lantern clarifies his point, it verges on the heresy that makes God depend on human love for His existence.

Conrad would have found a somewhat better analogy for the union of grace and free will in the force we call gravity, in which the strength of the attraction exerted by either body is directly proportional to its mass: a dropped stone exerts a pull on the earth —but this pull is incommensurable, or negligible, when measured against the pull exerted on the stone by the earth. And just as the pull exerted on the stone may have something to do with the fact that the stone was once part of the earth, so the attraction between God and an uncontaminated free will is based on the origin of human free will and reason in the Being of God. The pilgrim's reply to Conrad carries on this idea. In praising the uprightness of Conrad's family (a relative of Conrad was one of Dante's prime benefactors during the poet's exile—at a time later than the ideal date of the poetic journey, though earlier than the writing of the poem) the pilgrim says:

> '*Custom and nature so privilege it* [your family],
> *that although the guilty head* [Rome] *may twist the world awry*
> *alone it goes straight, and scorns the evil path.*'

* * * * *

The passage from Antepurgatory to Purgatory proper is a change in quality and condition, rather than merely movement in degree. With the opening of canto 9 the thematic and emotional preparation for the gate of Purgatory becomes intense. The change that will affect the pilgrim from the moment he enters the gate is foreshadowed by the theme of metamorphosis presented through Tithonus (line 1); Adam overcome by sleep, as in preparation for the making of Eve (line 10); the turning of day into night (line 7); and Philomela transformed (line 14). Adam, Tithonus as serpent, and the serpentine cold creature that stings with its tail (lines 5-6) remind us of the negative aspects of the Garden of Eden which lies at the summit of the mountain.

The transition into Purgatory proper requires transport in respect to both condition and place; it takes place mysteriously after the pilgrim has gone to sleep. This is suggested in the transcendental transports of the mind wandering freest from the flesh in dream, and in the physical transports of Achilles and Ganymede. The pilgrim, when he awakens, learns that he has actually been transported during his sleep by Lucia to the region of the gate. (Virgil again was of no help in finding the way for the pilgrim to move ahead; at line 46 he even mistakes the reason for the pilgrim's fright.) To recapitulate: the pilgrim's movement to the gate of Purgatory is achieved, first, in suggestive imagery; second, in dream or vision; third, in actuality. Virgil followed in Lucia's footsteps; before she left she showed him the open entrance by the use of her eyes.

From Babylonia, Egypt, Greece, and ancient Rome the Middle Ages had inherited and somewhat modified a great lore of dreams. Broadly, this lore was based on the belief that dreams were prophetic, either falsely or truly, depending on certain criteria. One of these criteria—that dreams just before dawn were sent under good auspices—Dante uses for his dream of the eagle and for the pilgrim's two later dreams in Purgatory: under Christian conditions such dreams received in a state of grace were considered a minor species of revelation.[1] (Dante's beliefs about dreams are described in *Convivio* 2.9; I shall more fully discuss the dreams of *Purgatory* below, in chapters 9 and 11.)

Lucia (see *Inf.* 2.94-108) has come to the pilgrim's aid before this. She has been identified as the Spirit of Contemplation, as the saint in charge of eye ailments, as divine grace prevenient, illuminant, or cooperant. Through these various identifications runs a common thread of association with light and seeing—an association which, however it may be symbolically identified, is adequate for our understanding her role in Dante's poem. The assimilation of Lucia in this dream to an 'eagle . . . with plumes of gold' adds an important complication. The eagle, the bird of Jove and then of the Roman Empire, is also associated by Dante with justice. (The imperial eagle appears [*Purg.* 32.109-17] in a misguided, or even evil, action in the symbolic pageant of Church history; the culmination of this figure of the eagle appears in cantos 18 and 19 of the *Paradise,* where over a thousand spirits of just and noble rulers assemble to form the head and neck of the imperial eagle.)

For this culmination we are not yet prepared, here, before the entry into Purgatory. Lucia, intelligence and light, *is* not the eagle: the pilgrim *is carried* by Lucia and *dreams* that he has been carried by the imperial eagle. There is a relation that I shall later try to clarify between the dream and the particular event it prophesies or prefaces; here I shall only say that this relation is not that of identity. In other words, and remembering that the dream takes place in the valley of inadequate princes, we can say that before the entrance to the process of purgation, the phenomenon of ruling (in its highest form, the Empire) is not yet to be equated with intelligence and divine light: the relation between light and ruling will be clarified when the pilgrim has attained the stage of progress marked by his being in the Earthly Paradise and will be consummated when, in this process, he has come to the midpoint of Paradise.

Before entering the gate with the pilgrims we might well pause for a sketch of the structure, function, and meaning of Purgatory.

The Ptolemaic structure of the earth was based on the pre-Socratic theory of the four elements: *earth,* surrounded by *water,* with the *air* above, and *fire* highest of all. Dante, keeping the essentials of the orthodox Ptolemaic structure, made some highly important alterations—important in themselves, but perhaps even more important in showing the freedom he took in working out the physical details of his poetics and his beliefs.

Dante moved Purgatory from its usual orthodox situation next to Hell and placed it in the hemisphere on the other side of the earth from that known at his time: it is a great conical mountain, reedy and marshy at the base, in the middle of the hemisphere of water and the direct antipodes of Mount Calvary.

Mount Purgatory is a solid mass of approximately the same size and shape as the cavity which is Hell. The concluding lines of the *Inferno* describe the simultaneous making of Hell and Purgatory when Lucifer-Satan was thrown from Heaven: Hell is the chasm that opened to receive him, and Purgatory is that part of earth that fled from his coming (the Earthly Paradise, at the top of the mountain, is the part that fled farthest). The fall of Satan created a tremendous hole and a tremendous splash. Purgatory, however, is far more regular in shape than Hell: the great earthquake that accompanied the Crucifixion shook down many of the walls and ramparts of Hell but only made the basis of Purgatory more secure. Although we may doubt that Dante pursued all the details of his physical creations, we may get an approximation of the size of the mountain from medieval notions of the diameter of the earth: Hell extends from just below the surface to the center and Purgatory is the same size—figuring the diameter at six thousand miles we arrive at three thousand miles, more or less, as the height of Purgatory.

The face of the mountain is broken by a series of narrow terraces —at most 'in width three times the height of a man'; it is not clear whether these terraces circle the mountain or are cut only into the side of the mountain which is exposed to the sun. Each of these terraces, or ledges, is devoted to the penance for a specific sin and to the cleansing or purgation of all tendency to that evil or sin— as each level of Hell is devoted to the punishment in suffering for a specific sin.[2] But in Hell the punishment is eternal; the sinner has chosen his sin and is completely immersed in it; he has no hope or thought of change. In Purgatory the duration of penance depends on the quality and extent of the sinfulness and on the energy with which the ardor of repentance attacks and eradicates the tendency to commit a given sin. The spirit being purged stays on each ledge until its own self-knowledge—not any external judge or jailor—realizes that it is ready to move up to the next level.

The moral-theological basis of the idea of Purgatory is nobly expressed by Aquinas (*Compendium Theologiae,* 145):

> To hold that sins are unforgivable is certainly wrong, even with the qualification that this indeed is not because divine power is unable to forgive, but because divine justice has so decreed that a lapse from grace is beyond repair.
>
> Divine justice does not treat men who still have their course to run as though they had finished. Only when their life is over can human beings remain fast in evil: unalterableness and immobility mark the end of a process. All our present life is in a condition of flux. We are always travelling and never in the state of having arrived—our thorough restlessness bears this out, and every vicissitude of mind and body. That we should stick in our sins is certainly not to be expected from the way divine Providence works in the world.

In Hell the punishment fits the crime. More precisely, the punishment is the physical fulfillment of the intellectual and emotional state which *is* that particular crime: thus the glutton lives in an area of flatulent odors and belching sounds. In Purgatory the spirits are first put into a physical state attuned to a given penance—as the proud are burdened with great weights to humble and lower their bodies, and the eyelids of the envious are sewn shut to prevent looking at the goods of others.[3] The penance is performed with the aid of what have been translated as the 'checks' and the 'goads' appropriate to each sin: the goads provide great examples of the virtue opposed to the given sin, that the penitent may have a good path mapped out for him; the checks provide notorious examples of the sin itself, that the penitent may be thus restrained from wandering off into the sinful tendency once more. The very terms check and goad—borrowed from the language of ox management, for the useful employ of that stupid, stubborn, but powerful beast—cast some light on Dante's view of the repentant sinner as one whose great powers for constructive good are likely to be cast away on aimless or destructive pursuits (other translations of his terms would be related to horse management). The arduous and disciplined ascent of the mountain is for the purpose of training man out of the morasses of vice and stupidity and bringing (or restoring) him to a state of enlightened innocency.[4]

The vices expiated by the souls in Purgatory are the same seven capital sins described by the churchmen of Dante's time; there was however no agreement as to the order in which these sins should be arranged, except that pride was always considered the worst.[5] Dante's arrangement of the sins in Hell seems to move from those that affect the smallest number of persons to those that affect greater and greater numbers; it is nearly the same thing to say that this movement is from the sins based on the senses and a minimal employ of reason to those with the greatest use, or rather misuse, of reason.

There is a steady decrease in severity of the sins being purged as we ascend the mountain to regain Eden: Pride, Envy, Anger, Sloth, Avarice and Prodigality, Gluttony, and Lust. The ten divisions of Purgatory consist of these seven ledges plus the two great groups in Antepurgatory (the excommunicate near the shore and the late-repentant near the gate) and the Garden of Eden at the summit.

Every soul entering Purgatory must spend some time on the ledge of pride, since pride is not only the greatest sin but the root of all the others; thereafter the soul spends whatever time is required on the six higher ledges.

Some explanation of these numbers is also needed. Dante and his age, like other ages, made much of the science of gematria—the significance, almost magical, of certain numbers. For Dante the especially significant numbers were one, three, four, ten, and one hundred. One is unity—God Himself. Three is the triune God: three itself is the creative act, of unity creating variety upon and out of itself (two would have made a Manichean duality out of the act of creation). Four is the sum of three and one. Ten is three produced upon itself (3×3), plus the original unity out of which three proceeded; one hundred is ten produced upon itself. Other significant numbers may be made from these by processes appropriate to the particular need. Thus the seven capital sins of Purgatory are generated (as we learn in canto 16) from the three errors of love: misdirected love, insufficient love, and excessive love. The two extremes divide into their own trinities, the center holds as a pivot: misdirected love generates pride, envy, and anger; insufficient love is sloth; excessive love generates avarice or prodigality, gluttony, and lust. Thus the three have become seven and are incorporated within a wider trinity: a like pair (the two classes of sinners in Antepurgatory, a region rather similar to Purgatory proper) and an unlike element (the Earthly Paradise, which has nothing to do with any purgatorial function). Thus the seven, two, and one now equal ten. By similar number-generative systems there are ten regions in the Inferno and ten regions in the Paradiso. There are, in the three canticles of the *Commedia,* one hundred cantos written in *terza rima,* triple rhyme.

* * * * *

Let us return to the passage at which we interrupted our progress. At canto 9, line 109:

Devoutly I flung myself at the holy feet;
through mercy asking that he admit me;
but first on my breast I struck myself three times.

Seven P's upon my forehead he inscribed
with the point of his sword, and: 'See that you wash away
these wounds when you are within,' he said

The pilgrim's beating himself on the breast in self-accusation is followed by the inscribing of the seven P's, one for each of the sins to be expiated in Purgatory (each P standing for *peccavi,* 'I have sinned,' or for *peccatum,* 'sin'). Each of the P's will be erased in turn as the pilgrim completes his stay on each ledge of the mountain.

As the pilgrim enters the gate (the hinges creak from disuse) he hears from within, but indistinctly, the *Te Deum laudamus*—

'so that now the words are understood, and now are not.' The sharpening of the pilgrim's senses keeps pace with the refining of his intellect and the deepening of his sympathetic understanding. Here, while he is barely within the gate of Purgatory, it is right that he hear a hymn in praise of God, but it is equally right that he not have a clear perception of the details of that praise. Like this is the unbearable brightness of the angel's sword and of the angels' countenances: the pilgrim's senses are not yet ready to take in all that the angels have to offer. The angels, we later learn, are properly of the circle closest to God in Paradise; that they may be assigned to other posts does not alter the radiance they have from their essential proximity to God. For man time and space seem to be of the essence of things; not so for God. (The concluding paragraphs of the *Letter to Can Grande* state this point of the simultaneous progress, in the forward movement of the poem, of the moral, spiritual, intellectual, and physical powers of the pilgrim.)

The dark saying of the angel about the two keys that open the gate requires poetic as well as theological elucidation. The angel is usually taken to signify the authority of the Church, receiving the ministration and care of the keys to Heaven as its delegated duty from St. Peter. The gold key, 'more precious,' is the key of the power of salvation and was bought with the blood of Christ. The silver key, however, is the one which actually 'frees the bolt' and 'demands much art and wit.' This silver key, we are usually told, is the Church's function of judgment and discernment. It may also be that in the phrase 'demands much art and wit' Dante is indirectly referring to the magnitude of the poet's job in revealing the details and occupancy of Purgatory. Like the angel the poet must 'err in opening rather than in keeping closed' the gates for those who beg to be admitted.

When, at the beginning of canto 10, the gate closes behind the pilgrim, he knows this by the sound alone: first, because one must here begin to be prepared for the condition of Paradise, where there is no possibility of deception, where one does not need to use one sense to check and confirm the impressions of another; more important, though, is the reminder that here is no possibility of looking back for any qualm of regret or doubt—these things have been utterly left behind with the decisive change in status produced and marked by entrance through the gate. As the inscription over the gate to Hell had read: Abandon all hope ye who enter here, so the sense at the gate to Purgatory is: Abandon all doubt as ye enter here.

Before the travelers come to the first of the penitent souls on this ledge, they have another of those curious climbs through a cleft or chimney in the rock (this is the sixth since the opening of the *Purgatory*). The Freudian would find birth-imagery in these clefts; an element of this idea was probably in the poet's mind. Perhaps more prominent is what might be termed Dante's path-imagery, a dominant image throughout the poem. The direct path, ordained by love and illuminated by reason, is that which leads man inexorably to God; but man himself casts many barriers into this direct way. In the opening lines of the poem the pilgrim had found himself in a dark wood where the direct way was lost. The tremendous theological apparatus and the guide-system of the poem are established to teach him the direct way; but even with this great assistance he meets many confusions and difficulties in the details of his path.

The clefts are prime examples of difficult traverses on this path; it is even a problem—to be solved differently each time—to locate the cleft. The opening lines of this canto look back to the *Inferno* and forward to canto 16 of the *Purgatory* to describe sin and error in terms of the path: 'the perverse love which makes the crooked way seem straight.' The cleft which the pilgrim encounters just after these lines about the crooked path is uniquely difficult, as might be expected from its position just inside the gate—difficult not only for the travelers but for readers as well. Are the rocks actually in motion, like the ancient Symplegades, or is the wave-zigzagging merely a vivid phrase for the exceptionally jagged and tortuous shape of this cleft? [6] The travelers finally come out on the first of the ledges on which the process of purgation is performed.

On each of the seven ledges, lessons of two kinds are presented to the penitents to help purge them of the particular sin and to strengthen them in the virtue opposed to this sin. These goads to virtue and checks on viciousness are presented in appropriately different ways, to different senses, on each ledge. (The terms 'check' and 'goad,' or they may be translated 'bridle' and 'scourge,' are used only on the ledge of Envy, but they are equally applicable on all the other ledges.) There is, except perhaps on the ledge of Gluttony, a symmetry in the number and arrangement of the checks and goads. This present ledge, of Pride, exhibits the most ingenious kind of symmetry. There are three examples of humility and thirteen of downfallen pride; but the thirteen are arranged in three groups of four parallel examples plus a final summary example which embraces and contains all the others.[7]

The examples—both checks and goads—are drawn from pagan and Christian sources, history and literature, ancient and recent: they are drawn from, and are intended to apply to, all known life. On each ledge the goads are first presented—the positive impulse before the negative deterrent. The first example of the goads is always drawn from the life of Mary: as the best of all pure created beings she provides the clearest and most imitable demonstrations of all the virtues.[8]

Each ledge also has its peculiar expiatory torment. In Hell the torments are the manifestation or continuation of the particular sin; in Purgatory the torments are corrective, as an oculist might design eyeglasses to overcorrect a certain flaw in the eyes and thereby arrive in time at a true condition of the eye muscles, or as a fisherman might hang weights from the tip of his rod to correct a 'set' in the rod after it had been bent too often and too strongly in one direction. The torments are in each instance closely linked to the matter and the method of the goads and checks, so that the corrective growth and the expiatory torment collaborate in a single pattern of purification.

The ledge of pride—in width three times the length of a human body—is of white marble engraved, in this first section, with scenes of notable humility. The first is a picture of Mary at the Annunciation of her lofty function. So full and so fetching is this picture[9] that the pilgrim could continue indefinitely to dwell on it; Virgil has to remonstrate with him to move on from her 'who turned the key to open the exalted love.'[10] Such notable praise and such infinite dwelling might seem to be an excess of mariolatry—to go beyond the place of Mary as mother of Christ. Yet what Dante is doing is only spelling out the details of Mary's function. This exalted love was the love first made fully available to man: the love of God manifested through the love of a woman for His Son. Simultaneously it is the love for man that God demonstrated through the birth and sacrifice of His only begotten Son. And through all this shines the humility of Mary.

Dante reluctantly turns his face from Mary and sees next, in a carving like that of the religious procession on Keats' Grecian urn, a picture which confuses the senses: the workmanship is such that the onlooker's eyes assure him that the figures are singing but his ears listen in vain for the song, and in the same way his eyes see the smoke rising from the burning incense while his nose vainly strives to smell it.*

The reality of the carvings increases, if that is possible, in the third picture. Movement can be seen: the widow at the bridle of Trajan seems to be shedding tears and above him 'the golden eagle moved visibly in the wind.' But this is not all: the woman seems to speak to the emperor and he to answer her—not in a simple single exchange, but each of them speaking three times. The astonishing explanation that the poet gives for this visible conversation—he realizes that some explanation is called for—is that God

. . . who has never seen a new thing
produced this visible speech,
new to us, because it is not found here.

*It is important to note that what Dante deems greatest in the plastic arts is something even closer to reality than photography could ever get; it is like the painting praised by Aristotle because the painted grapes deceived birds into coming to peck at them. This concept of what is good in the art of carving is possibly reflected in Dante's ideals of good poetry: from this concept of lifelike realism we may be expected to deduce Dante's notion about the nature of the literal meaning of his poem, about the kind of reality he wants and thinks his poem to be. It is a realism (lines 32-3) that puts to shame not only the greatest sculpture but nature as well.

This is as much as to say that the poet serves notice of his carte blanche to lay before us any marvel that his invention finds fitting.

But while the pilgrim continues to take deep delight in gazing at these images of humility, Virgil again calls his attention to something farther on—because Virgil above all has the mission of seeing the pilgrim steadily employed at the chore of getting on with his journey, but probably also because the poet wishes us to note that the pagan gets only limited pleasure or edification from the detailed and continued process of penance.

The poet rounds out this little section by another aside to the reader: the pilgrim has already been distracted from full absorption in the act and mood of penance and thereby has the chance to remind himself of the double attitude that many of his readers might have at this moment. Therefore, to console the reader and to ensure that he be not diverted from his good aim for Heaven by learning of the pangs involved in penance, he tells us:

Do not dwell on the form of the torment;
think what follows, and think that, at worst,
it cannot go beyond the Great Judgment.

CHAPTER SIX

The Poet in His Poem

[CANTOS 10.112 THROUGH 11]

At the end of the last chapter we noted that something done to Dante the pilgrim impels Dante the poet to address himself—as though stepping outside the illusion of the poem—directly to the reader. Not Dante the whole man but Dante the poet outside and controlling the operation of his poem—this *persona* of Dante-as-poet has a large role in the *Purgatory,* especially from this point on. We may pause, then, to summarize a few aspects of this role.

We no longer think of Dante as a mechanical summation of the Middle Ages. The universe he describes is the medieval-Ptolemaic cosmos, but many details of the structure of the earth and of astronomical relationships are his own. Dante is undeniably an orthodox Catholic and to a great extent bases his beliefs on contemporary doctrine as presented, for example, in the *Summa Theologiae* of Thomas Aquinas; yet in many ways Dante is a philosopher, perhaps even a theologian, independent of orthodox belief.[1] Similarly in what might broadly be called poetics, Dante owes a good deal to the teachers and models of his youthful poetry—the Provençal poets and their Bolognese and Tuscan followers of the middle and late thirteenth century: from them he acquired richness and fluency in the use of language, imagery, emotion.* From other writers, such as Alan of Lille, Lucian, Statius, Brunetto Latini in the *Tesoretto,* and—above all, he says—Virgil, he may have acquired structural concepts of a long narrative embodying many realms of the universe and many ideas. General concepts—allegorizing, gematria, a moral universe—notions about these were available for anyone living at that time.

* Dante's relations to medieval orthodoxy and poetry have been discussed in chapter 1; the development of these relations will continue through this book.

The *Commedia* unquestionably makes use of all these ingredients, but the result is everywhere marked by the writer's individuality to an extent rare in a long poem. (Perhaps only Pope's *Dunciad* is equally marked, to the point of idiosyncrasy, though in a way different from Dante's.) The form and purpose of the poem as a whole, and the organization of the parts within the whole, are Dante's—to so powerful an extent that we can legitimately say that for his plan Dante is indebted to no one but God. The poem is his, it is about him, we never lose sight or hearing of him for a moment—these are things we can never forget. No more should we forget that also his are (to a great extent) the arrangements of sins and sinners, the choices of whom to stop and speak with, the amount of time or of stress or of emotion to be expended on any given point of the poem. In other words, we find Dante's individuality (or originality, if you prefer) not only in the physical, moral, and political structures of the poem but even more notably in the psychological, emotional, and dramatic handling of each episode of the poem.

Such considerations as these lead us into a question: How much of what the pilgrim encounters in the three realms is intended to be, so to speak, standard procedure in the afterworld and how much is especially arranged or enacted for him alone? This question, which might seem almost whimsical if asked about any other work of art, must be seriously met for the *Comedy*. We must assume that for Dante the afterworld was constructed essentially as he depicts it, but we must see that indubitably the allegorical history of the Church as presented in the Earthly Paradise is enacted specifically for Dante, for the particular function of Dante as poet. We must be prepared, then, to find other aspects of the journey presented not as a picture of eternity but as the *curriculum vitae* of a poet.

Let us return to the text, then, and take Dante's aside to the reader, mentioned at the end of the preceding chapter, in a structural sense. 'Do not dwell on the form of the punishment; think of what follows . . .'—this is a reminder to the reader to be ever aware of what lies ahead in the poem, in the same way that the writer himself is aware, aware not only of the final cause of the world and of the poem but, more practically, aware of the poetically demanding structure of the episode we are in.

The sin of the first ledge is pride, the font of all seven capital sins, the sin for which all in Purgatory must undergo purgation. It is also, we seem to learn from contemporary accounts, the sin to which Dante was particularly prone. As a representative of Man, as himself, as an artist who must be proud of his work and workmanship, Dante knows that the climate of this part of Purgatory may give him especially strong twinges. The immediate prelude for this scene had begun in the emphasis on the senses in the second tercet of this tenth canto. Just after the travelers have entered the gate:

> *by the sound I heard it was shut again;*
> *and if I had turned my eyes to it,*
> *what would have been a fit excuse for this fault?*

The struggle between the senses is built up in the account of the carving of the ark (10.55-63): the triumph over Nature herself is directly attributed to art (10.33). The artistic effectiveness of these carvings—that is, the success with which they perform their intended function—completely absorbs the pilgrim so that he has to be called back to the needs of the journey by Virgil.

When the sight of these carvings is followed by the sight of the first group of those undergoing purgation, the poet is impelled into another direct outburst against the Christians who, blind in their vainglory, try to move forward by taking backward steps. The poet's image (at lines 124-9) aims at the unimportance of the individual: he is only an insect destined to be metamorphosed into a higher form which can then soar to the judgment seat. Pride is the will to fly before the equipment is there—as though the caterpillar were to attempt to do what only the wings of the butterfly make possible. Since Dante speaks, in lines 124-5, of many insects forming one butterfly, he is probably thinking in terms of social and political cooperation: as the Mystic Rose of the Empyrean is made up, petal by petal, of a multitude of blessed souls functioning with one purpose, so the rising to judgment may require a similarly collaborative act. A more closely related image is that of the Eagle formed by the collocation of courageous and just spirits, *Paradise* cantos 18-20.

The image at the close of this canto temporarily binds together a number of the themes I have just mentioned. It is an image, again from art, which gives the essence of the aesthetic theory called empathy. The travelers see coming towards them the souls suffering the torment of the proud by walking bent to the ground under the burden of the heavy stones they bear; the pilgrim tells the effect of this sight on him:

As, to support a ceiling or roof,
sometimes as a corbel, a figure
is seen joining knees to breast,

which, though unreal, causes real pain
in him who sees it; in this way
I saw those spirits when I gave full heed.

The pilgrim rarely reacts in this way to the spectacle of purgation. On the next ledge, for example, he feels sorry for the envious whose eyelids are wired shut, but his own sight is not impaired. Here, with the spectacle of the burdened proud, his own back aches as though it too were laden: so works an effective piece of art, according to the theory of empathy—a theory Dante might well have approved.

Canto 11 opens with a prayer from the proud souls—a prayer which stands in relation to the Lord's Prayer as the medieval 'sequence,' developed by artistic elaboration, stood to the alleluia. It is a prayer which makes clear, as the Lord's Prayer might fail to make clear, Dante's view of the weakness of man without divine help. This paraphrase also emphasizes the precise kind of humility Dante wishes to offer as counterpoise for pride—a humility not of weakness and of abasement but rather of confidence that man *can* do something, *can* have bread, and *can* advance himself; all this, though impossible without love of God, *is* possible with it. (Note, at line 15, the 'going backward,' which recalls the proud, at 10.123, who put their faith in backward steps.) [2] Throughout the *Purgatory* we shall continually come upon Dante's great faith in man's intelligence, his powers of reason; but in all these passages we must keep in mind what Dante posits here, as we enter upon our cleansing journey through the cornices: his firm belief that without His will our wit is naught.

Generally Dante's view is that men themselves provoke sin by their faulty seeing and erroneous choices; rarely, particularly in the *Purgatory,* does Dante advance the popular view that sin comes from testing and tempting by the devil. Is this present mentioning of the devil to be explained by the final tercet of the prayer offered by these penitent souls? Here they say that the prayer is not for themselves, who no longer have need of it, but for those still alive: as though they were saying, in an excess of self-abasement, 'Our sin came from our own guilty selves; the sins of others are perhaps caused by a great evilness outside them.' Even the horse-image, at this point, is put into the use of this mood; at lines 19 to 21 the figure is that of the devil as rider subduing the easily managed horse of human virtue.

In short, this whole version of the Lord's Prayer is (still like Buonconte's version of his death) special and dramatic in the sense that it is these souls, in this situation, who think it proper to pray this way, with these asseverations. All these details of pliability and humility (which, as suggested, are necessarily excessive) are right for this dramatic situation—and probably not exactly right for any other. Perhaps they are not even right for any other poet's portrayal of penitent pride.

* * * * *

Virgil, a cosmopolitan Roman, has by now begun to know his way about this region formerly unknown to him. We have seen his earlier helplessness in Purgatory; gradually he has become acclimated so that he first becomes able to hide his lostness and then increasingly acquires a facsimile of the broad wisdom he had been able to utilize in the *Inferno.* This kind of character development, which Dante is able to employ whenever one of his actors remains on the stage for more than a canto or two, is one of the subtlest devices of the poem for emphasizing the continuous development occurring in the pilgrim himself. Virgil, then, combines a pious compliance with the prayer of the proud souls * with an elaborate, almost courtly-unselfish, request for information about the road ahead. (Again, of course, the path upward lies through a cleft in the rock.)

From this point, line 58, through line 108, lies the climax of this episode, that is, the developed use of the themes I have been tracing since the opening of canto 10—a use, as I have suggested, to demonstrate the particular relevance of the sin of pride to Dante himself. Three of the souls on this terrace are singled out as representatives of the three forms of pride with which Dante was most familiar—Pride of Ancestry, of Art, and of Power.

The first proud soul to tell his story says many things which might apply to Dante himself [3]—'an Italian, born of a great Tuscan . . . my ancient family and the noble deeds of my ancestors made me so arrogant that, unmindful of our common mother, I held everyone in disdain.' This account touches the pilgrim, but only externally—he bends down to hear the story from the stooped penitent. Then, with a beautiful modulation, as though by a little pride of family he was led into a great pride of art, the act of bending to hear the first spirit puts him in position to recognize another of the spirits, one who is expiating a sin of pride in artistic achievement. But this penance the pilgrim completely shares: as he listens to the long story of the artist Oderisi, he walks along bent down in the same way—more precisely, the relation between Oderisi's penance and the pilgrim's penance is much the same as the relation between the corbel statue and the person who sees it, at the end of canto 10.

Dante the pilgrim recognizes the spirit, whose penance he has already been impelled to share, as Oderisi of Gubbio, the honor of the art called 'illuminating'—(as the art of Dante the poet is another sort of illuminating). Oderisi talks of the relation of the artist to his art, of evolution and progress in the arts—and we listen; but when

* Notice how, in line 38—'let you move the wings'—he picks up the image which the poet had used at lines 124-6 of the preceding canto, even though it is difficult to figure out how Virgil could have overheard the poet's thought of this metaphor.

his speech closes, and with it closes the episode we have been examining, we realize that his excessive humility and the disparagement of all human endeavor are dramatically apt bits of rhetoric rather than the convinced voice of the poet himself.

Oderisi begins by acknowledging that he has been outstripped by a successor in his art: alive, he would never have been so fair-minded, since his only wish then was to excel—a wish that he and we can now see as a confusion between aggrandizement of the art and aggrandizement of the artist himself. Not only in his own branch of art but also in others the same succession has taken place: Cimabue has lost the lead to Giotto,* Guinizelli has taken the poetic palm from Cavalcanti, and perhaps there is another who will exceed both of these. It is wonderful to see how Dante the poet struggles between humility and pride in the words he gives here to Oderisi: 'perhaps,' not 'certainly,' but 'a one is born,' not 'one will be born.' [4] The pride seems to win: Dante is, as everyone in his day would have known, directly in the poetic tradition of Cavalcanti and Guinizelli with his early poems and there fairly competes with them—but with the poem we are now reading he far exceeds the aims and the achievements of his predecessors. This conclusion of Dante's might seem to us to be tinged with arrogance, or at least to contain the kind of thing that a man should leave to others to say. I believe though that we are wrong and Dante, along with Shakespeare in his sonnets, is right: humility is a fine thing (although even at this point we must remember that Dante's conception of humility might be quite different from ours), but humility does not call for hiding one's light under a bushel or falling into the kind of appraisal that permits mock modesty to pass over into inaccuracy of judgment.

The final six tercets given to Oderisi (lines 100-17), together with the earlier one about the vainglory of human talent, take us into the mood of *Ecclesiastes*—all, all is ashes! This mood is dramatically fitting—that is, we must realize that the process of penance or purgation involves a pendulum motion, in which the sinner must

* An interesting side issue here comes with the application of the image in the preceding tercet: how long Cimabue's leaves remain green will depend on the quality of his pigments and on the care taken of his paintings by posterity.

swing as far in the direction opposing his sin as his sin had originally taken him from the clear and rational center: thus is balance restored and purgation accomplished. Oderisi is familiarly sententious here: 'earthly fame is nothing but a breath of wind,' 'a thousand years . . . in relation to eternity.' But when he asks the question, what human achievement can make any difference a thousand years later? the answer comes unspoken from one of those present: well, for example, the achievement of a poet like Virgil.

Oderisi's exordium is, then, theologically apt at this point, even though it represents as false an excess of humility as his life on earth had presented a false excess of pride—he swings the pendulum to its other extreme. His exordium has another important function. As I have already intimated, Dante performs some swings—interesting at least technically—between an illusion of literal reality within the journey-pattern of the poem and another, balder kind of reality which copes with the fact that this *is* a poem and will be read as something brought into existence by a man named Dante. The poet's asides to the reader are only the most obvious of the indications of this second kind, or level, of reality. In the episode we have just completed Dante uses a parallel device, both subtler and more important than the aside to the reader. We had been more and more forcibly, since the opening of canto 10, drawn into direct contact with Dante the poet and the man outside his poem; there have of course been other ideas in these same lines but none so forceful as those presenting Dante himself. Oderisi's exordium, then, would provide a denouement to this episode: as a denouement in a play provides a slow departure from the world established by the play, a gradual return to the other worlds that the spectator must live in, so does the end of Oderisi's speech return us from the world of Dante himself to the business of his poem in the process of purgation.

CHAPTER SEVEN

The Paradoxes of Envy

[CANTOS 12-15.81]

The tension and the concentration shown in the speech of Oderisi have been resolved; the poet's personality, drawn powerfully into his poem by the demands of the situation—the penance for pride—has been allowed to recede. The next major episode, opening in canto 15 and coming to its peak in canto 17 at the center of the canticle, will raise the most profound intellectual questions and be involved with the most powerful emotions we have thus far met in the *Purgatory*. But until we come to canto 15, the two or three intervening cantos serve as a level place in the narrative—the story continues but there are no great involvements of any kind; it is one of the relaxed places that Poe predicated as inevitable in any long poem.

Conversation with Oderisi continues to the end of canto 11, but nothing new comes out—we have only a few tags of familiar themes: Florence, once proud, is now a prostitute; our fame is like the color of the grass which comes and goes; humility and repentance, even at the last moment of life, bring salvation.

At the opening of canto 12 the process of penance continues. Neither the pilgrims nor we can spend as much time on the ledge of the proud as we might spiritually require. The poet reminds us that not only the shock of the penance is necessary, as well as the realization that the sin and the punishment belong also to us, but that time spent in the performance of penance is equally necessary. This the poet provides as well as may be:

In even step, like oxen which go in yoke,
I walked beside that burdened spirit,
so long as my sweet teacher allowed it.

And then Virgil once more hurries the pilgrim on—almost as though his function as guide in the *Purgatory* were primarily his ability, as a poet who has completed a poem like this one in size and scope, to remind the pilgrim-poet that the demands of any moment must never be allowed to transcend the need to move to the end. The immediate shock of this purgation is now over—the pilgrim stands erect in body, as a man should walk, and walks lightly. But his thoughts 'remained bent down and shrunken.' The examples of humility had affected both body and mind; the effect on the mind remains.[1]

The checks on pride are also in the form of sculptures on the path. These are presented in an elaborate rhetorical structure, almost a distinct set piece, comprising thirteen tercets, arranged 4, 4, 4, and 1, with the examples of the punished proud constituting a curiously involved pattern of Biblical, historical, and mythological figures—a pattern that might well indicate that Dante was well aware of the varied origin and status of his exemplary figures.

In the first group each of the four tercets begins with *Vedea,* 'I saw'; in the second with *O;* and in the third with *Mostrava,* 'It shows.' The lines of the thirteenth tercet begin with *Vedea, O,* and *Mostrava.* Is there any point to this curiosity of arrangement? Perhaps; treated as an acrostic these letters give us *VOM,* that is, *UOM,* the contracted form of *uomo,* 'man.' In other words we have here, constructed and reiterated, an equation: pride = man.

Yet it is not this schematization that remains as the effect of the passage. Rather is it the mood almost of a warm sadness for these fallen proud ones—for these who fell because of what Troccoli calls *una specie d'involontaria esaltazione*—'a kind of involuntary exaltation.' (The phrase is better than the theology: without the exercise of free will there could be no sin.) There is reproach for the pride, but there is no gloating for the fall. Even for Satan—first among the proud as Mary had been first among the truly humble—we have only the quiet, but tremendous, reproach that he 'was created nobler than any other creature.'[2] The pilgrim, we remember, comes upon these sculptures with his thoughts 'bent down and shrunken'; are we to assume that a rousing invective against pride requires a goodly portion of it in the speaker?

The last tercet of the set piece reproaches (and this is the only violent tercet of the thirteen) the city of Troy; the bitterness is repeated in the sardonic coda to this section:

> *Now be proud, and go with haughty head,*
> *children of Eve, and do not bow your faces down*
> *lest you see your evil path!*

These lessons of fallen pride are for all children of Eve; yet the examples culminate in the proud and base city of Troy—Dante's readers would not forget Troy's part in founding Rome.[3]

This ledge of the proud brought low has already called forth a number of images of the human desire to soar or fly (e.g., 10.124-6; see also my comments on canto 4, at page 107). Now comes another such apostrophe after the angel has kindly told them of the ease of the path ahead of them. (Notice how different is this angel from the one guarding the entry-gate.) The pilgrims are led to another cleft in the rock; the angel 'then beat his wings upon my forehead.' The result of this touch is the removal of the first P, the badge of pride. The pilgrim however becomes aware of this only through internal process: he first notices that now climbing is easier than walking on the level ground had earlier been, as though a great burden had been removed from his back; he asks Virgil to explain it; he then by feeling his face learns what Virgil had been able to perceive by looking. The canto closes on a charming and simple note. Dante feels in vain for the seventh P—'observing which my leader smiled.'

The opening of canto 13 takes us to the second ledge, the terrace of the envious. (The correlation, in one sense mechanical, between physical ascent and moral ascent is stated essentially in the reference to 'the mountain which frees from evil by being climbed.') Virgil, as usual, feels the urgent need to move ahead, as though without his presence the pilgrim might turn into poetic sightseer (as he had done when Virgil, not yet aware of the law and custom of Purgatory, failed to interrupt his meeting with Casella). Virgil, it seems at first, does not need to question a local inhabitant about the course to follow. True, but we must also see why. The point is that he *no longer* needs help. He looks steadily at the sun, not for moral or intellectual guidance as the Christian pilgrim might, but to take his bearings, remembering from the first terrace the relation of the sun's position to the path they must take. Notice in his words that the sun is a warming and guiding light in a purely reasonable and secular sense, as to a navigator or pilgrim concerned only with physical guides to his course:

> *'O sweet light, trusting in which I enter*
> *upon the new road, lead us,'*
> *he said, 'as we need here to be led.*
>
> *Thou warmest the world, thou shinest upon it;*
> *if other reason urge not to the contrary*
> *thy beams should ever be our guide.'*

It is necessary to observe Dante's presentation of Virgil carefully at this point. As we continue we shall see Virgil giving more and more detailedly accurate statements of the significance of things present and even to be encountered at a later stage in the journey. He seems to be turning into a true guide—one who has been there before and can enlighten through his expert knowledge. This, as I have already said, is a theological impossibility. The question, however, should be more accurately stated, not 'Why does Dante do this?' but only 'How?' In answering this question we see that Dante's treatment of his pagan guide is theologically impeccable, we get a deeper concept of why Virgil was selected to be a guide, and, incidentally, we acquire a new respect for Dante's dramatic and constructive skill.

Come back to the sun. If Virgil's use of the sun for guidance had occurred on the first terrace, it would have been the act of a guide who knew the necessary principles through some prior knowledge. When he does it on the second terrace, it is the act of an exceptionally shrewd and observant man who can notice and remember details even amidst all the confusion of a first meeting with a complicated situation. The poet, I believe, wants us to be aware of this important point he is making about Virgil. It is the difference, on the one hand, between native shrewdness, wide experience, and a knack for immediate and accurate deduction-from-example—all these are qualities Virgil must and does possess; and, on the other, a prior knowledge of the physical and moral structure of Purgatory. Such a knowledge Virgil could have only from prior direct experience, which he had not had; or from prior vicarious experience (but we can assure ourselves that his companions in Limbo knew even less of Purgatory than he did); or by inspiration, that is, grace, which we can be equally sure he had no way of possessing.

Dante has taken pains to expose this trail he is laying out, starting from Virgil's utter lostness during the first hours in Purgatory and leading up to the great authoritativeness with which he will be speaking towards the end of the *Purgatory*. Not only this passage we have just been looking at but one just a few lines earlier conduces to this point. At 15.40 the pilgrim had asked:

> '. . . *Master, tell me what heavy thing*
> *has been lifted from me, that hardly any*
> *fatigue is felt by me in climbing.*'

Virgil answers:

> . . . '*When the P's which have remained,*
> *though nearly extinguished, on your face,*
> *shall be, like the first one, wholly erased,*
>
> *Then your feet will be so conquered by good will*
> *that not only will they feel no fatigue,*
> *but it will be a delight to them to be urged upward.*'

This certainly looks like foreknowledge. How did he get it? But let us rather look at what Virgil has actually done. A few moments earlier, the angel had brushed the pilgrim's forehead with his wing. The pilgrim, unable to see his own forehead, at the moment knows of no effect of this act. Virgil, with eyes, sees; Virgil, always knowing the uselessness of speech until it is called for, says nothing. After they start to climb, the pilgrim says that the effort of climbing has been decreased and asks what heavy thing has been taken from him. Virgil tells him but, being Virgil and aware always of law and process even when he had not known what that law was, he tells the pilgrim something he himself did not know until that moment: we have finished with one terrace, one P is removed, you feel lighter; there is another terrace in sight above us (we could even deduce the number of terraces from the number of P's), more P's removed, more lightness to come—even to the point of joy in the ascent.

Virgil, on behalf of the pilgrim, is the one who notices details that, in one way or another, as with the P's, the pilgrim is excluded from observing. Even more important, Virgil is the one who can be thinking his private thought, putting things together, coming to conclusions, while the pilgrim is busy with other and equally necessary trains of thought, which must be carried on at the same time. Remember what the poet himself had told us about multiple souls at the opening of canto 4: when one part of the soul, or mind, is thoroughly occupied, the other parts, or faculties, are free—that is, detached, nonfunctioning.* Virgil sees, like Tiresias in *The Waste Land;* unlike Tiresias, he has not previously experienced either the actuality or the pattern of what he is now observing.

* * * * *

Let us return to canto 13, with an enriched feeling even for the simple little statement that follows Virgil's words about the sun:

As far as here is counted for a mile
so far there had we already gone,
in a short time, through our ready will.

* This is a very interesting point that we may not stop for: it denies what might be thought of either as a counterpointing of thought or as a concept of subconscious

These two are companions, walking the same distance side by side. But dwell on the different thoughts and motives in their heads. The pilgrim still measures distance by his earthly standards; only Virgil himself knows (and will later apply to a problem) what he is thinking. They both go quickly because of their ready will—Virgil's the quick perceptive will of someone intent on storing up observations and facts because one never knows when they may prove useful; Dante quick because of his will operating in sensitive perception and obedience to the divine will, the sum of all. This response to the divine will is, of course, the pilgrim's participation in grace, which provides hope and destination for his journey. Virgil's only destination is his return to Limbo, where we can imagine him as providing new material for the speculations of Plato and Aristotle, who will now be able to discuss the content of purgation but still with no understanding or feeling of its meaning. Those in Limbo will continue to have desire without hope.

The beauty of the first cornice is completely missing from the second; pride, the greatest of the sins, has at least the grandeur of egoism. Envy, as conceived by the Middle Ages, is only mean and sordid. Grandgent[4] suggests a possible source for Dante's form of punishment for envy, in a book the poet unquestionably knew. In the *Magnae Derivationes* of Uguccione da Pisa the poet had read: *'Invideo tibi,* idest non video tibi, idest non fero videre te bene agentem': *'I envy you*—that is, I do not see you [*in* plus *video*]; that is, I cannot bear to see you doing well.'

The stitched eyelids of the envious show not only that Dante considered envy an eye-sin but also that he was thinking of the aggressive and destructive qualities of this sin. The hawk ravens until he is blinded; then he becomes docile and, so to speak, capable of being socially useful.

This fierce aggressiveness of the open-eyed hawk is particularly set off by the gentle seeing of the pilgrim in the lines which immediately follow (13.73-5), and by the considerate courtesy with

levels or wells of thinking. I believe that Dante's own example throughout the *Commedia* and apart from the four senses of the poem (which are a different thing entirely) affirms what he is expressly denying in this passage.

which he greets the spirits a few lines later. Dante is sensitive to the situation; his reaction is that of a warm human being whose emotions respond with agonizing quickness to suffering he can do nothing to remedy, and let us remember the need Dante has for his own powers of sight. Virgil keeps his eyes and ears open, but an important corner of his eye is always on his companion; his duty lies not in the situation but in his ministrations to the pilgrim's needs. Dante, sighted, walking amidst the sightless, is embarrassed and fears to be giving offense. Virgil, rather, sees that there is a question on Dante's mind, but by no mysterious means—he sees this when the pilgrim turns to him with the same look that he has so often used before. When the pilgrim asks for one of the spirits to speak with him he shows that he has learned some of the deductive technique of his guide:

Among the others I saw a shade expectant
in look, and if someone should ask 'How?'

that is, how he knew the shade was expectant, he would answer:

'Its chin it lifted, after the manner of the blind.'

This whole terrace of the envious is of lower intensity, almost of lower interest, than are those above it and below it. A few explanations may cooperate to explain this. A lowering of dramatic tension between two intense episodes seems a possible artistic necessity, something that Dante might deliberately have allowed to remain. Dante himself, if we are to believe his words at 13.133-8, was not greatly moved towards this sin, and so his emotional involvement in it may not have been great enough to move him to deep insight into it. The examples he cites, both as checks and as goads, and the envious spirits we meet, all seem to exhibit a sin which lies somewhere between pride and anger without having much clear character of its own. Finally, the answer may lie mostly in the fact that envy is a meaner sin than either pride or anger: it makes the gestures of anger without the violence and has the motives of pride without the self-centered concentration.

The spirits on this ledge are covered with haircloth cloaks of the same murky, livid shade as the rock against which they lean—so that the pilgrim has to be admonished to open his eyes wider before he can distinguish them. What a complex comment on the nature of envy is their situation! Alive, they might have envied another's cloak which through its beauty stood out from those about it. Now they all wear the same and are all indistinguishable from their environment—and none of them can see any of these things. As it had once been easy for them to weep at the welfare of another, so it is now difficult for them to weep even at their own pain. As they had once been active busybodies in the affairs of others, so they are now seated, immobilized. (The slothful, two cornices higher, perform their penance in ceaseless activity.) As their former acts had been in derogation and depreciation of others, so now they need the support of each other's shoulders and of the mountain itself (the mountain, in this sense, of common weal).

The first encounter on this ledge is the most revealing of those that take place here. Sapia, the Sienese, defines her sin as being 'much happier at others' harm than at my own good fortune.' A moment before this, when the travelers had been met by the goads against envy we had had, as I mentioned above, an anticipation of this rather unsatisfying definition. The first of these goads, Mary's saying to her son at the wedding in Cana, 'They have no wine,' may be taken in many ways, but it is difficult to see how any of them could well serve as an opposite to envy—is it Mary's kindliness, or consideration for others or for the proprieties of the situation? [5] The second goad may be a bit clearer: here we have the willingness of both Pylades and Orestes to sacrifice anything, even life, for the other. The third goad is unequivocally 'Love those who have harmed you.' These examples, together with Sapia's statement, seem to make envy consist in a dereliction of duty or of altruism, but to whom?—to your fellow-guests at a feast, to your best and only friend, to your enemies, to your fellow-townsmen? The range of possible duties may be broad enough to cover the whole of mankind: envy consists in not wishing well for those with whom you have any bond whatsoever, even the bond of hate and harm.

The pilgrim's emotion towards the penitents here is deep but with a great amount of detachment, of what has come to be called 'distance.' Their punishment brings tears to his eyes (only in this detail he shares their localized suffering) as it would touch any living man with pity, but he does not share in the penance; rather he feels embarrassment at his difference, is aware that his difference might possibly cause offense. Here we have what may be the most meaningful hint of what lies at the opposite of envy—not so much a feeling sorry for the sufferings of others (which is Aristotle's concept of pity, as in the *Poetics*) but an embarrassing regret at not sharing in these same sufferings. Envy, then, like the other major sins is a social sin—it consists in doing the opposite of what one ought to be doing for the welfare of one's family, one's townspeople, one's fellow-men.

This may make the sin of Sapia clearer. Instead of praying (her only obligation as a woman?) for the victory of her townspeople in a battle (Dante is against war, but he recognizes, realistically, the need for battles) she prays against them, and not only takes joy in seeing them put to rout but piles on top of this a related sin. She cries out to God, 'Now I fear Thee no longer.' This is pride, the reverse of humility towards God's help, the reverse of an acknowledged need of God's help. Perhaps this is the poet's way of reminding us that, as is required by his ethical system, not only is pride the greatest of all sins but that pride is contained in all sins—in diminishing measure, of course, as we ascend the mountain. Pride is the source of all the other sins; all the other sins are special applications of pride—from lust, which is the presence of pride in one restricted area of life, to envy, which is the presence of all of pride except its center of total egocentricity. Envy falls short of pride only by faltering enough in its self-sufficiency to steal a look at the qualities or possessions of others. Perhaps Sapia's clearest display of the arrogance of pride is her calm assumption that the Sienese were defeated through her prayer.

Sapia is guilty of late-repentance as well as of an element of pride.

She would have gone to the Antepurgatory of the late-repentant had not Piero the comb-seller, a humble man, prayed for her: this is perhaps of further significance in defining her sin by setting it against its opposite. Her repentance alone would not have brought her directly to Purgatory; she has come here because she was able to call forth an altruistic, unenvious prayer from someone. (If, as the commentators suggest, Piero's good will towards her was the result of a charitable act of hers towards him and other citizens of Siena, her ill-willing prayer against the Sienese is set within an even clearer context of charity and unselfishness.)

Is there a breath of envy in the question she asks the pilgrim?

> *'But who are you, who go asking about our condition*
> *and bearing eyes unsewn,*
> *as I believe, and speaking with breath?'*

If there is, we may still pity her, as she suffers the worst torment inflicted anywhere in Purgatory.

The pilgrim's answer to Sapia, as I implied before, is of Dante the man outside his poem and keeps us aware of the multiple characters of Dante in respect to this journey. He is, says the pilgrim, only slightly tainted with envy:

> *Much greater is the fear from which is suspended*
> *my soul, fear of the torment below* [on the terrace of pride],
> *for already now the burden from down there weighs upon me.*

Dante, the pilgrim in the poem, has been purged of pride and of the necessary fear of it; to say 'already,' in expectation rather than in retrospect, is relevant only to the author, not to the character within the poem.

Sapia remains Sapia to the end: she is unselfishly glad of the favor that has been extended to the pilgrim in permitting him to make this journey while alive, but she would also like this favor extended to herself by means of the pilgrim's prayers after his return to earth. And her final word is a gibe at her fellow-townsmen, though perhaps now she is more selective than before: not all of them but only those ambitious of wealth now receive her ill will.

Sapia reminds me somewhat of La Pia: both have a tight little self-sufficiency which may be Dante's concept of *das ewige Weib.* La Pia, actually whining with no greater dignity than her neighbor Buonconte, yet manages to give away less of herself and of her essential weakness; Sapia, for all her mean envy, throwing herself about with great gestures—praying to God to defeat her town, assuming that she has moved God to this defeat by her prayer, and then saying, 'That's all, God. You may turn it off now. You have our permission to leave.'[6] And with it all, able to inspire pity in a little seller of combs. And able to utter what, in its context, may be the most sardonically witty line in the *Commedia:* of her inland townspeople, who organized a great burrowing project to find a subterranean river in an attempt to become a maritime power, she says:

'. . . it will be the admirals who will lose the most.'

* * * * *

Envy is a sin of the intellect, as are pride and anger. Clearly the meaning here, if we are to cover all three of these sins, is that of various misuses of the intellect: in anger, not using it where it should be used; using not enough of it, as in envy, which does not see that disparaging the good of others brings no good to oneself; or totally misdirecting intellect, as in pride, which tries to secure for the individual those things which are inescapably social or which rightly belong to a higher individual or power.

Sapia and the goads towards the opposite of envy reminded us in another way that envy is an intellectual sin: as we shall see, only by the sharp use of the reader's intellect can he form any idea of the nature of this sin. The following canto continues this idea and technique, presenting even one of the poem's political invectives with comparative calm.

At the opening of canto 14 one of two spirits who have overheard the pilgrim's conversation with Sapia asks who he is. He answers:

'. . . Through the center of Tuscany there flows
a little stream that rises in Falterona,
and a hundred miles are not enough for its course.

From its banks I bring this body;
to tell you who I am would be to speak in vain,
for my name as yet is not well known.'

It seems at first to be a humility befitting this ledge that makes the pilgrim refuse his name and conceal the name of his town in a puzzle. Yet his questioner readily enough recognizes this as mock modesty and appropriately reproaches him; we also see, when we remember his thoughts of Florence, that he is trying hard not to express ill will towards his townsmen but does not yet know how to do this.[7]

The two questioners, Guido del Duca and Rinier da Calboli, pick up this theme inadvertently begun. The plaints of Guido del Duca fall into two sections which dovetail very neatly—the first bitter and violent, the second nostalgic and melancholy; the first on Tuscany, the second on Romagna. But together they form an outcry against the degeneration of Italy, against the mad race for material things that has destroyed common sharing and gentleness; together they add another subtle touch to Dante's concept of envy: these condemnations of Tuscany and Romagna seem to differ little from the invective of canto 6, but they serve as a first step in a logical, cause-finding analysis of the condemnation expressed passionately in canto 6.

Guido del Duca's first speech falls into three parts of approximately four tercets each—first on the river and the inhabitants of its shores, then on the beasts they have become, and finally a prophecy about the city of Florence. He first tells us that in the cities along the entire course of the Arno:

'Virtue as an enemy is shunned
by all, even as a snake, either through the ill-luck
of the place or through the evil habit that drives them on:

whence so changed in nature
are the dwellers in this miserable valley
that they are as though Circe had them in her pasture.'

The inhabitants have been turned into the beasts they truly are, as though by an incantation of Circe, either through a curse on their environment or through their use of bad habits as goads instead of checks—they have accepted a reversal, a transvaluation of values by treating virtue, rather than vice, as the snake to be shunned. The beasts that Guido names are social animals, living amicably in groups so long as there is abundant supply of food; when food becomes scarce they are prepared even to feed on each other. As Guido takes us from one city to the next going downstream, the animals he names become first more fierce and ravening and then more sly and vicious in their will to prey on each other. This parable of economic cannibalism Guido completes in a prophetic statement to Rinier:

'I see your nephew, becoming
a hunter of those wolves, on the bank
of the fierce river, and terrifying them all.

He sells their flesh, while they are yet alive;
then slaughters them like old cattle:
many he deprives of life, and himself of honor.

Bloody he comes forth from the sad wood;
he leaves it such that a thousand years hence
it will not be re-wooded to its primal state.'

This 'sad wood' (*trista selva*) is one of Dante's most emotional images: it reminds us of the *selva selvaggia* of the opening lines of the *Commedia.* The wood seems throughout the poem to be an image essentially of torturing ambivalence—shadowy, cool, beneficent, vital; and yet dismal, frightening, a reminder of death. (Notice, too, the structural use of rivers.)

In Guido's next speech he identifies himself and goes on to give his explanation of the cause of envy:

> *'My blood became so afire with envy*
> *that, if I had seen a man becoming glad*
> *you would have seen my face spotted by malice.*
>
> *Of my sowing I reap this straw.*
> *O human race, why do you set your hearts*
> *there where sharing must be excluded?'*

Guido's explanation is essentially that something has happened to change men from sharers to rending wolves—either some curse or some wrong choice.[8] Thus far, of course, this explanation can easily be reconciled with original sin by means of free will: Guido may use untheological imagery but his thought remains theological. However this is only when he is speaking of the Tuscans. They are all evil and—almost—always have been. When he turns to speak of his own region, the Romagna, his explanation of the evil of the Romagnols is entirely in terms of the decay of the generations:

> *'This is Rinier . . .*
>
> *And not only his family has become stripped*
> *between the Po and the mountains, the seashore*
> *and the Reno,*
> *of the good needed for truth and for chivalry;*
>
> *for within these boundaries is a fulness*
> *of poisonous growths, so that only slowly*
> *would they now be rooted out by cultivation.*

. . . O Romagnols, turned to bastards . . .

the ladies and the knights, the toils and the sports
of which love and courtesy enamoured us
where hearts now have grown so wicked . . .

Bagnacaval does well to bear no sons . . .'

These are the words of an old man: 'since our day nothing has gone right.' This thought may be only another aspect of the envy he is confessing and so may fit his dramatic role. But Dante himself, like many another man intensely dissatisfied with the present and working hard for a better future, does not avoid an occasional nostalgic glance at the glories of the past; an example of this may be the treatment of his ancestor Cacciaguida in Paradise.

There seems to be an important, if subtle, connection between these two long speeches of Guido del Duca. The first speech turns men into beasts and connects this metamorphosis with the curse of the river that flows through the region (compare with this the metamorphosis produced by another Tuscan river, the Elsa, *Purg.* 33.67-8). The second speech is based on the perversion of natural growth and product—families and lands decay and produce unnatural, poisonous growths and bastards.

What in the first place connects these speeches is the emotion that inspires them—an emotion that grows to cut off speech itself in the last tercet Guido utters. This emotion is another expression of envy's opposite: envy is delight in the ruin of others (as Sapia has just shown); the negative opposite of envy then is grief, even invective grief, at the spectacle of others' decay and ruin [9]—as the positive opposite is joy at others' well-being.

But a deeper relation between the speeches comes from the tercet that connects them:

Of my sowing I reap this straw.
O human race, why do you set your hearts
there where sharing must be excluded?

This outcry is cryptic enough to call forth a question from the pilgrim in the next canto, but we may partly deal with it here. The burden of Guido's complaint is the corruption or perversion of what should be among the highest of natural-social processes. Land should produce crops but not of poisonous weeds; plants and families should produce scions of increasing nobility; rivers should promote commerce, amity, and fruitfulness instead of robbery, hatred, and barrenness. This perversion of process is related to *usura,* which Dante condemns so fiercely in the *Inferno:* both are perversions of breed. It is probable that this concept in the *Purgatory* embraces and transcends the comparatively jejune evil of *usura; usura* suggests no feasible social cure for itself; the rest of the *Purgatory* might be said to be aimed at outlining a remedy for the evil described by Guido del Duca.

The checks on envy are presented to the travelers in voices, as the goads had been. The first voice is that of Cain, who slew his brother in jealous rivalry and despairs that every man's hand is against him. The second voice is that of Aglauros, turned to stone because of jealousy of her sister preferred by Mercury: she, like Cain, was defeated in a jealous rivalry with one whose success should rather have inspired rejoicing.

Virgil's comments, which close the canto, seem at first to be an impossible mixture of images from equitation and fishing. We soon recognize, however, the image of man's-nature-as-horse, which needs to be subdued by a bit (i.e., the checks on sin); and the concept of the devil as adversary, tempting human fish which take the bait he offers rather than the lures of God (i.e., the goads towards virtue). We should also notice that the poet Dante puts these confused and comparatively simplist ideas into the mouth of the pagan Virgil (as, earlier, similar ideas were expressed by Buonconte and the proud penitents). The fishing (or hunting) imagery comes in with particular aptness as continuing the river and animal invectives of Guido.[10]

Among the minor puzzles presented as we are finishing our stay on this ledge is the problem of how the second P is removed from the pilgrim's brow. We know from Virgil's words at 15.79 that it has been removed, but there is no mention of its being removed by the usual method, brushing by the wing of an angel, with the singing of the appropriate beatitude. Did the P vanish when the pilgrim's eyes and brow were touched by the level rays of the sun and, at the same moment, by the brilliant light of the approaching angel? * (Does this angel work by light only, light that can penetrate the wire-closed eyes of the penitents?) Did the P vanish when the pilgrim put his own hands to his brow and eyes to shield himself from the unbearable light? Does the pilgrim himself, or the penitent himself, remove the second P by the enlightened selfishness—a step up from envy—of protecting his power of sight? Did the P vanish when with joyous voice the angel said: 'Enter here on a stairway less steep than the others'? Since the checks and goads on the terrace of envy have been presented by means of voices, is the angel's voice enough to remove this P, to lessen thereby the pilgrim's heaviness and make the way less steep? These remain the three possible moments of vanishing; the poet does not resolve the question.

As the travelers climb to the next ledge, the pilgrim, made unusually thoughtful by what he has seen and heard among the envious—he has attained purgation of this sin but not yet attained complete understanding—asks about Guido del Duca's words on 'exclusion' and 'sharing.' Virgil is able to tell him that he is making the mistake of thinking of nonmaterial things in terms of material things: the laws of supply and demand are not the same for both categories. Material things are diminished by sharing; hence envy inflames the desire to see the misfortune of others—'envy moves the bellows of your sighs.'[11] With love, love of the divine—and even the pagans in Limbo could know this by being excluded from anything like it—the greater the number of those who share, the more there is for each. The pilgrim's reply[12] is that this answer clears up nothing for him:

* At 15.21, in an image of incident and reflected rays of light, the poet says that their angles are equal, 'as science and experiment show.' This may not prove that—contrary to our view of the Middle Ages as completely authority-ridden in science—experiment (or experience—*esperienza*) is necessary before the laws of science can be accepted; but it shows at least that there is some thought of confirming such laws by the methods of experiment. We might also remember that Aquinas said (*Sum. Th.* Ia.i.8, ad 2), 'In the field of human science the argument from authority is weakest.'

'How can it be that a good thing shared
can make more possessors richer
than if it is possessed by only a few?'

Virgil's reply to this needs full quotation:

'. . . because you still fix
your mind only on earthly things,
you draw darkness from the true light.

The infinite and ineffable good
that is on high runs toward love
as a ray of light comes to a bright surface.

As much ardor as it finds, so much it gives,
so that however widely love extends
eternal goodness still gives increase upon it,

and the greater the number on high who comprehend,
the more there are to love well, and the more love there is,
since, like a mirror, one gives back to another.'

This explanation—and Virgil again finishes it by saying that if it is not clear, his companion must wait for further enlightenment until he meets Beatrice—is nothing more than Virgil's statement of a moment earlier but now expanded by being put into the form of an extended, almost epic, metaphor. True, it is a metaphor much like that which the poet himself will use when he comes to Paradise, but—particularly in the second quoted tercet (lines 67-9)—it has some theological as well as optical infelicities and sounds unpleasantly like the economic theory that money attracts money.[13]

The final lines spoken on this terrace (15.79-81) maintain the mood of paradox to the end: the process of purgation deals with wounds which, unlike earthly wounds, 'are healed by being painful.' Perhaps, though, the painful part of the wounds is all that is evident to the pagan; the joy in suffering, which is the unique quality of penitential suffering and is the mark of grace and hope —this joy does not exist for Virgil.

CHAPTER EIGHT

The Dead Center

[CANTOS 15.82 THROUGH 18]

The travelers have reached the third ledge, where anger is purged. Here the checks and goads are presented through ecstatic visions, imagined sights and sounds which resemble the way the angry man in his anger is transported out of his normal senses. From ledge to ledge the poet changes the method of presenting goads and checks, not from a principle of elegant variation but to show that each sin tends to be ruled by a different means of perception.[1]

The goads here teach a lesson of gentleness, gentleness that should serve where anger might seem to be required. The first of these lessons is again from the life of Mary—Mary quietly reproaching the child Jesus when he inconsiderately 'tarried behind in Jerusalem, and Joseph and his mother knew not of it' (*Luke* 2.43-50). The second check is also on the domestic level but has a wider scope, with a sense of social and political responsibility: the wife of Peisistratus, ruler of Athens, urged him to kill the bold young man who had dared kiss their daughter in public; more alert to the demands of love than to a chance to flaunt his power, he answered:

> *'What shall we do with him who wishes us ill*
> *if he who loves us is condemned by us?'*

The third lesson to the angry deals with the martyrdom of St. Stephen who, as he fell beneath the stones of his slayers, prayed that God pardon his persecutors.[2] A thoughtless child, an irate wife and an overbold young man, a mob of slayers—for each of these there is the soft response, turning away the wrath from one's own lips, rejecting the anger that one might think himself justified in feeling.

This set of visions is expressed in some of Dante's most beautiful verse, as in the trance-like sounds of the first line (15.85),

Ivi mi parve in una visione
estatica . . .

But Dante's emphasis is on the unreality of these visions-with-sound. They arose within the pilgrim's mind in the same way as dreams or hallucinations. When they are at an end his mind 'turned outwardly to the things which are true outside of it.' Not until that moment did he recognize that the things seen in the visions were 'errors' (*errori*). Yet this emphasis on their unreality is finally and completely cancelled through the rhetorical description of these errors as *i miei non falsi errori*—'these not false errors of mine.' In other words, we conclude with the truth of *these* visions but do not destroy the general possibility that visions may be false. (This may have some bearing on the three dreams the pilgrim has in Purgatory.)

Virgil's refusal to hear the content of the pilgrim's visions comes either from the fact that he too has experienced * them or from the opportunity he now welcomes to read the changing expressions of his companion's face (his ability to do this is one of his highest and proudest accomplishments in Purgatory). In the terrace of the envious there had been a recall of the proud, in Dante's own fear of the punishment for this sin (13.136-8); here we have, in the same personal terms, an anticipation of the next sin, of sloth, in Virgil's speaking of his obligation to 'spur the slow and slothful to use their waking hours' (15.137-8).[3]

The canto closes in an atmosphere overcome by the climate of the angry—smoke which takes away sight and the pure air, and reminds us of the murky noisomeness of Hell. This reminder is picked up at the opening of canto 16; here it is built up into the amazing statement that never in Hell itself was there so complete

* The extent to which Virgil experiences the processes of purgation remains an open question.

a shutting off of the light. Not only is this smoke a thick veil for the eyes; it is of so harsh a texture that

> *. . . it did not permit one's eye to stay open:*
> *so that my wise and faithful escort*
> *drew close to me and offered me his shoulder.*
>
> *Just as a blind man goes behind his guide*
> *that he may not stray and that he may not run against*
> *something that might hurt him or even kill him:*
>
> *so I went through the bitter and foul air,*
> *listening to my leader, who said*
> *often: 'See that you are not cut off from me.'*

This is a curious episode. Part of the significance is clear: Dante wants the reader to cast himself back not only to the murk of Hell but equally to the condition in which the pilgrim was thoroughly dependent on his guide—to an extent we have not seen since entering Purgatory. Virgil, as he should, remains aware of his mission; but is there not a tinge of fear for himself, or of anger, in his admonition to the pilgrim?

The penitent spirits pray for the mercy and gentleness of the Lamb of God; the praying spirits themselves are gentle and considerate of one another. These spirits are learning to relax the knotted tensions of anger (16.24)—it is interesting to see how often Dante's metaphors for sins or emotions find corresponding metaphors in the psychological vocabularies of our day.

The scene with Marco Lombardo is carefully staged. From the tinge of asperity which appears in Marco's greeting (to remind us again that we are on the cornice of the angry) we proceed to a conversation notable for its *gentilezza,* courtesy (as a feasible opposite of anger), and finally to the bitter reproaches of Marco's closing words to remind us that the abolition of anger need not extinguish the flame of righteous indignation.

The agreeableness, even open sweetness, of the conversation with

Marco is of course particularly apt on the cornice of the penitent wrathful, but this tone does not begin until the pilgrim says to Marco: 'You will hear something marvelous if you follow me,' and continues with a mixture of threat and wheedling:

> . . . *'With those swaddlings*
> *that death dissolves I travel upward,*
> *and came here through the anguish of Hell;*
>
> *and if God has received me into His grace*
> *so far that He wills me to see His court*
> *in a way quite outside what is customary today,*[4]
>
> *do not conceal from me who you were before death.'*

It is perhaps the pilgrim's phrase *la sua corte,* 'His court' (16.41), that sets this new mood in motion. Dante is more likely, when speaking of heaven, to refer to it as a city ('the Rome of which Christ is a Roman') or a cloister than he is to use the metaphor of a king's court; perhaps something courtly in the tone, or perhaps only the aristocratic flavor of a Lombard accent,[5] has suggested the court to the pilgrim.

The courtly tone is picked up by Marco in his reply at 16.46-9 and culminates in the pilgrim's words, as of one knight to another, at 16.52-3:

> . . . *'By my faith I bind me to thee*
> *to do that which thou askest of me.'*

Lombardy, says Marco, at 16.115-7, was the province of virtue (*valore*) and courtesy.[6] Possibly this chivalric framework even suggests to Marco the notion that man's free will exists in a condition of battlings with the heavens (16.77).

Before examining the substance of Marco's discourse I should like to take up two general Dantean problems that are apropos: the structure of exposition (which I shall come to in a moment) and the question of time. We must remember that, whether the gauge is an internal human clock or the clock of eternity, there is a time-quality in the process of purgation: penance on each terrace is a process which comes to a close for each spirit to let him move to the next level. To translate this into earthly terms: of the spirits we meet on each terrace some are beginning their course while others are ready to graduate. Marco, it may be, is near the end of his course. He seems to show this in his opening words, which betray a preoccupation that has nothing to do with the sin of anger, but might have something to do with his term on this terrace. It is also relevant that the terrace of the slothful is the next above: Marco might be preparing his spirit to deal with the sin of sloth at its essence, which is a distortion of time-values.*

The problem I named a moment ago, the structure of exposition, has to do with Dante's technique of expressing philosophic abstractions in a direct form of human growth and development. Virgil will give an exposition of 'love' in the next canto, but before he can do this he needs some doctrinal information about free will that he does not have as yet. It is information that requires a comparatively impersonal context; it could convincingly be transmitted in a friendly atmosphere but certainly not in one of angry murkiness. In a certain sense, then, and remembering that this information about free will could not easily have been given earlier, Dante is for the moment almost ignoring the moral environment of this terrace in order to make this necessary preparation for the substance of the next canto.

What we are dealing with here is a rather complex notion but one that I believe to be of great importance in understanding the episodic structure of the poem in its relation to the intellectual progressions by which, through successive and incremental clarifications of a given doctrinal or spiritual question, the poet justifies his whole poem.

* Such considerations as these might well be damned today by being called 'academic' (which is worse than 'medieval'), but it is well to remember that this kind of question, dealing with the details of how long one suffers pain on each terrace, might have been the most real and the most important of the issues of the poem when it was discussed by Dante's contemporaries.

Let me restate this principle. If Dante could have uttered a few statements to express essentially what he had to teach, then the rest of his poem would have been so much unnecessary padding or else another kind of poetry. Dante had convictions that he intensely wanted to convey to his readers. Even when these were theological, spiritual, or political ideas familiar in his day, his method of conveying them is his own, based on his notions not so much of cause and effect as of preparation-statement-consequence—in short, on his concepts of dramatic process.

This is not only a question of how a poet may provide the best intellectual preparation and prerequisite for a given profound and complex idea; it is even more a question of the social and emotional environment he must establish to enable an idea to become a living and effecting thing. The reader encountering a given concept restated on different levels of the *Purgatory* does not have to lift himself by his bootstraps to each higher level: each statement is real and is related to all the qualities of its stated environment; the transitions from one to the next, if emotional rather than intellectual as we follow the experiences of the travelers, are nonetheless real and effective. Only infrequently do we have to make a transition arbitrarily or on faith. When the pilgrim is carried to the gates of Purgatory while he is unconscious, we have to supply, in some way undictated by the poet, the means by which those spirits in Antepurgatory—all of them so obviously, in one way or another, unready for the acceptance of the painful and joyous labor of purgation—somehow *do* become ready for the process. Such an episode as this is infrequent, but is so startling when it does occur that it may obscure the paradox that even where the progress seems to be completely methodical and gradual we are still undergoing, almost constantly, significant saltatory elevations, epiphanies.[7]

Let us turn to this example at hand. Consider these three moments in the progression. In the first (canto 14.86-126), Guido del Duca has told us, in a context of envious and destructive competition for material things in an economy of scarcity, that the world is wicked because good fathers have produced bad sons and worse grandsons. In the last of the three moments Virgil, in canto 17, will give us his schematization of the first four capital sins in terms of their characteristic distortions of divine love; these sins constitute, or are included in, the abstract scheme which explains, or is at the basis of, Guido's finding fault with the world. But we should not think of the third moment merely as an explanation of the first; the relation between third and first is something other than cause and effect—third and first even seem to be mutually exclusive explanations of the same phenomena. Perhaps if we look at the middle term, the Marco episode we now have before us, some of these questions will be resolved.[8]

The problem is the cause of wickedness. Guido had explained evil by an Ovidian pattern of the Ages of Gold, Silver, Bronze, Iron. The pilgrim here (16.58) agrees that the world is indeed deserted by every virtue, but besides Guido's explanation he mentions two others that people use: 'the stars and . . . below.' This latter explanation is of course the idea of the devil as the source of all evil; 'the stars' are divine influence, exerted either directly or mediately, which may be discovered by some astrological technique.[9] Marco, hearing this, sighs and finds the world as blind as ever. It is wrong, he says, to consider every cause as originating in the heavens; if this were so there would be neither free will nor justice, and there would consequently be no need for exulting over good or for sorrowing over evil. The heavens (in the sense of stellar influences) may initiate both good and bad impulses in men; but each man has, in addition to those impulses, a light from God to help him distinguish between good and evil and also a will that is free to choose between them. Man's free will may be sorely tested in his first battles with evil impulses from the heavens, but every conquest of these impulses helps set up good habits which make the succeeding battles easier to win. Man's free will is subject only to God, Who is a force higher than the heavens, and Who is even the creator of minds (angels) that are not subject to stellar influences.[10] The cause for evil, then, is in men themselves and not in the influence of the heavens. (We must see that this does not contradict what he had said a few lines earlier about the heavens sometimes trying their hardest to set evil impulses in motion.)

To prove this, Marco reveals a secret about the growth of the soul—a secret that has the warmth and simplicity of a folk myth. The soul, says Marco, is like a little child when it is created, laughing and weeping for no cause; God, the creator of the soul, loves it. This love, manifested even before the creation of the soul, is the only thing known by the newly created soul, which therefore instinctively turns to whatever proves pleasurable—to continue the mood of delight in which it was created. Unless a guide or check is provided, such a person will not be able to distinguish between pleasures that are lasting and those that are trivial or even ultimately harmful. Laws are necessary to impose restraint and guidance on desire. Such laws exist, to be enforced by the Church and by an equivalent temporal power. The Church, however, has come to ignore the rightful separation between Caesar and Christ and is now seen to be striving only for material things; who can blame the people if they follow their guide, the Church, and are thereby led astray? Nature is not to blame: nature has been corrupted by nurture—the bad leadership of the Church is to blame for the world's disorder.

If this seems a dubious explanation, says Marco, consider the results. Italy was once courteous and valorous. Now, after the dispute between Emperor Frederick and the Pope, Italy can safely be traversed, Marco says with heavy sarcasm, by anyone provided he is enough of a villain. Three old men still left in Lombardy who display the old-time virtue rebuke Italy by their existence and long to be dead. Like Guido at the end of his speech, so overcome by the bitter picture he has drawn that he would rather weep than speak further, Marco dismisses the pilgrim abruptly, with actions closer to rudeness than anything the travelers encounter on this terrace.

What are we to make of this long speech by Marco the Lombard? In the first place we must note that, of the three popular explanations the pilgrim cites for the cause of evil, only one, the devil, is ignored by Marco: the other two, stellar influence and the decadence of the generations, are incorporated in his answer. Another part of his answer, the failure of the Church to recognize the separation of authorities and consequent failure to serve as a strict moral guide, we have also had before (and will continue to have as an important theme throughout the *Commedia*). The new element in his answer is the account of the creation and development of the individual soul and the reason for the soul's being led from the start by what Freud would call a 'pleasure principle.' In other words, Marco has contradicted no part of the earlier explanations of the world's disorders; but he has added something new which holds all the previous explanations together—no matter how irreconcilable they might have seemed; or, rather, he tries to build up a unified explanation to replace the broken and varied explanations which are in themselves other symptoms of evil.

Still, are there not, in Marco's discourse, three explanations for the world's evils, with the relations among them not made clear? In 16.67-84 it is *you* (the individual man) who are to blame; at 16.94-105 it is 'evil leadership . . . which has made the world sinful'; and at 106-28 it is Rome that is solely responsible for the evil leadership.

The ultimate aim of Marco's speech is obviously the condemnation of the Church for having attempted to contest with the Emperor for secular power and so having become the 'shepherd who . . . may chew the cud but lacks the cloven foot.' (Milton, in his attack on ecclesiastical authority in *Lycidas,* echoes this passage even to the boldly confused imagery.) Marco's statement brings up a number of questions. The main reason, he says at line 112, for the separation of secular and spiritual powers is that one may check the other, but he does not suggest how or whether the Emperor is to check the Church in spiritual as well as in secular matters. The problem is further complicated by the geographical distance between the two rulers: the division was originally set up when both God's part and the world's part could presumably be ruled from the single city of Rome. The initial—and probably greatest problem—is presented at line 95: the Church, as a ruler in spiritual things, is needed as one 'who can discern at least the tower of the true city.' The true city, the City of God, must be figured forth, must be imitated, so far as possible, in the City of Man. To what extent, then, is the Church, in helping to establish and continue the spiritual basis of the City of Man, to abstain from any role in the social and political institutions which are, in turn, to be based on the spiritual structure? This is a theoretical and practical problem which, in its various aspects, neither Marco nor Dante is obligated to answer, certainly not at this point in the poem. However, it is the very problem which had started the whole quarrel centuries earlier when the Church felt obligated to step into political issues in order to safeguard religious rights and institutions. Marco's rhetoric offers no solution.

As we must expect, this statement by Marco is not the final word in the *Commedia* on the subjects of free will, the nature of evil, or the role of the Church. It is a statement suited to the level we have attained when we have reached the middle of Purgatory: blaming the devil has essentially been left behind; the role of stellar influence has been made more complex and brought into relation with grace and free will (see 16.73-5). As we move ahead in the *Commedia* these great themes will receive greater solutions.

* * * * *

The opening of canto 17 reminds us that we are still in the murky atmosphere of the angry, with the filmed-over eyes characteristic of such strong emotion; but in the choice of the mole as the animal whose eye-skin is imaged we also have a hint of the slow, as though subterranean, tendencies of the slothful we are soon to encounter.

This opening imagery of the mole is followed by an apostrophe to fantasy.* This address to fantasy is expectable enough but receives impetus from the form of fantastic vision in which the goads against pride have already appeared and in which the checks on pride are shortly to appear. There are, however, one or two exceptionally interesting details in this apostrophe. The first is the utter absorption of self produced by fantasy, an absorption which recalls

* This use of 'fantasy' is the technical medieval term discussed in chapter 1, in the section on 'The Philosophy and Poetry of Love.'

the discussion, at the opening of canto 4, of the possibility of multiple souls. But we now go further; the earlier discussion told us that absorption in the sensations of one sense denied for that time perceptions by any of the other senses. Here we go entirely beyond the realm of the senses; in fantasy the senses give no impressions. Stimuli come, even to the spirits here in the murky dark, from a light formed in heaven 'either by itself or by a will that directs it down.' * [11]

Three checks to anger are now presented by means of these 'fantastic visions'; after each of them is a comment on the quality of this means of experience. After a vision of Procne, the mother impelled to filicide and worse, the poet says:

> *. . . my mind was so confined*
> *within itself, that from without came nothing*
> *which was then received by it.*

This is merely a stronger repetition of what we had had at line 16. Then comes a fantasy of cruel and proud Haman, scornful and fierce even as he died:

> *And as this fantasy broke*
> *within itself, like a bubble*
> *when the water fails of which it was made,*
>
> *so there arose in my vision a maiden . . .*

Fantasy seems here to be a self-contained afflatus (as from the breath of a Muse) with a very thin and short-lived separation from the consciousness of the recipient.[12] Finally:

* These latter alternatives are equally tantalizing. If the light forms itself in the heavens, is fantasy then something connected with the stellar influences we dealt with in the preceding canto? (See p. 53 for the role that Mars or Venus plays in the action of the imaginative faculty.) If the light is formed by a will that directs it down, is this God's will, directly inspiring the poet? If not God's, whose? If we get no direct answers to these questions, we at least get some related hints in the section which immediately follows.

As sleep is broken when suddenly
a new light strikes the closed eyes,
and, broken, wavers before it wholly dies away,

so my imagining collapsed
as soon as a light struck my face,
a light far greater than that which is in our use.

Fantasy, then, is like sleep in being cut off from sensation—but not entirely. When the sensation is powerful enough, as the brightness of the angel is here, it will penetrate to the mind.[13] Does this suggest a comparison, a weighing of relative powers, of nearnesses to God, between the angel of the terrace and the source of the fantasies? We *are* told here that the effect of the light is on the will of the pilgrim; this might be a suggestion that the fantasies affect the recipient not so much against his will as in an area where the will is nonoperative, and that the fantasies must yield, must disappear, before an act of the will. (The Avicennist-Averroist psychology makes such a separation as this between the operative areas of will and fantasy.) This does suggest that they come from some source considerably inferior to God Himself, if we are to believe Marco's statement (16.79-80) that even free will is ultimately limited by the authority of God. At the same time, we gain a new insight into the nature of the purgatorial process: on this terrace at least, purgation could not take place without the temporary surrender of the individual free will to the effects of the place, since these fantasies could be cancelled at any moment by the will of the spirits undergoing penance.

Virgil's comment on the angel who has produced this light shows that he has by this time regained most of the sureness and standards he had lost on entering Purgatory.

'This is a divine spirit who directs us
on the way of ascent without our asking,
and with his own light he conceals himself.

He acts toward us as a man should:
for whoever waits for the request, when he sees the need,
already prepares himself unkindly for refusal.'

This is a rich situation: Virgil applauding the conduct of the angel, as one Roman gentleman of another. Virgil's comment is of course perfectly in keeping with his medieval function as a guide to good conduct: to many medieval writers, with their customary total disregard of historicity, Aeneas was a well-nigh perfect knight—even the blots on his conduct (chiefly his behavior towards Dido) were necessary parts of his higher duties. But Virgil's comment also continues the demonstration of how accurately he has surmised the operations of Purgatory, and thereby prepares us for the discourse we shall encounter later in this canto.

With the angel's kind invitation the travelers pass through the stairs leading to the next terrace. The fanning of the angel's wing removes the third P, and the beatitude of the peacemakers is sung. At this moment the last rays of the sun disappear below the horizon, and, just as Sordello had warned them, their strength to move disappears at the same time, leaving them like a stranded ship. (The image of the ship is picked up just below, at 16.87, and transformed into something like the Ship of State or, at least, of Society: it is a sin to slacken work on the oar which helps pull one's weight in the boat.) Powerless to move, hearing no sounds, the travelers are thus fittingly introduced to the terrace of the slothful.

At this time, so as to put to good use the hours they are forced to spend here until the return of the sun, Virgil explains in terms of the single concept, love,* the sins which hitherto have been presented mostly in isolation of each other.

No being, creator or created, we are told, is ever without love, both instinctive (natural) and willed (or rational).[11] Instinctive love, which arises from the process of creation, can never err, either in object or in amount. Rational love, which is directed by

* 'Love,' thus used, is a somewhat different concept from our uses of the word today—broader, or differently focused. See the discussion in chapter 1, pp. 26-54.

will or choice, can err in three different ways: by being directed at a bad object, by being insufficient, or by being excessive when directed at a good object. Love properly directed and properly measured can be only a source of spiritual good; improperly directed or improperly measured, love makes the creature work against his Creator. Love thus defined is the basis of every act, good or bad.

In seeking the motivation or end of bad acts, Virgil considers the three forms of love wrongly directed against an object—that is, the three possible objects of hatred: one's self, God, one's neighbor. The first two are impossible: love can never turn against the welfare of its subject (one's self); love can never operate to cut one off completely from one's Creator. Consequently hatred can be directed only against one's neighbor, one's fellow-man; we love evil only when it is to be visited on our fellows.[15] This evil occurs in three ways: the proud hope to excel by destroying the greatness of others; the envious wish others to sink; the angry enjoy and plan the suffering of others. These are the three terraces of purgation that the travelers have already passed through.

> '. . . *now I want you to understand the other love*
> *which runs toward the good in wrong degree.*
>
> *Each one confusedly apprehends a good*
> *in which the mind may find rest, and desires it:*
> *therefore each one strives to attain this.*
>
> *If insufficient love draws you toward the vision of it,*
> *or the gaining of it, this cornice,*
> *after due repentance, torments you for it.*
>
> *There is another good which does not make*
> *men happy;*
> *it is not happiness, it is not the good*
> *essence, the fruit and root of all good.*

The love that abandons itself too much to this good
is mourned above us in three circles;
but how it is conceived thus threefold

I do not say, that you may discover it by yourself.'

The vagueness, redundance, and limping conclusion of this description of the three terraces not yet visited stand in contrast with the clear pattern into which Virgil had fitted the sins of the three already experienced (17.112-23)—a contrast which goes beyond the poet's desire not to give away too much of the later chapters of his story.

One further point we must note. True, the sins of the first three terraces are clearly described, yet notice how they shade into each other. In the ordinary uses of the words 'pride' and 'envy' we would have little trouble in characterizing a given act or a given man as marked by one or the other of these sins; Virgil's definitions explain the motivation towards each sin and at the same time blur the distinction between them. The definitions, in short, are valid, but they seem to be aimed at destroying any essential difference between the two terms. Is this the intention of the poet? Is he demonstrating that the level we have now reached, where we are above these three sins in our physical journey, enables us to realize that these first three sins are actually only one one motive, one impulsion, which may take on various appearances because of the differences in situations and persons? In other words, are we beginning to consolidate distinctions—are we to see that the distinction of the category of misdirected love into the three specific sins of pride, envy, and anger may have been arrived at by an existential process from below, not by a planned process from above, by human freedom of choice rather than by divine fiat?

I strongly doubt this. I think, rather, that Dante has planted in this discourse of Virgil's a number of reminders of his paganism—that is, of his inadequate knowledge of theology as well as of God. In addition to the dubious details I noted above, we have others more serious to deal with.

The form of Virgil's first sentence is not clear (perhaps intentionally so), but it seems to say that both Creator and created are impelled by both natural (or instinctive) and rational (or elective or willed) love: this is dubious theology, since elective love is by definition (as Virgil himself says at 17.95) capable of error.

> '. . . *Neither Creator nor creature, then,'*
> *he began, 'my son, was ever without love,*
> *whether natural or rational; and this you know.'*

(It is a trick of the skilled orator or demagogue to start with the weak points of his argument and to prove them by simply saying: 'All you bright people know of course that these things are true.')

Again the structure is not clear in the relation between the tercet 17.97-9 and that of 17.100-2; this haziness is localized in the difficulty of determining the antecedent of *egli,* 'it,' in line 97: the 'it' cannot possibly refer to anything but 'love' in the preceding tercet, although many—if not most—translators and annotators try to have it refer to 'willed love.' Their only possible basis is that 'this *must* be what Virgil (or Dante) meant.' This correction may be necessary, but a simpler solution is to see that it is the dramatic character, Virgil, who is saying, at lines 100-1, that it is possible for the created one to love the Creator excessively. Similar doubts can be described for the notions Virgil expresses in 17.100-2 and 17.106-8: in both these places the concept Virgil expresses is perhaps not so much pre-Christian as pre-*dolce stil nuovo.*

Virgil's concept of the errors of love in this discourse may be described as faithfully Aristotelian—which, from him, is not surprising but which, for a Christian poem, is not the last word.

* * * * *

This explanation at least of the first three vices is, says the pilgrim, clear to him—except that he does not understand the term on which the whole chain depends, the concept of 'love.' In the following canto, then, Virgil resumes his explanation of the forces which move men. Before he picks up his argument, however, there is an interesting continuation of the byplay between the travelers at their game of sharpening wits, but always in the direction of greater mutual kindliness and consideration. Virgil looks in his companion's face to see whether the explanation was adequate; it wasn't, but the pilgrim hesitates to speak lest he offend Virgil; reconsidering the kindliness of Virgil then gives the pilgrim courage to ask. Only at the end are there two slightly revealing touches: if the pilgrim understands 'all that your explanations contain or describe,' why does he have to ask for more information on the one word which was at the center of every point that Virgil had to make? [16] Then Virgil, beginning his new explanation, says to his companion:

> *'Direct . . . toward me the keen eyes*
> *of your mind, and there will be made manifest*
> *the error of the blind, who make themselves leaders.'*

With this wise warning in mind let us now look at Virgil's discourse.

The first nine lines, which comprise a definition of love (18.19-27), are nothing more than a paraphrase, slightly tamed and scholasticized, of what Marco had told the two travelers (16.85-93): on the whole, the terms chosen by Virgil to express this 'pleasure principle' are less exciting and less precise. He continues with a metaphor: as it is the nature of fire to rise so it is the nature of the soul captivated by a desire never to rest until 'the thing loved makes it rejoice.' This explanation ignores the possibility that the thing loved *cannot* make the soul rejoice: a rather large possibility when we view the number of souls in Hell and Purgatory—all of whom are there because the object of love, or the extent to which the object is loved, is such as to make the soul *not* rejoice. Further, says Virgil, there can be no question of praise or blame for the soul if it choose well or ill. On this basis the movement of the soul in love is instinctive and uncontrollable—in fact, this is the moral creed of Francesca in canto 5 of the *Inferno* (or the creed of the more naive forms of courtly love). However, Virgil indicates that he is satisfied by his own explanation: [17]

'Now you may see how deeply
the truth is hidden from those who aver
that every love is a praiseworthy thing in itself,

because in truth its material may seem
always to be good; but not every seal
has value, even if the wax is good.'

Here, in a rather curious image, he tells what has already been told, by Marco among others, that the soul may become subject to bad kinds of love: the 'good wax,' like the naturally good soul, may receive a deep impression even from a worthless seal. The origin of this image of impressions in sealing wax can be recognized by looking back at lines 22-23. The seal is seen then to be the object perceived by, and so causing an impression on, the soul. We shall meet this image later: it is almost certainly to be associated with the courtly-love concept of *immaginazione,* the image-making faculty or activity, as described above at p. 40.

The pilgrim answers:

'Your words and my attentive mind,'
I answered him, 'have revealed love to me;
but that has made me more full of doubt:

for if love is offered to us from without,
and the soul proceeds on no other basis,
she has no merit whether she go straight or crooked.'

Virgil had said that while the stimulus to love comes from without, love itself rises within the soul. The pilgrim, asking 'if love is offered to us from without,' is altering and extending his teacher's statement. We must notice that in what follows, Virgil makes no clear effort to deal with the situation in which 'love is offered to us from without'—for example, in the form of divine grace.

Virgil's answer falls into six parts: (1) for the full answer, which involves faith, you will have to wait until you see Beatrice; (2) the specific quality of any soul is discernible only in its operations and results (we are back with Virgil's earlier insistence that man can know only the *quia*); (3) an example of (2) is to be found in the instinctive form of love; this form does not merit either praise or blame, since it is immovably there for all; [18] (4) also innate is the virtue that counsels (Marco's 'light from God') and shows good and bad loves as such; (5) every kind of love may be kindled by necessity, but every soul has (4) and the power given by free will to resist bad loves; (6) same as (1).[19]

Virgil's statements in cantos 17 and 18, then, are methodical, reasonably clear and cogent treatises on subjects presented sensuously by Marco; further, Virgil is lacking in the biased direction which makes all Marco's remarks on the soul, free will, and love serve only as a preamble to his attack on the Church for neglecting her function in man's nurture. But does Virgil add anything to what Marco had said about love? *

Having received these answers the pilgrim, for the first time on this terrace, allows himself to succumb to the quality of the place. When the travelers first arrived here the descent of the sun took away the power of movement from Dante's legs, but this enforced physical immobility was countered by the great intellectual exertion that the pilgrim demanded both from himself and from his companion. Now, however, with his questions answered to the extent of Virgil's ability, the pilgrim becomes somnolent, 'like one who lets his mind wander.' (This we can see, remembering the various faculties of the pilgrim, opens him to the dream he will soon have.)

The canto closes with a rather summary catalogue of the goads and checks to the slothful. The sin of sloth seemingly was even

* Looking back to Marco's conversation, and forward to the dream in canto 19, I am taken with a feeling of wordiness and circularity about the speeches of Virgil in cantos 17 and 18—a wordiness almost separable from the fact that he actually says so little that is new. I am tempted to associate this inconclusive wordiness with the nature of the place—the terrace of the slothful—in which he is speaking. Or with the possibility that here, at the center of the activity of Purgatory, we have a dead spot as at the center of a cyclone—yet never entirely dead, because bits of paper and the like will be carried about and about lazily.

less interesting to Dante than envy had been—probably because he was even less susceptible to it. Sloth has lost status since the Middle Ages: nowadays, under the name of laziness or sluggishness, or perhaps neurasthenia, it is most likely to be dismissed as glandular or temperamental in origin (although we must probably identify acedia with the Pascalian 'void,' and with Baudelaire's *'ennui,'*—for him a destructive and disruptive demon). In Dante's day, under the name of acedia (in Middle English, 'accidie'), sloth warranted serious treatment as one of the capital sins. Aquinas, for example, defines acedia as 'a certain sadness by which man is made slow to spiritual acts on account of physical difficulty'; he also speaks of acedia as 'weariness of doing,' and 'sorrow over apparent ill which is real good.' In Dante's classification sloth is at the center of the seven sins; and, in Virgil's scheme, as resulting from insufficient love (that is, insufficient attraction towards any definite line of conduct), it is a point of inaction between the three sins of the mind and the three sins of the flesh. It is a sin equally of body and of mind: the mind, or spirit, lacks the will to commit itself either to vice or to virtue; the body follows, doing nothing, itself not strongly enough moved by any stimulus to impel the mind either towards good or towards bad. It is not laziness although one of its accompaniments is usually laziness; it is often a state of being unduly bothered by fussy details, or feelings of inadequacy, which inhibit the completion or even the starting of any considerable task. Ultimately, perhaps, it is always an infirm trust in the value of the work to be done.

The goads to industry, to commitment to a cause, are performed by a great rushing throng; two in the vanguard shout as they weep, one of a rapid action by Mary, the other of a rapid and efficient series of actions by Julius Caesar. The others shout: 'Quickly, quickly, let no time be lost through insufficient love.' Virgil, never wasting a chance, asks these spirits the way to the nearest opening by which to pass to the next ledge. The spirit, who in life had been Abbot of San Zeno, answers courteously enough, with an apology for his brevity, and with a rapid instance of official corruption in the Church. This is the only conversation with a penitent spirit on this cornice of the slothful (the briefest converse on any of the cornices) —in full accord with the industriousness with which they must expiate their sin. Aquinas calls *verbositas* a sign of sloth and traces it to the wandering of the mind about things forbidden, which is one of the 'daughters of Acedia.' [20]

After the remaining spirits have passed by, the pilgrim once more yields to the spirit of the place—this time by yielding to random thoughts, rambling in his mind from one to another, until finally

> *. . . I closed my eyes for wandering,*
> *and transmuted thought into dream.*

CHAPTER NINE

The Flesh, sans World sans Devil

[CANTOS 19 AND 20]

The idle thoughts of sloth we saw passing into slumber and dream. The dream is narrated at the beginning of canto 19, a dream that serves as general preamble to the sins of the flesh (in former days dreams looked forward, not backward, as they do now). In idleness and darkness—the idleness imposed by the absence of the sun—comes this dream of the Siren.

Impotent darkness and motive light play a great part in the pilgrim's dream. He sees there a woman who is more than ugly—she is almost the perfection of nonfunctioning impotence: she stutters so that she may not speak straight; she is cross-eyed so that she may not see straight; her feet are crooked so that she may not walk straight; her hands are maimed so that she may not use them; her flesh is sallow so that she may attract no man. But by gazing on her the pilgrim makes her seductive. This is more than an instance of ugliness becoming attractive by becoming familiar; rather is it a creative process in which the gazer brings into existence that which was not alive before, 'as the sun comforts the cold limbs that the night has made heavy' (remember the necessity for the sun emphasized throughout Purgatory—a necessity much greater than comfort), or as the poet animates unpromising material:

I beheld her; and, as the sun comforts
the cold limbs that the night has made heavy,
so my look loosened

her tongue, and set her whole body straight
in a short time, and colored
her wan face just as love desires.

The dream is presented in a context of darkness, especially relevant because of the cornice of sloth and of the entrance to the sins of the flesh. Even more pertinent is the discourse, at 17.13-8, discussing the relations between vision or fantasy and man's will.

Of the qualities shared by all three dreams the most prominent is a kind of egocentricity—more precisely, a self-created self-importance. We have already noted the great exaggeration in the first dream: the pilgrim *is* carried but he had delusions of grandeur in thinking he had been carried by the eagle (who as described here is Zeus himself and very nearly to be equated with God the Father) and in thinking that he had been carried up to the Sun (or to the Heaven of the Sun).[1] A heightened self-vaunting appears in the second dream: here the dreamer is responsible for giving beauty and motion, almost life, to the Siren. The third dream will be treated later, but we may here note that although the pilgrim's ego is not there the center of attention, Leah and Rachel (who constitute this dream) seem to differ from one another mainly in the ways in which they exhibit their narcissism.

The dream of the Siren combines ideas of artistic creation with substance of concupiscence (directly in her words, indirectly in the entire tradition of the Siren)—a combination that seems to add up to a solipsistic concept of an art that is self-produced and self-consumed. There are overtones of this same concept in the Leah-Rachel dream.

Virgil plays varied roles in the three dreams. In the first, the Lady who carries the pilgrim to the gate of Purgatory does a job that conceivably might have been Virgil's. In the second dream Virgil destroys the charm of the Siren, but only at the spurring of the Lady. The connection, if any, is not made clear between his three attempts outside the dream to wake the pilgrim and his single successful attempt within the mechanism of the dream. In the final dream Virgil—soon to vanish—plays no part at all.

The straightness and color that give the Siren the appearance 'that love desires' (19.15) came from the creative eyes of the pilgrim upon her. This may be a gloss on Virgil's words about the origin of love, as spoken in the previous canto; his most nearly pertinent words are at canto 18.19-33, especially (lines 22-4):

> *'Your perceptive faculty from a real object*
> *derives an impression, and unfolds it within you,*
> *so that your soul is made to turn to it . . .'*

Here, in gazing at the unseductive Siren, the pilgrim's soul has gone through rather a different process. His perception of this object created rather revulsion than attraction; continued gazing alters the object, which then becomes a different thing-to-be-perceived.

This process is of course quite understandable in the light of the Capellanian theory of love (above, p. 39). We actually see this theory of love evolving as we trace the stages in which Virgil expresses what he has seen and surmised. The concept of love he presents in cantos 17 and 18 is conditioned—one might say determined—by the experience the travelers have had of the sins of the mind: in these sins love is diverted from its true course by being diverted to a wrong object—but this wrong object is fixed upon by an act of the will. What is to be said when the wrong object is chosen not willfully but by an error (that is, a deception, a self-deception) of the senses? The sins of the flesh are usually called sins of 'disproportionate love'; but does this disproportion not come into existence unwillfully—that is, by an act of wrong seeing which makes the unattractive attractive?

Such seems to be the point of the pilgrim's dream. It is a dream that serves as a modulation from one kind of sin to another—of this there can be no question. But we must be sure to see the terms, the qualities of this modulation. The essence of unattractiveness, unable to move anyone towards herself, is transformed, by looking, into the opposite of this: the Siren, in myth, is an archetype of the desired, of that which can divert anyone's motion to herself under any circumstances.[2] Finally, by the aid of an external revelation of objective accuracy (Virgil, alone, was useless here until moved by another), the essential unattractiveness, repulsiveness, is again perceived.*

One phrase of the Siren's is generally belabored. She says, at line 22:

> *'I turned Ulysses from his wandering way*
> *with my song . . .'*

This line has given the critics the mission of discovering where Dante could have gone astray from the Homeric truth of this story (since he did not know the *Odyssey* directly): the source of the error has been found in a reference by Cicero to the Siren, a reference which, if properly misunderstood, might have led Dante to believe that the Siren succeeded in turning Ulysses from his journeyings and in destroying him. There seems to be a simpler and better explanation for this line, for even if we grant that Dante could well have misunderstood Cicero we would have trouble with the Ulysses of the *Inferno,* who had obviously reached home after his wanderings (and we must remember that those who were turned aside by the Siren never turned back). Quite simply, the Siren is lying; obviously she has to, not only because telling of her failure with Ulysses would be bad self-salesmanship, but because essentially she is a lie. The remainder of the tercet in which the Ulysses lie is found is equally a lie; she has not yet closed her mouth upon her lies when the Lady from Heaven appears to expose her lies. Tearing the concealing covering from her reveals the lie.[3]

It is especially important to see this point because thus far in the *Purgatory* we have been notably free from lies. Lying is not one of the cardinal sins. Lying, however, in various forms of deceit (including that by Ulysses himself), occupied specific places in Hell. Lying does not need a specific place in Purgatory because it may be a part, or at least an accompaniment, of all the cardinal sins, but

* Only one thing we are not told at this point: Why does this perception-deception take place? The poet evidently insists on this part of the process; otherwise the Siren would have made her first appearance in all beauty. He even stresses his loosening of her tongue, in which lies the magic of her attractiveness.

particularly of those of the flesh. So this figure of the Siren warns and reminds us. It might also remind us that sin lies not in the needs of the flesh perceived accurately but only in a self-deceiving mode of perception.

Aroused from his dream by the stench of the Siren, the pilgrim walks in thought, the weight of the thought physically bowing his body:

> *. . . I bore my forehead*
> *like one that has it burdened with thought,*
> *one who makes of himself a half-arch of a bridge.*

Is this the same kind of thought, dwelling idly on an object rather than reasoning industriously to its quality, that produced the false attractiveness of the Siren? The figure could not of course be changed to that of a *whole* arch (*arco*) of a bridge (notice the *arco,* 'bow' as well as 'arch,' which ties this in with the bow-and-arrow image), but it is worth noting that here thought is able to carry the pilgrim only half over the stream of his meditation (as he by himself cannot, later, bridge the stream to Matelda). With gracious and kindly manner the angel of the entrance invites the travelers to pass through, cleansing the pilgrim of another P by the touch of his wings. But the thought remains even after they have passed through, directing the pilgrim's gaze to the ground in the force of his preoccupation. (Is this gaze on the ground to remind us of the punishment of the proud and of Dante's own concern with this sin?) Dante's vision has made him dread what lies ahead in their journey, but Virgil reminds him that he has already seen how to be rid of the temptations of the Siren-witch. At this, Dante's eyes lift from the ground to the summit and the sun.

This little epilogue or coda to the dream of the Siren—just before the travelers mount to the next cornice—is presented with great portents. Not only is the pilgrim unusually thoughtful but his preoccupation continues after he has been purged of the P of this cornice. Virgil starts his questioning (19.52-4) after the travelers have 'mounted a little above the angel' of the cornice of sloth:

'Did you see,' he said, 'that ancient witch
because of whom alone they now weep above us?
Did you see how man frees himself from her?'

Accepting for the moment Virgil's statement that the Siren (or what she represents) is solely responsible for the sins of the three upper terraces, let us see what *is* involved in freeing oneself from her blandishments. The parties seem to be three: one (the role of the pilgrim) himself creating the alluring qualities he is then tempted by; the second (the role of the Lady) acting as protecting daemon or guardian angel; the third (Virgil's part) the, let us say, earthly teacher carrying out orders to expose the self-delusion of a certain kind of fantasy. This done, man can spurn the earth and like a falcon rise to his heavenly repast. The imagery, the very words, at this point echo Virgil's earlier statement (14.145-51) after the conversation with Guido del Duca. But some of the mysteries of this episode remain: the process of self-delusion into sin is not made explicit.

On the next terrace the avaricious and the prodigal are found together. In Aristotle's scheme avarice and prodigality are equally misuses of the good which resides in the proper use of money and material goods. This is one of the few instances in Purgatory where Dante uses the Aristotelian system in dealing with a specific sin. The avaricious perform their penance by weeping and lying on the ground with their faces down (there may be here, as with the sin itself, some reminder of the envious). This penance is explained a few lines later when one of the spirits, questioned by the pilgrim, first identifies himself as Pope Adrian I and then says:

'What avarice does is shown here
in the purgation of the inverted souls,
and the mountain has no punishment more bitter.

Just as our eye did not lift itself
on high because fixed on earthly things,
so here justice has plunged the eye to earth.

Since avarice quenched our love
for every good, whence our good works were lost,
so justice here holds us bound,

hand and foot tied and seized;
and so long as is the pleasure of the just Lord
so long shall we stay immobile and outstretched.'

Adrian's statement that 'the mountain has no more bitter penalty' is interesting: is he being self-pitying? or is the punishment of the envious, which *seems* worse than this, actually less bitter because being deprived of sight becomes greater torment as one comes closer to the sun and Eden at the summit of the mountain? Note too that only here does the duration of the punishment seem to depend on the pleasure of God; elsewhere the individual soul, as we shall learn in the next chapter, knows of itself when it has worked out its penance.

Adrian also continues the imagery of the Siren by expressing himself in terms of the eyes—eyes fixed in the wrong direction until they were unable to perceive what is worthy of love. Is there a further reminder of Ulysses and the Siren? In punishment these souls are bound hand and foot, free only to cry out; so too was Ulysses in the Homeric story.[4]

Before the canto comes to its close we are told that earthly dignities do not survive into the afterworld; Adrian tells the pilgrim that understanding the implications of the phrase, 'They neither marry nor are given in marriage in Heaven,' should have told him that all similar earthly relationships are only for the earth (remember also Cato's words about Marcia). Yet Adrian's last words qualify this statement. Speaking of his niece, Alagia,[5] still alive, he says:

'*. . . and she alone is left to me in that world.*'

Earthly relations, then, do not exist *in* the other world; they do exist *between* the worlds. How otherwise explain any interest shown by the other world in this, or by this world in the other?

* * * * *

At the opening of canto 20 Dante uses an image which describes part of his function as a pilgrim—the image of a sponge thirsty to be filled. Adrian had asked the pilgrim to move on—his stay hindered the weeping with which repentance had to be ripened. The pilgrim, his 'lesser will contending vainly against the better' will of a spirit belonging in this part of Purgatory, regretfully broke off his conversation with Adrian: 'I drew the sponge unfilled from the water.'

What follows the image of the sponge seems perhaps unconsciously related to the imagery of soaking up water. The penitents are described as 'distilling through their eyes, drop by drop, the evil which possesses the whole world'—that is, their tears come from their grief, are the result of the greed which they, when alive, shared with the rest of the world. Then, with the wolf recalling the beast met at the foot of the mountain at the opening of the *Inferno* and also the wolves we met at 14.49 (so that by now besides its significance of greed the wolf refers to Florence as well as Rome—but the greed and the reason for it are the same everywhere):

Be thou accursed, ancient wolf,
That hast more prey than all the other beasts
for thy hunger endlessly deep!

O heaven, through whose revolutions it is believed
that conditions down below are changed,
when will he come who will make the wolf depart?

This second tercet invokes the heavens through which the power of God is mediated, but the prayer or objuration is self-conscious: 'through whose revolutions people believe . . .' The prayer is rather a peculiar one. It does not ask that avarice be removed from the hearts of people; it asks that the wolf be driven away—this is to be a renewal of the poet's prayer for someone to overcome the material ambitions of the papacy and so set up the Church as a better guide for mankind, by the reasoning in Marco's discourse at 16.94 sqq.

The goads and checks on the terrace of the avaricious are presented in the plaints and prayers of Hugh Capet, the only spirit with whom the travelers speak in canto 20. The goad is in the direction of virtuous and blissful poverty, with examples from Mary at the birth of Christ, from Fabricius, and from St. Nicholas of Myra in his gifts to the maidens that they might live with honor rather than in shame. The pilgrim moves up to speak with the spirit who has been weeping as he told these tales of honorable poverty and, in trying to learn who he is and why he is here, speaks (with peculiar inappropriateness on this cornice) of a reward if the spirit complies; the spirit with dignity refuses the bribe, presumably of prayer, but complies with the request because of the grace manifested in the pilgrim through his being there while yet alive.

Capet gives a long recital of his progeny, the Capetian monarchs, whose ambitions, in Dante's view, were as responsible as the papacy's for the ruinous greed of all Europe; sadly he says:

'I was the root of that evil tree
that darkens the whole Christian land,
so that good fruit is seldom plucked from it.'

There is a completion here of the Biblical saw of the love of money being the root of all evil: the fruit, when the root is a great monarch, is the demoralizing of a continent. (Outside of Dante's special view of history it is difficult to say whether the French monarchs were more responsible than any others for the unhappy wars of the two or three centuries before Dante's day.)

Hugh closes his section of history by a prayer to God for the day when his suffering and penitence will be completed and he will be able to see that God's vengeance on him (which is his phrase for the evil descendants he incurred by his greed) is not only just but sweet.*

* Hugh (we probably should say Dante) is wrong, the commentators remind us, in many of his statements. Dante's history is likely to be fuller of errors as he gets farther from the Italy of his own time. This is an interesting point—not only in accord with Aristotle's formula that poetry is more philosophical than history, but on the related line of how far the demonstrable wrongness of many of the poet's factual statements affects the moral and emotional qualities of the poem.

He then returns to his account of the functioning of this terrace. By day the spirits recite, as the pilgrim had earlier heard Hugh, the goads toward virtuous poverty; by night they recite the contrary examples, of the punishment of the avaricious.[6] They tell of Pygmalion, not the sculptor of Galatea but the brother of Dido and murderer of her husband (their uncle, Sichaeus); of Midas and the greedy request which made the people laugh at him; of Achan, who stole the booty and was punished by Joshua; of many others whose greed was punished either by violence or by ridicule. This is the first group of sinners mentioned, even in the checks, as being punished by ridicule. We may recall that the comedy of manners, the comedy of mockery of vice, has chosen to ridicule the sins of the flesh more often and successfully than the weightier sins of the intellect.

The final episode in this canto is a terrifying earthquake which shakes the mountain. A shout is heard on all sides, at first terrifying and then understood as the spirits' singing of *Gloria in excelsis Deo*—a chant of exultation but with still no explanation of what has happened. When the trembling ceases, the spirits resume their lament, and the travelers resume their way. But:

No ignorance did ever with such assault
give me desire for knowing,
if my memory does not err in this,

as I then seemed to have while thinking;
nor because of our haste did I dare to ask,
nor could I see anything there by myself:

and so I went on, timid and pensive.

Thus the poet closes the canto—the mystery of the earthquake remaining a mystery.

* * * * *

In many ways, these two cantos—19 and 20—have been another plateau in the emotional and intellectual progress of the travelers:

the pilgrim has had a dream, he has talked with Adrian I and Hugh Capet (neither among the more striking personalities of the mountain, although Hugh's talk is part of the important political mission of the poem), but nothing striking followed the dream. Perhaps this is as well: the details of the dream are so melodramatic that they are likely to distract the reader from its intellectual content unless he can coast along for a canto or two and then have the impact of the dream return even stronger for the delay.

Both Adrian and Hugh Capet are comparatively gentle and melancholy men; by definition of their place in the poem they had been greedy and avaricious men—somewhere between the wolf and the pig—but nothing of this appears in the way they are presented. This fact, together with more thought about the dream of the Siren, may lead us into one of the fundamental paradoxes of the *Purgatory,* a paradox absent from the other two canticles. The paradox may be thus stated schematically: the arrangement of the sins in Purgatory is from the most to the least intellectual—from pride, the greatest perversion of intellect towards sin, to lust, the least participation of intellect in sin; yet, as we have already seen, the requirements of Dante's narrative scheme call for a constant deepening and clarification of the nature of sin and purgation, of the love which is the motive force of the universe, and of the mishandlings of this love which turn into sin. In other words, the less intellectual the sin, the more intellectually must it be treated in Dante's scheme for the *Purgatory.*[7]

We began to catch sight of this paradox on the terrace of the slothful. Here, where intellect and flesh are both close to slumber, we had Virgil seizing the opportunity for the most abstract discussion of sin and virtue thus far in the poem. The dream of the Siren, in which gazing creates a metamorphosis for the beholder (not 'beauty is in the eye of the beholder,' but 'beauty is created by the eye of the beholder'), a metamorphosis visible not only to the beholder but to the others present as well—this seems to reinforce the idea that the sins of the flesh have an origin somewhere in a process of cooperation between the intellect and the senses. But the action of the intellect comes first: the senses passively perceive, then the intellect transforms the object, and finally the senses return to find a newly created object of delight. These are sins of the flesh from which the devil as tempter has disappeared—the Siren is an ugly object, not a tempter, in herself. In a way, even the world has disappeared—the world as social, emulatory context for sin. If, then, we were asked at this point in the *Commedia* to describe the essence of the sins of the flesh—considering the prologue to these sins in the pilgrim's dream and then the two subsequent scenes with Adrian and Hugh Capet—we would have to find this essence in thought and senses dwelling unduly on an object of sense and thereby, almost like the act of a Narcissus, transforming what should have been a minor, functional, and passing object into a self-created obsession.

CHAPTER TEN

Three Poets

[CANTOS 21 TO 24]

Canto 21 introduces us to Statius, who at this moment has become free to move from his terrace and now accompanies the two travelers as they mount; he will for a while remain with the pilgrim after Virgil has come to the end of his stint.* Who is Statius, to undertake such a role?[1] In medieval or Renaissance Europe such a question would not have been asked: he was known then as the poet of two Virgilian epic poems, on Achilles and on the story of Thebes, read by every educated man. Although he was probably not a Christian (he lived during the second half of the first century A.D.) the Middle Ages generally believed that he was: Dante underlines this belief by having Statius say that his conversion was prompted by reading Virgil's Messianic Eclogue.

The very mode of meeting Statius promises something out of the ordinary. The pilgrim has almost invariably accosted one of a group of spirits to ask for his story; Statius (we do not learn until later who he is) comes from behind so that the travelers are not aware of him until he speaks: 'Brothers, may God grant you peace!' Even for Purgatory this is an unusually friendly and comradely greeting; conversation continues while Statius is told that the pilgrim is yet alive while making this journey, a journey which will continue into Paradise: '. . . you will see that he must reign among the good.' Virgil is also unusually detailed in his explanation of his function as guide, as though this were already a premonition that he will soon have to turn this function over to someone else.

* Until one reaches a realm where direct revelation prevails, a poet may be the best guide: he can explain and clarify without otherwise limiting freedom. In Purgatory, where every ascent of the mountain requires the step-wise assent of free will and enlightenment, Dante chooses poets as the guides for his pilgrim; why Statius was chosen rather than another poet we shall see as we proceed.

Virgil's statement of why a guide was needed for the pilgrim is put in puzzling terms:

> *'. . . his soul, which is the sister of yours and mine,*
> *coming up, could not come alone,*
> *because it does not see as we do.'*

The common ingredient in the souls of Virgil and Statius—an ingredient which Dante's soul lacks—is the transformation, whatever all its details might be, caused by death. There is, then, a mode of seeing in the afterworld which is provided by death without grace but not by grace without death. However, the quality of Virgil's peculiarly limited knowledge is shown in the next few lines. 'I was summoned,' says Virgil, 'from the wide throat of Hell to show him the way, and I will continue as far as my knowledge can take him.' But evidently this knowledge still has essential gaps, even within its spatial scope, for he must immediately ask Statius for the explanation of the mystery with which the previous canto had come to its close—why had the mountain trembled?

A notable collection of images is contained in this little section. At the beginning of this canto the poet speaks of the 'natural thirst which is never quenched' tormenting him (for the explanation of why the mountain shook) as he followed Virgil. This thirst remains unslaked until Virgil asks Statius to explain the shaking; then, at line 39, merely the hope that the question would soon be answered 'made my thirst less burning.' Mixed with this imagery of man's natural thirst for knowledge is an incidental reminder that not all sorts of liquid can serve to slake this thirst: at line 36 is a mention of the 'wet base' of the mountain—this wetness, because of its position in the scheme of the universe, quenches no thirst. Added to these images of thirst is the peculiar metaphorical statement that Virgil's question 'threaded the needle's eye of my desire.' A needle is threaded, its eye is completely filled or satisfied by the thread, only in order that a function may be performed—the function, in this instance of re-motivating the pilgrim's hope that his thirst will be quenched. It is obviously a queer collocation of images, yet the first part and the second part together express with the utmost cogency Virgil's function and Dante's need: Virgil accurately and completely, with no need of a word from Dante, sets in motion the apparatus of the place so that Dante's desire to know can be sated to the extent attainable at this point in the voyage. He threads the needle so that others may mend the fabric of knowledge.

Statius' answer to the question is circumstantial; he relates the quake to the meteorology of Purgatory and to the inner relation between free will and divine justice that permits the souls in Purgatory to complete their purgation. The mountain has its own holy rule of nature; the climatic variations of earth have no effect except in Antepurgatory, below the three steps which precede the entrance to Purgatory proper. (Dante incidentally gives two samples of the scientific thought of his time: lightning is dry vapor; earthquakes are caused by winds somehow compressed in the earth.) The quake, then, observed by the travelers, has an etiology different from that of earthly quakes. When a soul is ready to complete its purgation and mount to heaven, the shouts of all the other spirits on the mountain and the shaking of the mountain itself signal the jubilation over another blessed soul. We are reminded here that Mount Purgatory and Mount Calvary are exactly antipodal—as are the earthquakes of each. The triumph of a blessed soul is expressed in the sympathetic tremor of Purgatory. The quake of Calvary at the time of the Crucifixion expressed the recoil of the earth from the shock of human evil—a jar which passed down into the center of the earth and broke Hell into its cliffs and ruins and parapets (cf. *Inferno* 12.34-5; 21.106-14). This is one of the few but powerful reminders of the underlying function of Christ in the great process of human growth portrayed in the *Comedy*.

We are not told by what means of communication the other souls are informed of the lucky soul's readiness; but we can probably supply an answer to this question from canto 15.52-7 and 67-75. Here we had learned that heavenly sharing differs essentially from earthly sharing: in place of the competition which makes each man's earthly possessions lessen the share available for others, heaven provides more and more bliss according as there are more and more blessed souls to share in it and return their sharing to the All-Creator. In Purgatory then there may be a premonition of this knowledge: every soul there is aware of the fact that each soul risen to heaven increases each portion of available bliss.

How is the soul made ready to rise? Statius tells us that, as we have known before, the free will of every soul in Purgatory desires ascent to heaven, as prerequisite condition for its being in Purgatory; but this free will is 'conditioned' by divine justice to remain in penance. Just as sin (freely chosen during life) formerly kept the soul from the attainment of its true desire, so now does justice (freely recognized and therefore chosen as token of penitence) keep the soul from attainment of Paradise; for each soul the delay is temporary—each delay is actually (when we remember that earthly time and other-worldly time have no earth-knowable relation to each other) equal in duration to the other. It is not that, at the end of the penance, divine justice relents and permits the soul to rise; it is rather that at the end of the proper time the cognitive soul, with its free will, for the first time freely agrees with all the qualities and details of the divine justice. As Statius says:

'Of the cleansing the will alone gives proof,
which surprises the soul, when ready to change its cloister,
and aids it so to will.'

The soul indeed had desired Paradise before this time, but the varied contaminations of the pure freedom of the will had previously inhibited perfect collaboration between will and desire.

We now learn of the identity of our informant [2]—until now he has been only a soul who, perhaps because of the liberation he has just undergone, has been exceptionally friendly, informative, and informed on what lies ahead (to the extent that his words give a foretaste of the feeling of Paradise). He tells us first when he lived,[3] then his proud and forthright claim to fame:

'With the title which lasts longest and honors most
I lived yonder,' answered that spirit,
'greatly famous, but not yet with faith.'

(It is significant that Dante, as well as Statius, assumes that the phrase, 'the title which lasts longest and honors most,' need not be explained as equalling 'poet.') Then comes a little section which, in displaying the warmth and affection of friends-in-art, reminds us of the meeting with Casella * at the beginning of the *Purgatory*. Like a thousand others, says Statius, he was inspired to poetry by the *Aeneid*—'which was a mother to me and the nurse of my poetry' (the Muse in all her images remains feminine); to have known Virgil he would have been willing to spend more time in Purgatory (and we must remember what a tremendous statement this is). These words

. . . turned Virgil to me
with a look that silently said, 'Be silent!'
but the virtue that wills cannot do all it wishes,

for laughter and tears follow so closely
the passion from which each springs
that they least obey the will in those who are
most truthful.

At the pilgrim's involuntary smile Statius became silent and looked into his eyes 'where the soul is most fixed.' Caught in this dilemma, where one bids him be silent and the other bids him explain his smile, the pilgrim sighs. Virgil then gives him leave to speak. The canto ends with details that recall Sordello as well as Casella:

Already he was bending to embrace the feet
of my master when Virgil said, 'Brother,
do not do it, for you are a shade and are looking
at a shade.'

* These two meetings, together with half a hundred equally notable in the *Comedy,* might constitute a little anthology of Aristotelian recognition-scenes.

And he, rising, 'Now you can understand
the measure of the love that warms me toward you
when I forget our emptiness

and consider a shade as a solid thing.'

For the first time the travelers have a third with them as they pass to a higher terrace (and the next canto) and the pilgrim loses another of the P's. As the three walk along they talk as might three Florentine gentlemen, with elegance and kindliness and wit.[4] Virgil's peroration is indeed only a nobler, more virtuous paraphrase of Francesca's words to the travelers in canto 5 of the *Inferno;* there, in excusing her guilty passion, she had said:

'Love, that exempts no one beloved from loving . . .'

Here Virgil says, likewise echoing the amatory theory of the Provençal poets, but adding the significant element of virtue:

'. . . Love,
kindled by virtue, always kindles love for that other
if only its flame is shown forth.'

And thus, when Virgil learned at Juvenal's arrival in Limbo that Statius had formed such affection for him,

'my good will toward you was such
as had never yet bound one to an unseen person,
so that now these stairs will seem short to me.'

This friendship now serves a paradoxical purpose: it makes the question, 'Why are you being punished on this terrace?' which had never before seemed impertinent, now seem a difficult one to ask; on the other hand, the friendship makes it possible for Virgil to take the liberty of asking such a personal question. Such subtleties of emotion and consideration we have rarely met before this in the *Comedy*.

Statius is able to smile and inform them that prodigality as well as avarice had been punished on the fifth terrace. Virgil has another question. When Statius wrote the sad story of Thebes, from the content of the poem

> *'. . . it does not seem that you as yet had faith*
> *without which good deeds are not enough.'*

(Evidently Juvenal, or another, has recited for Virgil the content of the *Thebaid*. The detail of the double-horned flame, at *Inferno* 26.53-4, is borrowed from this poem; the pilgrim's question in these lines assumes that Virgil knows the reference.) Virgil continues:

> *'If that is so, what sun or what candle*
> *dispelled the darkness for you, so that afterward*
> *you set your sails to follow the fisherman?'*

(Juvenal, or another, must have informed Virgil at the same or another time of the mortal as well as the ghostly employment of St. Peter; this may account for many of the shreds of Christian doctrine that Virgil has been able to display on this journey.)

In imagery both real and touching, Statius answers: You directed me first to the sources of poetry, and then, though not a Christian yourself, through your inspired poem, you enlightened me about God:

> *'You acted like one who goes by night,*
> *who carries a light behind him and helps himself not,*
> *but makes those persons wise who follow him.'*

The Messianic Eclogue, the preachers of the new faith, the persecutions of the Christians by Domitian—all these cooperated to persuade Statius to receive baptism—but secretly, through fear; this lukewarmness in his faith kept him for four centuries on the ledge of the slothful before his ascent to the ledge of the prodigal.*

* This biography of Statius is almost wholly an invention of the Middle Ages and of Dante himself. Statius in his own life was even less admirable a character—essentially a timeserving occasional poet.

Statius then asks the whereabouts of some of the older Roman poets; they, with many others, says Virgil, are with him in Limbo. In this listing of Greeks and Romans in Limbo, Virgil names, first, dramatists and epic and lyric poets and then—with equal status—those whose existence was as characters in the poems of Statius and others.

The tercet at 22.127-9 gives point to this entire episode, starting from the encounter with Statius, and even to the choice of Statius for his function in the poem:

> *They proceeded in front, and I, alone,*
> *behind them; and I listened to their discourse*
> *which gave me understanding* [intelletto] *in poetry.*

Discourse between the two epic poets, one just before and the other just after the lifetime of Christ—discourse imagined both within and without the scope of the *Commedia*—such discourse would have provided much food for Dante's poetic development.

The first indication the travelers have of the quality of this terrace comes when they encounter a tree whose branches decrease in size from the top down, so that it cannot be climbed.[5] The pleasant fruit and the leaves of the tree are sprinkled by a clear rivulet that falls from a high rock and is dissipated before it reaches the ground. On this terrace of the gluttonous, then, neither the sustaining fruit nor the clear water is available for consumption. From the tree comes a voice within the leaves which shouts forth the goads towards abstemiousness in diet: Mary, the ancient Roman women, Daniel, the Age of Gold, John the Baptist—all these gained in purity and wisdom by being spare in food and drink.

The same point is made at the opening of the next canto. When the pilgrim starts to look closely through the leaves of the tree, 'as a man does who wastes his life hunting birds,' Virgil once more hurries him on his way.[6] The poet (Virgil or Dante?) may be expressing his scorn here for those who hunt and fish, or for those who hunt obscure etiologies (if the pilgrim is looking for the source of the voice that shouted); but the birds are also a table delicacy particularly banned from the thoughts of this terrace.

The spirits purging themselves of gluttony are emaciated almost beyond conception: their eyes are like rings without their stones so that these two O's, with the haggard nose between and the deep lines of the cheeks to either side, read *omo,* man.

> *Who, not knowing how, would believe*
> *that the fragrance of an apple or of water,*
> *generating desire, could have such an effect?*

The poet is speaking here of the apple and the spring water in two senses: the fruit of the tree they have just passed, with the water falling on it, does produce, as we learn in a moment, the desire for food and thence the emaciation of these penitents. However, to the extent that this tercet deals generally with the origins of gluttony, the poet is here speaking with ironic naïveté: apples and spring water never produced or fostered a glutton. Gluttony rather requires human thought devoted to discovering what, in a pastoral poem, might be considered endless elaborate substitutes for apples and water. Or, in the terms I suggested a few pages back, we have here a demonstration of how the sins of the flesh originate in an exaggerated application of the intellect to something which should be a comparatively simple action, or sphere of action, of the senses. Finally, and consistently with this last point, we have here a reminder of the fruit trees of the garden in which Adam and Eve found themselves not quite to the point of saying that the original sin was gluttony, but certainly to the point of reminding us that, after free will had decided to perform the original sin, the action following that decision was an act of gluttony, of eating something more than should have been eaten, something beyond the needs of simple nourishment.

One of the shades, recognizing the pilgrim, shouts loudly, 'What favor for me is this?' (In this method of recognition and greeting there is some likeness to the encounter with Brunetto Latini, in *Inferno* 15.) This spirit is Forese Donati, with whom when younger

Dante had exchanged, as has often been a poetic custom, a series of poems in which each tried to outdo the other in nastiness.

Forese explains the functioning of this terrace. The justice of God has given to the fragrance of the fruit and to the spray of water on the leaves of the tree a power to cause craving for food and drink. However, it is not desire for sustenance that keeps these spirits (who are punished here because they cared too much for their stomachs) coming back to the tree; it is rather, as we have seen before, that the spirits' recognition of the justice of the divine decision makes them find solace in the pain produced by the tree. And Forese likens this desire-pain with the feeling of Christ on the Cross, crying out in agony and yet willingly performing this part of his function of redeeming man. The blood of Christ's veins comes as an appropriate rejoinder to the gluttony which brought these spirits to this place; perhaps their purgation by becoming emaciated is to be connected with the state of Christ, his veins emptied of blood.

Forese, dead five years, would still be at the level of the negligent in Antepurgatory were it not for the prayers of his widow, Nella—Nella, highly to be praised for devoutness, love of her husband, and modest life. (Dante may be making amends here for some of his youthful poems which had not treated Nella respectfully.) [7] Forese then contrasts with the modesty of his wife the shameless immodesty of the Florentine women in general. If these knew the punishment the heavens have in store for them they would already have their mouths open to howl; and this punishment will come before their infants have time to grow to be youths.

This bitter invective against women who go with their breasts uncovered comes rather surprisingly on this terrace—it seems to have nothing to do with gluttony. Yet we can see how it follows from the praise of Nella; more important, it is an instance of what we have seen before when the sin of one terrace is hinted in the account of the previous terrace—as though to keep us reminded of the interconnections of all the sins. Lust and gluttony, Venus and Bacchus, especially have been related sins—and not only in Florence. Terence, who perhaps by accident was inquired after in the preceding canto, wrote the *locus classicus* for this association: *Sine Cerere et Baccho friget Venus.*

Forese interrupts himself to ask about the pilgrim, not merely out of the usual curiosity about his presence in the body, but also as one friend who has not seen the other for some time. It is important that the question, as asked on this basis of intimacy, has come up comparatively so late in the *Purgatory;* for under these circumstances, the question being asked by a rowdy friend of his youth, the pilgrim can tell of himself in terms of a metamorphosis, a new life—at a dramatically greater distance from the old life than would have been possible at an earlier point in the journey. The pilgrim says indeed that the memory of their early days together would be for both Forese and himself 'a heavy burden' (as of pride); the consciousness of this burden, but not the burden itself, remains. Perhaps it is as a recall of their youthful elaborate puzzle-making poetizing that he so fancifully specifies, in lines 118-21, the moment of the full moon when Virgil rescued him from the dark wood.

Dante continues with a deeply touching tribute to Virgil—as though here where gluttony is purged he finds it best to expunge old debts, both pleasant and unpleasant, from his account (a few moments earlier he had handsomely apologized to Nella Donati). Virgil's comforting, he says, has brought him from the dark wood and deep night of those who are truly dead (that is, the spirits in Hell or the condition of being morally and intellectually lost, as in canto 1 of the *Inferno*) up to here where, in a paradoxical pattern of directions, circling the mountain straightens out what the world makes crooked. (Or is it that a poet must be circuitous to straighten the crooked ways?)

> *'So long, he says, he will bear me company*
> *until I shall be where Beatrice is;*
> *there I must remain without him.'*

Kindly and loving though this tribute is, we must be prepared to find in it a further refining of the poet's estimate of Virgil's function. Virgil, under the aegis of Diana and Apollo, the twin lights of pagan antiquity, *led* him through the deep night of those who are truly dead; but in this realm, where the crooked world is set straight, Virgil functions in *comforting*. The pretense of Virgil's being a leader in Purgatory has been dropped, even by Virgil himself—as though he too were being cleansed, or at least modified in the direction of self-knowledge, by his journey through this realm.

Placing this appraisal and tribute at this point, where we have been reminded of the rowdiest—that is, least responsible—period of Dante's personal and poetic career, may add still another clarification to the use of Virgil in this poem. Virgil, as Dante says in many ways and in many places in the *Inferno* and *Purgatory,* was his poetic mentor; but so were Guinizelli and Cavalcanti and Arnaut Daniel and many others. How did Virgil differ from these? Certainly in the uses of language, in the workmanlike details of the art, the later poets were more useful to Dante than Virgil. But Virgil had moved beyond his early bucolic and georgic poems to one great poem embodying what might be called total responsibility—responsibility to the political and cosmic functions and obligations of man (to the extent he could know them) as well as to his personal and lyric functions.

Dante too had to strike out into this great field, to cope with new and even greater responsibilities than those of Virgil. Christianity had not so much changed men as set their every concern in a new context. Dante's plan then—to incorporate everything existent into one poem—segregated the things of the universe on three layers and found Virgil's example variously useful on the first two of these layers. It is obviously inadequate to equate Virgil with Human Reason. Others besides poets are reasonable men (for example, Aristotle—the Master of Those That Know), but only a poet must organize his reasonable insights into a work of art—reason constituting the *ratio,* the plan, the form, the argument, of his poem. And Virgil, of the poets known to Dante, had utilized a *ratio* nearly comparable to Dante's intention. It is then not so much in details that Dante made use of Virgil as a guide; Arnaut

Daniel, for instance, would be more useful for these—for details of such subjects as love and the beloved even more than for the technical details I mentioned a moment ago. Virgil's *ratio* would be greatly useful to Dante on the first layer of his treatment of the world; striking out into the less familiar world of the *Purgatory* (less familiar because infrequently organized by poetic plan) Dante would find Virgil's kind of perception helpful in seeing unclear structures and would find Virgil's companionship perhaps even more helpful as solace and a shoulder to lean on where the way was most obscure, but—to state the matter most bluntly—Virgil has nothing to do with the plan, the *ratio,* of the *Purgatory,* nothing even to do with ascertaining the plan of it as he goes along. Towards the end of the journey, when Virgil's perceptiveness becomes useless, but before his presence becomes sadly a burden (as his presence and example had at an earlier time relieved Dante of the great burden of his youthful inadequate concept of poetry), Virgil is partly relieved by another poet, Statius. Statius, who in his time had also followed Virgil in the true *ratio* of a poet, although himself inferior to Virgil as a poet, was a Christian and so could remain longer as companion to Dante. In canto 26 we shall see the final statement of the function of Virgil.

Canto 24 completes this little episode—actually in itself only a prelude—beginning to deal with Dante's quality and function as a poet. The three travelers, accompanied for a time yet by Forese—three of them poets and the fourth at least a rhymester—walk on rapidly, 'like a ship in a fair wind': their speech itself rapid, as though lending breath to their sails (we have dealt with ships before this in the *Purgatory;* the most relevant one at this point is perhaps 'the little vessel of my mind' of the opening lines of this canticle). They speak of many things, but the only talk reported by the poet is that of the pilgrim with Forese. After a mention of Forese's sister Piccarda (our minds are thrown ahead to one of the more beautiful episodes of the *Paradiso*), Forese names many of the shades they meet, the poet Bonagiunta of Lucca, politicians and prelates, and Bonagiunta again, who returns the talk to the subject of poetry. Bonagiunta, we note, is named before the princes and prelates, and his name is given specifically—to avoid confusion with any nonpoetic Bonagiunta.

In the preceding two or three cantos we have had the work of Virgil and of Statius accurately defined; it is time now to begin a precise definition of Dante. The full discussion of this point too comes with canto 26. Dante is defined here as the writer of the canzone beginning *'Donne, ch'avete intelletto d'Amore,'* * ('Ladies that have intelligence of Love'), a poem in the sweet new style, the *dolce stil nuovo.* In this style, says Dante, the fantasy-building of the older poets is eliminated:

'. . . I am one who when
Love inspires me, take note, and go setting it forth
as he dictates within.'

Bonagiunta, on hearing this definition, says he now sees the difficulty that held back the three poets of the old school—Jacopo da Lentino (who commonly called himself the Notary), Guittone of Arezzo, and Bonagiunta himself—from attaining this sweet new style:

'I see clearly how your pens
follow closely him who dictates, that is, Love,
which certainly did not happen with ours.

And whoever sets himself to search beyond this point
sees no difference between the one style and the other.'
Then, as if satisfied, he was silent.

On this cryptic definition by the pilgrim (including Bonagiunta's response to it) must depend a good part of our understanding of the kind of poetry written by Dante in the *Commedia:* it is a

* Remember that a short while back, at 22.127-9, the pilgrim said that the discourse of Virgil and Statius gave him understanding (*intelletto*) in poetry.

definition, above all, embracing a concept of the nature of poetic inspiration and of the relation between this inspiration and the art of the poet as embodied in allegory or the like. This is a complicated subject; at this point we need note only this: that Dante says he differed from his predecessors and contemporaries (and from his own earlier poetry, including that of the *Vita Nuova* and *Convivio*) in the immediacy with which his art expressed his inspiration. This difference is, however, as indicated by Bonagiunta's response to it, an absolute one—expressing a completely new kind of poetry. In relation to the distinction Dante draws in the *Convivio* between the allegory of theologians and the allegory of poets,* what is defined here is almost certainly neither of these kinds of allegorical expression but something utterly new—perhaps to be seen as some kind of synthesis of the two earlier species.

* * * * *

In describing the spirits as birds flying with great speed in a flock (lines 64-6) Dante reminds us again, on this terrace of the gluttonous, how close is the terrace of the lustful: this image of the birds is much like that describing the lustful in canto 5 of the *Inferno*.

Before we leave Forese there is time for one further reminiscence and prophecy of the bad state of affairs in their beloved city of Florence. Forese, like any good friend, asks, 'When will I see you again?' Dante's answer, ambiguous as to the time of their next meeting—it will not be 'before my desire brings me to the shore' of Purgatory—blames Florence for his despair:

'for the place where I was put to live,
from day to day is more stripped of good
and seems doomed to sad ruin.'

* In writings interpreted by the 'allegory of theologians,' e.g., the Old Testament, the literal meaning is historically true and the allegorical meaning is the fulfillment of the earlier event in terms of the Christian dispensation. In the 'allegory of poets,' the literal meaning is a fiction designed to hide, except from the skilled, a kernel of truth.

What bitter love is there, what dull hate is there, what belief in the impossibility of a second motherland as of a second mother, in the line, 'the place where I was put to live'!

Forese, predicting the death of his brother Corso (significantly he does not name him), uses imagery which looks both forward and backward in the poem. Death comes to Corso Donati dragged at the tail of a riderless beast—recalling the 'vicious beast' of canto 6, the 'untamed and wild' beast with no proper rider or no rider at all, the beast that is Italy with the wrong ruler. Besides the beast (which returns just below at line 94) Forese uses a peculiar image, of the revolutions of the heavenly bodies, to denote the time the pilgrim must wait before this prophecy will become clear:

'Those wheels have not long to revolve'
(and he directed his eyes to the sky), 'before you will see clearly that which my words to you can no further clarify.'

In a little while, that is, in canto 29, we shall see a splendid image involving animals and wheels—the pageant of the Church Militant in the Garden of Eden.

Forese, because he is losing too much time from the performance of his penance by traveling at the slow pace of the pilgrim, strides on ahead, leaving Dante with Virgil and Statius, 'who were such great marshals in the world'—and leaving behind another encounter with the crowded, interrelated, unpredictable little cosmos, the city of Florence. This appellation of 'great marshals,' *'del mondo sì gran maliscalchi,'* 'marshals in the world,' or 'of the world,' can refer only to one thing. Virgil and Statius were not as, for example, Aeschylus had been, famous soldiers; but they were great marshals of the facts of the world in which they lived, marshals of the *ratio* of a great poem: when Forese, his youthful companion in one kind of poetry, strides off on the path he must take, Dante follows—or by this time, walks beside—the two marshals of another concept of poetry.

The remainder of this canto returns to the business of the terrace. As at the beginning, so at the end of this terrace there is a green and laden fruit tree, this one even more sharply than the other rejecting the prayers and tears of the spirits who come to it. Just as the pilgrim, in the opening lines of canto 23, had looked closely through the leaves of the other tree, so here the spirits lift their hands to the leaves, 'begging someone who does not answer.' The unusually symmetrical structure of this terrace may be a symbolic indication of the importance of right measure as a corrective to gluttony: to a greater extent than with the other sins the content of this sin is, in its right measure, an essential of life. The last line of the canto, containing the beatitude fitting this sin, blesses those 'who hunger always in right measure.'

From this second tree comes the voice speaking the checks to gluttony: Eve (as I suggested earlier, gluttony, wrong measure of the nutritive goods of life, while not itself original sin, was the first act of sin by man); the centaurs who gorged themselves and fought Theseus; and the Hebrews who made themselves unfit to fight by kneeling to drink water and so drinking more than a good soldier should. The centaurs are a foreshadowing exemplum here: in the story of their origin, as the poet reminds us, they were the offspring of Ixion and a cloud—Ixion, invited to eat and drink with the gods, grew heady from this unwonted food and attempted to assault Hera; Zeus, wishing to learn the extent of Ixion's intentions, substituted a cloud for his wife. As suggested earlier, we have another instance here of the traditional linking of the sins of gluttony (especially in strong drink) and lust.

The canto closes with the touch of the angel's wing that removes another P from the pilgrim's brow and with the singing of the beatitude celebrating those

. . . whom so much grace
illumines that the love of tasting
does not kindle too great desire in their breasts,

and who always hunger in just measure.

But before the angel's touch there is a final touch to the theme of the three poets. As the three walk along, 'each in contemplation, without words,' they are startled by the voice of the angel. Each of them, secure in the friendship and guidance of the others, has walked on, and there is no leader among them, none to watch out for the road. It is only the initiative of the angel that shows them at this point the way to ascend. The pilgrim, for one, is not yet ready—if one ever can be—to proceed without paying attention to the way; we are also reminded, in terms of the light-imagery that occurs with such frequency, that the light of Paradise, as reflected in the countenance of the angel, is still too powerful for the pilgrim's vision to tolerate.[8] He must still depend on his ear for guidance, as a young poet listens to his predecessors until his eyes are strong enough to let him see for himself:

. . . so I turned back to my teachers
like one who guides himself by listening.

* * * * *

The two trees on this ledge remain somewhat of a puzzle. The second, we are told at 22.116-7, is a scion of that 'tree which was eaten of by Eve.' The origin of the first tree is not specified—it may or may not be the same as the other.

The only clue to the meaning of the trees comes from their functions. They are speaking trees, one reciting the goads and the other the checks to gluttony. It would be tempting to see them as separate scions—one the Tree of the Knowledge of Good, the other of the Knowledge of Evil—each expressing partially what the parent tree will express in reciprocal fullness.

Another part of the function of the trees is that they, with an economy of means unique thus far on the Mountain, also are the source of the pain, or penance, on this terrace. Forese had told us (23.61-75) that the scent of the fruit and the spray of the water kindle within the penitents a desire and a pain; similarly, the second tree (24.106-14) 'holds on high what they desire' and 'mocks so many prayers and tears.'

This source of pain in the trees is also, curiously enough, a source of desire—almost of temptation; this is the only terrace on which such temptations exist towards the sin being purged.

Here, I believe, is the solution. Something that has had to happen imperceptibly up to this point of the ascent must now become explicit. We started at the base of the Mountain with raw, earthy material for future bliss; we are soon to be at the crest of the Mountain, fully prepared for paradise in eternity. Is the transition from base to crest to be accomplished merely by the sloughing-off of one specific sin after another? Or is a positive growth also to take place in the soul? Partly we have already answered these questions; we have described the goads as directing the soul towards development of the area left empty by the removal of the sin. Now, with the aid of these curious trees, we may supply a better answer: it is essentially an answer, in Dante's terms, to the question 'What is sin?' and involves a re-examination of such terms as 'free will' and 'love.'

'Free will,' it might be said, has two, nearly contradictory senses, depending on whether the free willer is unenlightened or enlightened. In the first sense, free will opens up a multitude, almost an infinity of choices of conduct in a given area. At the other extreme, free will provides no choice at all in the usual sense: it only fosters the choice of the single right line of conduct. It is this latter sense of free will, rarely exercised on earth, which marks the eternal unchanging exercise of the souls in Paradise (or, in Dante's allegorical sense, of the persons who have in life attained a paradisiac level of enlightenment).

'Love,' in the sense of that which impels us towards anything, is, as we learned from Marco Lombardo, an undiscriminating drive, a pleasure principle; its only essential taboo is the doing of conscious, willed harm to oneself (or to God)—even suicide is undertaken after one has weighed, however mistakenly, the better and the worse for oneself.

Love, then, impels one towards gratification of desires while free will chooses the means thereof. Enlightenment, available through grace (*gratia*) to anyone, determines whether the choice made will result in harm or in good—not merely the eventual harm or good of Hell or Heaven but the immediate, earthly harm or good of inaccurate or accurate choice of means of gratification. The emaciated souls on the terrace of the gluttonous as well as the flatulent bloated gluttons of Hell have missed the mark in aiming to satisfy their desire for food.

What have the two trees on this terrace to do with these questions of free will, love, and sin? The answer lies, as I have suggested, in the successive epiphanies provided by ascending the Mountain. What is two must become one: * the Tree of the Knowledge of Good and Evil (that is, of choice between the two) will become in the Earthly Paradise, as it was before the Fall, the Tree of the Knowledge-of-Good-and-Evil † (in which there is no choice since there is no need of any). Here, at the last terrace but one before the Earthly Paradise, we are getting close to, and must be prepared for, the paradox of the one choice which is also the infinite choice. (I shall return to this subject in chapter 14.)

Dante, as we shall see after we enter the Earthly Paradise, presents this essential idea of his *Purgatory* in other ways as well. The most important of these is the premise of the good within each sin—more accurately, of the good object-of-desire which, when wrongly aimed at, leads into sin. The terrace of Lust provides a clear preparation for this point by indicating the thin conceptual line between good and bad enactments of sexual desire.

* Only at the semienlightened level of gematria does 'two,' the principle of duality, become the principle of evil—below two, multiplicity; above two, one.

† This tree, the scenic center of the pageant-history of the Church, is often called the Tree of Justice. This is not so much a wrong as an inadequate appellation: this tree, in what happened to it in the history of the Garden of Eden, is the means by which divine justice was transmitted to man. The tree itself, however, in its pre-Fall quality, can have no earthly name—since all human awareness of it is in terms of the dichotomy existing after the Fall. Understanding the tree in its primordial quality requires either supernal revelation or the progressive epiphanies towards superearthly comprehension provided by the process of Dante's poem.

CHAPTER ELEVEN

The Function of Fatherhood

[CANTOS 25 THROUGH 27]

While on the terrace of the lustful the three travelers engage in two notable conversations: one, in canto 25, centering in a long speech by Statius on the nature of generation and the etiology of the soul; the second, in canto 26, dealing with Provençal and Tuscan poetry—two subjects that seem reasonably disparate and dissociated. Yet, through details and images, these two subjects tightly merge in a common idea—that of fatherhood. Seeing this, we next see the reason of such an idea on the terrace of the lustful: one way of stating the major function of Purgatory is to call it a means of restoring human talents to their proper courses and functions —here, to demonstrate that the activity which, when aberrant, turns to perversions of lust, has a true course in the process of desire-generation-fruition, of which one notable aspect is the relation of fatherhood. The same theme occurred in simple form in the speeches of Guido del Duca in canto 14. Something comparable was done on the preceding terrace: among the gluttons, who use the vital desire for food in wrong ways, the idea of symmetry and proportion is prominent and culminates in the prayer for 'right measure' at the end of canto 24.

The idea of fatherhood has of course already been presented in the poem. Virgil has many times been called father by the pilgrim; presumably the dominance of the idea of fatherhood in cantos 25 and 26 is connected with the imminent departure of Virgil—after he leaves, the pilgrim's guides (or intercessors) will all be feminine (with the exception of the brief prayer by St. Bernard of Clairvaux near the end of the *Paradise*).

The final clarification of Virgil and of the father-relation is necessary to purge the reader's mind of one concept to make ready for another. This new concept, of guidance by a woman rather than by a man, is of course to be connected not only with the medieval veneration of Mary but with its correlatives, the particular idealization of woman to be found in the *dolce stil nuovo* and in certain parts of earlier poetry in Sicily and Provence, as in the concept of Lady as *domnei.*

Canto 25 begins with the three poets wrapped in their own needs but now walking as equals:

> *. . . as a man does who does not stop*
> *but goes on his way, whatever may appear,*
> *if the spur of need pierces him,*
>
> *so we entered by the gap, one in front of the other.*

This sturdy independence is interrupted when the pilgrim is again beset by a need to have a question answered; then he becomes as a fledgling stork who 'lifts its wings to fly, but does not dare to abandon the nest.'[1] Virgil is still alert to the needs of his charge, with the same alertness that had made Dante give him the beautiful tribute of canto 23.118-30. Two of the details in these lines from canto 23 give the essentials of the fatherly function: 'he has led me through the deep night. His comforting has brought me up.' We have also seen, with a mixture of feelings, the slow attrition through the *Purgatory* of Virgil's function as leader—more precisely, the pretense of his being a leader—while his function as comforter has remained. Now, however, that is about to vanish. But why is this role of guide, or of father, so important?

Our modern concern with the individual has, in some aspects of our lives, become transformed into an obsessive and destructive separative force. In the frantic desire to be and to encourage individuals, we often try to set moving, with freedom and independence, persons and ideas that are barely able to stand alone. The aim of individualism, of democracy itself, is to permit each man to stride out after his own star. But what we are doing is to start the free stride before the person can distinguish between star and tinsel. The medieval Church may have erred on the side of overpaternalistic shielding from evil; but is it better to let the six-year-old grow where he will and choose the good comic books from the bad? Even those who have discarded, as outmoded, a distinction between good and evil must still recognize a difference between better and worse. This difference is too precious a necessity to be attained by trial and error. The entire world may disappear one of these days while we, individually and nationally, walk our proud separate paths.

Perhaps the deepest lesson to be learned from the form, as well as the contents, of Dante's poem is this process of education, of leading forth—the lesson that tutelage never ceases; it merely changes form. In the *Inferno* the pilgrim is a child, led by the hand while he is learning to avoid mortal dangers. In the *Purgatory* he is a youth, comforted and encouraged by his teacher as he walks a prescribed path, but already his powers of vision and discernment have been sharpened to the extent that he himself is often able to locate the next stage of the path. In the *Paradise* his guide is his star: having been taught to use his eyes and his judgment, the mature man can see that there is one clear direction in which he must go. (This idea of education and growth is, of course, essentially Platonic; it is to be found in his myth of the cave more easily than in the other places where readers look for Plato's theory of education; it is deducible from the *Timaeus,* which the Middle Ages knew.)

Let us return to canto 25. We were at the point at which the pilgrim is encouraged by Virgil to ask the question he has been 'burning with desire' to ask, about the fearfully emaciated spirits they have just encountered on the terrace of the gluttonous. This question, seemingly simple or even gossipy, soon calls forth one of the most important philosophical lectures in the canticle. 'How,' the pilgrim asks:

> '. . . *how can one grow thin*
> *there where the need for food is not felt?'*

Virgil answers by presenting two analogies, neither of which has much relevance to the problem: the first, an example of sympathetic magic, has to do with the myth of Meleager, whose life span was dependent on the life of a log of wood; the second, a linkage of material substances and their images, mentions the correspondences between one's movements and the reflection of those movements in a mirror. 'If you think' of this, he says, 'what appears hard will seem easy.' Perhaps so, but he evidently feels unsure that his answer has met the question and so:

> '. . . *that you may become easy within your desire,*
> *here is Statius, and I call upon him and beg him*
> *to be now the healer of your wounds.*'

Statius' long reply (25.31-108) brings in much more than seems to be called for by the question. Let me present an outline of the reply and choose certain aspects of it to examine.

After two tercets of preamble there are four major divisions of his speech: in the first (25.37-51), we learn of the process of human generation; in the second (25.52-62), of the development of the embryo; in the third (25.62-78), of the origin of the soul of each individual; in the fourth (25.79-108), of the qualities of the human soul surviving death.

The first tercet of the preamble is addressed to Virgil: it is rather a peculiar apology for being unable to deny Virgil any request even when it involves so-to-speak classified material—of the substance of revelation. The second tercet, to the pilgrim, says that his words will cast light on the 'how' that had been asked about: Virgil had made a flat statement (at canto 3.31-9) about the kind of thing that is not available for human knowledge * [2]—it is precisely this that Statius is now about to explain.

* Virgil had said:

> *'To suffer torments, heat and cold,*
> *bodies like ours a Power disposes*
> *that does not want Its workings revealed to us . . .*
>
> *Be content, o human race, with the* quia . . .'

We are now getting ready to leave behind the need for being content with the *quia*, the facts as they can be observed.

The blood of man, says Statius, is of two kinds: one kind circulates in the veins; the other is perfect and remains in the heart. Here it exerts a formative power over the rest of the body and, after being further refined in the heart, descends to the organs of generation: this is the semen, which is without the impurities that give color to ordinary blood.[3] The male perfect blood, the active principle, combines with the passive blood of the female 'in a natural vessel.' The active blood first coagulates, and then quickens with life the passive blood.[4]

Then begins the second part of the process. Here Statius, or Dante, describes the development of the embryo in terms which have a curious resemblance to the present-day embryological theory of ontogeny recapitulating phylogeny: a medieval embryologist might have thought of this as a recapitulation of the six days of creation, if not of the pre-Socratic concept of the three kinds of soul. The first stage of the embryonic development resembles the soul (the active life force) of a plant, but differs in being able to develop beyond this stage. The next stage resembles a sponge, midway between plant and animal; then the embryo begins to acquire the members which will make it resemble its begetter. The third clear stage sees the embryo become an animal, and the fourth a child.[5] The change from third to fourth stage led Averroes astray because, seeing no specific organ for housing the potential intellect, he thought of this intellect as something separate from the soul in its development from vegetative and animal to human.

The third part of this process, Statius warns, must be closely hearkened to:

'Open your breast to the truth which is coming
and know that as soon as in the embryo
the articulation of the brain is perfected,

the First Mover turns Himself to it, rejoicing
over such a work of nature, and breathes into it
a new spirit filled with powers,

which draws what it finds active there
into its own substance, and makes a single soul
that lives and feels and revolves about itself.'

As soon, then, as the brain is perfected, God breathes a soul into the embryo.[6] In describing this part of the process Statius (like Virgil at a weak spot in an explanation) resorts to argument by analogy. To make clear this remote breathing, Statius reminds his listeners of the heat of the sun (likened to God) which becomes wine (with all its sacramental as well as secular life-giving power) when joined to the juice of the vine (the nonfermented juice, likened to the animal or vegetable condition of the soul). For further clarification Statius uses the pagan myth of the three Fates: when Lachesis, wherever she may be, has no more thread for a person, he dies.

The final portion of Statius' speech uses this account of the origin of the soul to answer the pilgrim's question. After death some of the faculties, both human and divine, are mute; but memory, intelligence, and will are keener than ever before. The soul, coming to the shore of Acheron or of Tiber to start its further course, uses its formative power just as the soul had functioned in passing from the sponge to the animal stage while in the body: that is, the soul now uses this power to make the air around it take on the shape of the living limbs (Statius here makes an analogy with the process by which the air, when moist, adorns itself with the varied colors of the rainbow). This new aerial form, which follows its spirit just as the flames follow their fire wherever the wind may take it, develops the organs of every sense—it can speak, laugh, sigh, and weep. Finally, it takes on the appearance that desires or other impulses impress on it; this is why the souls of the gluttonous, feeling the desire for food that is part of their penance, take on the shape of extreme emaciation.

One of the more important general observations we must make from this account of the soul * is to notice once more how far we

* The process of embryonic development was known to some extent by the ancients: Aristotle and his assistants probably had managed to do more dissection of the human embryo than had the entire medieval period. However, the similarity

have gone from Virgil's stern admonition that man must be satisfied with the effects and not seek to know origins. Dante makes clear his point about the limitations of Virgil's knowledge by having Statius deal with precisely the same questions that Virgil had said could not be answered. Why and how the spirits suffer torments, heat and cold—these are the questions answered in detail by Statius. The Power that, according to Virgil, does not want Its ways revealed has revealed through Statius some of these ways to Virgil himself.

At the end of Statius' speech the travelers have come to the last turn of the terrace, between the purging fire on the one side and the abyss of emptiness on the other. The spirits going through the flames, having sung their hymn to the God of supreme clemency, loudly shout the goads against lust—from the life of Mary and the life of Diana—and celebrate husbands and wives who were chaste. With this singing, this shouting, this celebration of chastity (all these while the spirits are in the midst of the flames), the last affliction, the last wound—the sin of lust—is healed. Here near the summit, in the final cleansing, the fire which is the means of purgation is probably less the burning of lust (penance equal to sin) than it is a proximate form of heavenly love (the greater love consuming the lesser), and therewith an example of the thesis we treated at the end of the previous chapter: that we are approaching

between this theory and that of the present day in regard to the development of the human embryo must be taken in the proper light. The Aristotelian or Dantean explanation is not an empirical scientific statement so much as it is a support of the theory, at least as old as Pythagoras, of the three forms of the soul—the vegetative, the animal, and the human or rational: the human being possesses (or in its development has possessed) all three. We met a reference to this theory at canto 4.1-12, where Dante says that the human being has only one soul. To reconcile this with Statius' account we must know that each later form of the soul displaces its predecessor.

Other parts of Statius' physiological theory we may look on with condescension, if we please. It is not Dante's fault that his age knew less than ours about human morphology. We may, if we like, treat, for example, the first part of Statius' statement as metaphor rather than intended fact; then we can see in his account of common and perfect blood a remarkably apt metaphor for the embryologist's distinction between somatic and germ tissue.

the top of the mountain, where sin is to merge with the hitherto hidden good impulse within it.

* * * * *

At the opening of canto 26 the poet lets us know, with his usual delicate touches, that here among the lustful we are again on a terrace where the sin comes especially close to home. In the opening tercet, as the travelers walk along the rim between the fire and the deep drop, Virgil, his 'good master,' often says to him, 'Be careful, and profit by being warned' (a succinct statement, perhaps, of Virgil's concept of a teacher's function and limits). Then, the means by which the spirits on this terrace learn of Dante's body are uniquely complicated and handsome. The sun shines down on the scene; its light makes the ruddiness of the fire less bright—the light of God, as reflected and transmitted by the sun, diminishes the brilliance and impressiveness even of these fires. The pilgrim's earthly body coming between the sun and the fires, instead of casting its usual darkening shadow, permits the fire, where his body has been interposed, to regain its ruddiness—approaching such ruddiness as the fire has in darkness, when the light of the sun is withdrawn. The spirits, noticing this reminder of their former state, when their own bodies could make the fires of lust gleam more brilliantly, make a comment which might have seemed absurd before the last part of Statius' speech in the preceding canto: 'He does not seem to have the body of a shade.'

One of these spirits,[7] distinguishing himself from the others (we shall soon learn that he is Guido Guinizelli, the last of Dante's poetic fathers), addresses the pilgrim, to ask how he makes of himself 'a barrier for the sun.' But before he reaches this question, his comments summarize a number of the images and concepts we have been noticing in the past canto or two. One of these is the image of thirsting for knowledge (as in the opening tercets of cantos 21 and 22): not only the speaker himself but all the other spirits around him thirst more than for cold water. Curiously combined with this thirst for information is a burning: he is of course burning with the penitential fire, but he also reminds us that the poet has recently used images of burning for information, as at 25.13-5, where his desire to ask is 'kindled to the point of beginning.'

These themes of hunger and thirst keep us in mind of the increasing hunger and thirst of the pilgrim as he mounts the hill of purgation—in Dante's terms equally purgation from vice and purgation from ignorance. The elimination of ignorance—that is, the passing out of a state of nonknowledge or of faulty knowledge—increases both the scope and the desire for knowledge: this is a paradox resembling the problem raised by Guido del Duca (at 14.87) when he spoke of 'common sharing,' a problem resolved by Virgil (at 15.67 sqq.) in explaining that the greater the number of souls partaking of the divine bliss, the greater the share for each. So in the pilgrim's ascent of the mountain: the greater his knowledge, the greater his thirst and desire for more. The pilgrim, at 26.58, speaks of the grace that a lady has won for him to permit him to bring his mortal body through this world. His statement 'I am going upward to be no longer blind' expresses this entire process in a few words: the purgative ascent of the mountain is for the end of enabling the pilgrim to see clearly what a man must see.

The pilgrim then learns the meaning of the crowd of spirits he has been watching: two groups of them have been moving in opposite directions, and as the groups meet each other, one shouts 'Sodom and Gomorrah,' and the others speak of Pasiphaë. Then they continue on their path, as cranes fly off in the direction that best suits their taste—a notable difference of control from the cranes in the circle of the lustful in Hell (at *Inferno* 5.48). These two groups of spirits, we learn, comprise the two divisions of lustful sinners: the homosexual, and those who indulged their normal heterosexual desires to abnormal extent and, by not observing human restraints, became as beasts. For this reason the example of Pasiphaë, who became as a beast in the pursuit of her lust, is an appropriate check; all the more because her lust was fruitful only in producing a monster, the Minotaur.

The spirit now names himself as Guido Guinizelli. It is the pilgrim's turn to act now as Sordello and Statius had acted at hearing the name of Virgil. The earlier poet, who has guided and helped the later, is here, as invariably, spoken of as a father. The pilgrim speaks of his emotion

> *when I hear, naming himself, the father*
> *of me and of others, my betters, who ever*
> *wrote sweet and graceful rhymes of love.*

Later in the canto we shall return to this theme of fatherhood; here I want to point to a curious detail. Immediately before these lines I have just quoted, the poet uses this image to portray his feelings at hearing Guido's name:

> *As, in the sadness of Lycurgus,*
> *two sons became on seeing again their mother,*
> *became I, but not so high do I rise*
>
> *when I hear, naming himself, the father*
> *of me . . .*

The details of this story are significant. Hypsipyle was entrusted with the care of the child of Lycurgus, King of Nemea. She left the child for a short time in order to show a band of thirsty Greeks the fountain they sought. While she was gone a serpent killed the child. (This combination of woman and serpent is especially interesting as we approach the Earthly Paradise.) Lycurgus on his return was at the point of killing Hypsipyle when her two sons rushed in, embraced and rescued her. The pilgrim, then, is saying that his feelings at seeing Guido are analogous to those of the two sons in their mixture of grief, love, and eagerness to face danger to rescue their loved one; but he does not rise so high as the two sons, since he does not rush in to rescue Guido from the flames. A moment's thought about the process of purgation would of course have told the pilgrim that not even Guido would thank him for such a rescue; however, the poet is telling us of an emotion that is prior to thought, and then of a self-awareness that is prior to action. The collocation, finally, of the terms 'mother' and 'father' leaves us with a question: Under these same circumstances would the pilgrim have risen as high as the sons of Hypsipyle if the loved one in danger had stood not in a father's relation to him but in a mother's?

The pilgrim attributes his love of Guido to

> '. . . *your sweet verses*
> *which, as long as modern usage shall last,*
> *will make precious their very ink.*'

Guinizelli's poem, the canzone *Al cor gentil ripara sempre Amor,** was the source of the *dolce stil nuovo*—a style which, in sweet and telling rhyme, often philosophical or metaphysical in style, combined the courtly love of the troubadour and Provençal poets with a spiritualized love of woman—of Mary as woman, of the Mary in all women.

Guido is deeply affected by the pilgrim's love of him, but he modestly points to Arnaut Daniel as more deserving of Dante's love, for excellence in the mother tongue. Even here we have the quarrels of poets and of critics memorialized: for some, says Guido, were fools enough to prefer other poets to Arnaut:

> '*They turn their faces to rumor rather than to truth,*
> *and thus fix their opinion*
> *before they listen either to art or to reason.*'

That is, art in the form of the poems themselves; reason, in the form of knowing critical opinion about the poems as well as understanding the *ratio,* almost the 'philosophy' of the poems. Thus, continues Guido, did many of our fathers do in praising Guittone d'Arezzo, praising him alone, until most of them came to recognize that Guittone's successors were greater than he and thus 'the truth won out with most.' We are reminded that there are generations of fathers: they may be right in their own generation but must be re-

* For a translation of this poem of Guido's and a discussion of the qualities of the sweet new style, see chapter 1, 'The Philosophy and Poetry of Love.'

placed when later needs and greater possibilities arise. This theme, which we had already met in the pilgrim's talk with Oderisi in canto 11, of generations following generations, of fathers, guides, artistic leaders succeeding one another, is now presented with transcendent force. Guido's final words to the pilgrim are:

> *'Now if you have such ample privilege*
> *that you are permitted to reach the cloister*
> *where Christ is the abbot of the college,*
>
> *say for me there a* Pater Noster *to him . . .'*

Why should Guido use this image to name Christ? Neither Guido nor Dante has any ecclesiastical connections which would suggest such an image as an appropriate one. But the word 'abbot' (*abate*) meant originally 'father' (Syriac *abba*). What is more natural, therefore, than for Guido to use this relationship as the source of his image? The pilgrim has come along to call him father; he in turn looks upon Arnaut Daniel, who was *his* poetic father; after the mention of the fathers who preferred Guittone, with the reminder that fathers too must pass away or at least be succeeded by other fathers, it is well-nigh inevitable that he think of Christ as *abba,* father. It may be, says Guido, that the pilgrim has sufficient grace, in this process of mounting ever higher, this process of obtaining ever higher and greater leaders, to attain to the presence of Christ Himself in the one college, or group, that does not pass away; if he does, let Dante say to Christ a Pater Noster, a prayer through Christ to His own Father, or to Christ as Father. (Guido's theology here may be naive, but the pattern of fathers is clear.)

Let us however notice a detail in this ever mounting paean to fatherhood—a detail of immense germinal power for all that follows in the poem, in the final cantos of the *Purgatory* and the entire *Paradise.* Christ is the abbot of the college, a monastery from which women are excluded. In the association we have been examining between poetry and fatherhood there has been a notable avoidance of the mention of women—with but one exception: the allusion to Hypsipyle. True, these poets—Virgil, Statius, Guido, and Arnaut Daniel—all dealt with women and love in their poetry, but their relations to one another are entirely patrilineal or are at least in a world in which women seem to have no creative poetic function. We know that Virgil will cease functioning as a guide in the next canto and will soon be replaced by Matelda and Beatrice. Are we then to surmise that not only each individual father but that fatherhood itself, on the earthly level, is finally an expendable function, necessary through boyhood and youth to keep the son-student away from useless or destructive paths; but not necessary as a guide during maturity and not able to provide the mature person with a light to direct his course?

This possibility seems to be suggested in another way when we look at the sin for which Guido Guinizelli and Arnaut Daniel are being punished. Is Dante's basis for placing these men in the realm of the lustful the fact that both of them made love-poetry an end in itself instead of making of love a theme for celebrating all the glories of God, or at least a theme correlated with the political and social picture of their times? Love, Dante might say, is a theme in itself only when considered under its greatest aspects—as the force which turns the universe.

* * * * *

The angel guarding the exit from this terrace sings *'Beati mundo corde,'* the last of the beatitudes.* The angel on the terrace of the lustful (we are never told that the final P is removed from the pilgrim's brow except through the implication in the closing lines of canto 25 that the fires themselves heal this last wound) then warns the three travelers that they can go no farther unless they pass through the flames of this terrace—all must be cleansed of and by the fires of lust; but Dante's hands clasp each other in anguish

* It is interesting to note, in connection with the paradox I spoke of in chapter 9—that in Dante's scheme the sins of the flesh are necessarily increasingly intellectual—that Aquinas (at *Summa* ii-ii 9. viii, a. 7) says that this beatitude corresponds to 'the gifts of intellect.'

and fear of pain at the prospect of going through the flame 'which has burned so many.'

Virgil remains near Dante through canto 29 and is finally mentioned in canto 30, but he does not speak after canto 27. In this canto where he speaks his last words his role is larger than it has been for some time. Here is the moment which finally resolves the idea of fatherhood: in sum, Virgil the father has guided well through a thousand dangers, he has not told an untruth by minifying any of these dangers; yet all his cogency and all his efforts to get the pupil to test his statement that the fire will not harm him—all these do not move the pilgrim. Virgil says:

> *'Put now, put aside all fear;*
> *turn this way and come onward securely.'*

The persuasive rhythm and repetition of this whole speech of Virgil's are almost magical in their effect, as though with it a small boy might be charmed hypnotically. The pilgrim, in a sense, returns to obdurate boyhood, though he knows better:

> *And I yet fixed, though against conscience.*

What we must see here is that at this point all the pilgrim's trust in his teacher-guides and all that he himself has learned do not suffice to get him past this fire. For this fire is the last barrier before manhood and maturity; this fire purges the last remnants of vice, of ignorance, of inexperience. Yet it is more than a means of purgation, goad and check combined: it is also the realm of fire through which one passes to reach the supermundane universe; it is a foretaste, almost a sample, of the power of God's *caritas.* One leaves the fire to go freely where his will freely takes him. The purged spirits are prepared, after leaving the fire, to depart for their final destination in Paradise. But what can Dante's goal be? He as yet has no station in Paradise. He has experience, training, purgation—but to what end? Virgil, it has sadly been clear for a long time, cannot illumine the present path, let alone the path ahead.

Actually, what is needed is not only an illuminating light but a goal, a star—something to fix the value of traversing the path. This is not a role that can be filled by a teacher-father, not even by a teacher for a young teacher: it is the purpose of men taught, not the purpose of teaching. And so Dante, in spite of his educated conscience, stands firm.

But then Virgil remembers what had been the motivating force for himself in undertaking this journey, what had had the power to take him from an eternity of Limbo:

When he saw me stand still fixed and stubborn,
a little disturbed he said, 'Now see, my son,
between you and Beatrice is this wall!'

The idea of the pilgrim as child is an important part of the paradox at this point in purgation. The sin of origin is nearly removed from the pilgrim by this time; he has nearly become as a little child that he may enter heaven. Yet we must be aware at the same time that his purified maturity—his power to observe and judge and choose with accuracy—is greater, for example, than Virgil's. So that, while the reminder of Beatrice is enough to give Dante reason for entering the fire, Virgil is like one who does not know the true relation between cause and effect and returns to a playfully exaggerated statement of the child-theme as a new tempting to win Dante's entrance to the fire:

Then he shook his head and said, 'What?
Do we want to stay on this side?' then smiled
*as one does to a child that is won over by an apple.** [8]

The references to Pyramus and to the mulberry turned from white to red emphasize the change of state that lies immediately ahead for the pilgrim—a phoenixlike death and transfiguration in the purging fires. Exit from the first six terraces has found the pilgrim purged of one sin after another; exit from the seventh terrace will find him

* The 'apple,' of course, as well as the 'child,' keeps us close to the idea of Eden.

purged of all tendency to sin—the earlier changes were in degree, this one in quality. Even Virgil's persuasiveness partakes of this difference in quality: never before has it been so extended or so necessary as at this, the final manifestation of his eloquence as he prepares to be eliminated from the narrative.

At this moment Virgil regains his earlier relation to the pilgrim: those who had temporarily taken his place step back—Guido Guinizelli and Arnaut Daniel had stepped back into the refining fire, and Statius ceases to be important when the need is for the child's tutor: Virgil

> *. . . then stepped into the fire ahead of me,*
> *begging Statius to come behind,*
> *who, for a long way before, had divided us.*

Then:

> *When I was within, into boiling glass*
> *I would have flung myself to cool off,*
> *so immeasurable was the burning there.*
>
> *My sweet father, to comfort me,*
> *went on speaking ever of Beatrice,*
> *saying, 'Her eyes already I seem to see.'*

The pain of the burning is as severe as anything the poet can imagine; the comforting by Virgil helps in the way in which a child is helped by the touch of his mother's hand when he is in the pain of a dentist's chair—the comforting indeed at this point seems to be that of a mother rather than that of a father. The pilgrim, as child, needs this sweet affection, but is he truly enough of a donkey to be deceived by Virgil's blatant little carrot-lie about Beatrice: 'Her eyes already I seem to see'? Or is Virgil, at this moment, also touched by the same need that his graduating student is experiencing, the need for the guide-light, the eyes of such a woman as Beatrice? *

* * * * *

* The eyes of Beatrice, as we shall learn in the Earthly Paradise, are not lightly achieved or endured.

For the third time the travelers are overtaken by the descent of the sun and perforce make themselves comfortable for the night, each on a step of the mountain. The image Dante uses here to define the relationship between the pilgrim and the two poets ('sages' he calls them at line 67) is that of an agile, wanton goat who at nightfall is guarded by two herdsmen—certainly an uneconomic proportion of cattle to herders. Probably the mountainous terrain suggested the goat, but it is worth noting that the usual pastoral image of a sheep or lamb is not used here. The pilgrim is indeed at this time agile and independent; soon his herdsmen will not be able to hold him down.*

That night Dante dreams again, his third and last dream in Purgatory, in the sleep 'which often announces events before they occur.' This dream is the most difficult of all three to deal with; only one thing seems certain—that the traditional interpretation is possibly quite misleading. In this interpretation Leah represents the active and Rachel the contemplative life. Leah, we see from the dream, represents the active life by singing all day and gathering flowers to make herself a garland; Rachel's kind of contemplation consists of never leaving the mirror all the day because she likes to see her beautiful eyes.

The Middle Ages greatly concerned itself with the choice that some men might have to make between an active and a contemplative life—a choice represented by symbolic figures particularly after Boethius' time. When the allegorical, or figural, interpretation of the Old Testament became popular, Leah and Rachel were most often used as the symbols of this choice.

Of this traditional meaning, then, there can be no question. The only question here, as elsewhere, is Dante's use in the *Commedia* of conventional allegory. Perhaps the most direct way of dealing with this question here is to ask, remembering always that dreams point forward, why at this place is there a choice between activity and contemplation? Is this choice being presented to the pilgrim? For immediate choice or at some point in Paradise? The more specifically

* The wantonness of the goat is perhaps a foreshadowing of the peculiarly strong and yet sinless context of desire in which the pilgrim will encounter Matelda.

one asks this question, the more nearly absurd it becomes. The reason of the process of purgation which the pilgrim has just completed is that the need (which includes the possibility) of choice has been removed: choice is a product necessarily of uncertainties, of taints or lacunae in the will or in the reason, or of imperfections in the situation. To say that any of these conditions prevails at this point on the mountain—remember we are through with the purgatorial terraces and are entering the primordial, pre-sinful Garden of Eden—would be bad logic and worse theology.[9] Even Virgil attempts to define the place with greater precision than this: he says, at line 140, after the dream:

'Free, upright, and whole is your will . . .

Therefore I crown and mitre you over yourself.'

(This latter line I shall come back to; for the present let us see only that Virgil is announcing that Dante is in total spiritual and temporal control of himself.)

Our inquiry into the nature of this dream may be divided into three parts: first, another general view of all three dreams in the *Purgatory;* second, a look at the characters of Leah and Rachel; and third, a look at the way in which this dream fits into the dramatic progress of the poem.

All three dreams come at moments of decisive advances, almost transfigurations, in the poem: the first, at the gate of Purgatory; the second, at the entrance to a new class of sin (the sins of the flesh, with the paradox we noticed that made them seem rather sins of the thoughts); the third, at the entrance to the Earthly Paradise. The three dreams have a peculiar relation to time—a kind of double focus. These dreams all come, it seems, just before dawn, at the time (according to antiquity and the Middle Ages) when dreams are likelier to be true than earlier in the night. We are specifically told, at 27.93, of the 'sleep which often announces events before they occur.' The question is, how long before? In the first dream, so far as we can judge, the pilgrim's dream of being carried aloft by the eagle is simultaneous with his actually being carried by Lucia. On the other hand, the dream seems to figure forth not merely his being carried to the gate of Purgatory but rather his being carried, like Ganymede, to heaven or at least to the realm of the gods. (Remember that Ganymede was carried to the heaven of Mount Olympus, which like the Garden of Eden is at the top of a mountain; the scorching fires through which the pilgrim is carried by the eagle remind us of the later fires before the entrance to Eden.)

The time quality of the second dream is also double: the Siren is all the sins of sense, upon which the pilgrim is immediately entering for purgation; but she is specifically connected with the sin of lust, the terrace of which lies some time after the dream.

The third dream has a pastoral tone that we shall meet again in the next canto, just after we enter the Earthly Paradise; more important, Leah and Rachel have a resemblance to a certain antinomy of Matelda and Beatrice that develops only in the last canto or two of the *Purgatory*.

The dreams differ from one another in respect to the degree of the pilgrim's involvement. In the first dream he is entirely and literally caught up, transported. In the second dream, the pilgrim is not caught up except by his own act (or thought—the terminology is difficult to pin down); the pilgrim is still a major actor but a little less the center of the stage than he had been in the first dream. In the final dream he is only a witness and auditor; his qualities as person seem nearly irrelevant to the dream.

The three dreams have an important but peculiar connection with sexuality—again in a way which makes the sequence seem schematic. In the first there is an ambivalence of sex not only in that Ganymede was transported to Olympus to be the homosexual love of Zeus but also in the image the poet uses at canto 9.34-9—his feelings at awakening were like those of Achilles when carried in his sleep from Chiron to Scyros: remember that Achilles' mother carried him to Scyros in her arms to prevent his joining the forces assembling for the Trojan War; and that the remainder of her plan consisted of disguising him in women's clothing. Notice a curious dissociation of personality: Dante dreams detachedly of Ganymede, and himself turns out to be partly Ganymede.

In the second dream the element of sexuality is of course dominant, lust run hog-wild. Of sexuality in the third dream I shall have more to say in a moment; here let us only remember that Jacob, taken by the charms of Rachel, worked that he might obtain her in marriage; and receiving, by a deception of her father, the sister Leah instead, had to work another seven years for the one who had attracted him.

Laban's two daughters, Leah and Rachel, undeniably provided the early Middle Ages with a convenient allegory of work and meditation, of the active and the contemplative ways of life [10]—of the choice clearly presented in one of the great formative books of the period, Boethius' *Consolation of Philosophy*. It is of considerable importance, in the general question of Dante's relation to medieval symbolism (which has directly to do with the problem of what do his characters 'mean,' and even with the question of what does the *Comedy* 'mean') to see what it is that makes the Leah and Rachel we meet in the *Comedy* unlikely to be representatives of action and contemplation. Two other general questions may also be illuminated by such an examination: the relation of Dante to medieval lore and belief; the problem of discovering what Dante meant by the 'literal sense' of the *Comedy*.

Dante introduces the dream with the important detail of the hour at which it occurred—remember that the dreams which came at dawn were those most likely to be sent under heavenly auspices. But of the multitude of ways in which he might have specified the hour, he chose to do it in terms of Cytherean Aphrodite 'always burning with the fire of love.' This specification of 'Cytherean' rather than 'Uranian' Aphrodite (like the 'concubine of Tithonus' used to specify the hour of the first dream) remains as a strong suggestion of profane love to introduce the dream. Then:

Young and beautiful there appeared to me in a dream
a lady walking over a plain
gathering flowers; and singing she said:

'Know ye, whoever asks my name,
that I am Leah, and go moving about
my beautiful hands to make a garland.

To please me I adorn myself at the looking-glass;
but my sister Rachel never stirs
from her mirror, and sits all day.

She likes to see her beautiful eyes,
as I to adorn myself with my hands:
for her to see, and for me to do, is satisfying.'

The reader unaware of the traditional interpretation of these young ladies would see Leah as a pleasant lily of the field, whose not-toiling and not-spinning seem to bother no one; but he would probably see Rachel as a young woman whose advanced narcissism may work itself into manic depression if she is not forced by someone into a more wholesome kind of regimen. Of course this kind of interpretation is no more applicable than the traditional one I spoke of a moment ago.

The two final tercets of this dream seem to hold the heart of it. The two sisters we see here exhibiting two ways of reflecting beauty. Leah 'reflects a pleasant image': the original of the image lies elsewhere; by adding garlands of flowers to herself she, as image, brings herself into accord with the original. In Rachel this process of reflecting beauty is self-contained: she is herself the original—the image reflects her. Rachel 'sees' to reflect an image of beauty; Leah must 'do' before she can reflect the image.

Before we can decide on the reason for this reflecting of beauty and the point of the two different ways of doing it, we need to bring two or three things to bear on the question. For one thing: in the complex Biblical story of Leah and Rachel, Jacob has what might be called preference—a will to choose—between the two sisters, but is without freedom of choice in respect to his spouse. It may even be relevant to remember Jacob's position as founder, with divine sanction, of the ecclesia in Israel; Jacob's ladder, a continuum from earth to heaven, would serve almost as a perfect image of the system and purpose of the *Comedy*. The results of Jacob's choice might also be remembered: Leah, the wife thrust upon him, was fruitful; his choice, Rachel, was barren.

The context of themes and ideas within which the dream comes forth is also to be considered. We have just been in a rapid sequence of one father succeeding another, finally with the suggestion—in the allusion to Hypsipyle—that we may have come to the point in the progress of the pilgrim that requires a woman as guide-companion. (We know of course that soon Beatrice—or Matelda—will come to take over the guidance of Dante.) The present question then might well be: What woman or what kind of woman is required? The little introduction to the dream falls into place, with Cytherea's burning with the fire of love reminding us that the pilgrim, just before this choice between Leah and Rachel was offered to him (if it *was* offered as a choice), passed through the fires purifying desire.

Let us bring in the matter of the time-relationships, the time-qualities of the dream. There will be, very soon after the dream, an encounter with two women who bear a certain relation to Leah and Rachel: Matelda and Beatrice. But the time-relation seems to be backward as well as forward. The description of Leah as 'young and beautiful, going over a meadow gathering flowers and . . . singing' is almost a formula for the young heroines of late Latin and medieval poetry; soon, however, we are to meet Matelda doing these very things. Somewhat less clearly, the picture of Rachel's activity (if so it can be called) suggests the picture of My Lady Philosophy as she came to offer Boethius, imprisoned, the choice between an active and a contemplative life. Nowhere in the progress of the *Commedia*'s journey does the pilgrim have a choice of such magnitude put before him—or, actually, any sort of choice beyond a determination to speak with this spirit or with that one. His progress, from the desperate prison in which he had found himself at the beginning of the *Inferno,* on to the Empyrean, is everywhere determined by the form and law of the place.

A final word on the dream [11] of Leah and Rachel must wait until after we have looked at the next episode.

The concluding section of canto 27 contains Virgil's valediction. As the pilgrim wakes up, finding his two masters already awake, Virgil says to him:

> *'That sweet fruit for which on so many branches*
> *the labor of mortals goes searching,*
> *today will satisfy your hungerings.'*

The word here translated 'fruit,' *pome,* is the same as that used to name the fruit of the two trees on the terrace of the gluttons; it is the word for the apple eaten by Eve.* This is the fruit of knowledge and light, barred from those who have not yet purged themselves of gluttony, that the pilgrim on his entrance to the Garden of Eden will be able to use to satisfy his hunger and thirst. Remember how often in the past six or seven cantos, as we neared the end of the purgatorial process, the poet has used images of burning with desire or with thirst, or having the unslaked sensation of an incompletely filled sponge—all to describe the one thing, a need to have his questions entirely answered. Virgil's statement that the pilgrim is approaching the place where this satisfying of desire will be accomplished is the greatest of his gifts to his pupil—

> *. . . never were there gifts*
> *that were equal to these in pleasing.*

Virgil's promise to the pilgrim of course continues to show his peculiar limits: Dante will this day enter the Garden of Eden and have his hunger satisfied—but only to the extent that the Earthly Paradise is capable of satisfying. Virgil's vision—or projection beyond what is present to his eyes—still does not extend to the

* It is also the word used metaphorically by Virgil to denote Beatrice at line 45 of this canto. Does this establish a relation between Beatrice and Eve? or between Beatrice and that which Eve sought?

Heavenly Paradise and the even deeper hunger that it alone can slake.

Hear finally Virgil's summation of what he has done in leading the pilgrim through the limited punishment of Purgatory and the eternal punishment of Hell, together with his understanding of what lies ahead of the pilgrim:

> . . . *'The temporal fire and the eternal*
> *you have seen, my son, and you have come to a place*
> *where I, by myself, discern nothing further.*
>
> *I have brought you hither with subtlety and with art;*
> *now take your pleasure as your guide;*
> *you are free from the steep ways, free from the narrow.*
>
> *See there the sun that shines on your brow;*
> *see the tender grass, the flowers and the shrubs*
> *which the earth here produces of itself.*
>
> *Until the fair eyes* [of Beatrice], *now rejoicing, come—*
> *which, weeping, made me go to you—*
> *you can sit or walk among them.*[12]
>
> *Expect no further word or sign from me;*
> *free, upright, and whole is your will;*
> *it would be wrong not to do as it prompts you.*
>
> *Therefore I crown and mitre you over yourself.'*

This final speech by Virgil sums up not only his function as guide in the poem but also the highest potentialities of enlightened paganism. It may even be a speech in which Dante is setting straight, with clarity but without reproach, certain overeager qualities of the humanism of his day.

Limited as are Leah and Rachel in their respective ideals, their practicing ideas, the highest vision of Virgil—that which he now offers as the opportunity open to his pupil—is the ideal of enlightened paganhood. This ideal is the freedom for pleasure, for the creation and enjoyment of beauty, under circumstances which entail no conceivable harm or damage to anyone: the person fulfilling such an ideal, in full development of his faculties, free within and without, spends his life in isolated increase of the world's store of beauty. This dream, at its highest, can rise above the economy of scarcity we have talked about and can conceive of a common sharing in which each such free man welcomes and invites the activity of others like himself. Pleasure, innocent pastoral pleasure, is then not only the goal but the obligation of such a development as Virgil conceives he has aided the pilgrim in attaining: with the pilgrim's will free and whole, he says, 'it would be wrong not to do as it prompts you.' Therefore, he now makes the pilgrim emperor and pope over himself.[13]

This last statement has troubled many commentators who, to resolve the difficulty they find, have had to twist a statement from the *Monarchy* into giving Virgil the right to absolve the pilgrim from complying with secular or ecclesiastical authority. This freedom from authority might seem to be feasible at this point where the pilgrim has regained the primal state of innocence, carrying him back before the Fall, before the time when man needed both kinds of authority to inhibit the sin he had originated by his Fall. This explanation is not false, but it is incomplete: authority, and the need for it, are present in the pilgrim's further journey (think only of the decisive role played by Beatrice and by the Tree in the concluding cantos of the *Purgatory*). The question of Virgil's last line can be resolved only by realizing the fullness of his dramatic character in the poem.

His act of crowning and mitring the pilgrim is not so much an unseemly arrogation of powers as it is a gift of the highest thing within his knowledge and hence within his power. It is the donation, as I said a moment ago, of the highest fulfillment of the pagan vision, couched in the language of 'emperor and pope' that Virgil has acquired in his own journey through Hell and Purgatory. The dream about Leah and Rachel fits into the pattern of this, not as playing into Virgil's hands but as resembling Virgil in the way it is limited by the altitude of the place. The dream casts us forward into the Earthly Paradise, where even Virgil can go. The life here is of utter freedom for pleasure-without-harm, but, as an end-in-itself, it ignores one of the deepest paradoxes of the Christian mystery, that existence in the Earthly Paradise before the Fall was an incomplete use of man's talents, that man had to fall and then struggle to rise again before he could fully use his God-granted talents for organization and direction or could require the redemptive function of Christ. (This is of course the same kind of paradox that lies at the basis of Christ's passion: was His suffering the point of His existence?) The Earthly Paradise is necessarily of limited scope, that is, of limited knowledge—but it is not limited in goal, in the sense that every spirit there (except Matelda?) is destined, is aiming, for a higher place. Leah, Rachel, Virgil—these are, literally, earthbound. This is the meaning and the function of Virgil. It is, though not completely, the function of Leah and Rachel: remembering what was said a while back about the twofold relations of the dreams to time-fulfillment, we can expect to find not only an immediate fulfillment of the dream in Virgil's speech to the pilgrim but also a later fulfillment—perhaps in the remaining cantos of the *Purgatory,* perhaps not until we reach the *Paradise.*

The question might once more be tentatively raised: What is this higher thing, this thing beyond the Earthly Paradise? In a practical sense Dante, who has to write a third part to the poem and has to hold the reader's interest through that third part, cannot defeat his own purposes by revealing the fullness of his vision before the second part is over. Nor should we try too hard to steal a look at the end, to see how everything comes out. However, we have already intimated what will be involved in the future of the pilgrim, as he changes from male to female guides. Leah and Rachel, Hypsipyle, even as far back as the mother of Achilles—these have been women whose lifting, guiding, or choosing function has been established for the pilgrim; Matelda and Beatrice are soon to come.

Virgil even, in his words on the grass, flowers, and shrubs of the Earthly Paradise, carries us into a realm of primordial myth, the myth of the Earth-Mother as a self-fertilizing being, with no need of the male fathering function: *

> *'See there the sun that shines on your brow;*
> *see the tender grass, the flowers, and the shrubs*
> *which the earth here produces of itself.'*

This tercet deserves quotation in the Italian:

> *'Vedi l' il sol che in fronte te riluce;*
> *vedi l'erbetta, i fiori e gli arbuscelli,*
> *che qui la terra sol da se produce.'*

The word *sol* you will notice occurs twice, with a serious play not uncommon in Dante: the first time it means 'sun,' the second time, 'alone'—with a redundance which does not show in the translation. Literally this line, the last of the tercet, says, 'that which the earth alone by itself [*or,* from itself] produces.' This redundance, it seems to me, is intentional and emphatic, to make sure that the reader sees the point about the self-fertilization of the earth, and that he is also reminded that in traditional nature-myth it is the male sun that fertilizes the female earth. In this tercet the sun illumines the pilgrim's brow and provides the light by which the flowers may be seen—but it was not needed to produce the flowers. For the nonce, fatherhood is not a needed function. Fatherhood has for the moment done all it can in illuminating the path of the pilgrim; to attain further heights he now needs the function of the woman—whatever this may be.[14]

* Perhaps more importantly we are reminded of the two habitats of Adam: Eden, that produced fruits without toil; the rest of the earth, where man produced his food through the sweat of his brow.

CHAPTER TWELVE

The Paradox of Innocence

[CANTOS 28 TO 30.108]

At the end of canto 27 Virgil had given the pilgrim full control over himself, both secularly and ecclesiastically. As he enters the Earthly Paradise this control seems immediately to be translated into the beauty and freedom of the place.[1] Two moments, however, of his stay in the Earthly Paradise—one at the beginning, the other near the end—seem to be inconsistent with this condition of purified power: the first is the feeling of desire—one had almost said lust—that is stimulated in the pilgrim by the sight of Matelda, guardian of the place; the other is the schoolboyish abasement he exhibits before the stern reproofs of Beatrice. An attempt to understand these two moments—and particularly how the second is related to the first—may clarify some of the great puzzles of these concluding cantos of the *Purgatory*.

We are reminded, in lines 22-4, that this is an entrance upon a new thing by the ways in which this entrance into the woods resembles that of the opening of the *Inferno*. But the woods of the Earthly Paradise—beautiful, calm, reassuring, free of fear—are as different as could be from the dark and terrifying *selva selvaggia* of the *Inferno*. The setting of the Earthly Paradise is painted with the deliberate beauty of a flowered landscape of Botticelli. A sweet unvarying breeze is blowing. (After what we have learned of the mountain's immunity to changing weather this too will need some explanation.) However, this wind does not rustle the leaves enough to disturb the joyous sound of the birds.

The river which flows through the woods is clearer than any water on earth in spite of the perpetual shade through which it flows, but this phenomenon of clarity without the light of heaven is only one of the peculiar qualities of this river. On the other bank of the river is a solitary lady who, like Leah, sings as she gathers flowers.[2] (She is also like Proserpine, of whom we shall be reminded in a few lines, when she was ravished away by Pluto.) The pilgrim's greeting of this lady is less in the tradition of the *dolce stil nuovo* than in that of the earlier mode of courtly love:

> *'O fair lady, you who warm yourself*
> *in the rays of love, if I may believe your looks*
> *which are wont to be a witness of the heart,*
>
> *may you be pleased to come forward,'*
> *said I to her, 'toward this stream,*
> *so that I can understand what you sing.*
>
> *You make me remember where and how*
> *Proserpine was at the time her mother*
> *lost her, and she lost the spring.'*

The courtesies of these first two tercets are handsome enough, although perhaps a shade too elegant for this situation. But the image in this third tercet is curious indeed. The pilgrim seems to be putting himself vis-à-vis Matelda in the same relation that Pluto bore to Proserpine: Pluto was the only one who saw 'where and how Proserpine was at the time her mother lost her,'—that is, when Pluto ravished her away. Dante's first view, then, of Matelda is described in a context of passionate, even violent desire.*

* There is also something curious and powerful in the last two quoted lines. Other ways of describing Proserpine at this moment were surely available to Dante; naming the moment in terms of 'the time her mother lost her' connects it with the theme of fatherhood we have been dealing with, of father yielding place to mother. But this is a mother who has lost her daughter, as Eve, Great Mother, lost, or sacrificed the welfare of her children at the same time that she (Ceres? Proserpine?) lost the beneficent glories of spring. ('Spring,' we must remember, is in the Italian *primavera,* which in its parts, *prima* and *vera,* is 'first truth.') So that we have here in these lines a confusion of seasons and gardens and mothers and the First Truth, which was lost—a confusion that is rather a welter of the great feelings and ideas that are about to be straightened out in the course of the next three or four cantos.

Matelda, Dante next tells us, fulfilled all his wishes by coming to the bank directly opposite him. But even though she comes with eyes downcast, 'like a virgin,' her mode of walking, with the mincing steps of a woman dancing, is not devoid of seductiveness. She then delights him by lifting her eyes. Dante reminds us here that the eyes are the transmitters of love's burning glances by his use of an image even more surprising than that of Proserpine:

I do not believe that so bright a light shone
under the eyelids of Venus, pierced
by her son, quite against his intention.

This refers to the time when Venus, accidentally wounded by one of Cupid's arrows, beheld Adonis and—such was the power of the arrows—immediately looked upon the young man with great desire, as she would have looked upon any other man seen under these circumstances. Is this the kind of undiscriminating love the pilgrim sees in the eyes of Matelda?

She smiles at him from the other bank, in her hands some of the flowers which this part of the mountain produces without seed: these are the flowers we noticed in the previous canto as testifying to the no-need this region has for the function of fatherhood. The separation between Matelda and the pilgrim is but three steps (like the three steps at the gate to Purgatory), but not even the Hellespont was more hated by Leander for keeping him apart from his beloved Hero. (Leander, however, overcame his hate of the Hellespont by swimming nightly to Hero.)

Here, in quick sequence, we have three images, and they are the only ones used by the poet to describe the pilgrim's reactions to the sight and sound of Matelda: of ravished Proserpine, of Venus enamoured of Adonis, and of Leander impelled to swim a stream for love. Notice also that in the second of these images the poet is saying that Matelda returns this love. The love may be thoroughly spiritual—or at least aesthetico-spiritual—but the three legendary illustrations used by the poet are all derived from stories of notably fleshly love. At this point, however, Matelda offers to satisfy the pilgrim's curiosity about the qualities of this place and, as usual, such an offer is enough to drive all other thoughts from his mind. The poet drops these suggestions of aroused fleshly desires; but we must stop to look for a meaning within the three images of desire.

These three images are all powerful and clear; they all conduce to the same point; perhaps most important, they come in rapid succession just as we have entered upon the Earthly Paradise. Do they not direct the reader to the problem of the nature of man in this region—either before the Fall or just after entry by means of ascending through the terraces? *

The pilgrim, under one or the other of these two conditions (we shall soon see him nearly identified with Adam), strongly exhibits a quality that may be described as desire without sin. We have noticed before that each of the capital sins has a vital good at the center of it, as though it were a tainted or diseased fruit growing up around a wholesome core: without sexual desire, the process of human (or animal) reproduction would be primarily intellectual rather than primarily natural (or instinctive); without the habit (or instinct) of eating, individual life would be impossible; avarice and prodigality are corrupted exaggerations of the need for some amount of getting and spending in a social order; sloth carries to extremes a wholesome caution; anger, we had noted on the very terrace on which it was purged, may have a center of rightful indignation against wrongdoing; envy has, deep within it, a concern over what is happening to one's fellows; pride may have begun in an idea of the worth of man as individual.

Dante would not need to show the pilgrim divested of the diseased layers of sin, exhibiting notable instances of each of the primal (or capital) virtues. He has, however, begun with the most dramatically effective instance—the virtue within the vice of which he had most recently been purged. While the virtues within gluttony and avarice-prodigality would be awkward to exhibit here

* These latter conditions are probably similar; but there is, as we shall see, a third condition: after the process of human history has begun to unfold in the great pageant, man is something other than merely sinless.

(and I believe they are ignored), the remainder of these core-virtues may be seen developing within the pilgrim as he undergoes his final metamorphosis within the Earthly Paradise—especially in the final scenes of abasement in front of Beatrice from which the pilgrim rises ready to mount to Paradise.

The pilgrim has been troubled by the flowing of the water and the blowing of the wind: these, which would be natural phenomena on earth, he had earlier learned (canto 21.40-60) were disturbances that were not permitted above the level of Antepurgatory. Matelda explains the water and the wind. (Is it a little, harmless joke that she promises to remove his wonder by dispelling the fog that has enveloped him? Fog is a product of water and wind.) Her explanation, as happens so frequently in the poem, involves much more than the fairly simple question seems to call for. Not only the meteorology of the Earthly Paradise but the moral and spiritual qualities of the region come into her answer.

The wind and the water are quickly explained. What the pilgrim has earlier learned is true: the mountain is free of atmospheric change. But the earth's blanket of air revolves with the revolution of the heavenly bodies, as set in motion by the Primum Mobile—in Dante's cosmology the earth, of all created bodies, is still, while the rest of the universe is in rotation (if, as in another theory of the time, the earth rotates, it does so at a slower rate than that of the heavenly spheres which surround it). The revolving air is not felt by those in the inhabited parts of the earth since it is dissipated by the atmospheric winds and the irregular contours of the earth's surface. (The inconceivably great speed of the diurnal spin of the Primum Mobile grows less as it is communicated to the lower spheres.) Here at the crest of the mountain the gentle but unremitting force of the wind serves to give an earthly foretaste, in sensual equivalents, of the delights of Paradise: the wind keeps the air in pleasing motion, gently moves the leaves of the trees so that they give forth a sound, and scatters the aromas of the flowering plants and herbs. Nor is the water of the river produced by mundane means, by the irregular evaporation and condensation which cause unpredictable rises and falls in the levels of mundane streams. The water of the Earthly Paradise is generated directly from the will of God, unchanging and certain. It flows in two streams, Lethe and Eunoe—'the forgotten sorrow and the remembered dream': drinking the water of Lethe removes the last traces of the memory and actuality of sin (although, as we learn in the *Paradise,* it does not remove the memory of the *experience*); drinking the water of Eunoe restores the full memory of good, of all good deeds.

For the first of these streams Dante had the Greek stream and the Greek story to give him the name and the idea of a cleansing stream of the dead; the name of the second stream seems to be of his invention (the Greek mystery religions spoke of a stream of *prememory,* as well as one of forgetfulness, in Hades). Here, in little, may be seen a pattern of Dante's poetic creation: first, an ingredient derived from pagan antiquity; second, a corresponding, and yet transcending, ingredient required by the enlarged vision of the universe in the Christian revelation. The Christian ingredient may or may not be at hand for the poet in Christian doctrine or tradition; it makes little difference whether or no. Where it is lacking, as in the present instance, he coins the thing and the name; where it is present, as in the instance of the four cardinal virtues (available to pagans before Christ) and the three theological virtues, he uses or reorganizes the traditional concept to fit into the patterns of his poem.

But this account of the wind and water of Eden is more important as the occasion for Matelda's words on the idea of the Earthly Paradise. Here God, Whose pleasure is unalloyed in following every path of His will, had created a place in which man might come as close as possible to living in the path of God, where man's enlightened, beneficent pleasure would be identical with the free exercise of his will. Through his own fault, says Matelda, he exchanged the innocent laughter and play of Eden for the tears and toil of the world; yet the place remains, with a difference. Then, it was a gift to man; now, having lost that gift, he can regain the place only by the highest use of all his talents. And note what these required talents are—in noting them we can once more see the precise quality of Dante's Christianity.[3] Dante pays, at appropriate places, due deference to the ascetic, the monastic, life as a path whereby the individual person may attain paradise, both earthly and heavenly. But Dante himself has attained the Earthly Paradise only by a tremendous collaboration of all the forces of humankind—and more. Empire, city, church, the guidance and companionship of pagan and Christian poets, the force represented by Beatrice (we shall have to defer until the next chapter a definition of what this force comprises)—all these and other gigantic attainments of mankind had to be called upon to forward and elevate our pilgrim on his path. These forces, true, are all one—the force of God's creative love—but broken, confused, diffused first by man's fall and then (again) by his efforts to regain the summit he had once inhabited.[4] Dante's plan in the poem is therefore a method by which he can simultaneously clarify and synthesize (better, unify) the phenomenology of the world.

An illustration of this technique closes the canto. In Dante's scheme, as we have seen, the development of an idea often entails successive explanations of the same thing, each explanation made more accurate, more clear, and more inclusive by the one that follows. Matelda courteously (courtesy is proved by the event: even though Virgil and Statius are being corrected, they receive the correction in this place with smiles) adds something to her remarks. The pagans in their poems had a confused picture of the Earthly Paradise: in his incomplete vision on Parnassus (rather than a true vision on Purgatory) the ancient poet celebrated the Golden Age of man as a state from which he gradually decayed. The Earthly Paradise, imperfectly conceived, gave the pagan poet his notion of the golden age; the water of these streams, imperfectly conceived, gave this poet his 'nectar.'

At this the pilgrim turned to his poets, no longer for guidance of any kind, and saw that with smiles they had received this kindly reprimand by Matelda. Virgil has smiled before, but it has been with a stern Roman smile, or perhaps one with a touch of sardonicism or superiority. Only here, so soon before he is to leave, does he smile with a completely good-natured abnegation of self.

Then the pilgrim turned his face—his eyes, his attention, his will to learn and to receive pleasure—to the fair lady.

* * * * *

Canto 29 sets the stage for the greatest climax of the canticle—the coming of Beatrice in canto 30. Again Dante's staging is magnificent—or perhaps, since 'staging' is here a metaphor, we may as well use a more accurate metaphor and term Dante's accomplishment here the orchestral marshalling of his themes in massive recapitulation and simultaneous development to a climax.

Matelda, having finished her explanation, continues her song—a song of thanks for those whose sins have been remitted: the imagery of remission in this psalm is perhaps ambiguous. 'Blessed are those whose sins are covered': the word for 'covered' (*tecta*) means 'roofed over,' 'protected.' She wanders along the stream, moving upstream (here again the comparison with a nymph suggests the amorousness of pastoral poetry). Suddenly the stream, as Dante keeps pace with her on his side, takes a bend so that the pilgrim is now facing the east.

The great pageant [5] which now follows is generally taken to represent the history of the church or, with Carroll, the Procession of the Spirit. Such traditional interpretations are a great convenience in suggesting a direction for the reader's thoughts but mean nothing unless he, so to speak, re-evolves or re-induces the interpretation for himself: he sees what the details are, tries in one way and then another to fit them together, and finally arrives at a consistent explanation which disregards no significant detail. Thus a reader moves from scanning the poem to experiencing it.

Immediately after the pilgrim, following the stream, has turned to the east he sees a light from that direction, brilliant as lightning but increasing in intensity instead of vanishing.* It is still early

* The part of the poem now commencing is, it soon becomes clear, of a different order of writing from anything we have yet encountered. Earlier we have had only an occasional symbol mixed in with the (fictive) realities. From this point on to the end of the canticle the proportion is nearly reversed: the pageant, for example, is almost entirely symbolic. My method of proceeding must change accordingly: I shall try to give a running translation of the symbols into things-

morning; the sun would appear from this direction were it not for the heavy boughs of the forest. This light functions as the sun even within this shady forest; no such light had appeared to the pilgrim in the dark forest of the *Inferno,* except indirectly as Virgil came to execute the mission given him by Beatrice.

But the light alone serves only to raise the question, 'What is this?' The sweet melody that is the next phenomenon is described by a characteristic Dantean device: instead of trying to describe the quality of the sound or even its immediate effect on him he tells the thought that came as an intellectual sequel to the effect—he reproves Eve for her disobedience which had the effect of cutting him off, both in the past and in the future, from the delights of such music. This mention of Eve has another important function —that of reminding the reader of the ambivalent nature of women: if responsible for the fall of man they are also responsible—through Mary, Beatrice, and others—for his redemption, for his being set on the path by which one can struggle and regain primal innocence. More than this, the very terms in which Eve's disobedience is described state the paradox of the fall of man: the 'boldness of Eve who did not endure to remain under any veil,' that is, under any cover concealing things that might otherwise be seen. (We shall soon meet Beatrice under a veil.) This veil of not-knowing, under which Eve refuses to stay, is perhaps to be linked with Matelda's song in the previous canto: there it was sins that were covered; here it is the power of sight, of knowing. This concept of Eve fits with what we have previously seen: Eve brought the fall of man, but without the Fall man would have remained at the level of the Earthly Paradise, not to rise above it. (In the view of St. Augustine, without the deed of Eve man would have remained in the Garden of Eden until Judgment Day and would then have been translated to Paradise: Dante, it might be noted, neither ignores nor denies the Day of Judgment, but it must also be noted that it cannot play a significant part in the structure of his poem.)

symbolized, as a needed preliminary to any other analysis of or comment on the progress of the poem.

These 'first fruits of the eternal pleasure' stimulate the desire and the expectancy of still further joy. But before his pen can cope with the glories it must next describe, Dante offers a little prayer for help. This prayer, as usual, is to the same Muses that the pagan poets invoked, but there are two interesting touches: first, by calling the Muses 'most holy virgins,' he emphasizes in them qualities compatible with Christian values; second, by calling on these virgins to help him 'put into verse things hard to conceive,' he puts into question his fiction that the literal level of the *Comedy* is based on some species of direct experience. (This will be resolved in the final canto when we learn that the poet has impressed on his memory even things he does not understand—thus the fiction is preserved.)

As he commences the actual description of the oncoming pageant he makes a side remark on the nature of perception which tempts one into applying it to the progress of the poem. At a distance, he says, he thought he saw seven golden trees; closer, they turned out to be candlesticks: when he was close, 'the common features in different things, because of distance, no longer caused confusion.' Intellectual progress, or the journey up the mountain, it might seem from this, is not a process of more inclusive syntheses or generalizations but is a process of particularization, of refining differences, or rather, of discarding misleading similarities.

Still as preamble to the pageant comes a reminder that the pilgrim has a new guide—at least, has finished with the old guide. He turns to Virgil to share admiration with him, and is answered by a look of amazement—it is difficult to say how much should be made of this difference between 'admiration' and 'amazement,' but that there is some difference is made certain by what follows: Matelda takes over Virgil's function of reproaching the pilgrim for dawdling over one detail—

> *. . . 'Why are you still*
> *so eager only to see the living lights*
> *and do not pay attention to what comes behind them?'*

That the pageant represents the history of the church we may accept as a good hypothesis, but—as I remarked a moment ago—let us re-evolve this symbolism. Twenty-four elders (elder books), a few lines later, 'the chosen people' (the books of the Old Testament), sing:

> . . . *'Blessed art thou*
> *among the daughters of Adam,' and*
> *'Blessed to eternity be thy beauties.'*

Is this blessed one Matelda, Beatrice, Mary, the Church? It may be that it is not necessary to decide this question; not that they are all the same but that they have enough in common as feminine principle to function in equivalent ways (the Church as woman was a commonplace of the day through the interpretation of the Song of Solomon as a lovesong of Christ to his bride, the Church). Then, just as one guiding star succeeds another, four creatures (the four gospels) in green for hope follow the twenty-four elders in white for faith. The crown of green leaves marks the triumph of the four, whether as poets or as athletic contestants; their six wings—i.e., three pairs mark their triune power of flight. Their feathers, beautiful as a peacock's, are full of living eyes, to see and be seen.

It may be that Dante's impatience to get on—'To describe their form I will not waste rhymes, Reader, for another need urges me on'—is an indication that here, with the twenty-four and the four, he is doing something he rarely does: he is using commonplaces of current allegorical symbolism without trying in any considerable way to manipulate them, to comment on them, perhaps even—as he occasionally does—to reverse their import. And so, since his readers can find the same material in accessible places, he need not bother with it.*

* Equally, of course, he is expressing here, as in a number of other places, the urgency for concision forced on him by his plan to present the universe within a hundred measured cantos.

Contained within the four apostles is a chariot drawn by a griffon, an animal generally symbolizing Christ.[6] The animal symbolism of the Middle Ages is particularly rich and interesting in connections with the figures for Christ. To depict His wide range of qualities not only existent animals but fictitious or composite animals had to be utilized. For example, His dual nature as man and as God, had to be figured forth either by a real animal with some duality visible in it (such as the two-colored coat of the leopard) or by a synthetic animal such as the griffon or the cameleopard (sturdiness of the camel plus the speed of the leopard), just as His agility and strength could be figured forth either by the tiger or by the unicorn. The griffon is earthbound, though with strength, nobility, and force, through its lion's body; as it is heaven-directed through its eagle's head and wings. It is worth noting that the griffon draws the chariot by its neck, where the two bodies (and the two qualities) join or are merged with each other, and not by its chest as do most draught animals. The wings of the griffon rise so high as to be out of sight, in the heavens. As they extend upwards the wings do not harm, do not disturb, the bands of color that introduced the pageant and serve as a canopy over all. As the seven candlesticks (like and yet unlike the seven-branched candelabrum of ancient Hebrew symbol) seem to represent the seven gifts of the Holy Spirit[7] (wisdom, understanding, counsel, fortitude, knowledge, piety, and fear) so are the paths of light subtended by these candlesticks (paths which extend farther back than the sight of the poet can reach) contained within the ten commandments, the ten steps which carry one from one outside band of light to the other. These lights, these commandments, that is to say, are not controverted or disturbed by anything in Christ's heavenly qualities and powers. Rather, he is in some ways contained within them.

The symbolism of the sun comes in at this point for an important comment. The sun in pagan worship had often been the direct symbol of the Great God or even the thing worshipped in itself. In Christian symbol the sun is only the vehicle through which God directs His light upon the earth; the sun provides illumination and stimulates growth but only as a means, a means eventually to be transcended. Here, in the Earthly Paradise, one's vision is sufficiently cleared and liberated to be able to cast ahead to the time, not far off in the journey, when the pilgrim will come to the sun and pass beyond it. In Dante's terms, then, this is another way of saying that the sun is not the final illuminant, even that the sun because it is ultimately inadequate must in some ways be imperfect. As a way of expressing this the poet tells us that not only the greatest secular monarchs had no chariot to compare with this but that even the chariot of the sun itself (as told for example in the story of Phaëton) had no comparable perfection, was even expendable or destroyable within the—as yet—mysterious justice of Jove (or God) in behalf of the earth's welfare.

By the right wheel of the chariot come dancing the three theological virtues:[8] Love (*caritas,* dearness or charity), pure but of the same color as the fire that purged the lustful; Hope, green through and through; and Faith as white as snow. Faith and Love take turns in leading the dance; Hope never leads, since she could not even exist without the prior existence of her two sisters. The movements of the dance are guided by the song of Love—Love which gives measure and order to life.

By the left wheel are the four cardinal virtues[9] (Prudence, Temperance, Fortitude, and Justice), which the pagans themselves had known (remember that in the shape of stars they illuminate Cato in the first canto); Prudence has three eyes in her head, not only because the prudent one needs such extra means of sight but perhaps to suggest that through this virtue the very pagans might have had an inkling of threeness, of the Trinity, of the three theological virtues. Prudence needs the ability to see past and present together and to have at the same time an eye to the future.

The remaining figures in the procession denote the minor books of the New Testament: these seven are garlanded not with the white lilies of faith, as had been the books of the Old Testament, but with the red roses of love or charity (the Latin word embraces both meanings). The two old men, opposed in attire and in technique of cure, are St. Luke and St. Paul—Luke the beloved physician, author of the Acts of the Apostles; and Paul, the militant proselytizer, who cures by assaulting and wounding the soul. Then come—according to the most likely identification—the writers of the four 'Catholic epistles': James, Peter, John, and Jude. Finally, in sleep, walks the St. John who saw the vision of the Apocalypse, the final book of the Bible.

The close of the canto seems to me of tremendous significance:

And when the chariot came opposite me,
a thunderclap was heard; and these worthy people
seemed to have their advance forbidden,

and together with the first banners they halted.

It is not enough—at least with such a writer as Dante it is not enough—to say that this is a dramatic necessity, that the procession must pause in order to put certain functions to work vis-à-vis the pilgrim, as again in the following cantos. A mechanical necessity such as this would, for example, not have utilized the thunderclap—quite apart from the point that no poet has to be tied down by such mechanical difficulties. No, the entire procession—Scripture, Church, even Christ—comes to halt specifically for the pilgrim at the behest of God's thunderclap.[10] This interpretation may be a little easier to assimilate if we look ahead to the next canto to see that here, where Dante's name is mentioned for the only time in the entire poem, we must realize that the entire pageant is being staged for the intensely personal transaction that Beatrice has to execute with Dante. If Scripture, Church, and Christ are to be thought of as universal and transcendent, Dante reminds us that by the same token all three exist for every individual being.

* * * * *

At the opening of canto 30 the seven candlesticks are presented in an image as the Septentrion (Ursa Minor, the Little Dipper), of which the lower star (the North Star) guides vessels to port; but the Septentrion of the candles differs from the one visible to mankind in being not subject to rising or setting or in being veiled by any atmospheric disturbance—only sin has acted as a veil to hide it from men. Just as the North Star directs the mariner on his way, so do the candles make everyone aware of his duty. At the stopping of the candles and the chariot all the persons in the procession turn to the chariot as to their peace—as Dante will later say, in providing a perfect reconciliation between free will and the will of God: 'In His will is our peace.'* They sing and offer benedictions: from the Song of Solomon, 'Come, my spouse, from Lebanon' (in the Vulgate text, the word *veni,* 'come,' occurs three times)—in the traditional interpretation, this is Christ's call to His Church; 'Blessed art thou who comest'[11] (is this for Christ? for Dante?); and 'Give lilies with full hands' (are these the same lilies as those of canto 29.84?).

The appearance of Beatrice is expressed in terms which transcend even the beauty and majesty of what we have thus far seen in the pageant. In the coming of the candlesticks, at 29.16, there had been only an implied statement that their light was like that of the sun; at the coming of Beatrice the comparison is explicit—her brilliance, like the sun's, can be steadily looked at only when it is veiled, by a cloud of flowers in the one instance, by a cloud of mist in the other. The lady appears in the three theological colors we have already seen—white, green, and red; but it must be noted that another color is added—olive—which will be explained below (at line 68) as Minerva's leaves, the leaves of wisdom and of peace.

Here comes what is probably the most touching emotional climax of the entire canticle—all the more touching because it brings to a ringing resolution the themes of father and mother which have been building for the previous six or eight cantos. The presence of Beatrice, even before the pilgrim can see her clearly, 'through a hidden influence which came from her,' revived the great power which had pierced him even before he was out of childhood. And

* This line is sometimes called a sophistic reconciliation of human will and divine will. When it is taken as true at the level of Paradise on which it is spoken (*Par.* 3) or at an equivalent level in earthly life, the sophistry vanishes.

the first effect of this power is to make him fear as a child fears, fearing that which he can neither understand nor cope with, so that he turns to the left, to Virgil

> *. . . with the trust*
> *with which a little child runs to his mother*
> *when he is afraid or afflicted.*

In the *Inferno* Virgil had been able to serve as a substitute for a mother, but now, now that Beatrice has appeared, Virgil her deputy has vanished. And the pilgrim, for all the power of Beatrice, for all the urgent need impressed upon him to look forward always to the next event, the pilgrim must yet halt everything to mourn for his lost father:

> *. . . Virgil had left me bereft*
> *of himself, Virgil, my sweetest father,*
> *to whom I gave myself up for my safety;*
>
> *nor could all that our ancient mother lost*
> *keep my cheeks, cleaned with dew,*
> *from turning dark again with tears.*

His tears over Virgil are deep indeed: deep enough that the bliss of the Earthly Paradise cannot prevail against them; deep enough that even the stern admonition of the angel at the gate to Purgatory cannot prevent him from being cast back for the moment to a state preceding his entrance to Purgatory, before the time when his face had been cleansed by the dew of Antepurgatory.[12]

Dante's mourning over Virgil is unmistakably sincere, over Virgil as a poet and companion with whom he had spent so many great hours both within and without the *Comedy;* but this sincere mourning is still compatible with an important dramatic preparation presented simultaneously with it. This is a preparation for the most startling thing that happens in the Earthly Paradise—the stern reproach to Dante for the sinful or wasted life he led after the death of the earthly Beatrice. True, this reproach has its theological explanation as a necessary step in the pilgrim's contrition; but the supposedly blissful atmosphere of the Earthly Paradise provides a problematic context for these bitter recalls, even though this is before he has drunk of Lethe.

The pilgrim's mention of his cheeks being darkened again by tears directly recalls the traces of sin and suffering with which Dante emerged from Hell in Canto I of the *Purgatory*. Beatrice's first words to him sternly pick up this same theme in the tone of a mother telling her child that if he thinks he has something to bewail he must wait until she gives him something truly to weep for. Even the repetition, 'do not weep yet, do not weep yet,' has this mixture of fostering love and minatory reproach. This mixture prevails to the end of the canto; a sense of the immediacy of guilt, the consciousness and shame of sin, is so strong as to create a feeling that the serpent still lurks somewhere in the Garden.

The terms in which Beatrice is described complete the chain of images begun in the previous canto. At 29.91 we read of the New Testament as the star which succeeds that of the Old Testament in the heavens; in the opening of canto 30 we had an extended image of the candles likened to Ursa Minor, functioning to help the helmsman guide the ship to port. Now at 30.58 we have Beatrice presented as the admiral of this voyage, not only as the commander in chief but as one whose glance encourages to their labors those who man all the vessels of the fleet, from wherever she may happen to be stationed, either ahead of the others or behind them. All this she is able to do while still veiled, before the power of her eyes is made completely manifest to the beholder. Even in her words she impresses one as having more in reserve than in expression. And yet her words seem as scathing as words in this situation could be:

> *'Look at me! I am indeed, I am indeed Beatrice.*
> *How did you dare to approach the mount?*
> *Did you not know that here man is happy?'*

What can this mean but that Dante was so overladen with sin at his approach to the mountain that the purgatorial process itself has not been able to cleanse him, and that consequently he contravenes the law and quality of the place by being unable to be happy even here after the completion of this process?

The pilgrim receives the fullness of the blow. His gaze, unable to meet even her veiled eyes, falls; but here, in the stream of the cleansing of sin, he sees only the shame of his own countenance and must turn to the grass, to the green grass of hope. And indeed in a moment the angels will sing, 'In Thee, O Lord, I have hoped,'—but significantly, do not go beyond the line which says, 'Thou hast set my feet in a large room'—that is, the Lord has responded to the hope and trust put in Him but His response has not inhibited the free will of the one praying: He has given to the praying one the fullness of the earth to choose as he wills. The stern pity and reproach of Beatrice had been the attitude of a mother who must at times seem cruel; her attitude had frozen the pilgrim as the harsh north winds freeze the snow on the trees of the Apennine mountains. But as this snow, melted by a warm wind from the south, trickles down, so was the pilgrim's frost melted by the pitying song of the angels, pity clearer than if they had spoken 'Lady, why do you shame him so?' And as his frost gave way before the angels' pity, so was it transformed into the sighs and tears of weeping.

Beatrice's next words are set in a great context, of lecturing the angels as well as the pilgrim: their pity for him has also been evident to her, and so her justification of her sternness must be as clear to the angels who observe in their eternal day, as to the pilgrim who observes with his earthly senses and with the intermittent light of the sun. The pilgrim has already made the first stage of his contrition by his weeping (but remember that it was the pity of the angels that made his frozen feelings melt to tears); now, by an act of understanding, of intellect, he must bring himself to a point at which his sorrow exactly balances his sin.

CHAPTER THIRTEEN

The Great Confessional

[CANTOS 30.109-31]

Beatrice's purpose at this point in the journey is not so much to make the pilgrim aware of specific sins he has committed as it is to balance the greatness of his going astray at all against the greatness of the capabilities and opportunities which had been his original endowment. Now that he has been purged of the specific sins,[1] this balance sheet will be more starkly clear. Consequently she begins the charge against him by retailing the cosmic forces which operated on his behalf: the conjunctions of the heavenly bodies and the bounty of divine grace were such in their potential and promise that all good qualities might in him have come to marvelous fruition in his new life—*sua vita nuova*—which, as Dante tells us in the *Vita Nuova,* began after he met Beatrice. But—even exceeding the Biblical reminder that lilies that fester smell far worse than weeds—the more vigorous the soil, the ranker the crop of weeds, if it is not wisely and properly tended. This great reproach transcends its model—that in Book I of the *Consolation of Philosophy* in which My Lady Philosophy bitterly reproached Boethius for deserting her.[2]

While the pilgrim was a young man the eyes of Beatrice provided a light to show him the right direction. But at the death of Beatrice—when she was on the threshold of her second life—he gave himself to others: the enormity of his misdeed can be seen when one realizes that this change in Beatrice's state (a change to greater beauty and virtue after flesh was gone from her) should have made her more dear to him than before. Instead he followed false ideas of good, which never fulfill their promise, and he could not be recalled to the good even by her appearances to him in dreams and other visions. She does not yet specify what his sins have been but says only that they had taken him so far from the path of salvation that only one step could be taken to save him: to do what she did in giving Virgil the mission of showing him the punishments of those in Hell—note the gentle phrase, which yet is adequate description, in calling them the 'lost people.' (This of course justifies only the journey through Hell: we need something more to explain the need of the journey through the other two regions.) For such a sinner it is only just that the full penance of tears be paid before the waters of Lethe may be drunk: but there is almost excessive sternness in Beatrice (for reasons of personal affront?) as she measures out the pilgrim's weeping to the last judicial drop.

Without pausing Beatrice now turns the point of her speech toward the pilgrim: note here how closely the poet observes his own images as they come forth—in the earlier part of this speech Beatrice had directed the point at the angels; therefore only the edge, as in a dagger, had at that time been presented to the pilgrim. The accusation before others is in itself not enough; Dante must acknowledge the truth of it, and more explicitly than he already has through his tears. Twice he tries to speak, but confusion and fear have so disturbed his senses that the most he can utter is a voiceless 'yes,' while Beatrice sternly exhorts him to speak up. He breaks under the tension of her questioning as a crossbow breaks when pulled too tight 'so that the shaft hits its mark with less force.' (Is this the culmination and denouement of all the bow-imagery we have met as related to questioning?)

With asperity and sarcasm she rewords her question: What hindered you from the good and attracted you to the bad? Finally, with sighs and tears he is able to answer, in words that paraphrase her accusation at 30.127-32:

> *'. . . present things,*
> *with their false pleasures, turned my steps away*
> *as soon as your face was hidden.'*

This is as good a place as any to pause to discuss briefly the traditional identification of Beatrice as Revelation. We have seen enough of her to be able to judge of this identification, and we need some idea of her before we can proceed much farther. What qualities and powers have appeared in her words and actions? First, with the aid of God's thunderclap she was able for the sake of directing herself to the pilgrim to bring to a halt Scripture, Church, and Christ: this seems to establish for her a primacy among the entire assemblage, with the possible exception of Christ. She served as inspiring direction to Dante when he was young; she died and he went astray; in her reborn and transfigured state she was able to lift him higher than ever before, after first leading him (via Virgil) through greater sin and suffering than he had previously experienced.[3] Perhaps all this we can fit into the notion of Beatrice as Revelation if we treat Dante as Everyman, her first life as the Old Testament, the interim period as Everyman's passion reflecting Christ's, and her new life as revelation in the New Testament. This can be worked out although some of the details may offer trouble. But we run into deeper difficulty when we try to rationalize the personal, almost vindictive tone that Beatrice takes: it surely is not the function of Revelation to drain the last drop of contrition from wayward man, especially when he has already been purged of the capital sins. As I said at an earlier occasion of this sort, it is necessary to be aware of these traditional identifications, but it is even more important to see where they begin to falter and fall short. Let us then continue with Beatrice, a Beatrice who may be partly an allegorical figure but who is much more a rounded fictional figure.

Beatrice hears the pilgrim's admission of straying after false pleasures but is far from satisfied. His failure to confess, she says, would have been in vain: his sin would not thereby have been concealed from such a judge—*tal giudice*—as sits in this our court—*in nostra corte*. (This all-knowing judge might seem to be God Himself, but it obviously is Beatrice who claims both the jurisdiction and power of prosecution for herself, in addition to her previous personal connection with the case.) True, a confession such as he has made will dull the cutting edge of justice (remember the point and the edge of the opening lines of this canto). But his nose must be rubbed still more in his sin, to make him stronger another time. Note that Beatrice, more concretely than any other we have met, continues to emphasize the fact that the pilgrim is to return to his first life after the completion of his journey. He must put aside his tears and hear what the effect of her death should have been for him.

She says, in frank (almost Platonic) recognition of her earthly endowments, that neither nature nor art had ever produced such beauty for Dante as her body had displayed; and if death had come between Dante and her fair body, how could he then lower his sights to any other? At the first assault of other things—necessarily false and evanescent—he should rather have lifted his sights even higher, to follow Beatrice in her transfiguration. (From the 'delusions,' reminding us once more of the Siren, we may assume that Beatrice is referring to another girl.) She then shifts to another image, that of the bird able to fly and avoid traps: a young bird may be distracted by idle snares (as a young man may be lured by a young girl or two or three other such brief vanities), but for the full-grown bird the net should be spread and the arrow should be shot in vain. She points to the pilgrim as a full-grown bird by telling him to lift not his chin but his beard—that he may suffer all the more intensely by looking at her as well as by listening to her.

Here, in the words of the poet himself, is 'the venom of the argument,' with almost a fishwife spite in this last remark not only *ad hominem,* but *ad barbam hominis.* However, he is able to look as she commands and to see—as no doubt she wished—that as she had surpassed others on earth so she now surpasses her former self:

The nettle of repentance so stung me then
that, of all other things, those that had made me
love them most now became most hateful to me.

So much remorse gnawed at my heart
that I fell, vanquished; and what became of me,
she knows who gave me the cause of it.

But when he recovered from his faint it was Matelda who was at his side, not Beatrice, 'who had caused this.' And it was Matelda who led him into the water of Lethe, made him drink thereof, and led him out to the embrace of the four cardinal virtues. All this while Beatrice has had her eyes turned toward the griffon, 'which is one in two natures.' The pilgrim has not yet come far enough to be directly aided by Beatrice: the pilgrim, as in the unconscious leap to the gate of Purgatory, is lifted by another intercessor than Beatrice. Her function is to teach or inspire him to ascend without external aid.

What is this shaft of venom that Beatrice hurls at Dante? For one thing, it relieves her, at least temporarily, of any mission of functioning as Revelation. Coming as it does so soon after our meeting her, it embodies Dante's insistence that whatever allegorical qualities his persons may have, the major characters in his poem are above all real people. There is no difficulty in finding allegorical significances in Beatrice's reproaches, but all these significances are secondary to our first and dominant attention to the lashings out of a woman whose self-esteem has been wounded: not the pride in excess of attainment, which is a sin, but the self-esteem which is a full awareness of all one's talents. Let us look at the sum of these talents of hers.

The commentators have generally approached this question by referring to the 'false images of good' of canto 30.131 and the *pargoletta,* the young girl, of 31.58, as connoting the temptations of worldly philosophy and sensuousness that drew Dante from the memory of Beatrice; the *pargoletta* may be a real young girl or an allegorical one, and may or may not be identical with the *donna pietosa* of the *Vita Nuova.* I believe, however, that the question may be most economically met by recalling the pertinent details of our long approach to Beatrice in the course of the *Purgatory.* Virgil, Statius, Guido Guinizelli, and Forese Donati are probably the most important milestones on this course: with the first three of these we saw significant advances in Dante's practice and scope of poetry. With Forese there was a backward step—almost a fall—but a necessary step to bring Dante's poetry to a more intimate relation with his life and times. It is for this backward step that Beatrice hurls her venom at the poet. (Obviously this step backward in poetry may well have involved an attachment to a girl inferior to Beatrice.) [4]

What I am speaking of here is a close connection, rather an inseparability, among the life, the ideals, and the poetry of the dedicated poet: as his life, so his poetry—and correspondingly for all the other interconnections. (And this life, these ideals, this poetry concern themselves with the full moral, social, political, religious, philosophical, and spiritual range available to man.) Abandoning the true ideal, then, means for Dante and Beatrice abandoning the best life, the direct path, the proper scope and quality of poetry. Dante's concept of poetry, as he worked it out in the course of his development, added to the cosmic, social, and political scope of Virgil the Christian epic qualities of Statius, and employed as inspiring center for it all the gentle, spiritualized, woman-centered idealism of the *dolce stil nuovo;* but whether Beatrice thought so or not, the realistic, even coarse note added by his poetic play with Forese was another necessary ingredient.

It is because of this inseparability of life, ideal, and poetry that Beatrice in her attack is able to move without break or transition from one of these areas to another: from the 'first shaft of fallacious things' to the 'young girl or other vanity,' and to the mention of the pilgrim's spiritual and poetic wings.

This explanation of Beatrice's wrath places it on a level far from that of a jealous or spurned woman: this total guidance of him that she was able to provide, and that he ignored, merits such high emotions. On the other hand, we seem to be getting farther from the definition of Beatrice as Revelation: Revelation, for the community, for the congregation, has no direct place such as Beatrice is now displaying in the development of an individual.

The remainder of the canto (from line 103) deals with the pilgrim's preparation to gaze upon the unveiled Beatrice. After the pilgrim has bathed in Lethe and has drunk of its waters, to remove from him the last traces of a tendency to sin, of even the memory of sin, he is led by Matelda to the dance of the four cardinal virtues. 'Here,' they say, 'we are nymphs, and in Heaven stars.' Here where the vision of the onlooker is not yet completely divorced from the earth, where it is even strongly tinged with sensuousness (as we saw in the way the pilgrim had originally looked at Matelda), here the virtues have the sensuous, even sensual, appearance of nymphs; in Paradise, where the senses need no such enticements, they appear in their true shape of stars (we had caught a glimpse of them, from afar, in this shape at the very beginning of the ascent, as they illumined the countenance of Cato). The cardinal virtues existed for the pagan world and were ordained as Beatrice's handmaids even before she came to the world, before she was born into her temporal existence. Acknowledging that the three theological virtues will better prepare him to meet Beatrice's gaze, these four lead him near her as she stands close to the griffon and encourage his eyes for their coming ordeal by reminding him that Beatrice's eyes are 'the jewels from which Love once shot his arrows.' (Note the reminder in 'arrows' of the shafts we have previously met, for example, at lines 55 and 63 of this canto; there is also a nearly irrelevant reminder of the arrows and eyes in the image of Venus, at 28.64-6.) That Love once shot his arrows from her eyes imposes on the pilgrim the obligation of the pilgrim to respond to this love, as we have noted in our comments on the ideas of courtly love. While a thousand desires hotter than the flames of lust bound the pilgrim's eyes to hers, Beatrice's eyes were still fixed on the griffon.

What the pilgrim now sees reflected in Beatrice's eyes not only gives precise definition to the function of Beatrice but is the climax of the entire *Purgatory:*

> *A thousand desires hotter than flame*
> *bound my eyes to the shining eyes*
> *which still were fixed upon the griffon.*
>
> *As the sun in a mirror, not otherwise*
> *did the twofold creature shine within them,*
> *with the attributes now of one, now of the*
> *other nature.*

Think, reader, if I marveled
when I saw the thing itself remain still
and yet change in its image.

While full of joy and wonder
my soul tasted of that food
which, while satisfying, gives hunger for itself.

What the pilgrim beholds is the resolution, the sensuous enactment, of the paradox of the twofold nature of Christ—'I saw the object remain still and yet change in its image.' The joy and wonder of this sight are foretastes of the bliss of paradise, where not only this sight but all others will have the eternal paradoxical quality of satisfying all spiritual hunger and at the same moment stimulating new hunger.

This resolution of the dual nature of Christ is the predecessor, within the appropriate limits for this place, of the parallel scene at the end of the *Paradise,* in which the Trinity is made visible and resolved. (We should also note that the resolution of duality is not final, as the resolution of trinity is: a time element—'now with one, now with the other nature'—keeps the present scene on a human level.) Here in the Earthly Paradise, for the first time in the poem, we have come to the point at which man is getting ready to transcend his pure humanity, is getting ready to know the divine as well as the human, to know them through the person of Christ, Who mingled the two natures in the one person. Here, also, duality is no longer what it always is when in purely human terms: unresolved duality is the source of the Other, of the alternative path which can lead only to evil.

We must also see *how* the pilgrim saw the dual nature of the griffon. A few moments before this he had looked at the griffon directly and reported what he saw: two kinds of animal, lion and eagle, merging at the neck. He saw, that is, not Man-God but man-and-God—two discrete natures. It is only with the mediation of Beatrice's vision—in Beatrice's eyes—that he is as yet able to see the unified duality of Christ.

Notice, finally, the precise and emphatic definition of how Beatrice functions. The twofold creature shone in her eyes 'as the sun in a mirror, not otherwise . . .' An observer may look at, may comprehend, the sun when seen in a mirror even though his eyes would be paralyzed by the sun viewed directly (and the sun is in itself only a mirror by which the light of God is conveyed to earthly eyes). Beatrice's eyes do not create truth (the light and vision of Christ), but they are the needed means for the transmission of truth to the pilgrim at this stage in his journey. It was probably this function of Beatrice that gave rise to the concept of her as the symbol of Revelation. To call her Personal Revelation would be more accurate, although it is theologically an awkward or impossible concept; but even this would be far from describing her prime functions in the poem. The part she plays in the pageant, and the message she gives to the pilgrim in the final canto make the symbol of Revelation at best somewhat off center of her functions.

But the pilgrim has not yet looked into Beatrice's eyes. The three theological virtues now dance forward and show their higher rank in what they take as their right to say: while the cardinal virtues had addressed the pilgrim, bidding him look at the eyes of Beatrice, the three speak to Beatrice directly, asking her to turn her eyes to 'your faithful one, who, to see you, has taken so many steps.' Forgotten for the moment, washed away in the stream of Lethe, is Dante's sin of divagating from the course of Beatrice. He has been contrite in his heart, he has confessed with his mouth, and he has received satisfaction of his deed. The canto closes with the request and the fulfillment, with the light of Beatrice now rivalling the sun's:

'Of thy grace give us the grace that thou unveil
to him thy mouth, that he may discern,
the second beauty that thou hidest.'

O splendor[5] *of eternal living light,*
who has grown so pale beneath the shade
even of Parnassus, or has drunk at its well,

that would not seem to have his mind encumbered,
when trying to depict you as you then appeared
there where the heaven in its harmonies shadowed you forth,

when in the open air you revealed yourself?'

What poet, he asks, would not seem awkward in trying to describe her splendor, no matter how he had reinforced his skill by time spent on Parnassus, the mountain of the Muses, no matter how deep he had drunk of the Muses' well of inspiration? The answer is: that poet whose light comes directly from his Beatrice and not indirectly by means of the Muses.[6]

CHAPTER FOURTEEN

The Dropping of the Veil

[CANTOS 32 AND 33]

But Beatrice is not yet to be directly gazed at. All his senses, says the poet, are suspended, excepting his eyes in their attempt to satisfy ten years' thirst for Beatrice: her holy smile has drawn him completely back into the old net (but this is a different net from that of canto 31.63—the concept of a net as restraining the free flight of a bird was seemingly obsessive with Dante). He is warned by the nymphs, but almost too late, that he is gazing too fixedly: he is temporarily blinded by looking on her, as one is smitten by the sun. Notice the change from line 121 of the preceding canto—there she was only the mirror; now she is as the sun. (We are still reminded that Beatrice is not the ultimate source of light; Beatrice herself [at *Par.* 18.21 and 23.70-2] later warns the pilgrim to this same effect.) Before leaving this idea of Beatrice as light, Dante here brings it to a peak: from being blinded by the sight of Beatrice the pilgrim regains his sight to look at what is a little light compared with the greater light of Beatrice—this lesser light is nothing other than the sun and the seven candles at the head of the glorious army.

* * * * *

From here to the end of the canto we shall be concerned with an elaborate pantomime in which the poet figures forth a history of the Church. By means of this pantomime, in two great scenes, Dante is able to express a double idea of the Church: first, the essential function of the Church throughout the purgatorial process and through the further preparation of the soul for its entrance to heaven; second, the material decay into which the Church as institution had fallen through her usurpation of temporal functions. For most of the play Beatrice is at the pilgrim's side and, now that his trial and cleansing are completed, begins to function as his guide by directing his eyes to what he should observe and by answering and encouraging his questions. His eyes, we must remember, have already acquired a power of insight transcending that of humanity by means of the *sight* of the twofold nature of Christ, even though this sight was granted to him via the medium of Beatrice's eyes: hope has been defined as the expectation that *faith* will be transformed to *sight*.

The pilgrim has been without vision for a while after being blinded by the sight of Beatrice. Slowly his vision returns to the scene. The army, 'the glorious host,' reforms its ranks, reverses direction, and marches back into the woods. Matelda, Statius, and the pilgrim follow the chariot. All come to a halt at the base of a sturdy tree, while the pilgrim hears murmurs of 'Adam!' The tree, devoid of flowers and foliage, is of great height and, like the trees on the terrace of the gluttonous, 'its branches . . . spread wider as it rose.' In coming to the tree the army had moved 'perhaps three flights of an arrow' when it halted to let Beatrice descend from the chariot. Symbol and allegory here are dense and difficult. Some commentators see in the movements of the chariot a parallel to the movements of the Church—founded in the east, moving west to the Atlantic, and then retracing its way over Spain, France, and Italy (the three arrows) to Rome. This seems an unlikely explanation: these movements take place before Christ has hitched the chariot to the tree, that is, before he has founded the Church. Let me suggest a more likely explanation.

Either by the will of Beatrice or by the will of God this great play is being presented before Dante that he may, as she warns him at line 103, carefully observe what he sees, to write it down after his return 'for the good of the badly living world.' For Dante's methodical mind this requires an explanation of things from their beginning, a rolling back to the beginning of time on earth. This is indicated at lines 17-24, where it is said in three or four different ways that it may not be mistaken. In simplest terms, we have come from the beginning of the poem through a historical, moral, and spiritual process which must temporarily be reversed. Everyone, everything, keeps pace in this rewinding of the process—the sun, the pagan and the Christian virtues, Christ, Matelda, even Statius. But the extent of this reverse travel is measured, not by Christ or the sun, but by Beatrice. Why? And what are the three flights of an arrow? In canto 31 imagery based on arrow flights is used so often and so insistently as to make it likely that there we were being prepared for what happens here; the idea of the arrows of canto 31, at lines 16, 55, 63, and 117, is not a simple one, but all its parts seem to come from the complex of life-ideal-poetry in the universe, as measured also by the three canticles of this poem, the three kinds of life-ideal-poetry that Beatrice sees as necessary for Dante to experience before he can return with clear sight to earth. Are not these three, then, the three flights of an arrow which must be reversed before we can get back to the beginning of everything? Even the word 'perhaps' ('perhaps three flights of an arrow') seems to fit into this explanation: we have had, here in the Earthly Paradise, a foretaste of Paradise but not Paradise itself, so that the pilgrim cannot be sure of the precise measurement of the distance they go back—two of the arrow flights are clear and complete, the third unit is something he must guess at.[1] This journey back is not easy: Matelda, Statius, and the pilgrim (who are the three weakest of all those participating) take the easiest possible way by following the 'wheel which turned with the lesser arc.' But the griffon is not strained by this job: he 'moved the sacred burden without displacing his feathers.' When Beatrice, then, descends from the chariot—Beatrice, the center and measure of Dante's poetry and poetical conceiving—we are at the starting place for the *agon*. And that this is the starting place is signalled by the choral murmur of 'Adam' which arises.

Adam is named here as the first of men, as the man responsible, in the view of medieval theologians, for the *transmission* of original sin to mankind. Aquinas says (*Summa Theol.* I-II, 81, 5) that if Eve alone had fallen, the burden of original sin would not have passed to the generations of man. But it is impossible not to see the murmur of 'Adam' as naming in some way the pilgrim himself—the pilgrim restored to a condition of primal innocence and now ready to serve as Man, as a participating spectator in the great historical pageant now to ensue.* [2]

The tree which now serves as the center of the action is generally explained as signifying Law or Civil Authority or Empire.[3] This is too narrow a definition. When Adam was, there was no distinction between spiritual and secular authority. The tree rather, it seems to me, represents something prior to any establishment of civil law (we must remember that we are still near the beginning of things and must keep our chronology in order): perhaps we will come closest to defining it by borrowing from *Genesis* and seeing the tree as that of the Garden of Eden when this tree still combined the quality of obedience in an obscure way with the quality of the knowledge-of-good-and-evil—what might be paraphrased as the objective and subjective awareness of God's justice. The knowledge of good and evil, as later to be codified in law (perhaps both natural and civil), did not come into existence for Eve and Adam until the precept of blind obedience had been contravened (we touched on a point related to this in chapter 12 when we looked at the paradox of Eve's behavior: would Paradise itself have come to function without her sin?). This total, or primal, obedience is of course prior to the dichotomy of good-and-evil; it is therefore prior even to justice. The tree, then, is, so to speak, the origin of law rather than law itself: in the words of the griffon, at line 48, the tree is, or contains, 'the seed of all justice'—which even the divine part of the griffon abstains from lessening.†

When the assemblage gathers around the tree (which, like the wings of the griffon, rises inexpressibly high) the 'others' shout to the griffon:

* The name 'Adam' means 'man,' 'man of the earth,' or 'man of red earth.'

† All three of the trees in Purgatory are in the puzzling form of having their roots in the ground but their branches increasing in size as they ascend the trunk. This symbolism should give little difficulty. Like all other earthly things these grow from earth, with their foundation in the ground. But these three trees, a unique link between divine justice and worldly performance, grow *as though* they were rooted in heaven. Roots and trunk of a tree provide the sustenance and support of it; branches, leaves, and fruit perform the practical and aesthetic functions. These two aspects may seem to be reversed, but a little thought will straighten out the paradox.

'Blessed are thou, griffon, not to break
with thy beak this wood sweet to the taste,
since afterwards the belly writhes from it!'

The griffon (with his beak? of the heavenly part of his nature?) does not break, or command to be broken, the wood (that is, the structural basis) of the tree: rending the fabric of obedience may be sweet at first but thereafter, and eternally, the bellies of those that follow are set on edge. (There is even an image here of the dual constitution of Christ: the beak is in the divine half of his body, the belly in the lion, the human half.) After Adam, of course, there was no fruit of the tree to eat.

And it is to the tree that he brings the pole he had drawn, allowing the chariot to remain fastened to the pole. Here, most likely, we may read a parable of Christ's fastening the Church to the tree of obedience and knowledge (two qualities which are inseparable) by means of the pole, the Cross on which He met His earthly death (the griffon will vanish from the scene in a little while).* With this joining of tree, pole, and chariot a great renewal takes place.

As with the revivification of spring, with the great light of the sun and the stars of Aries, the bare tree comes to life once more and takes on a color between violet and rose, the color of imperial

* There was a well-known legend in the Middle Ages that the Cross was made from an offshoot of the forbidden Tree. Dante, at 32.51, seems to be using this legend; when the griffon has dragged the pole to the 'base of the widowed bough'

to it he left bound that
which came from it.

Carroll says of this passage (*op. cit.*, p. 471):

. . . into this legend Dante read a curious *moral* sense. The Tree, as we have seen, represents the justice of God; and, since the Cross is made of the Tree, it also represents justice. In the Sixth Canto of the *Paradiso,* the Emperor Justinian says all the great achievements of the Roman Eagle grow dim before that which it accomplished under Tiberius, namely, the Crucifixion of Christ. This is its crowning glory, because it is God's 'vengeance for His wrath,' the supreme act of His justice. The justice of the Empire, and the justice of God in the Cross, are therefore one and the same; and this appears to be what was in Dante's mind when he says that the pole of the Chariot was made of the wood of the Tree. The Church is drawn by the same justice of which the Empire is the symbol.

purple. In other words, the fruition of Christ's joining the Church to the latent powers of obedience and knowledge is the Empire, but the Empire grows out from the tree—it is not the tree itself. At this mystery of birth, those standing about sang a hymn unearthly in both words and music—a poem of such magic and such mystery as to send him into a charmed slumber. This slumber he describes in rather a cumbersome image: if he were able to describe how vigilant, hundred-eyed Argus fell asleep, he would then have a model for describing how he himself fell asleep; however, since he did not have the opportunity of watching Argus fall asleep, he has no model to follow (except by using this image, which perfectly expresses what he wants to convey).

Dante's three previous slumbers on the mountain have been, so to speak, natural, the sleep that comes at the end of an energetic day. They have also been connected with the complete inanition that overtakes the mountain when the light of the sun vanishes with nightfall. And with each of these three slumbers has come a dream. But this time the pilgrim's slumber is not natural but induced by the hymn, is not disturbed by a dream and, most important, the purpose of the slumber is not to work a mystic change within him or to transport him to a new place (as happened in the first of the dreams and in the swoon that preceded his being dipped in Lethe)—but to permit a mystic change in his environment. When he awakes, the griffon and the figures representing Scripture have disappeared.[4]

The mode of his awaking is interesting. A light (which must be nothing other than the accompaniment of the ascension of the griffon) tears the veil of his sleep (as Eve who, at 29.27, did not endure to remain under the veil of ignorance) when he hears a cry ordering him to arise and reprimanding him for sleeping. Is the cry Beatrice's, thinking that he should be ready to witness this ascension before which his powers have failed? Or is it Matelda's, still supervising the propriety of the pilgrim's behavior? The pilgrim's mode of arising is described in an elaborate simile, which seems also to explain the slumber. Referring to *Matthew* 17.1-8 the poet compares his slumber and awakening to those of the three disciples who witnessed the Transfiguration of Christ: they were overcome by the flowers only of the tree (this tree is the Cross-in-anticipation, the flowers the premonitory transfiguration before the Crucifixion) while the fruit that causes rejoicing in Heaven is not only the translated Christ but also the souls saved through Christ (there is inescapably a side reference to the tree we have just been dealing with in the Earthly Paradise, although no fruits of the renewed tree have yet been mentioned). To the transfigured Christ there came Moses and Elijah to talk with him; then, while Peter

. . . yet spake, behold a bright cloud overshadowed them: and behold, a voice out of the cloud . . . And when the disciples heard it, they fell on their face, for they were sore afraid. And Jesus came and touched them, and said, Arise, and be not afraid. And when they had lifted up their eyes, they saw no man, save Jesus only.

In this way did the pilgrim return to his senses: with this difference, that he neither saw nor had to ask after Jesus, because this re-running of the film of history has clarified and justified the Ascension of Jesus. He sees Matelda and asks after Beatrice; she shows him where Beatrice sits, on the roots of the tree and beneath the new foliage. The foliage of the Empire shelters her, or at least is over her, but her seat on the roots of the tree is of higher rank than the imperial throne. Matelda's words continue; she tells that certain of the company surround Beatrice and that the others have ascended with the griffon—but the pilgrim's attention is only for Beatrice.

Beatrice, as she sits surrounded by the seven nymphs with their candlesticks, speaks pointedly to the pilgrim:

'Here you will be for a while a forest dweller
and then you will be with me forever a citizen
of that Rome in which Christ is a Roman.

Therefore for the good of the badly living world,
fix your eyes on the chariot, and what you see
be sure that you write down after your return.'

If, in the first of these tercets, Beatrice is speaking of the immediate future (the forest being that of the Earthly Paradise) she is merely outlining events to come within the fiction of the poem. If she is referring to a *paulo post futurum* (the forest being the *selva selvaggia* of human life) she is going beyond the confines of the poem into the life of Dante, exiled citizen of Florence.

The first possibility is made inadmissible by the 'forever' in line 101: in the ensuing journey through Paradise with Beatrice, Dante is not to stay there forever—*senza fine*. It is, then, unmistakably clear that the image of the forest is to be identified with life on earth—dark, confused and confusing, but now also green with hope and rich with fruit. At some time after his return to this life on earth Dante will become a citizen of that heavenly empire of which Christ Himself is a citizen. Beatrice's idea of the didactic purpose of the poem, at least in relation to the Church and the Empire, could not be more baldly stated than in this way of describing Christ: even in heaven, as on earth, there is a rendering unto Caesar.

The seven acts, or scenes, of the ensuing pageant are on the simplest level of unilateral symbol. Not that any one of these scenes bears its identity on the surface but that there is no question here of multiple meanings: A (the scene) simply represents B (the intended meaning). The point of the pageant is also clear: it is to trace the episodes, or causes, in the degeneration and enfeebling of Church and Empire alike. Let us first rapidly identify the episodes.

The first act of this play of the Church is violent. The bird of Jove, the imperial eagle, descends 'from the highest region,' that is, falls from the heavens themselves; but the descent is abrupt and destructive, breaking not only flowers and leaves but the bark of the tree (the griffon, you remember, had been praised for not breaking the wood of the tree; probably the later writhings of imperial bellies resulted from this impious assault on the fabric of the tree in the early years). The eagle's fall ends in the chariot, which is buffeted as by great storms. The reference here seems to be to the vicissitudes of the Church under the early Emperors, who were corrupt disobeyers of man's as well as God's laws. Thus in this episode describing the aggressive descent of the imperial power we have an initial step comparable to the fall of man: in this episode the beginning of destructiveness for both Church and Empire is presented.

The hungry she-fox which leaps into the chariot, false belief or heresy (probably Gnosticism), is easily driven off by Beatrice: we are here still in the early years of the Church where false doctrine had little to feed upon, few adherents to win, and so the clarity of Beatrice's sight has the power to drive this danger away.

The eagle descends once more for the third scene, but this time to leave the chariot feathered with his own plumage. This clearly refers to the donation of Constantine (in which Dante and his age believed), giving to the Church a large share of the material goods of the Empire and thus voluntarily resigning a good portion of its possessions and powers. At this a soft voice from heaven (whose if not the griffon's, Christ's?) mourns for this heavy burden that the chariot now has to bear.[5]

The dragon that emerges from the earth between the very wheels of the chariot, to strike the body of the chariot with his tail and remove part of that body as he withdraws his tail, is almost certainly Satan, father of schismatics, withdrawing considerable segments of the congregation of the Church (either in the schism of the Eastern Church or in the growth of Mohammedanism, possibly both—Dante and his age thought of both of these faiths as schisms from the one Church). The model for this episode is almost certainly *Revelation* 12.3-4, in which the dragon is described as drawing down with his tail 'the third part of the stars of heaven.'

What remains of the chariot next covers itself with a rank growth of feathers, the secular wealth and power first given by Constantine and then amplified by the donations of Pepin and his son Charlemagne (the poet is not even sure that these gave with good intent) finding rich soil for growth; almost instantaneously both wheels and pole are covered with the feathers—both the motive power of the Church and the very mystery of the Crucifixion (through unholy uses of pieces of the Cross?) are made squalid with materialism. These later donations, which were also accepted as historical by Dante's age, greatly accelerated the metamorphosis of the Church into a temporal power competing with the other temporal rulers.* In canto 33.38-9 the poet attributes to these gifts the last two degradations of the Church:

> . . . *the eagle that left the feathers on the chariot,*
> *through which it became a monster and then a prey.*

In the sixth episode of the pageant the chariot grows seven heads, most likely the seven capital sins, in the forms described in *Revelation:* the first three having two horns apiece (one to harm oneself, the other to harm one's neighbor) for the sins of pride, envy, and anger; the remaining four sins, which harm mostly the sinner himself, have one horn each.†

The next and final scene shows 'an ungirt harlot,' rich and 'secure as a fortress on a high peak,' sitting in the chariot. Her lover, a giant (generally taken to be the kingdom of France—Philip the Fair, especially notorious for his intrigues with Pope Boniface VIII, was nicknamed Goliath) sits beside her, and occasionally they kiss each other. But the eye of the harlot is ever ready to wander, even to the pilgrim as he sits watching. Does Dante here have the honor, or the dishonor, of representing Florence, or all of Tuscany, in its intrigues with the papacy? More likely this flirtatiousness of the harlot—the papacy at its lowest depth—is the wandering of her eye after any man: the prostitute, even in the course of her bargain with one man, must keep an alert eye for her next, or for a

* There may be some connection here with the frequent identification of Matelda with the Countess Matilda of Tuscany. Her great donations to the Church, at her death, were probably the largest single incentives to the struggles between Pope and Emperor within the bounds of Italy.

† A quite different interpretation of this sixth episode has been given, in order to meet the objection that this moral degeneration is not a specific historical event, as are all the others. Dr. Moore (*Studies in Dante,* 3rd Series, pp. 206-8) cites this interpretation from Butler (*Purgatorio,* Appendix B, p. 430): the seven heads 'denote the seven electors, three of whom were mitred—the Archbishops of Mainz, Trier, and Cöln—and four temporal princes. It must be remembered that these were originally appointed (circa A.D. 1000) by the Pope, and hence they are appropriately made to spring from the Church.' This papal appointment of the electors of the Emperor would certainly have seemed to Dante to be a criminal perversion of the right relations between Church and Empire.

better, partner. The jealous giant beats his inamorata (as Philip mistreated and tried to murder Boniface VIII at Anagni) and then

> *. . . loosed the monstrous chariot, and dragged it*
> *through the woods,*
> *so far that he made of it a screen between me*
>
> *and the harlot and her bestial chariot.*

In the removal of the papal seat to Avignon, under the control of the French king (the Babylonian Captivity) the worldliness and spiritual confusion of the papacy (the wood as screen) brought it to a lower level than before: the move, so far as Dante could see, reduced almost to zero the already small possibility that the Church could be led along better paths through the force exerted by those like himself, with a program that he felt could be the salvation of the Church as well as of the daily life of the secular realms—this is another facet of the brief flirtation of the harlot with the pilgrim.[6]

* * * * *

A few pages back I spoke of the emotional climax of the canticle as occurring in the passage beginning at canto 31.118. For Dante himself perhaps the most important climax of all comes in the last canto: this is the vatic climax, the summit and resolution of the accumulation of insights and wisdoms mounting through the course of the canticle. The *Purgatory,* it has become a partly true truism to say, deals with moral man, while the *Inferno* deals with emotional, and the *Paradise* with spiritual man. The central concern of moral man, man in his daily social relations, is civil government and civil law: it is for this reason that it is fitting and necessary to have the resolution of the *Purgatory* comprise the great pageant of Church and Empire. At the same time, let us not oversimplify for the sake of a sentimental phrase: all three canticles, and almost equally, are emotional, moral, and spiritual—it may be going dangerously far even to say that each of these is a respective emphasis of one canticle. The difference between one canticle and the next is rather to be sought in terms of levels of insight, what I would prefer to call 'levels of wisdom.' But nearly every statement one can make about the *Commedia* is a partial statement.

With this in mind, then, we may make the statement that the point of the progress through Purgatory is to come to Beatrice's prophecy in the final canto with the assurance that what she says will be taken as inspired and veridical. This may require some explanation. The structural underpinning of the *Commedia* is a sequence of 'statements,' of the form 'this is thus-and-so,' 'this one is here,' or 'this is why this is thus-and-so.' To an extent too great to be ignored Dante uses external data, referents or supports, for these 'statements.' Of this kind are his cosmology ('the universe is laid out thus and so'), and the skeleton of his theological, moral, and spiritual concepts (he finds of course more than the skeleton of these in the religion and customs of his day, but we must allow room for the significant ways in which he modifies these), and the historicity of his characters (this applies equally of course to the known qualities of legendary characters: 'Aristotle is thus-and-so' and 'Dido is thus-and-so' have about the same kind of validity as 'statements'). In short, these are materials for gaining credence that were at hand before Dante wrote a line of his poem.

What Dante, in writing his poem, adds to these given sources of credibility may be subsumed under two related heads (the various ways in which Dante wants the *Commedia* to be credible deserve a thoughtful essay): first, the functional status he gives to his characters, particularly to the long-lasting characters such as Virgil and Statius, adding to or subtracting from their known historical qualities by his method of depicting them; second, the functional 'status of the place'—a modification of what I have been calling the 'wisdom of the place.' This latter can best be defined by an example. What is said by the angel guarding the gate to Purgatory is better worthy of full credence than what is said by Sordello or by Virgil at this same time and place in the journey (through the angel's superiority of function) or by Sordello or Virgil at an earlier moment in the journey (through the angel's superiority of place). These two categories are obviously interdependent.

To return to Beatrice and her prophecy: She obviously has, as the last 'authority' speaking in the canticle, the highest status of place. But more important is her functional status—actually her status of place would not carry conviction without the support (or demonstration) that comes from her superiority of function. This superiority of function rests of course on the sequence of guides: each guide, culminating in Beatrice, functions because he or she can carry the pilgrim to a higher level than could the unaided previous guide. The superiority is visible, *inter alia,* in the degree and kind of deference that each guide received from his predecessors and the other characters concerned in the progress. Of these, of course, none receives any deference comparable to Beatrice's; none has power comparable with hers; power, of course, in Dante's terms, being here equated with illumination. On these considerations, then, we may return to the statement that the line of progress through the *Purgatory* is for the sake of substantiating the validity of Beatrice's prophecy; the substantiation comes not from asserting that Beatrice is Revelation and hence to be believed—rather it comes from the entire emotional and intellectual build-up of the poem. (And this is something more than another way of arriving at the same place.)

My suggestion, then, is that the prophecy of Beatrice is for Dante *a* fruit or *the* fruit of the structure of validity or credibility (this is of course not to be confused with the literal sense, or level, of the poem) that serves as one of the chief lines of movement in the poem. A corollary to this suggestion, and perhaps a confirmant of it, lies in the elaborateness of the texture in which the prophecy is set in this, the final canto.

We had seen, at the close of canto 32, the degradation and disgrace of the papacy culminating in the dragging of the harlot off to a position of being masked by the confused forest (which is like the *selva selvaggia* of *Inferno* 1). For this the seven virtues weep and mourn antiphonally—'now three singing, now four,' as though the atrocious treatment of the Church is to be deplored separately (though equally) by those within and by those without the Church.

Beatrice, listening, suffers grief very nearly as great as that of Mary at the Crucifixion (this is momentarily another of those places in which the identification of Beatrice as Revelation seems sound: Revelation, at the straying and suffering of her Church, is entitled to feel nearly the grief of Mary at the suffering of her Son).

Beatrice rises to her feet to speak. She is glowing like fire—the fire of indignation, it would seem, but we have often been reminded in the past few cantos that red is the color of love-charity as well as of love-lust or love-passion. Beatrice's words, with some significant modifications, are those of Christ to His disciples: the phrase *sorelle mie dilette,* 'my dear sisters,' is patched into the Latin of the Vulgate not only because of the requirements of the *terza rima* but also to indicate that the quoted words are being made integral with the situation. Too, Beatrice omits the final, explanatory clause of Christ's statement—'because I go to the Father.' Beatrice of course could not possibly have uttered this final clause in her situation, but the omission of it is striking and leaves the reader as though looking for an expected step that has suddenly disappeared. To utter these words Beatrice has left her seat on the roots of the tree (Revelation divorcing herself from obedience?) and is preparing to walk away. She does this by placing the seven virtues in front of her (so that, literally, for a little while they, her sisters, do not see her) and, still without a word, placing the pilgrim, Matelda, and Statius behind her. This new procession has the same general order as the first, but without its glory: Beatrice, we must note, occupies the place of the chariot. Not until nine or ten steps were taken did she let her eyes meet the pilgrim's. Exhorting the pilgrim to come up to her, then to question her freely and without confusion, without fear and shame, she then speaks in a way that, so to speak, cryptically clears up some of the obscurity in what has been occurring. From this point of vantage we may now look back at the chariot, the harlot, and the giant.

We may start by knowing the emotions inspired in the pilgrim after the episode at the end of canto 32—at least the emotions Beatrice believes were, or should have been, inspired in him. He has said, embarrassedly stating his curiosity about this scene:

. . . 'My lady, my need
you know and what is good for it.'

Note that this, at line 29, is the same language he has often used in half-fearfully asking Virgil to explain something. Her answer is:

. . . 'From fear and from shame
I want you now to unbind yourself
so that you no longer speak like one who dreams.' *

This suggests an important point about the level of truth and actuality presented throughout the *Purgatory,* as well as the entire *Inferno,* and decreasingly in the *Paradise*—the point deals with the relation between dream and actuality. Dreams, at least those of the right kind and time, are 'true,' as experienced reality is 'true.' But what this 'truth' is, is generally seen only in the light of hindsight: in this sense, the entire plan of the *Commedia* might be called an ordered arrangement of reality—the meaning of things is to be sought in the functional relations between them: these relations are incrementally explained, deepened, and extended as we move on the journey in such a way that each subsequent explanation embraces and contains the prior one without destroying it. Beatrice is here saying that now is the time for the pilgrim to free himself from the emotions which produce the dreamlike (that is, inadequately clear and specific) mode of perceiving things and expressing them. (This is a significant point, too, in respect to Beatrice's role in Dante's life-ideal-poetry complex.) The emotions she specifies are especially interesting (in the Italian there is a lingering emphasis from the fact that 'shame' and 'dreams' are the rhyming words in the tercet—*vergogna* and *sogna,* rhyming with *besogna,* need, in the previous tercet): fear and shame stand in a decisive relation to Aristotle's 'pity' and 'fear' (whether or not Dante knew of the terms Aristotle used to describe the function of tragedy is of no concern). Pity and fear have a connection which might be called

* Remember here Virgil's words at 27.142: 'I crown and mitre you over yourself.'

solipsistic-altruistic: one pities another for being in a situation which would cause fear if the one were himself in it. The connection between fear and shame is of a different order: the fear is still a trembling before consequences, but the shame is for the wasted and destroyed potentiality of doing other than good—one feels shame only in a situation in which one must say to a higher authority 'I knew better,' 'I should have known better,' or 'I once knew better but I forgot.' In other words, the Aristotelian dyad may remain in a state of frozen, hopeless sentiment—it need not, but it will unless something else is added to the situation. Dante's (or Beatrice's) dyad is more than optimistic—it involves a reproach to the man for not using those powers in him which would have prevented both the fear and the shame. Shame is never a matter of 'I've now learned my lesson and will henceforth do better'; shame is a knowing of the lesson but being led away from it by something inferior.

The pilgrim's talking as in a dream, then, from which Beatrice 'now' wants him to free himself (presumably by means of what she is about to say; this we shall come to in due time), is connected with the fear and shame he felt at watching the story of the chariot—probably most of all at the point at which the harlot brought him into the play. One point more before we go back to the giant: Beatrice's first statement after she has admonished him to issue from his dream is:

> *'Know that the chariot the serpent broke*
> *was and is not . . .'*

and that a rescuer,

> *'. . . sent by God, will kill the thievish one*
> *with that giant who sins with her.*

The chariot was and is not; the harlot will be killed. Let us now return to the episodes of the last third of the preceding canto.

What we may now see described from line 109 to the end of the canto is what the pilgrim sees, the pilgrim 'at the feet of her commands,' as Beatrice is at the feet of the tree of obedience, the pilgrim whose eyes and mind are directed to what she wished him to see—possibly even (since there is no clausula to complete 'what she wished') the pageant is something created by the power of Beatrice's will as the most efficient way of expressing to the pilgrim what she so earnestly wished him to know. The chariot, tied to the tree by the griffon, was first attacked by the eagle of the Roman Empire and then by the she-fox of heresy: the first attack in energetic malevolence, the second in ravening rapacity. But it is the next plunge by the eagle that for the first time works visible harm: the wealthy plumage that the eagle leaves behind is a burden for which the chariot was not designed. The feathers proliferate after the later donations, and the chariot now brings forth other strange crops on the pole and body—those on the pole are sins against neighbor as well as self, sins against the social end of the Crucifixion. The harlot, it is now clear, is not the Church herself but another of these products of the evil miscegenation between State and Church. The chariot has truly become, as at line 158, *il mostro,* a 'monster,' through this unnatural offspring.

Return now to line 34 of canto 33—'the chariot the serpent broke was and is not.' The serpent, the dragon of the preceding canto, tore the bottom out of the already weakened chariot; the giant and the harlot completed the destruction begun by the eagle's impregnation: the Church no longer exists. (We have seen the chariot replaced by Beatrice in the re-formed procession.)

Then comes the climax of the prophecy. The eagle will not forever be without an heir,

> *'for I see with certainty and therefore state*
> *that stars already near,*
> *immune to all impediment and all hindrance,*
> *will bring a time*
>
> *when a five hundred ten and five*
> *sent by God, will kill the thievish one*
> *with that giant who sins with her.'*

The heart of the prophecy is usually taken to be the identification of the 'five hundred ten and five'; the start on this job seems to be turning the number into the Roman numeral—DXV—which gives the word *dux* by a simple transposition customary in the numerical mysticism of the day. That is, a leader will come within a short time who will be the rightful heir to the Roman Empire and who will put a decisive end to this criminal behavior of the papacy and the royal house of France. That Dante was thinking of a definite man seems almost certain; it is equally certain that the man he had in mind never acted as Dante hoped he would and that the many attempts made to put a name to him have been vain. The number it seems must remain an unsolved puzzle—perhaps, along with the greyhound of the *Inferno,* the only such puzzle of the *Commedia.*

The name of the man may remain unknowable, but his quality and function are adequately clear. This is no millennial coming, no messiah; it is Dante's guess, almost certainly about a man living in his time, that here is one who will straighten out the one problem which for Dante lay at the heart of the material, moral, and spiritual ills of Europe—the strong and effective secular leader who would require the development of an equally strong spiritual leadership.

Beatrice admits that the prophecy is obscure and therefore, since it does not permit clear functioning of the mind, is unlikely to gain credence; but events themselves will resolve the enigma. The citation of the Naiads, at line 49, as solvers of riddles, is explained on the basis of a textual error that existed in Ovid manuscripts of Dante's time: the correct reading is now accepted as being Laiades (for Oedipus, son of Laius) rather than Naiades. The riddle in the allusion would then be the famous riddle answered by Oedipus, and propounded by the Sphinx at the suggestion of Themis, goddess of justice. But the answering of Beatrice's riddle will not have the dire consequences of the answering of the Sphinx's riddle. Themis, when the riddle was answered and the Sphinx thereby destroyed, sent a wild beast to destroy the fields and animals of the Thebans, since there had not yet been a satisfaction of that miscarriage of justice which had originally caused the sending of the destructive Sphinx to the city of Thebes.

Beatrice again anxiously insists on the importance of what the pilgrim is now learning and on the need for accurate reporting:

> *'Take note; and as the words come from me*
> *so relate them to those who live that life*
> *which is a race unto death,*
>
> *and bear in mind when you write them*
> *not to conceal how you saw the tree*
> *which has here been now despoiled twice.'*

The first despoiling of the tree was of course that by Eve and Adam; the second can be only that of Jove's eagle (the aggressive acts of fox, dragon, and giant are all directed at the chariot). This makes it clear that it is incorrect (as, for example, do the editors of the Temple Classics translation) to identify the tree as the Tree of Empire; Dante's knowledge of history, as well as his sense of accuracy, would not allow him to exculpate the historical empire and emperors from blame for the state of things in the Church in particular, and Italy and the rest of Christian Europe in general. The acts of earlier emperors in unwisely fecundating the Church might well, in Dante's historical sight, be responsible for the impotency of the emperors of his day.

For eating of the fruits of the tree Adam suffered on earth for 930 years and in Limbo for 4302 years until Christ (Who Himself in turn had to undergo His suffering because of His mission of trying to free man from the onus of Adam's sin) came to Hell to rescue him. The sum of these two figures is 5232, in which year of the world, according to the chronology of Eusebius, the Crucifixion took place and, therefore, also the Harrowing of Hell.

Beatrice continues with an elaborate reproach of the pilgrim's recalcitrance of mind, a reproach in which (unless we here figure forth the pilgrim as the ideal auditor of the poem) we are struck with the curious phenomenon of a poet accurately writing the lines which sternly analyze his inability to observe and analyze correctly. We are, of course, rather to see this reproach as attempting in advance to cut the ground out from under those readers who might struggle against accepting the ideas of Church and State which the poet is here expressing through the medium of Beatrice's prophecy:

'Your mind is asleep if you do not see
that for a special reason this tree
is so high and so inverted at its top.

And if your idle thoughts had not been
like Elsan waters about your mind
and your delight in them a Pyramus to
the mulberry,

by so many circumstances alone
you would recognize in the tree, in a
moral way,
the justice of God in the interdict.

But, although I see your mind
is made of stone, and, stony, is darkened
so that the light of my words dazzles you,

I still wish that you take them with you, at
least outlined
if not written down, for the reason
that the pilgrim's staff is brought back
wreathed with palm.

Let us explain what needs explaining in this passage. The tree is high because it communicates with heaven, it is of heaven; it is an inverted tree, almost as though it grew from heaven towards earth. Its roots are in earth (in the special sense in which the terrestrial paradise is of earth)—the substance of it is derived from the earth. The tree reaches to heaven, but because of its inverted growth may not be used to climb to heaven: obedience and knowledge of good and evil are not in themselves adequate for attaining heaven. By these circumstances the pilgrim ought to be able to see the social, the moral function of the tree: God's justice has its earthbound replica (as in imperial organization) but the two functions, the secular and the spiritual, are not to be confused, in the sense that one might try to attain the end of the one by progressing along the other. This is the interdict, the prohibition against climbing this tree as well as against rending the tree: Jove's eagle, by rending the fabric of the tree, began the latter-day mischief, as Adam by his act had committed the original mischief; Christ had been commended for not borrowing from the substance of the tree even for building or enlarging the chariot.

These qualities and significances of the tree the pilgrim was directed to write down as proof of his visit to higher realms, as a pilgrim who has visited the Holy Land thereafter bears a staff wreathed with palm leaves from these lands. Beatrice describes two related obstacles to Dante's understanding the meaning of the tree: the first is his Tuscan heritage; the second is the extent to which his mind has been formed by the Church. The first image is based on the Elsa, a river of Tuscany, in some stretches so heavily saturated with lime salts as to petrify objects placed in its waters. The second image—'your mind is made of stone, and, stony'—reveals the point more easily in Italian: *nello intelletto fatto di pietra ed, impietrato* * inevitably leads us to the Peter on whom, as a rock, the Church is founded. Both these inhibitory biases of the mind, says Beatrice, Dante soaks up with alacrity just as the mulberry tree (formerly having white berries) turned its berries to red when spattered with the blood of suicidal Pyramus: the mulberry in itself was not guilty of any crime, but had perforce been silently present through the earlier episodes of Thisbe's adventure—if the mulberry tree had been able to cry out in truth-telling protest, the death of Pyramus † (and also of Thisbe) would have been averted.

* For an additional interpretation of this line see chapter 1, p. 54.

† Pyramus and the mulberry were used, at 27.37-9, to indicate the force of Beatrice's name for the pilgrim.

This seems to define the position of Dante with peculiar accuracy in the relations of Empire, Church, and Florence: of course it is being done through a poetic machinery that permits him to express these ideas while one of his fictional persons is reproaching him for not having the freedom of mind even to understand them.

These words are marked on his brain, says the pilgrim, as accurately as wax is marked by the seal (Dante has used this same image before, canto 18, lines 37-9, where the point was rather that the seal and its imprint may be worthless even though the wax may have had value), although the more he tries to understand these words of hers, the more they evade him.

His inability to understand she attributes to 'that school which you have followed'—its doctrines can but badly explain her words. What is 'that school' which he has followed? On our answer to this depends a very large segment of what we make of the entire *Commedia*. Is it, as one group of critics maintains, the school of profane philosophy, as described in the *Convivio?* This would make Dante's aberration from Beatrice entirely a philosophical wandering, a wandering away from Christian tenets. Is it the poetic school of Virgil, also deprived of Christian revelation? Or, finally, is this the orthodox school of theology, as summated by Aquinas himself? And how is this reproach about the 'school' to be squared with the reproaches of cantos 30 and 31, reproaches which seem to center in the *pargoletta?*

If these are two separate reproaches, the earlier for a moral and the second for a philosophical or poetic or theological errancy, we must note that they are divided by the pilgrim's complete contrition and drinking of the waters of Lethe—waters which removed the last trace and memory of sin. Does Lethe remove physical sin and leave intellectual sin untouched? Or has Beatrice so contrived things that she may continue to have something with which she may reproach the pilgrim? Neither of these seems likely.

Beatrice is reproaching him for a single fault; the present instance is for intellectual deficiencies produced by his course of life, as the earlier instance was for the explicit turning of his steps to an evil path (30.130). The evil has been removed by his contrition and by Lethe, but nothing has yet been supplied to replace it with good. Beatrice herself (at 30.115-20) had spoken of Dante as rich soil sown with bad seed and so producing a rank growth of weeds. The weeds have been removed, but the soil still needs proper cultivation and seeding.

We have already seen the reproach for the poetic errancy, but we are now at a higher level—concerned with the total program in which his moral and poetic development will be employed.

To understand this point we must recall the dates of certain events in Dante's life. Up to the year 1300, the date of the action of the *Commedia,* Dante was a Florentine, brought up in Tuscany, and a Guelf in politics. (Here we have the relevance of the Tuscan ossification and the papal petrifaction discussed in connection with lines 67-75 of this canto.) In short, the pilgrim's school is that which preaches papal supremacy, with both spiritual and temporal jurisdiction. Aquinas, in his *De Regimine Principum,* had provided the theological foundation for this school.

It was from this school that Dante was to break away—at some time after 1300—decisively in the *Monarchia.* The results of this breaking away we have of course been tracing throughout the *Purgatory,* especially in the scenes in the Earthly Paradise. And let us not forget that Beatrice's other reproaches and Dante's other self-transformings are also involved in this, or—as the point is made in the form of the poem—the moral, ideal, and poetical transformations are preparatory for the spiritual and theological.

The point, then, of Beatrice's final reproach is that the pilgrim with a great splendor from on high to show him the way has been delinquent by permitting the customs or habits or prejudices of his native region to be his guide: in one way or another he has been parochial when the light guiding him was ready to illuminate the universe.

Beatrice completes her reproach by demonstrating to the pilgrim that his guilt is proved by the very fact that he has no consciousness of guilt nor does he remember being estranged from her: he has but to recall, she says, that he had earlier known what she was talking about and had then drunk of the water of Lethe and had had his memory washed of sin; his forgetting proves that he committed this sin, just as lingering smoke proves that a fire has been present. But this discarded inadequacy of his old school and his present opportunity to avail himself of another school make the pilgrim's progress certain from this point upwards. True, Beatrice continues by saying that hereafter she will simplify her words to the extent necessary to have them clear to his dull vision; but we must also note that Beatrice has the opportunity to say only six more lines to the pilgrim before we reach the end of *Purgatory*—what she says to him thereafter is to be in the clearer light of Paradise.

Ahead, the seven ladies, the seven virtues, stop at a dark pool from which, somehow, the Tigris and Euphrates, the great beneficent twin rivers of earth, take their origin. Before the name of this water is told there is nearly a disagreement between Beatrice and Matelda—there are certainly a reprimand and a self-justification. All this is called forth by the pilgrim's question about the water: Beatrice's only reply is a curt 'Ask Matelda'—this is obviously part of the indoctrination that Matelda should already have given the pilgrim. She has, she says, and can only think that drinking Lethe's waters has made him forget this piece of information. And Beatrice:

> *. . . 'Perhaps a greater care*
> *which often deprives one of memory*
> *has darkened the eyes of his mind,*
>
> *but see Eunoe which rises there;*
> *take him to it, and, as your custom is,*
> *revive his weakened virtue.'*

Notice how precise, almost jealous, the two women are over their respective levels of teaching and guiding; but also note how the poet has given to each of them the proper kind of argument. Matelda excuses herself in the fact of Beatrice's reprimand; but the excuse, instead of blaming the pupil, finds something gone amiss with the educational tools she has to use—for it is not a proper functioning of the Lethe waters to cause this kind of forgetting. Beatrice, although not contradicting Matelda's explanation, offers an alternative, a more reasonable and more charitable explanation: the pilgrim has after all, in the events of these recent moments, had enough serious and touching things happen to him to make his forgetting of a river name understandable.

The pilgrim, drinking of the waters of Eunoe, which restore the blissful powers of innocence to him, would like to spend at least some time singing of the 'sweet draught that would never have sated me'—but he has run out of space. The pages, the lines allotted to the second canticle, are full, and he cannot violate the curb of his art by stretching his plan at will. And so, with echoes of the plants and waters of the opening of this canticle, and with the mention of the stars that culminates each of the canticles:

I came back from the most holy waters
born again, like young plants
renewed by their young foliage,

pure and ready to mount to the stars.

CHAPTER FIFTEEN

Perspective from the Ziggurat

Process and Person. Our journey through the *Purgatory* is over. Like the pilgrim we have come to an open place where we may pause to think of what we have traveled through and to look ahead to what comes next.

As we have moved on, from the first canto through the thirty-third, I have often spoken of the process of the poem without perhaps ever making quite clear what I meant by this phrase. The process of a poem (or of any other serial work of art) is the difference in the state of things before the beginning of the poem and then just after the end of it; it is nearly a mathematical concept. It can be examined and described in many ways: in the *Purgatory,* for instance, it is the difference in the moral, intellectual, and other qualities of the pilgrim between his grimy, bedraggled condition of canto 1 and his enlightened condition, with a powerful message for his country, after canto 33: he is a better man and he knows more at the end than at the beginning. Another process is the series of changes that occur in, or are imposed upon, the reader as he travels thoughtfully and emotionally through the canticle. The term 'process' is related to the form of the poem: in the *Commedia* we would thereunder examine the systematic way, tercet by tercet, section by section, episode by episode, canto by canto, terrace by terrace, in which these changes are produced.

We met the pilgrim on his exit from the pit of Hell; recall the range and kind of experience he had had there. We watched him display a wide range of feelings in his journey through Purgatory: the shy warmth of his meeting with Casella; his incessant burning curiosity; his deep fear of the fires before the Earthly Paradise; the groveling shame and the rapture of his *rencontre* with Beatrice. Ahead of him lie the emotional and intellectual glories whose brightness keeps pace with the ascent through the spheres of Paradise. But perhaps, in the part of the journey we have accomplished, it is the steady friendliness of his relations with Virgil that stands out most clearly: it is a friendliness with elements of many feelings, from almost childlike submission and dependence to a tacit and humorous protectiveness of his guide's deficiencies. This relation includes many qualities of opposition, but it is certainly one of the warmest and deepest friendships in all literature. Nor would it be a simple process to trace: it is counterpointed—as are many of the other processes in the *Commedia*—by a species of contrary motion. The moments of greatest dependence on Virgil in Purgatory come near the end of the journey, when the pilgrim looks to him as a frightened child looks to his mother; the moment at which the pilgrim shows the greatest protectiveness for his guide is probably at the beginning of the canticle, after Virgil's fiascos with Cato.

Considering these complex processes in the growth of the pilgrim may also throw some light on the important question of the choice of personages within the *Commedia*. Each person the pilgrim meets has, of course, his exemplary role as specific sinner, penitent, or saint; but with the entire panel of history and literature open before him, Dante has to use additional yardsticks for his choices. That they are known gluttons or prodigals or angry ones is not enough; their other characteristics must fit into place in the episodic structure within the total plan of the poem. They are, for instance, proud ones who can begin or continue a dealing with the artist, or they are prodigals who throw additional light on a theme dealing with the evolution of greatness in poetry.

The *Commedia* abounds in memorable personages; that the pilgrim's meetings with them are more memorable than the persons in themselves is to be attributed to the developing power of Dante's plan for the poem: each encounter, in its prelude and in its aftermath, falls into its place in the increasingly clear emotional and intellectual rhythms of the poem. In the introductory chapter I likened the movement of the *Commedia* in various ways to tale, to lyric poem, to novel. All these likenesses exist within a complex structural pattern which owes formal responsibility only to itself.

The unremitting progress up the mountain; the division into cantos and episodes; the segments established by the three sleeps and dreams of the pilgrim; the bracketing of the sins into groups of three, one, and three; the juxtaposition of like and unlike elements to produce a division of the areas of Purgatory into two, seven, and one for the summary number of ten—these set up rhythms of varying scope and intensity within the single gigantic timeless beat in which, in the closing lines of the *Paradise,* the entire journey begins and ends.

The Process of Purgation. The process of purgation is completed —and a little more—in the concluding cantos of the *Purgatory;* the end of the process is signalled by the dropping of Beatrice's veil in order to make a certain part, or level, of truth visible to the pilgrim. (Remember how often in the course of the canticle the poet warned us that here or here the veil was growing thin.) We spoke of the final stages of the process as (1) a temporary transmutation of the pilgrim to primal man (or everyman), and (2) a clear re-identification of this primal man as Dante the poet. The process of the canticle is to purify and transform the pilgrim, but the end is to make him all the more essentially Dante Alighieri.

The checks and goads on the various terraces have played their specific parts in straightening and clarifying the course of the pilgrim. (A companion paradox to this process is the fact that on the mountain we must go round-and-round or back-and-forth in order to go straight.) The goad has driven the spirit towards good, the check away from evil. The example from the life of Mary kept presenting an unattainable instance of unselfishness; while the sewn-tight eyes corrected an overuse of the eyes in wrong, outward, envious directions and forced the vision inwards; and finally the punishment of Cain repelled the auditors from a like career. I have likened the parts of this process to an attempt to correct a set in a fishing rod that has been played too often in the same direction. The goad towards good is an intentionally exaggerated bend in the direction away from the set established by evil; when the force of this bend is removed or lightened, the rod (or spirit) tends to spring back, past the center straight line, to the evil set. The check acts to stop this reversing spring. And we must remember that while Dante the pilgrim experiences each goad and each check only once in his journey, for the penitent souls there is repetition of goad-and-check until the straightening, the purgation, has been fully achieved. Another analogy for the process—and this is possibly the one which gave Dante the concept—is that of plowing with oxen: to keep them in a straight line the driver must constantly apply exaggerated goads in one direction and exaggerated checks in the opposite direction.

The notion of the straight line appears in a multitude of forms in the *Commedia:* in the arrow of the bow-and-arrow imagery, linked with the images of light which always goes straight to its target, and also linked (via the word *arco*) with the bridge which is the most direct way of crossing an obstacle-stream (which in turn provides a link with the river- or water-imagery). The straight line itself is the *diritta via* which the pilgrim had lost at the beginning of the poem and is finally the unimpeded, unswerving path of the pilgrim drawn to God by love in Paradise.

A difference between Hell and Purgatory may be repeated here to illustrate the process of purgation. The proud in Purgatory and the hypocrites in Hell are presented in much the same situation—both are forced to go along bent over to the ground. Hypocrisy *is* and *remains* the act of bending lower than one should; the proud penitent *needs* the bending-forward as corrective to the pride which had made him bend backwards even to the ground in his effort to be taller than he really was: the eyes of the proud are set so high above the straight-ahead horizon that they permit only a backward view.

This important point has, I believe, been sometimes mistaken. Dorothy Sayers, for instance, says (*Purgatory,* p. 15) that the culprit must be convinced of his guilt and that he is being punished by a just tribunal. This concept deals with the element of satisfaction for sin but not adequately with the actual purgation of it. Rather, it seems to me, the penitent recognizes the principle and the applicability of justice to his particular instance; and in that recognition is willing to do his share, in his own person, to rectify the injustice. He thereupon takes into himself some portion of that principle of justice (and its corollary, enlightenment)—justice which, as Dante everywhere indicates, is the structural principle of God's creation and which recognizes when something is right as well as when something is wrong, and is to be trusted to do, as well as know, the proper thing each time.

This principle of justice is social and cooperative as well as individual. Constantly in the *Purgatory,* unlike the *Inferno,* we encounter all the simple as well as all the complex ways in which people help each other. More even than the *Paradise* the *Purgatory* is a parable of the simple kinds of friendship—an honest *quid pro quo.* We must not forget, for example, what Virgil receives for his labor of guiding: he is introduced to realms and concepts he would otherwise have had no way of knowing. What greater reward could a philosophical poet ask for?

In addition to the straightening out of individual sins and sinners (or sinners as individuals) we are nowhere in the *Purgatory* permitted to lose sight of political and institutional sins. From the great invective against Florence (the sinning city) through Marco Lombardo's reproach of the papacy as a sinning institution into the pageant of Church and Empire in the Earthly Paradise the poet keeps burning before us the ill-doings of spiritual and temporal rulers and institutions. But no cure or corrective for these institutional sins is prescribed until the final episode of the canticle.

Here the cure seems to Dante to be self-evident. Not only the incumbent Pope but also the papacy in its present condition has been eliminated from the prerogative of ruling, through this last fling with the King of France. Dante does not explicitly say here that the incumbent Emperor has equally eliminated himself (and in fact most attempts to identify the 'five hundred ten and five' concentrate on one or two of the emperors holding office just after the turn of the century)—but the lesson of the pageant, in the progressive intercorruption of empire and papacy, calls for a new condition of empire as well as of papacy.

Finally we must see how correction of individual sin and sinners, thus paralleled by a mounting theme of institutional sin, has also been paralleled by a theme of the rising grandeur, purity, and power of the pilgrim-poet. It is this last theme which in a sense comes to embrace all the others. The culmination of the *Purgatory* is Beatrice's admonition to the pilgrim to clear his eyes and memory in order that Dante, the pilgrim-poet, may write down the great things he has seen in the Earthly Paradise, to prove to men the extinction of Church (and presumably of Empire) under present conditions: 'it was and is no more'; and then to offer—still as a poet using the most effective means at his command—hope of rebirth and reconstruction.

Speculations and Prospects. What are these means, these resources, at the command of Dante? The eloquence, the dramatic and architectonic skill of the master-poet—these are solid, clear, and profitable subjects for study and restudy.

But Dante, like Plato, is *vates* as well as sober poet: veils are dropped or momentarily twitched apart for us; we are crowned and mitred for dalliance among the flowered fields of the Earthly Paradise; strange tongues and stranger numbers are chanted for our puzzlement—are we to accompany Dante on his audacious and saltatory speculations only at a safe and comfortable distance?

Our minds should be able to prove that they have been stretched by Dante, even to the extreme of following him into the pathless woods of fantasy. One's approach, however, must be sober.

Dante's writings before the *Commedia* offer a great many unexplored relations to the *Commedia* when examined by two or three of the hypotheses I have already made: that Dante's growth is Platonic, which means (a) that his level of insight is never the same in two successive works and (b) that the later work embraces and refocuses the insights of the earlier one rather than abolishing them; in other words, that the Dante of the *Commedia* bears the same complex relation to his earlier works that he himself bears to the dogma and the poetic practice of his time.

On this point I shall merely suggest two such inquiries. It is, I believe, correctly agreed that the *Commedia* is the work projected in the concluding words of the *Vita Nuova:*

> After writing this sonnet, it was given unto me to behold a very wonderful vision; wherein I saw things which determined me that I would say nothing further of this most blessed one, until such time as I could discourse more worthily concerning her. And to this end I labor all I can; as she well knoweth. Wherefore if it be His pleasure through whom is the life of all things, that my life continue with me a few years, it is my hope that I shall yet write concerning her what hath not before been written of any woman. After the which, may it seem good unto Him who is the Master of Grace, that my spirit should go hence to behold the glory of its lady: to wit of that blessed Beatrice who now gazeth continually on His countenance *qui est per omnia saecula benedictus. Laus Deo.*

What changes in Dante's concept of his duty will account for the difference between 'as she well knoweth' and the violent upbraiding Beatrice delivers in the Earthly Paradise? Why does the future poem here receive the name of 'vision' while it is almost explicitly *not* a vision when Dante writes it? Is this citation from the *Vita Nuova* the explanation of the puzzling masculine form *Benedictus qui venit* at the coming of Beatrice in the Earthly Paradise?

The *Convivio,* as we have already seen, is the most promising and yet the most dangerous of the earlier works to deal with. It is promising because in it we have the mature Dante as poet, as dramatist, as philosopher, as theologian exploring and questioning his own poetics, dramaturgy, philosophy, and theology. It is dangerous because its very incompletion tends to set up (possibly) false dichotomies in the reader's mind—on the type we saw demonstrated by Singleton: if Dante does *A* in the *Convivio* he must consequently be doing *not-A* in the *Commedia.*

Let me therefore suggest only the most rewarding and dangerous study of all connected with the *Convivio:* an attempt to construct Dante's unwritten treatise on the nature of allegory.

That Canzone XIII (*Poscia ch' Amor del tutto m' ha lasciato*) is indeed the one around which Dante intended to write his account of allegory seems likely. For in this canzone we clearly have the basis for the method and means of allegory, the need and origin of allegory, and the burning relation between the allegorist and his allegory. Working out what may have been the general lines of such a discourse would provide a great light upon the Earthly Paradise and indeed on the entire *Commedia.* This canzone, glossed, might well reveal that Dante's connection with courtly love, Provençal poetry, and the *dolce stil nuovo* is somewhat different from that usually conceived. For in this canzone (and we must of course consider the reciprocal light cast by the Earthly Paradise) we can see that Dante's *dolce stil,* while elevating woman almost to (or actually to) the status of the Virgin Mary, never forgets (as of course theologically it should not) the details of her sexual function; so too in the Earthly Paradise we must also come to see the clarity and unique purity of the sexual thoughts and feelings aroused by the pilgrim's and Matelda's first sight of each other, and by the whole ladder system of progress by which we rise to the unveiled Beatrice as the culmination of all that is achievable on earth as, temporarily, distinguished from heaven.

A rarely examined aspect of Dante's creation is the mythic, the Jungian unconscious. I treated some aspects of this in chapter 4, discussing nature-myth and folkloristic elements in the story of Buonconte. I suspect that much more of this kind of material remains to be perceived in the *Commedia* and that it gives the poem one of its deepest emotional powers. For in Dante this species of insight is never dragged in, or superimposed upon something else, as it often is in the greatest of modern writings, in *Finnegans Wake* or in the *Magic Mountain.* In Dante the mythic is part of his literal and rational exposition of the cosmos; it comes, so to speak, from God's subconscious mind rather than from Dante's.

The great example of this in the *Purgatory* is the mountain itself. The mountain—and remember that Purgatory as a mountain is Dante's idea—is perhaps in the first instance a creation of Dante's literalizing mind: the fall of man, the greatest fall man ever made or could make, must be from the greatest height conceivable on earth. More: the fall was from this greatest summit to the water-level surface of the earth; sinners fall from the surface to the even lower level of their choice; the greatest sinners, the traitors, fall to the greatest depth possible in the created universe, where they join Satan, who himself fell to this lowest spot from the heights of the empyrean.

The mountain itself is the mythic, kinesthetic, empathetic symbol par excellence of human earthly aspiration. It demands to be climbed, as mountaineers say, simply because it is there. One, however, does not simply, as in a dream, soar up to the summit; the arduousness of the ascent is posited by all the practical as well as all the theological qualities of the pilgrim's experience. (A German scholar has explored for us the aspects of 'Dante-Alpinist'; but the mountain itself will repay further exploration.)

Dante and Medieval Doctrines. The relation between Dante and current beliefs or traditions is infrequently simple: after seeing that Dante uses traditional material we must look closely to see whether he uses it in a traditional, extratraditional, or antitraditional way. Professor Spitzer describes the strategies of Dante when using traditional material. In an article on 'Speech and Language in *Inferno* XIII' (*Italica* XIX [1942], 81-104) he says (p. 99):

> In all the passages discussed, Dante has used a stylistic pattern that was familiar in a manner specifically adapted to a particular situation or character: the rhetorical device is never used for its own sake, 'in order to use the well-known rhetorical device of . . . ,' as philologists like to reason; Dante recreates the given stylistic patterns by restoring their original strength. The *Amor che a nullo amato amar perdona* of the Francesca episode, followed by two other lines with an anaphoric *amor,* inserts itself easily into a well-known medieval pattern used by all preachers and orators . . . ; it is nevertheless an eternal expression of the nature of love—so much so that the modern reader (even the medievalist when he happens to be 'just' a reader) does not even sense the presence of an old pattern.

The larger aspects of Dante's relation to the doctrines of his day are soon presented: on such and such points he is in full compliance; on others—such as the location and nature of Purgatory—he boldly departs. A third, more elusive, relation we might exemplify in those parts of theological doctrine which he nowhere contradicts or violates but which provide neither emotional nor formal incentive for his poem. It is difficult to see or to describe this last relation, but it is often this which largely determines the quality of the *Commedia.*

There is, for example, no question about Dante's accepting the doctrine of original sin, of the Incarnation, and of the Last Judgment. He alludes to the Last Judgment a number of times, but what its effect is on the substance of the *Commedia* is speculative and lies wholly outside the poem—that is, the poem does not permit on this question the kind of answer that may be hypothesized for many other unanswered questions. It is possible, for example, to speculate on whether Cato is destined to go to Paradise or to Limbo after the Last Judgment, even though such speculation involves one in data and results that throw little light on the poem. On a broader scale, the Last Judgment will, it is obvious, terminate all the operations of Purgatory and will expose to the full awareness of all the eternal conditions of Hell and Paradise—but what real relation does this fact bear to the moving qualities of Dante's poem? Some relation, true; but how important is it?

Similarly with the doctrine of the Incarnation: no doubt it is everywhere implied in the texture of the poem. But if we did not know that this must be so, would we have been aware of it?

Dante's relation to the doctrine of original sin is yet more complex. Again there is no question about his belief in this doctrine. But, as we have seen in the Earthly Paradise, Dante leans heavily on the paradoxes in Eve's sin. We must notice, first of all, that he speaks of the sin of Eve rather than of Eve-and-Adam (although in this he was joined by many of his contemporaries) for the poetic reason of emphasizing the feminine virtues of Matelda and Beatrice: theology recognizes no essential difference on this point between man and woman, the priority of Eve's fall being balanced by the greater culpability of Adam; but for Dante the difference between a male guide and a female guide was of the poetic essence at this point in his structure of things.

The fall of man is a fact, a fact prerequisite to the existence and the passion of Christ as God-Man; but it is also prerequisite to the remainder of human history, including the realities of the current situation. To the poet dealing in facts, and not in theological hypotheses, the fall of man is the most important fact in history after the creation ('after' in rank rather than in time). But here is something else even harder to pin down. Dante's equation between sin and stupidity is so nearly absolute as to make evil a willful cantankerousness on the part of the men and women who have blindly elected such a course. (It may even be relevant here to note a difference between infernal and purgatorial sins: the Inferno contains a number of official sins, sins within the formalities of church or secular offices, such sins as simony and barratry; those in Purgatory are on a practical and psychological basis divorced from details or stages or of office.) But what other than the Fall provided the basis for the discrimination which must begin all use of reason, judgment, or intelligence? Before the Fall the differentia for men could be only between those things that God advocated or permitted and those things that He forbade. Working up to pure *libertas* by the haphazard exercise of *liberum arbitrium* is the way to salvation through a doubt-filled world—but how is such self-purification possible when the only choice is between obeying and disobeying?

The very idea of God's justice, of consequences of action, of right and wrong, of reward and punishment could be only nebulous until put into operation by the fall of man. Almost it would seem the gift of intelligence, God's highest gift to man (or, if you will, the highest after that combined free-will-and-obedience which existed only before the Fall and for which we therefore have no word) could be no more than potential until called into operation by the Fall. Man's highest achievements—including this poem that Dante was writing—as well as his lowest ignominies (which also had a place in the poem) would have had no history but for the Fall. Dante may himself have come to realize, ironically and practically, that his own greatest misfortunes—his fall from the vision of Beatrice and his exile from Florence—were indispensable in the sharpening of his wits and the broadening of his vistas, in his transformations from a Florentine love-poet and a local politician to a poet and citizen of the universe. Being thrust out of the petty paradise that

Florence had been for him may have given him, as he could know even in his bitter misery, the emotional and intellectual perspective needed for the creation of the *Commedia*. See the title of his poem as he wrote it for Can Grande:

Incipit Comedia Dantis Alagherii, florentini natione non moribus.

The 'condition of primal man' that the poet set up by the images of pure concupiscence at the pilgrim's entrance to the Earthly Paradise, by the likening to Adam, and by the rolling back of history may contain Dante's theology on the nature of original sin. Let me add two or three passages that bear on this question.

Dante follows the Greek Church Fathers (Irenaeus, Cyril of Antioch, Epiphanius) in allowing Adam seven hours in the Earthly Paradise; the Latin Fathers (Augustine, Ambrose, Basil) allowed him a longer time. (See *Paradise* 26.115-42: Adam here says that his sin was not the tasting of the fruit but disobedience, 'the transgressing, or trespassing, of the mark.') Aquinas had said (*Summa Th.*, II, 163, a. 1 *ad* 1):

Adam did not disobey the divine precept from mere wilful disobedience; for such a motive presupposes an already disordered will . . . What he first willed inordinately was his own excellence, and thus his disobedience sprang from his pride.

If Dante is following this belief of Aquinas—and he probably is—that pride was the stimulus to Adam's disobedience, there must still be an explanation of where the pride came from: it seems nearly as unfair to this new creature to saddle him with pride as it would be to have had him created with 'an already disordered will.'

Perhaps we may connect some of the things we have already noted in the *Purgatory* to suggest an answer to this problem. At 16.85-93 we saw the condition of the soul at its creation, the pleasure-principle by which alone it is guided. There is little reason to think that the creation of Adam's soul was of a different order from this; the difference is only that Adam was not a helpless infant at this moment but a grown man ready to, or rather obliged to, act and decide.

We have also seen, in the Earthly Paradise, the condition of primal man echoing the condition of Adam. What then is pride, as Adam's sin, but the willing of what Aquinas calls 'his own excellence,' the willing of what is intended to bring pleasure, but before experience and maturity are at hand to direct the intention, or will, along accurate paths of judgment?

Original sin, then, by the process of Dante's poem, seems to be more precisely defined not as pride but as an inchoate pleasure-principle action that might—in this one instance alone of human action—be called proto-pride.

Beatrice. The final purifying of the pilgrim is rewarded by the dropping of Beatrice's veil. The literal realness of Beatrice (whether the Portinari or another is not significant) has been insistently established by her treatment of the pilgrim; yet, in her unveiling she is (or provides) revelation for the pilgrim—if only personal revelation, at a level somewhat lower than that of the saints.

The simplest solution to this paradox might be to say that the veil she drops is her own. But Beatrice as Revelation and Beatrice as real woman are in fact inseparable within the structure of the poem. Without the force of Divine Wisdom and Will behind her the message she reveals to the pilgrim would have no effective force; if she had not been real she could not have played her part in the process by which fatherly guides yield place to the *donna angelicata* to create a new life for the poet. This *vita nuova,* with its corresponding new function, of Dante, was begun, interrupted, and then painfully reconstructed with Beatrice ever as the more or less clearly seen light. (Light, we must remember, is for Dante goal as well as illuminant of the way.)

In chapter 1, at page 25, I spoke of 'Christ as function'—Christ not so much apart from his theological role, as fulfilling the role with the utmost concreteness to fill a poet's need: action and contemplation of Christ, *theoria* and *praxis,* all together transformed into the substance of a work of art. In the same way is Beatrice here transformed into function: she has become the material of the poem as well as the incentive, or form, of it.

Nor is the revelation, or unveiling, of Beatrice a sudden, arbitrarily or divinely interjected occurrence into the pageant of cantos 30 through 33. It is gradual, accomplished by small leaps, foreshadowed by image- and theme-preparations, based on elaborate internal and external ascents by the pilgrim—in short, it depends on the process of the poem from its beginning up to this point. This process, idealized and formalized within a methodical poetic structure, is nevertheless parallel with the actual course of Dante's experiences: it is nothing other than his real life. Not that Dante's experiences included the fullness of all the sins he traverses in the *Inferno,* but his falling away from the light of Beatrice might well have involved him in the *reata* of all these sins. Stylized, slowed down—the descent into the Inferno is still a tumbling into a pit by one who has lost both his way and the light by which he might have regained it; he tumbles until, literally, he touches bottom—and falls no farther only because there is in the entire universe no lower place to fall to.

Then begins the curious and curiously rapid climb up from Satan's midriff. It is curiously rapid because the calendar of the pilgrim's journey seems to allow only a few moments for this traversal of half the earth's diameter, while the journey through the Inferno—the first half of the diameter—had taken two full days.*

But the greater part of its curiousness comes from its being unexplained: as such it becomes one of a small number of mysterious transitions—the pilgrim's finding himself in the *selva oscura* after he knows not what preceding action; the transport of the pilgrim by Lucia (if it is indeed she) to the gates of Purgatory; the pilgrim's acquisition of a new mode of movement in the first canto of the *Paradise.* All but the last of these examples show the pilgrim being attracted or drawn to a place where his conscious will has not taken him; yet none of these movements violates his freedom of will. The resolution of this puzzle lies of course in Beatrice: from his first trusting of himself to the pull of her attraction, a trust freely

* An alternative explanation for this part of the journey would have the poet Dante know that his travelers would gain a calendar day (expended in the climb) by coming into the other hemisphere. If this be true, the curiousness would only be transferred to the question of why he says nothing about it.

even if not clearly given, it was only a matter of time until he should release himself to be pulled or drawn up, by stages, to the point where he could meet her again directly. The last of my examples a moment ago—Dante's moving up through Paradise with neither explicit activity nor resistance by his will—is the motion he becomes capable of after he has encountered Beatrice and received her enlightenment without mediation.

Beatrice, throughout these activities, never loses the convincing quality of a woman—perhaps chiefly for the reason of her actions when first we see her. In the *Inferno* and in the first twenty-seven cantos of the *Purgatory* her name has often come up—sometimes as an awesomely powerful being, but often in some homely image. When she appears in the Earthly Paradise, to take her part in the great pantomime, her quality remains unclear until she starts to speak; then, the direct and intensely personal words she has for the pilgrim firmly establish her reality and even cast a shadow back over the symbolic pantomime, so that she comes into our minds with the same accentuated realness that Alice had amidst the pack of cards.

It is Beatrice who, real and prismatic, keeps the allegory moving through the single-faceted pageant. And it is Beatrice who, with humor and affection and majesty, guides the pilgrim through Paradise, to a point just short of the highest possible reach of human endeavor. Yet, we must never forget, Beatrice herself was created by Dante.

* * * * *

The poem and aim of Dante are a human revelation of the clarity and scope possible for the human mind. Doubt, murkiness, moral ambiguity leading to accidia, uncertainty of duty or goal or value—these are the stock in trade of the novelists and poets of the past hundred years. These are realities; no doubt. These convince us that Joyce and Kafka, Eliot and Rimbaud are writing for us: for these are the realities of our own lives. That there is another kind of real life is something that Dante can demonstrate to us, by process that can take us as high as his highest soaring.

Notes

CHAPTER ONE

1. The early commentators:

Chiose Anonime alla prima Cantica della Divina Commedia (ed. Selmi, 1865). This gloss is believed to be the earliest and has been guessed to be of 1320.

Il Commento all'Inferno di Graziuolo de' Bambaglioli (Udine, 1892). About 1324.

Chiose alla Cantica dell'Inferno di Dante Alighieri attribuite a Jacopo suo figlio (Florence, 1848). About 1324.

Commento di Jacopo di Giovanni dalla Lana (Milan, 1865). About 1330.

L'Ottimo Commento della Divina Commedia (Pisa, 1827). A little after 1330, perhaps by Andrea Lancia.

Petri Allegherii Commentarium (Florence, 1845). About 1340. A commentary on the whole *Comedy* by Dante's son Pietro.

Il Comento sopra la Commedia di Dante Alighieri di Giovanni Boccaccio. The substance of Boccaccio's lectures in 1373. It ends in *Inf.* 17.

Benvenuti de Rambaldis de Imola Comentum super Dantis Aldigherij Comoediam (Florence, 1887). 1375.

2. Karl Witte who, at the beginning of the nineteenth century, gave form to modern Dante scholarship, points out this danger in his essay on 'The Art of Misunderstanding Dante' (in *Essays on Dante,* translated by Laurence and Wicksteed, p. 21):

> True love loses itself entirely in its object, takes it where it finds it, pierces the intervening centuries and emerges at its side, to receive it on its own terms, without being so much as conscious of any requirements of its own. But there is a false love which is only directed to the counterpart of itself in all its environment. Kindled by the joy of finding its own sensations meeting it from outside, it treats the object it has found as a mere lay-figure to be generously robed in itself, in order thereby to acquire a larger bulk of material on which to lavish its affection. Dante has had his full share of admirers of this type.

3. Divine care supplies everybody with the means necessary for salvation, so long as he on his part does not put up obstacles. If a person, who has been brought up in the backwoods or among beasts, follows his conscience and

seeks good and avoids evil, then most assuredly is it to be held that God's internal inspiration will reveal to him the truths necessary for salvation or God will send him a preacher, as when Peter and Cornelius were brought together.—Aquinas, Disputations, xiv *de Veritate,* 11, *ad* 1, 1 (Gilby).

4. The question of how far Dante believed in an equal reality of all these beings is of some interest. Some of us might come to believe that Dante is as credulous as the most credulous of his day and thinks that meeting unicorns, sphinxes, and cameleopards is only a question of geography; or we might find that Dante is as hardheaded as a Yankee but is willing to attribute as much importance to the imagination as to any other human activity, and his only concern then with these creatures of the imagination is to decide which section of the universe should contain such activity and its creatures. Perhaps the fantastic animals we meet in the lower reaches of Hell therefore seem more real than those of Paradise or Purgatory; these latter are perhaps more clearly symbolic and used for direct allegory. The animals of Hell are creatures of the perverted imaginations housed there, imaginations more likely than any others to be realistically frightened by the dark structures of their own image-building faculties.

5. The validity of the Ptolemaic system had been violently attacked for at least a century before the writing of the *Comedy.* Aquinas himself supported the system with misgivings. He said that the Ptolemaic theory of epicycles may 'save the appearances,' but that this is not sufficient proof that the theory is true, 'for the appearances might perhaps also be saved on another hypothesis' (*Summa Th.,* Ia, 32, 1, *ad* 2).

6. This problem had been stated and solved by Boethius in the fifth book of the *Consolatio Philosophiae.* This book, says Hawkins (*A Sketch of Med. Phil.,* pp. 22-3):

. . . embarks on a discussion of the relationship of human free will to the divine foreknowledge and providence. The solution is found in the contrast of the temporal character of human existence with the timelessness of God, to whom all times are eternally and simultaneously present. This is where we find the justly celebrated definition of eternity as 'the simultaneous and complete possession of endless life.'

Aquinas also makes this point with perhaps a weak analogy:

When I see Socrates sitting down, my knowledge is certain and infallible, but no necessity to sit is imposed on Socrates by this fact. So God knows with certainty and infallibility all those things as present which for us are past, present, or future. And yet no necessity is thereby imposed on contingent events. (*De rationibus fidei ad Cantorem antiochenum,* 10.)

7. Aquinas: 'Just as we have come to knowledge of simple things through composite things, so we have to approach the knowledge of eternity through time' (*Summa Th.,* Ia, 10, 1).

This concept is, of course, older than Aquinas: '. . . St. Augustine considers the universe as a kind of unfolding, a *distensio,* which imitates in its flowing forth the eternal present and total simultaneity of the life of God' (Gilson, *Spirit of Med. Phil.,* p. 385).

. . . the future may be known in two ways: either in itself, or in its cause. The future cannot be known in itself save by God alone, to Whom even that is present which in the course of events is future, inasmuch from eternity His glance embraces the whole course of time, as we have said above when treating of God's knowledge (Q. 14, a.13). (*Summa Th.,* I, 86, 4.)

8. More accurately, of course, Satan is not Cause but privation (in Aquinas' sense) of Cause carried to its extreme; Satan represents the greatest disuse of greatest potential goods.

Aquinas' discussion of Aristotle's four kinds of Cause provides the sense in which Dante conceived these terms:

Hence God's universal causality must be defined in such a way that the proper activity of creatures is safeguarded. Now there are four classes of cause material, final, efficient, and formal. The material cause can be left on one side; it is not the principle of activity, but the subject receiving the effect of action. The others are co-ordinated principles of activity. Let me illustrate their role from the example of the production of a work of art. First is the end, the purpose the artist has in mind. Next is the efficient cause, the agent himself who applies the cutting edge of his craft. Last is the form embodied in the material, the chest or bed which is carved. Notice that the efficient cause acts through its own form (*Summa Th.,* Ia, cv, 5) (Gilby).

9. Let us consider his fullness of grace. The term *grace* suggests two ideas, not far removed from one another: first, of being in favour; second, of being given a present. For we give gratis to those who are after our own heart and to our own liking. We may like them either reservedly or unreservedly; reservedly, when we would give them what is ours, but without entering into intimacy; unreservedly, when we would draw them close to us according to the kind and degree of our liking. Consequently, anybody who has grace has received a gift, but not everybody who has received a gift is held dear. Hence two sorts of grace can be distinguished, one is only a free gift, the other is also a grant of friendship (*Compendium Theologiae,* 214) (Gilby).

10. Dante may not have agreed with Augustine on the predetermination of the elect, that their 'number is so certain that one can neither be added to them nor taken from them.' But neither would he have agreed with Augustine's opponent Pelagius in denouncing original sin and denying that the taint of Adam's sin and the consequent weakness of will were transmitted to the descendants of Adam.

11. Gertrude Leigh, in *A Study in the Heterodoxy of Dante,* argues vehemently that Dante was a thorough, if secret, follower of Joachim of Flora.

12. Most emphatic is Dante's belief in immortality. In the *Convivio* (II, 9) he says that 'of all the bestialities, that is the most stupid, most vile, and most damnable, which believes no other life to be after this life. . . . I believe, affirm, and am certain that after this I shall pass to another better life—there where that glorious Lady lives, of whom my soul was enamoured.'

In the *Inferno* (10.13-5) he presents as the touchstone of heresy the belief that makes 'the soul die with the body.'

Helmut Hatzfeld advances an eloquent statement of Dante's orthodoxy ('The Art of Dante's Purgatorio,' pp. 46-7):

In conclusion we may say that, while Dante's Inferno is a very 'earthly world' and the Paradiso a spiritualization which almost neglects the human element, the art of the Purgatorio consists in the creation of a very human, magic myth, including the poetization of theology, spiritual life, human relations, liturgy, landscapes, actions and situations. The real meaning of Dante's display of creative imagination and captivating symbolism in his Purgatory does become still clearer when we reduce his fantastic variations to their theme which scholars found very closely preformed in the sentence of Hughes of Saint Victor: 'The virtues drive out the vices . . . , the virtues finally taking over the place of the vices are called sanities or healings. The joy over the recovered health are the Beatitudes.' (Sermo XI, *De spirituali sanitate.*) . . .

Dante's painstaking in keeping strictly to the fundamental Catholic doctrine on purgatory is discernible in every line. Despite his apparent independence in the transformation of a traditional fire into a mountain, or in inserting an Earthly Paradise between Purgatory and Heaven, transformations more radical than the poetical changes in his Inferno and Paradiso, Dante's Purgatorio remains the dogmatic purgatory with its ontological truth. However, the formal truth is seen by a temperament and is broken by Dante's poetic prism into a bundle of most adequate, grandiose and symbolic images, radiating all the more his firm, vivid and unshakable faith (Par. xxiv, 142; xxv,

52-3). Therefore Dante's Purgatorio, although it owes its reality only to the magic wand of the poet, is in the fullest sense *littérature engagée*. Modern readers under its cathartic spell cannot help feeling already with Dante the thread sewing their envious eyes and the heavy stone destined to curb their pride (xiii, 133-138).

13. 'Reason may be hindered by concupiscence or by some other passion from applying a general principle to the case of some particular action' (*Summa Th.,* Ia, 94, 6).

14. Curtius, in *European Literature and the Latin Middle Ages, passim,* but especially at pp. 360-2, establishes a convincing basis for Dante's knowledge of Alan.

15. Ovid, plus Catullus and a half-dozen other classical and medieval poets, undeniably show up in certain phrases, certain parts of the attitude of lover to beloved—particularly when Ovid is fitted into the medieval pattern of *gentilezza,* courtly elegance. This in turn demands the explanation of the pattern of *gentilezza.*

16. The ideals of chivalry might provide this explanation if chivalry itself had a clear origin. Chaytor (*The Troubadours,* pp. 14-5) said that

> . . . troubadour love was constituted upon the analogy of feudal relationship. If chivalry was the outcome of the Germanic theory of knighthood as modified by the influence of Christianity, it may be said that troubadour love is the outcome of the same theory under the influence of mariolatry.

17. In recent years a number of works, speculative as well as scholarly, have tried, among many other things, to solve the question of courtly love by treating it as part of a larger question of religious, or specifically Christian, love. The most important of these are the three volumes of *Agape and Eros* by the Swedish theologian Anders Nygren; *L'Amour et L'Occident* by Denis de Rougemont (translated by Montgomery Belgion and published in England as *Passion and Society,* in the United States as *Love in the Western World*); and a book written partly in response to both of these—*The Mind and Heart of Love* by M. C. D'Arcy. An earlier book in the same field is Pierre Rousselot's *Problème de l'Amour au Moyen Age.* The most useful scholarly work is that by A. J. Denomy, as listed in the Bibliography.

18. According to Aquinas the *vis cogitativa* belongs to the level of sensitive life in man—the level that man shares with the animals. 'The physicians,' he says, 'assign to it a definite organ, namely the middle part of the head.' He calls the *vis cogitativa* 'particular reason,' since

it does not conceive universals, as reason proper does (*Summa Th.*, Ia, 78, 4).

Avicenna (Gilson, *Hist. Christ. Phil.*, pp. 200-2) describes three internal senses, together making up a single power of the soul: imagination, fantasy, and the 'common sense' (*sensus communis*). 'Common sense' enables us to distinguish colors from sounds, sights from smells, etc.: it is the common receiver of all external sensations and offers them, distinct from each other, to the intellect. 'Common sense' is localized in the inner part of the brain.

'Common sense,' then, receives forms from without; imagination and fantasy preserve them. These latter two are in the anterior part of the brain; the posterior part is occupied by the 'cogitative power.'

A summary of the moral and psychological problems raised by these theories of love is indirectly presented in a sonnet supposedly written by Guido Orlandi at the behest of a lady, to be submitted to Guido Cavalcanti. Orlandi's sonnet (quoted by Otto Bird, 'The Canzone d'Amore of Cavalcanti . . . ,' in *Mediaeval Studies* II, 150), which was answered by Cavalcanti's *Donna mi prega,* may be thus translated:

Whence is Love moved and where is it born?
What is the place proper for its dwelling?
Is it substance, accident, or recollection?
Is it caused in the eyes, or in the will of the heart?

Whence proceed Love's summers or its storms?
How does Love become a fire that devours?
On what is it nourished? I ask again:
How, when, and by whom was it made lord?

What sort of thing, I ask, is Love? Has it shape?
Has Love its own form or is it like others?
Is it life, this Love, or is it death?

They that serve it should know of its nature;
I thus ask you, Guido, about Love:
I hear that you are well acquainted in its court.

The relevance of these medieval scientific theories of love to most later love poetry has been recognized but far from adequately studied. For example, the poetry of the English Renaissance has been extensively read in terms of Courtly Love, but the Aristotelian-Avicennist-Averroist psychology of love (which is a somewhat different thing) provides more precise initial insights into the poetry of Wyatt, Sidney, and Shakespeare than does the allegory of love. Test the two methods as approaches to the 'Tell me where is fancy bred' or 'Who is Silvia?' Shakespeare's forthright use of medieval love-science in these little songs is matched by an equally fundamental, if more subtle, use of these theories throughout the corpus of Renaissance sonnets. This same science may even have provided a basis for Racine's theory of love.

19. In the dream of the Siren (*Purgatory* 19) we have a perfect enactment of this formula—with the Averroistic slant towards a deceiving relation between *visio* and *cogitatio*.

20. Dante shows direct knowledge of the troubadour poets. Arnaut Daniel (*Purg.* 26) and Sordello (*Purg.* 6 to 8) play their parts in the structure of the poem. (Cunizza, beloved of Sordello, we meet in *Par.* 9). Dante names six troubadours in *De Vulg. Eloq.*: Arnaut Daniel, Giralt de Bornelh, and Bertran de Born at II, 2, 9; Folchetto di Marsiglia, Amerigo de Pegugliano, and Amerigo de Belenoi at II, 6, 6.

21. In Dante's picture of Pier delle Vigne in the wood of the suicides there are some touches of curious particularity (*Inf.* 13). Not only is Pier a 'great thorn' but he controls the two keys of Frederick's heart—recalling the two keys of Peter, of the guardian of Purgatory gate. The 'harlot eyes' recall the wandering eyes of the harlot in the chariot of the Earthly Paradise.

22. These three sonnets are translated by Grandgent in *Dante*, pp. 116-8.

23. Such at least was the opinion of Dante and his generation. Guittone's sonnet to the Virgin Mary and Bonagiunta's canzone 'Of the true end of Love' are touching and simple poems that do not deserve these harsh judgments.

24. These two sonnets are translated by Grandgent, *op. cit.*, pp. 118-9; the next three sonnets are translated by Rossetti.

25. What Professor Singleton has to say of the theory of love in the *Vita Nuova* may be used here as an indication of what Dante's use of love in the *Comedy* will be. He says (*Essay on the Vita Nuova*, p. 114):

For the *Vita Nuova* is a theory of love, to be sure—but theory in an original sense of the word: a *beholding* of how things may be, and, in this case, how they may be in the order of their *rightness*. Dante, like the other poets of his generation, had written poems on themes inherited from Guinicelli and the tradition. But until he chose to surround certain of those poems with a prose controlling their meaning and ordering it toward an end, Dante had not faced the problem of whether love of woman, as the poems of Guinicelli and Cavalcanti and his own poems had represented it, might or might not be seen as good love, might or might not be seen in reference to and in subordination to love of God. And that is the problem which the *Vita Nuova,* as theory, faces and sees through. By making its beginning in the cult of troubadour love, with a God of Love and faithful servants of love who are poets each with his wondrous madonna, the *Vita Nuova* acknowledges its responsibility, sets up its problem resolutely. And the work ends facing God as no other beginning in troubadour love had ever done or would ever do—without recantation. The unique achievement of the *Vita Nuova* as a theory of love is the seeing how love of woman may be kept all the way up to God.

26. Aquinas deals with a closely related question, in discussing the problem of 'whether the devil can induce man to sin by internal instigations':

> The interior part of the soul is intellective and sensitive, and the intellective part contains the intellect and the will. . . . Now the intellect, of its very nature, is moved by that which illumines it for the knowledge of truth, and the devil has certainly no intention of exercising such an activity towards man. Rather does he darken man's reason so that it may consent to sin, and this darkness comes from the imagination and sensitive appetite. Consequently the whole interior operation of the devil seems to be confined to the imagination and the sensitive appetite, by moving either of which he can induce man to sin. For his operation may result in presenting certain forms to the imagination; and he is also able to incite the sensitive appetite to some passion or other. (*Summa Th.,* I, 80, 2.) (Pegis.)

Dante comes close to this doctrine (but without the agency of the devil) only in the dream of the Siren; see below, chapter 9.

27. The model for much of the detailed analysis of the *Comedy* is to be found in the extended commentary by Dante's son Pietro. Pietro's work shows a thoroughness lacking in many of those who came after him; it consequently seems fair to use his work to demonstrate the strait jacket qualities of such a system as this. This citation is from John Paul Bowden, *An Analysis of Pietro Alighieri's Commentary on the Divine Comedy,* pp. 100-1:

> Dante utilizes seven senses:
>
> 1. The literal or superficial, the meaning of which does not extend beyond the letter.

2. The historical, which tells of the events of history as though they were under the gaze of the reader; it contains the truth and things which are like the truth.

3. The apologetic, containing not the truth but some rhetorical invention for the instruction of man.

4. The metaphorical, as where Dante makes the wood speak in *Inferno* xiii.

5. The allegorical: the word 'Jerusalem' which historically is a city on earth, is allegorically the militant city of God. In an allegory one fact is to be understood through the medium of another.

6. The typological or moral understanding, when we direct our words to form morals, when through one action, another is pointed out as to be done. In this sense, 'Jerusalem' means the faithful soul.

7. The anagogic or spiritual, as when 'Jerusalem' means the Church triumphant in heaven. . . .

Some things cannot be understood literally without falling into error. What man of sound mind would believe that Dante actually went to those places and saw such acts except figuratively? The literal sense is not the figure, but that which is figured. When we read 'the hand of God,' we do not understand that God has hands but we understand God's operative power.

28. This belief in a double world, when it tends to the depreciation of the world of sense, is not far from Gnosticism.

29. Before Philo examined persons and things of the Old Testament as tropes of the soul and tried to prove that Greek philosophical ideas underlay the Testament there was an already established tradition of allegorical interpretation—stemming partly from the Stoic rules for the study of Homer and partly from Jewish haggadic exegesis.

30. Auerbach's idea of mimesis—figural representation—has had a great influence on recent Dante criticism and scholarship in this country. It is for the most part a healthy influence, reviving the importance of certain qualities of Dante's literary art that had fallen into the background. Auerbach has done a good work of synthesis without the particularization needed for Dante himself. Auerbach makes Dante a link between the figural interpretation of the Scriptures by the Church Fathers and the great vein of European realism, part popular and part literary. This is true enough, but Dante's uniqueness needs to be refined and restated after establishing these connections. His unique aim, form, and other major poetic aspects still need an accounting after *figura* has made its contribution.

31. Translated by Grandgent in *Dante,* pp. 255-6.

32. Gregory the Great justified the polysemous method by the effect on the hearer:

> First we lay the foundations in history; then by following a symbolical sense, we erect an intellectual edifice to be a stronghold of faith; and lastly, by the grace of moral instruction, we as it were paint the fabric in fair colors. . . . For the word of God both exercises the understanding of the wise by its deeper mysteries, and also by its superficial lessons nurses the simple-minded. It presents openly that wherewith the little ones may be fed; it keeps in secret that whereby men of loftier range may be rapt in admiration.

It was also Gregory who said that allegory 'is the device (*machina*) by which the soul is lifted to God.'

33. The literal statement is the immediate poetic replica of the experience—of the thing, the fact, the event that embodies and contains all the allegorical meanings. It is as though the poet himself realized the allegorical senses at a later moment than the direct expression of his feelings; the allegorical senses are consistent, or tell a connected story, not because he has in advance worked them out this way but because the experience-level itself (the literal level) is issuing from a tightly unified and consistent understanding-cum-feeling of the world.

34. Allegory is nearly absent from the great pageants of the Earthly Paradise. Here the literal meaning itself has turned into symbol: if there is any allegory at this point it is simply a reading of the symbols.

35. In *Commedia—Elements of Structure,* pp. 89 and 91-3.

36. A side-issue here, but one that may be decisive for this question of literal-and-allegorical, is the possible absence of one or the other of these senses. Aquinas often speaks of what we must call an absence of the literal level in a Biblical text—that is, the first sense of it must be, for one reason or another—a metaphor or one of the allegorical senses. For instance in the *Summa con. gen.,* III, 51 he says:

> This immediate vision of God is promised to us in Holy Scripture (1 *Cor.* xiii, 12): *We see now through a glass in a dark manner; but then face to face.* It would be impious to understand this in a material way, and imagine a material face in the Godhead; for we have proved that God is not a body. . . . we have proved that the divine substance cannot be seen by the intellect by means of any created species. Therefore, if God's essence is to be seen at all, it must be that the intellect sees it through the divine essence itself; so that in that vision the divine essence is both the object and the medium of vision.

Then, in *Monarchia,* Book III, chapter 4, Dante, while saying that the allegorical sense of a text may be very hard to find, comes close to saying that it may actually have none.

37. Geoffrey L. Bickersteth, *op. cit.,* pp. 36-7, amplifies a suggestion made by Gilson in order to pin this practical purpose down to the life of Dante himself:

> The *Divine Comedy,* as Professor Gilson not long ago reminded us [in *Dante the Philosopher,* p. 66], is both literally and symbolically a poem of penitence. Dante fell in love, chivalrously, with Beatrice when they were both very young, and his love for her did two things which were really one. It made him a poet and it made him truly virtuous. In other words, because he loved her he idealised, indeed, deified her and by so doing, that is, by means of poetry, he found salvation morally. But not long after her death he forgot her, fell into dissolute habits, and, had not he or, poetically speaking, had not she recalled her image to his mind just in time, or, in other words, had he not been made to realise by their contrast with that image the heinous character of his sins, he would have been lost without retrieve. The image or vision of her was heaven, that of his sins was hell. This poetry, in the shape of these two images, saved him again, and this time finally.

38. Gilson (*Spirit of Med. Phil.,* p. 447) provides a valuable note on the word 'analogy':

> The concept of analogy is one of those that offer the greatest difficulty to the modern reader of a mediaeval treatise; the mediaeval thinkers themselves were far from agreement as to its definition, and even St. Thomas does not seem to have attempted a full elucidation. We may regard it as having two functions, the one unitive, the other separative. An analogue is always drawn towards its principle in virtue of being an analogue, and at the same time departs from its principle in virtue of being no more than an analogue. . . .
> Without the doctrine of analogy the identification of God and being leads to pantheism.

39. 'Symbol' comes from a word which in one of its senses meant a watchword, or a password in a military camp. In early Christianity, a 'symbol' was a sign or test of membership in the Church.

'Allegory' as Dante derives it, comes from *'alleon-legein':* a reading other [than that which is written].

In both terms, then, there is a flavor of the secret password, of a significance or operation available only to the initiate.

40. The symbolic interpreter often seems to aim at stripping a work of 'nonessentials': developments of ideas, transformations of persons,

shifting and merging images—these and the like are cast aside in the search for 'what the poem is really about.'

Luigi Valli probably represents the final reduction of this hunt for symbols. An article, 'Il simbolo centrale della "Divina Commedia": *La Croce e l'Aquila*' (1921), was followed by *Il Segreto della Croce e dell'Aquila nella Divina Commedia* (1922) and then by *La Chiave della Divina Commedia* (1925).

His thesis is presented in the article (in *Il Giornale dantesco,* vol. xxiv [1921], pp. 11-30):

> In all the most characteristically symbolic passages of the *Divine Comedy* this idea is presented in wondrous variety of form: the Cross and the Eagle are both necessary to free man from the infirmity of original sin and to lead him to a state of felicity.

In the last of these three works—the Key to the Divine Comedy—Valli goes methodically, canto by canto, through the poem to show that each motive moment is reducible either to a cross-symbol or to an eagle-symbol: Church and Empire constantly oppose one another and yet cooperate in the long struggle to redeem man from sin and raise him to bliss.

41. Professor Singleton says something like this of the *Vita Nuova*—it is even more applicable to the *Comedy* (*Essay on the Vita Nuova,* p. 7):

> The circle refers to the fact that we know of the death of Beatrice at the beginning of the *Vita Nuova* and again at the end.
>
> By this same circle the poet who is her lover, and whose Book of Memory that is, becomes as it were two persons, distinguishable according to the principle of time so established. He is the protagonist of the action, moving forward along the line of events in their first occurrence. And then he is that same person who, having lived through all these happenings, looks back upon them and sees their meaning now as it was not possible for him to do at the time. As the first of these persons he knows nothing before it happens. But as one reading in a book of memory he knows the end, the middle, and the beginning of all that happened. This situation in time by which the poet becomes two persons is of first importance to the existence of this story as a form. For by that principle a *then* and a *now* are established for the whole action and, between those two poles of time, meaning jumps like a spark. Without this condition in time we cannot have this story. How, for instance, without this protagonist as he first was, knowing nothing of the end, could the death of Beatrice break in upon this story with the dramatic suddenness that it has?

42. These citations from Aquinas bear on the question of evil and sin.

That God permits evil to happen in this world he governs does not derogate from his goodness. In the first place, divine Providence does not change the natures of things out of recognition, but respects them. The perfection of the universe requires that some should be indefectible, while others should suffer changes according to their nature. Were evil swept away entirely, divine Providence could not regenerate and restore the integrity of things, and this would be a greater evil than the particular ills they suffer.

Secondly, gain to one is loss to another: coming to be spells dying away. The lion must eat, so the kid is killed; the patience of the just supposes persecution from the unjust. Take away all evil, and much good would go with it. God's care is to bring good out of the evils which happen, not to abolish them. Thirdly, goodness is set off by particular evils; bright colours are edged and emphasized by shade. (*Compendium Theologiae,* 142.) (Gilby.)

Evil denotes the absence of Good. But it is not every absence of good that is called *evil.* For absence of good can be understood either in a privative sense or in a purely negative sense. And absence of good in the latter sense is not evil. . . . Otherwise it would follow that a thing is evil if it lacks the good which belongs to something else. For instance, man would be evil because he lacks the swiftness of a wild goat or the strength of a lion. It is absence of good in the privative sense which is called evil. (*Summa Th.,* Ia, 48, 3.)

Aquinas gives demons a definite role in the sins of men. Not only did man's first sin come, but sins of men thereafter have come, by the devil's causation; the other causes of sin are 'free choice and the corruption of the flesh.' The various aspects of the devil's relations to sin are treated in the five articles of *Summa Theologiae* I, 114.

The distinction between mortal and venial sins is described by Aquinas at *Summa Th.,* I-II, 72, art. 5:

. . . he who by sinning turns away from his last end, if we consider the nature of his sin, falls irreparably, and therefore is said to sin mortally and to deserve eternal punishment. But when a man sins without turning away from God, by the very nature of his sin his disorder can be repaired, because the principle of the order is not destroyed; and therefore he is said to sin venially, because, namely, he does not sin so as to deserve to be punished eternally.

CHAPTER TWO

1. Michele Barbi (*Life of Dante,* trans. Paul G. Ruggiers, Berkeley, 1954) attractively summarizes this tone of the *Purgatory* and relates it to the preponderance of direct aesthetic concerns in this canticle. He says (p. 78):

> The poet himself, as though stimulated by the beauty of the place, delights in recreating that world of art for which he was especially molded by nature and in re-evoking the memories of his happier years. How many artists there are in this second canticle: Casella, Belacqua, Sordello, Oderisi, Statius, Bonagiunta, Guido Guinizelli, and Arnaut Daniel. What long discourses are held between Virgil and Statius about art and the creatures they have immortalized, while Dante follows them, listening to the conversations which give him 'an intellectual understanding of poetry.' We might say that Purgatory itself wishes to contribute to the glory of art, presenting, in one of its circles, a new kind of art beyond ordinary human skill which the astonished poet tries to describe in words: the bas-reliefs, which were a 'speech made visible,' and whilst seen in profile, 'the dead seemed dead and the living seemed alive.'
>
> In no other canticle are the emotions so sweetly expressed. . . . Even Statius, in the final act of mounting wholly purified to Heaven, would consent to postpone the blessed vision of God another year for the sight of Virgil.

2. At the beginning of canto 2 of the *Paradise* Dante provides a resolution for this image of the little ship:

> *O you who in your little ships,*
> *desiring to hear, have followed*
> *behind my keel that sings as it goes,*
>
> *turn to regain your own shores:*
> *do not commit yourselves to the sea; for perhaps,*
> *losing me, you would remain lost.*

We, the readers who are presumed to have followed the pilgrim through Purgatory in our own little skiffs, are warned against the mazing voyage through Paradise. A relevant ship-image is also found at the opening of the second treatise of the *Convivio.*

Between the ship-images at the beginnings of the two canticles, comes one in which the pilgrim himself becomes a ship drawn swiftly over the waters of the river Lethe. At canto 31.94-6, Matelda, he says,

. . . had drawn me into the river up to my neck,
and, pulling me after her, moved along
over the water, light as a shuttle.

3. Aristotle is probably the source of this concept. He stated that space would attain perfection if each point in it could be in all points at once: motion is the means of trying to achieve this goal.

Dante explicitly states the correlation between speed and virtue in the *Convivio* (II, 4, 69):

I say, further, that in proportion as the heaven is nearer to the equatorial circle, it is more noble in comparison to its poles; because it hath more movement, and more actuality, and more life, and more form, and it touches more of the one which is above it, and by consequence hath more virtue.

4. The most important part of Cato's admonition (1.97-9) is that the pilgrim's eyes be cleansed of any mist. The importance of clean sight is an image, or theme, that runs through the entire *Commedia* and is, perhaps most important in the *Purgatory*. The theme of cleansing is of course essential to the idea of purgation, but not until we reach the Earthly Paradise is the cleansing again of so simple a soap-and-water variety as this.

5. This is a sampling of views on Cato.

Giovanni Busnelli (*La Concezione del purgatorio dantesco,* Roma, 1906), p. 36:

The representatives [of Adam and Eve] and of the entire human family [on Purgatory] are two noble personages, Cato and Matelda; one is the guardian of Antepurgatory, in whose bailiwick are purged the souls of the seven realms or terraces (cf. *Purg.* 1.65-6, 82) of Purgatory proper; the other is the inhabitant and guardian of the terrestrial paradise. Both are outside the actual place of expiation, the man at the base of the sacred mountain, the woman at its summit.

(P. 36-9) . . . Cato represents man in his perfection . . . seems to be a renewed Adam, and is the antagonist of the immobile Old Man of Crete, symbol of corrupt human nature. . . . By the Old Man of Crete one descends into the Inferno; by the honest old man of Purgatory one mounts through the gate of St. Peter to Paradise.

. . . Within the freedom of the will, according to Richard of St. Victor, is comprised all the grandeur and the dignity of man, and herein consists all his likeness to God . . . Consequently Cato, representing man in his perfection, is a pure symbol of the perfection of free will, as it was established by God in man.

Benedetto Croce (*The Poetry of Dante,* trans. Douglas Ainslie, N. Y., 1922), p. 155:

Cato is the character by which the poet gives actuality to one of the sides of his ethical ideal. He is rigid rectitude, the fulfilment of lofty duty, which it seems cannot be achieved and cannot act upon others so as to make them also realize it, without a certain roughness, without the habit of a certain degree of reticence and diffidence on the part of one who is constantly watching himself and others.

Mario Casella, 'Interpretazioni—I. La figura Simbolice di Catone' in *Stud. Dant.* 28 (1949). 183-95, says at p. 187:

Cato represents the nobility of a soul internally aligned with God, spontaneously fixed on the means that will direct it to its proper end, by virtue of the reason that illumines it . . . But this liberty of practice, which increases and grows stronger in us to the extent that a life of reason and of moral virtue dominates the life of the senses or of the passions, this liberty demands a positive law to protect and defend it, and presupposes in itself a law or ordinance of reason which may or may not lead to a realization of the final end towards which we are essentially directed. This natural law or natural reason, which is directly expressed in us by the voice of our conscience, is inscribed in the very substance of our being, and in the created analogue of the divine creative reason which ordained itself in the act of creating. Thereby is fulfilled in us the function which Virgil fulfills in respect to Dante: the function of 'pedagogue' . . . and its terminus is the fulness of liberty, the enfranchising from all servitude and ultimately from all servitude to law. [This is the process initiated by the meeting with Cato.]

6. If Cato does not belong in the Inferno with—or near—the arch-traitors Brutus and Cassius who slew Caesar, or if he does not belong among those punished for suicide, his place would seem at best to be in Limbo among the other virtuous heathen. Line 90 seems to indicate that this had been his place, presumably until the Harrowing of Hell by Christ.

Cato is perhaps the most controversial figure in the *Purgatory*—if we may still use the word 'controversial' to refer to arguments and debates that have already been written down. The views about Cato range from shock that a pagan should be found here to a confident—and rather frequently expressed—identification of Cato with God the Father. This is based on *Convivio* IV, 5, 28. Virgil's speech in lines 74-5 seems to indicate that Cato is destined for Paradise after the Last Judgment. Perhaps; but even apart from Virgil's intent to cajole in this speech we must realize that he does not speak with full authority in Purgatory.

D'Ovidio says, *op. cit.*, pp. 58-9, that Cato died for political liberty, while the liberty for which the poet made his ultramundane voyage was peace of mind, dominion over his passions, purification of his passions (cf. *Par.* 31.85 and 89). Yet the suicide of Cato suggested a species of transfiguration, in which his search for liberty took on an appearance not greatly dissimilar from the spiritual liberty Dante was seeking.

7. *Monarchia* (II, 13) says that 'if the Roman Empire did not exist by right, the sin of Adam was not punished in Christ.' Aquinas also touches this point: 'One difference between Christ and other men is this: they do not choose when to be born, but he, the Lord and Maker of history, chose his time, his birthplace, and his mother.'

8. Grandgent (*PMLA* 17.1) demonstrates that Dante had originally intended to use Elijah as the guardian of Purgatory and that many traits of the Old Testament prophet were attached to Cato.

9. The question of Cato's ultimate destination has stimulated much scholarship. The majority view is presented by d'Ovidio, *op. cit.*, p. 83:

> And yet for Cato the case is quite simple. The salvation of this pagan [d'Ovidio assumes with Virgil that Cato is destined for Paradise at the Last Judgment] is such an anomaly, such a singular act of grace, that, without anticipating any other consideration, the singularity of this grace is matched by the singularity of the long wait.

This is the sort of not-quite-convincing sophistry that is provoked by the unanswered questions in the *Commedia:* the destiny of Cato and of Matelda, the prophecies about the greyhound, and the five-hundred-ten-and-five. However, d'Ovidio's discussion of Cato and of the many problems he arouses is probably the most brilliant and the most satisfying of all such discussions. See especially *op. cit.*, pp. 85-115.

On Dante's earlier use of Cato see *Mon.* II, 8: this passage is important but not decisive for Dante's ideas when it came time to write the *Purgatory*. On the general question of good pagans, damned or saved, see *Par.* 19.40-111.

On the question of why Antepurgatory needs a guardian, Aquinas may throw some light in dealing with the related question, 'Whether man was placed in Paradise to work and guard it' (*Summa Theol.*, I, 102, 3). Objection 2 of this article states: '. . . there is no need of a guardian when there is no fear of trespass with violence. Therefore there was no need for man to guard paradise.' The reply to this includes the sentence: 'Nor would man have guarded paradise against a trespasser;

but he would have striven to guard paradise for himself lest he should lose it by sin.'

10. Dorothy Sayers has some perceptive comments on Dante as dramatist. She says (*Purgatory,* p. 27):

> When we examine the structure of these concluding cantos of *Purgatory,* it is more than ever evident that we are in the hands of a born dramatist. Had he lived at a time when drama was the dominant form, the plays of Dante might be holding the stage to this day. His work has all the marks: the solid planting and setting of a dramatic action; the brisk economy of the dialogue; the instinctive avoidance of scenic incongruities; the sure recognition of the *scène-à-faire;* the knack of relieving a situation with a touch of high comedy; the ability to establish character in a line or two; the rejection of ramblings and embroideries; the knowledge of when to stop. It is this compact and sinewy quality in his narrative which holds the reader's attention. Other medieval poems delight by their surface texture; his, by its architecture.

11. D'Ovidio sees the two pagans somewhat differently without, however, negating my point about the inappropriateness of Virgil's manner under these circumstances. He says, *op. cit.,* p. 71:

> With a highly refined gentility, delicate and discreet, he proves himself here to be the same Virgil, sweet, insinuating, genteel and modest, that all his biographers depict and that his own poetry demonstrates. His elegant discourse, befitting a friend of Augustus, . . . By contrast Cato is always the severe one, immovable, the liege single-minded to his duty, as he is described by Lucan and others.

12. A similar and even more striking detail occurs at line 16. Here, in the parenthetical prayer to see this light again, Dante appears not in two but in three guises at least: as the pilgrim experiencing this feeling, as the poet aware of the rightness of such a detail, and as the man (in this sense embracing both pilgrim and poet) having everyman's wish at this point. It is perhaps curious that the wish to see this light once more is not directly connected with the experience of being a passenger on this boat; ordinarily such a passenger would have moved on before the next boatload's approach. Perhaps this is an early indication that a most important keynote of Antepurgatory is a dilatoriness towards duty.

13. That this kind of dallying is especially wrong in Purgatory, against the firm law of the mountain, is a lesson soon learned by Virgil. For the

remainder of the canticle we see him hurrying the pilgrim along at every opportunity.

CHAPTER THREE

1. Aristotle, *Ethics* iv.9:

> It seems too that the high-minded man will be slow in his movements, his voice will be deep and his manner of speaking sedate; for it is not likely that a man will be in a hurry, if there are not many things that he cares for, or that he will be emphatic, if he does not regard anything as important, and these are the causes which make people speak in shrill tones and use rapid movements.

Carroll, quoting this passage, comments (*Prisoners of Hope,* pp. 37-8):

> The chief interest of the words . . . is that they are characteristic of Dante's own temperament. His friend and neighbor the historian Giovanni Villani describes him as 'somewhat haughty, reserved, and disdainful, after the fashion of a philosopher'; and haughty and reserved men almost invariably have Dante's feeling that haste mars their dignity. It is an infirmity of temperament which he outgrows. Here at the Mountain foot his personal dignity is more to him than the purifying of his soul; but by the time he has climbed to the Fourth Terrace he has learnt that there is a haste without which there is no true dignity at all. . . . In the *Paradiso* he learns that the Angelic circles wheel round God with a swiftness which is in the exact measure of their love and service. In short, the dignity which counts itself harmed by haste is often only another name for sloth.

2. Virgil's inadequacy as a guide is foreshadowed in a number of places in the *Inferno.* The clearest of these is probably at the entrance to the City of Dis, at the end of canto 8 and the beginning of canto 9. Here Virgil falters, steps back, starts to say one thing and finishes another; is in 'doubt about the outcome,' longs for help. Perhaps it is also revealing that when the Furies threaten to call Medusa his only recourse (whether right or wrong) is to ensure that the pilgrim shut his eyes to the danger.

3. This problem is the most hotly, and most intelligently, contested question in Dante studies of the past century. Nevertheless, fashions here too may be discerned: in our own day symbolism and realism are more fashionable than allegory—hence the simplist equations, already mentioned in chapter 1, Virgil = Reason, Beatrice = Theology, etc.

4. The difference between symbolism and allegory has already been discussed in chapter 1, but may perhaps be thus simplified here: in both, when 'A' is said, 'B' is meant. In symbolism the 'A' always means the same thing in a given work, regardless of the context. The symbol may be traditional or, less frequently, may have been invented for the occasion. In allegory the 'B'—the thing intended—is the fixed thing and may be represented by anything the writer chooses, so long as the context makes his intention clear.

The symbolist is primarily interested in exploring the ramifications of the symbol (the 'A') to the extent that they illuminate the 'B.' The allegorist is primarily interested in the message he is trying to promulgate in a form which will make it alive and pertinent to his readers. Allegory is not necessarily a simplification of complex abstractions (though very often it is): it is rather a reaching down of moral and spiritual concepts into details that are like those of daily life.

5. Dante (at *Inf.* 19.124-33) takes pains to refute the popular view of Virgil as magician. In approaching the Bolgia that houses the diviners and sorcerers, Virgil is able not only to walk placidly over a narrow archway but is able to carry the pilgrim in his arms over 'the rough steep cliff which would be a painful passage even to the goats.'

The historical, as distinguished from the medieval, Virgil expected the redeemer to come from Rome, not from the East. He probably had the concept of the redeemer from one or more of these: Josephus, *Bell. Jud.* vii, 31; Tacitus, *Hist.* v, 13; Suetonius, *Vesp.* c. 4; or Dio Cassius, lxvi.

6. Professor Hatzfeld, in his article on 'The Art of Dante's Purgatorio,' discusses this point. He says, p. 38:

If some critics wonder why Virgil, the pagan, has such high powers as Dante's guide, one may conclude from the text that he, who practically led Statius and others to Heaven, is also capable of guiding Dante at least to Beatrice and to 'crown and miter' him (xxvii, 142). . . . Upon other occasions he assumes strictly sacerdotal attitudes, such as teaching (xii, 84) and imparting blessings (xxvii, 142).

The situation of a pagan, such as Virgil, guiding a Christian, Dante, leads poetically to the development of the motif of the blind leader. Virgil who must show the way to Dante does not know the way himself. Although he finds the wide road, he does not discern the narrow gates. Therefore he must ask continually, first Cato, later the angels and the souls, what path to take in this strange 'cloister of charity' (xv.57).

We may note that all the qualities and accomplishments here attributed to 'Virgil' are those invented for him by Dante.

Charles Williams (*The Figure of Beatrice,* pp. 146-7) discusses Virgil as guide through Purgatory in a way which carries formal aestheticism to a certain kind of irresponsible extreme.

Virgil is still the leading mind. It might have been thought that Beatrice would now take charge, but it is not so; and there are good poetic reasons. The first is that we had better not have too much of Beatrice. The poetic problem of dealing with Beatrice in the heavens is going to be difficult enough; we must not become accustomed to her too soon. The second is that it had in a sense been done. The discussion of Beatrice (or, more accurately, of her and of the Lady of the Window) in the *Convivio* is much like this journey; for her to lead through the *Purgatorio* would have been too much of a repetition. Thirdly, the re-establishment of her full supernatural validity is to be kept for Dante's purified mind. It is when he can see the Images clearly that he is to see her again. . . . The fourth reason was mentioned above; it is that Beatrice is herself the mountain. She is, as so many of her sisters have been to their lovers, the means by which purification takes place.

7. Dorothy Sayers (*Purgatory,* p. 93) provides a clear explanation of the *quia:*

Aristotle, and, following him, the schoolmen, distinguish between two kinds of demonstration: (1) the knowledge *that* a thing is, obtained by arguing *a posteriori,* from effect to cause: this is the demonstration *quia;* (2) the knowledge *why* a thing is as it is, obtained by arguing *a priori,* from cause to effect: this is the demonstration *propter quid.* In this life, finite minds cannot (11.32-6) know God as He is (in His quiddity), but only by His effects; and must therefore be content to know only the *quia* of His mysterious Providence.

But we must understand the complexity of 'in this life' for Dante's poem. Dante, while writing *in this life,* is utilizing the dramatic device of writing as though having experienced *the life to come.*

8. Vernon arrives at a similar conclusion though starting from a different point. (*Readings in the Purgatorio,* 1.94):

If God had wished man to know everything, He would not have forbidden our first parents to touch the Tree of Knowledge of Good and Evil. If they had not disobeyed, the human race would not have been doomed, and there would have been no need of the Incarnation of Christ and the Redemption of Man.

9. Although Dante often seems to take it upon himself to decide who is damned and who is saved, he has theological support at least for one's chances of being rescued from seemingly certain damnation. Aquinas (*Compendium Theologiae,* 145) had said:

> Divine justice does not treat men who still have their course to run as though they had finished. Only when their life is over can human beings remain fast in evil: inalterableness and immobility mark the end of a process. All our present life is a condition of flux. We are always traveling and never in the state of having arrived—our thorough restlessness bears this out, and every vicissitude of mind and body. That we should stick in our sins is certainly not to be expected from the way divine Providence works in the world.

We shall soon see an application of this doctrine in the last-moment rescues of Manfred and of Buonconte da Montefeltro.

10. For some reason the poet leaves some doubt as to whether Manfred is the 'leader of the fortunate flock.' He is identified, when he begins to speak, merely as 'one of them' (line 103); and there may be some contradiction between the description of the leader as 'modest in countenance' (line 87) and that of Manfred as 'of noble aspect.'

Carroll (*op. cit.,* p. 45) thus quotes from a book review by Edward Moore; Dr. Moore said:

> In the annals of that great family there is no name surrounded by such a halo of tragic interest—not even that of the great Frederick himself, unapproachable as he is in the loftiness of his genius and character—as that of Manfred, 'il bello e biondo,' whom his rough soldiers, whether Saracen or Norman, loved with almost feminine enthusiasm; whose name still lives in the traditional folk-lore of the uninstructed peasants of 'the land of Manfred'; whose tragic fate has inspired one of the most touching and splendid episodes in the divine poem of Dante.

11. The Church had identified this doctrine of two souls as part of the Manichean heresy; Aquinas refutes the Platonic (or pseudo-Platonic) theory in the *Summa Theol.* I, 76, art. 3 (see also I, 118, art. 2). We should note, however, that while Dante is here on the side of orthodoxy he bases his stand not on authority or theology but on his own experiences, the most immediate poetic criterion.

This doctrine of the single illumination and focus of the soul (ascending and growing clearer as the soul develops) is of course as important to Dante as it had been to Plato. Some light may be cast on this passage by Statius' discussion of the growth of the soul in canto 25. It is interesting that both these passages are associated with an image referring to ripe grapes and wine: 25.76-8 and 4.19-21.

CHAPTER FOUR

1. A modern social psychologist might make much of figures like Buonconte, Sordello, and Cunizza: these are lonely people, pushed aside by father, wife, husband, or brother. The dislocation of their family lives traps them in wider and wider social dislocations.

2. Dante fought on the other side in this very battle. See also *Inf.* 21.94-6.

3. It was widely believed in the Middle Ages that the soul of man is the great prize for which the powers of Heaven and Hell wage endless warfare. Of this warfare, medieval painting is full. See also *Inf.* 31.55-7.

> The full significance of Buonconte's salvation comes out only when set alongside the perdition of his father, Count Guido of Montefeltro, in Canto XXVII of the *Inferno*. . . . On the approach of old age he . . . made his peace with the Church, by which he had been several times excommunicated, and joined the Franciscan Order. So secure, indeed, seemed his salvation, that St. Francis himself came to meet his soul at death as one of his Cordeliers. 'One of the Black Cherubim,' however, appeared and successfully disputed his claim: ever since he gave the fraudulent advice to Pope Boniface, the demon had been 'at his hair.'—Carroll, *op. cit.,* p. 70.

4. In reference to *Purg.* 6, 26-7, Carroll says (p. 79):

> These words . . . suggest the conception of prayer held by Dante . . . If one is not mistaken, he indicates four distinct gradations in the power of prayer. The lowest stage is that of the souls before us. They have lost the power of prayer even for themselves, not to speak of others. Their whole conception of prayer is low and selfish, for that is certainly what Dante means by comparing them to parasites hanging onto the winner in a game of hazard. When we reach the Valley of the Princes, we shall find the souls there able to pray for themselves, but, so far as appears, for themselves alone. It is only when we get inside the Gate of Purgatory proper that we find spirits so far advanced in the unselfish life that they can pray for others as well as for themselves. . . . Finally, when Paradise is reached, the power of prayer is perfectly regained and so purified of every taint of selfishness that the saints pray only for others, as St. Bernard did for Dante.

CHAPTER FIVE

1. Charles Speroni's article on 'Dante's Prophetic Morning Dreams' (*Studies in Philology* XLV, 50-9), provides the following information: *The Divine Comedy* has seven allusions to morning-dreams—*Inferno* 26.7-9; 33.26-7, 37-9, 43-5; *Purg*. 9.13-9; 19.1-7; and 27.91-8 (also a reference in the first sonnet of the *Vita Nuova,* and the material in *Conv.* II, 9).

At least twenty-six handbooks were compiled in classical antiquity on the interpretation of dreams. Only one (the most famous) survives—Artemidorus's *Onirocritica.* Artemidorus does not mention morning-dreams but Moschus, Horace, Ovid, Philostratus the Elder, and Tertullian do. Aquinas believed (and had for authority *Job* 33.15-6) that men are instructed in dreams and that divination by dreams is lawful (*Summa Theol.,* II, 95-6).

* * * * *

On the way in which dreams are detached from the senses John of Salisbury (*Polycraticus* II, 14) sums up this doctrine, ultimately Pythagorean, in terms much like those of Dante: 'it comes about that the soul is lifted up above contact with the body that it may turn more freely upon itself and contemplate the truth.'

2. On the question of whether it is punishment, or something other, that the souls in Purgatory feel—see 23.72 and 21.61-6.

On the element of 'satisfaction,' that is, of purgation as the payment of a debt to God, see 11.70, 71, 88, 125; 19.125-6; 23.15; and 25.138-9.

3. A related difference between the sufferings of Hell and those of Purgatory has to do with their predictability. The demons in Hell (wherever they occur) have a good deal of spontaneity and their own brand of free will in their imposition of torments. The pangs of Purgatory are relatively standardized and according to clear rule: the sufferer knows what he is going to endure and, in a sense, for how long—up to the moment when there, on the mountain, he feels free to ascend to the next higher circle or to the Earthly Paradise itself.

Sayers (*Purgatory,* pp. 14-5) treats the differences between Hell and Purgatory as based on both artistic and moral grounds:

> The problem . . . was not how to make Purgatory a 'hell in reverse,' but how to avoid doing so: how to provide the desirable variety and surprise in two long poems whose subjects were so fundamentally similar.

Accordingly, the 'seven-sins' classification which lurks behind Cantos III-VII of the *Inferno* was discarded (if indeed it was ever really contemplated) and the classification into sins of Incontinence, Violence, and Fraud adopted in its place. The victims of Lust, Gluttony, Avarice, and Wrath already dealt with were relegated to the suburbs of Upper Hell, and the nether abyss was opened up behind the barriers of Pride . . . On the other hand this plan may have been intended from the start . . . It has the . . . great advantage that the use of two distinct systems of classification emphasizes the essential difference between Hell and Purgatory: in the former, *acts of sin* produce their cumulative effects, the soul remaining at the lowest point of degradation to which it has unrepentantly willed to descend; in the latter, the *stain of sinfulness* is cleansed, the penitent soul shedding off successively all those imperfections which cling to it against its better will. Hell is concerned with the fruits, but Purgatory with the roots, of sin.

4. Dante clarifies the function of these 'checks' in a lecture given to the pilgrim by Beatrice in the Heaven of Mercury. Here (*Par.* 7.25-7) she describes the fall of man:

> *Through not enduring for his own good*
> *a check* [freno] *upon his power of will* . . .

Dante probably had in mind a use of this term such as is exemplified in Augustine (*Op. imperf. c. Jul.* 70): 'The schoolmen named that supernatural grace of original justice which subjected the senses to the reason, *frenum concupiscentiae*—check on desire.'

5. Even the sins had changed since the early Church Fathers. Tertullian, at the beginning of the third century, listed the 'seven deadly sins' as 'idolatry, blasphemy, murder, adultery, fornication, false witness, and fraud.'

Of great importance for Dante's ideas of sin are the statements of Thomas Aquinas. Here are some clarifying examples:

Sin, the direct opposite of an act of virtue, is a disordered activity: vice, the direct opposite of virtue, is the condition of a thing out of its proper natural bearings. *Summa Theol.,* 1a-2ae. lxxxi. 1 (Gilby).

The division of sin into mortal and venial sins is not like the division of a genus into two species; they are not specifically different kinds of sin, determined by the objects to which they turn. The difference between mortal and venial sin is decided by the stage reached by the disordered turning away from God: it is here that sinfulness is brought to a head.

Two degrees of disorder may be marked. One turns the whole order upside down; the other leaves the principles intact, but muddles the details and subordinate pattern. The balance of health may be so utterly wrecked that life is destroyed; or it may be upset so as to cause sickness, but not death. The final purpose of life is the key to the moral order; our last end in practice may be compared to the first principles of reason in theory. When our acts are so deranged that we turn away from our last end, namely God, to whom we should be united by charity, then the sin is mortal. Short of that, the sin is venial. *Summa Theol.,* 1a-2ae. lxxii. 5 (Gilby).

There are two sides to every sin, the turning to transient satisfaction and the turning away from everlasting value. As regards the first, the principle of all sins can be called lust—lust in its more general sense, namely, the unbridled desire for one's own pleasure. As regards the second, the principle is pride, pride in its general sense, the lack of submission to God: *the beginning of pride is man's revolt from God.* Lust and pride in this pervasive sense are not called capital sins, because as such they are not special sins: they are the roots and sprouts of vice, as the desire for happiness is the root of all virtue. Disputations, viii *de Malo,* 1, *ad* 1 (Gilby).

One sin can be dependent on another in two ways: first, because of purely personal foible; second, because of its nature. The first connexion is merely of biographical interest, whereas the typological classification of capital sins looks rather to stock purposes; those, therefore, are called capital sins which are centred on certain key-points round which lesser purposes cluster.

They are arranged according to the special types of good which attract them and which repel them. The attractions are psychological, physical, and economic. *Pride* and *vainglory* come from wanting to be held in high honour and glory, and from preening oneself in the imagination. *Gluttony* comes from individual high living, *lust* from sexuality inborn to serve the race, *avarice* from the gathering of wealth. The repulsions are about good things wrongfully regarded as threatening our own proper good, and which, therefore, are grieved about or actively combatted. Spiritual values menace our physical pleasure, hence *accidie* or boredom, a sadness about spiritual good. *Envy* is similar; it resents another's good qualities because they lower our own self-esteem. To flare out at them is *anger*. Disputations, viii *de Malo,* 1 (Gilby).

Seven reasons for blindness, and seven sins. Here is a comparison—a swollen head, and this is pride; an overcast day, and this is envy; cross-eyed squinting, and this is anger; dust and grit, and this is avarice; heavy puffy lids, and this is sloth; congested veins, and this is gluttony; spots before the eyes, and this is lechery. *Sunday Sermons,* 38 (Gilby).

6. This passage has puzzled the commentators. Some, with reluctance, accept the rocks as actually moving. Others offer a variety of farfetched explanations. Permit me to offer a simple one.

The cleft that Virgil speaks of is what mountaineers call a chimney. If it is narrow enough one must mount or descend it à la Santa Claus. This one is considerably greater in diameter but jagged. If one were to draw a simplified cross section of it and start the pilgrims at X, it seems obvious that the only way to ascend is by the path indicated by arrows—in other words, always seeking the part of the curve that recedes from one and avoiding the part that advances towards one.

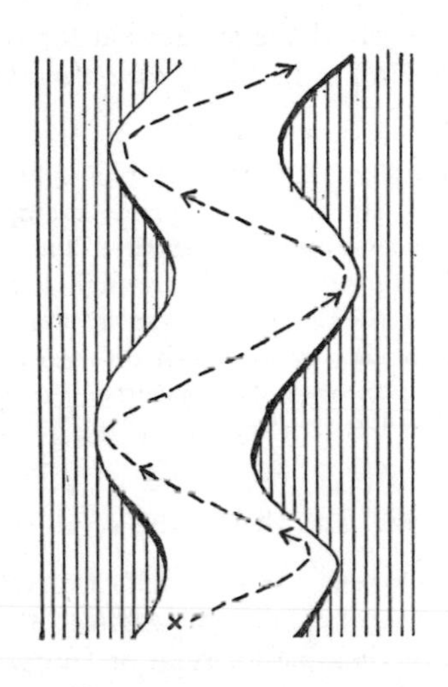

7. Carroll (*op. cit.*, pp. 153-5) quotes from Moore's *Studies in Dante* (2nd Series, pp. 251-8) to indicate the schematic arrangement of check and goad on the various terraces:

(1) 'Examples of the *Virtue* are found at the *beginning* of each *Cornice,* and those of *Vice* at the *end.*' . . .

(2) 'There is a studied correspondence between the numbers of these examples,'—that is, the numbers of 'scourge' and 'bridle.' . . .

(3) 'Sacred and profane instances are balanced and interchanged.' . . .

(4) 'The manner of their presentment is different on every *Cornice,* but each virtue and its related vice are similarly presented.' The modes are as follows:

I. Terrace of Pride—sculptures on the marble pavement and embankment.
II. Of Envy—voices in the air.
III. Of Anger—visions of the imagination.
IV. Of Sloth—voices of the penitents themselves.
V. Of Avarice—voices of the penitents, proclaiming examples of Liberality by day, and of Avarice by night.
VI. Of Gluttony—voices out of Trees representing Temperance and Intemperance.
VII. Of Sensuality—the two classes of the Sensual proclaim alternately in hymns and greetings examples of chastity and 'Luxury.'

8. Dante may have derived the suggestion for this function of Mary from Bonaventure's *Speculum Beatae Mariae Virginis*. Here, in lecture 4, he would have read:

Mary is most fittingly called the virgin so pious. For she is Mary who is not only devoid of every sin but also a prime example of every virtue. In short, it is Mary who was most immune from the seven capital sins. For Mary was most deeply opposed to pride through her humility; most effectively opposed to envy through her charity; firmest against anger through her gentleness; most staunchly against sloth through her industry; Mary was strongest against avarice through her poverty; she was most temperately against gluttony through her sobriety; Mary was most chastely against lust through her virginity.

Dante, we should also see, uses these same seven sins in the same order.

9. Were the craftsman's hand the rule itself of carving, he could not carve the wood otherwise than rightly; but if the rightness of carving depends upon another rule, then the carving may be right or faulty. *Summa Theol.*, I, 63, 1). (Pegis.)

Aquinas here, indirectly, provides a basis for understanding this perfection of God-as-artist, for here the craftsman's hand *is* the very rule of carving.

10. She who 'turned the key to open the exalted love' to mankind (line 42) reveals her feelings as clearly 'as a figure stamped on wax' (line 45). This close association of the 'key' image with the 'wax' image is interesting. In the previous canto we had encountered Peter's gold and silver keys, as the means of entry to Purgatory—that is, entry upon the individual journey-process which will end in the attainment of 'the exalted love.'

The wax-and-seal image becomes increasingly important as we go through the Purgatory. The image may have originated in Bonaventure's solution to the puzzling question of individuality. Matter, said Bonaventure, is common to all bodies, while form is correlative with the universal concept. Individuality, then, must arise from the conjunction of matter with form—matter as though it were wax and form a seal. The wax is not differentiated until it is impressed with a seal.

CHAPTER SIX

1. I might mention here only Gilson's work, as perhaps the most accessible and attractive on this general subject. Other works in my bibliography deal with Dante's relations, not only to such orthodox churchmen as Aquinas, Bonaventure, and Augustine, but also to such suspect or even heretical figures as Siger of Brabant, Joachim of Flora, Averroes, and Avicenna. Yet not all these together account for the philosophical and theological vision that Dante had in writing his poem.

2. These had put faith in backward steps because they were sick in mental vision—and so did not see that their steps were away from rather than towards an intended goal. This blinding by pride is anticipated in the image-fact in which Dante presents his first seeing of these souls: at line 114 we were told that his sight was confused.

3. We may notice here that, although Dante records, in *Par.* IX, that his great-grandfather Allighiero is actually in this Cornice at the time he visits it, yet family pride prevents him from giving any description of his ancestor in so undignified an attitude; but he devotes three whole cantos to his great-great-grandfather Cacciaguida, whom he describes among the Blessed in the Heaven of Mars. He puts into Cacciaguida's mouth the information about Allighiero's penance in Purgatory. Vernon, *Readings in the Purg.*, I, 386 n.

4. Note that at the beginning of this story of a proud one we have the evidence that he has already acquired humility: he had been proud of the greatness of his name, of the fame of his father, yet now he humbly says, 'I do not know if his name was ever known to you.' The 'perhaps' of line 98 may have this same humble function in respect to the poet's greatness.

CHAPTER SEVEN

1. Hanford Henderson, 'Dante's Angel of Humility,' *Italica* XXVIII (1951), 249-50, quotes Oelsner in the Temple Classics edition:

Towards the end of Dante's sojourn on each terrace, he hears one of the Beatitudes from the Sermon on the Mount. In each case, *except the present,* the angel of the respective circle is specifically named as uttering the words . . .

and solves the problem:

Why *should* the Angel of Humility let the chorus take this line? Because he was the Angel of Humility.

2. Although the sin of treason to God—as Satan's guilt is defined in the *Inferno*—was not definitely described there as identical with pride, we must realize from this use of Satan as the prime example of sinful pride that treason is to be taken as fundamentally, if complexly, a wish to displace one's benefactors.

3. In the previous chapter we had noted something of Dante's criterion of excellence in the plastic arts. We meet the same criterion here, at 12.67:

Dead seemed the dead, and the living seemed alive.

On this line Tròccoli comments (*op. cit.,* p. 91): '. . . this is like the new poetic, the timely esthetic canon that Dante helped originate and that he obeyed.'

4. Grandgent, *Dante's Divina Commedia,* Boston 1913, p. 109. Other illustrations might be added: Spenser's Envy is clad in a 'kirtle of discoloured gray' 'ypaynted full of eies' (*Faerie Queene,* Bk. I, canto lv, 31). It is the evil eye of Scripture; and it is written: 'If thine eye be evil, thy whole body shall be full of darkness' (*Matt.* 6.23).

5. According to Bonaventure, the opposite of Envy is Charity. Dante uses this same episode of Mary's loving solicitude as the first example of Temperance, at 22.142-4.

6. Even at their worst Dante's women always remind us of their relation to Mary and Beatrice—they can always direct and control—meekness is no virtue of theirs. Troccoli (*op. cit.,* p. 113) has this to say of Sapia: 'It is certain that the Sapia who here reports on her terrestrial

affairs is transfigured or, better, disfigured in her sinister merriment and in the expectancy and anxiety that yield her no peace.'

7. In the circle of Hypocrites in Hell, *Inferno* 23.94-5, the pilgrim says to the two 'Jovial Friars': '. . . I was born and grew/ On the beautiful river of/ the Arno in the great city.' Possibly this pride in Florence and the Arno is to be explained only in terms of his environment at the moment.

8. In various ways this theme of sharing is one of the most important in the *Comedy*. Man's failure to share, as seen in the realm of Purgatory, is transformed in the course of this canticle to heavenly sharing—the greater the sharing the greater the share for each. (In the next canto, at 14.44 sqq., we see the first step in the transformation.)

The infernal form of this theme is *usura:* not merely that usury is a profanation, or parody, of natural increase, as usually explained, but that increase in *usura* is one man's unilateral profit at the expense of another. Dante, whether right or wrong, saw *usura* (which today is simply the lending of money at interest) as a struggling for things that should rather be shared.

9. Tròccoli characterizes the speech of Guido (*op. cit.*, p. 116):

> Bitter and scourging, sharp and cutting, inexorable and harsh, this voice of Guido del Duca is one of the strongest in the *Divine Comedy,* in its precision and determination less agitated than that of a Brunetto Latini, less dramatic even than that of Cacciaguida because devoid of the philosophical gravity that marks that spirit in the Heaven of Mars.
>
> Guido's is the voice of Greek tragedy narrating the greed at the base of medieval affairs.

10. The rivers of the Purgatory—both those that are told about, as by Buonconte and Guido, and those that we actually meet in the Earthly Paradise—exhibit a mythic profundity and significance that is not exceeded even by the structural use of the Liffey in *Finnegans Wake*.

Dante's rivers seem almost invariably to be associated with ideas of metamorphosis: Buonconte's transformation, Guido's Arno that turns men (Circean-wise) into beasts, Lethe and Eunoe of the Earthly Paradise with the inner transformation effected by each, the Elsa that turns one to stone.

11. Carroll (*op. cit.,* p. 194) quotes Bacon on public or 'political' envy: 'It is a disease in a state like to infection. For as infection spreadeth upon that which is sound, and tainteth it, so when envy is gotten once into

a state, it traduceth even the best actions thereof, and turneth them into an ill odour.'

12. In introducing this reply the pilgrim says (at 15.58-9):

> *'I am more fasting from being satisfied,*
> *. . . than if I had kept silent at first . . .'*

This image, of hunger that increases the more it is satisfied, which might serve as a motto of all intellectual growth, is frequently used by the pilgrim as he makes his journey. Here it comes in as a peculiar counterpart to the goods—intellectual as well as spiritual—that are increased by sharing.

Walter Naumann in an article on 'Hunger und Durst als Metaphern bei Dante' in *Romanische Forschungen* (54.13-36) has made a good collection, organized into classes though with no attempt to generalize about function, of the relevant passages in the *Comedy*.

These images of hunger and thirst are indubitably to be connected with the 'economy of scarcity' which seems to lie at the base of the medieval concepts of, say, envy and gluttony. It may well be that the context of this 'economy of scarcity' is very much broader than these obvious examples—that even Dante's idea of pride (which he finally equates with tendencies toward treason, toward a wish to displace one's superior in rank) is in the same context: there is *not,* in the medieval world, plenty of room at the top.

13. Earlier, at 15.16-18, we had the combination of rays, water (picking this up from the previous canto), and mirror. Virgil's reply brings these three together once more at 15.67-9 and 75; similarly the idea of getting darkness from light (at 15.66) not only continues the theme of the perversion of natural things from canto 14 but also occurs in different form at 15.10-15 and 15.24.

CHAPTER EIGHT

1. 'The angry man sets his imagination to work round and round some slight or wrong, fancied or real, until by brooding on it, he is rapt away by his own inner vision, and loses the power to observe external things. Hence the apostrophe to the imagination in the beginning of Canto XVII.'—Carroll, *op. cit.,* p. 204.

2. The image in this tercet exemplifies what might be called the power of the dramatic eye in Dante. St. Stephen's death is, of course, not a burden to him. Yet he sinks to the earth. And why do men sink to the earth? Because they are burdened, in one way or another.

3. We must remember that the terrace of sloth is pivotal not only in being one between two groups of three each but also in the nature of the sin, which is an equipoise where there should be a definite attraction and movement to God.

4. Dante is again likening his journey with two earlier journeys through the otherworld, Aeneas's and Paul's, as he had earlier at *Inf.* 2.31-3. Dante's alone, he says, is comparable in modern times to these. Apart from the fact that Aeneas's was a pagan journey which saw, for example, nothing of Purgatory, we might wonder how Dante is classifying the other medieval comparable voyages—St. Brendan's, for example, or Alan de Lille's work. I do not believe we can decide how Dante felt about the 'authenticity' of these other works, but, as part of the problem of the literal meaning of the *Commedia* we must consider the assumption (or conviction or pretense) that the poet is here presenting about the God-given sanction to this poem. Probably to most readers today the issue becomes a little more palatable or a little more of a real issue if we relate the *Commedia* more closely to the *Aeneid* than to Paul's account of his journey; Dante's mention of Paul would then remind us that his own insight into the qualities of the otherworld has the immeasurable advantage over Virgil's in having the grace of the Christian revelation. As he concludes his statement to Marco Lombardo the pilgrim must say that he is asking for guidance:

'. . . let me know the right way;
your words will be our escort.'

5. Perhaps Guido's lament, especially at 14.109-10, had started this train of 'love and courtesy.' Similarly Marco's words at 16.47-8 continue (by chance for the pilgrim; thematically for the poet) the talk started by Guido of the world gone to ruin. (Marco's phrase, *valore e cortesia,* at 16.116, echoes two of the troubadours' catchwords: *cortesia, valors, proeza, mesura, pretz,* and *jovens.*)

The half-recognition of a Lombard by his accent gains probability from Dante's own preoccupation with the dialects of Italy, as shown in *De Vulgari Eloquentia.* In Hell, at 10.22-7, the pilgrim is recognized as a Tuscan by his idiom and a Florentine by his accent.

'Lombardo fui, e fui chiamato Marco.' This may mean either that Marco was a Lombard or that his family name was Lombardo. The first possibility is now generally accepted, although some of the early commentators placed Marco within the Lombardi family of Venice. (The notes in the Temple Classics translation follow this tradition.) Marco speaks a few lines later (16.115-26) of the degeneration not of Venice but of Lombardy.

6. Lombardy was also at this time a hotbed of contention between Emperor and Pope. This may account for Dante's putting a bitter complaint against the Church into the mouth of a Lombard, whose land had been rent by the Guelf-Ghibelline wars.

7. I believe that the thesis outlined in this paragraph is not only, in a sense, self-evident for the entire structure of the *Commedia* but is a way of stating Dante's idea of the process (or progress, or purpose) of a human life—for example, his own. I suggest, too, that application of this thesis would help solve the still-debated question of the relations among Dante's various works—specifically, such problems as that of the relation between Beatrice of the *Vita Nuova* and Beatrice of the *Commedia;* that of the nature and kind of allegory treated in the *Convivio* and then in the *Letter to Can Grande;* that of the concept of government in the *Monarchia* and then in the *Commedia.* In each instance the later idea embraces and enlarges (but does not cancel) the earlier. Here too may be found the reason for the noncompletion of the *Convivio:* that even before he had got well into this work glorifying philosophy, Dante had a poetic, operative vision of philosophy neither as end nor as tool but as functioning part of man's life.

8. Virgil's speech at 15.46-57 and 67-78 is not of the same order of importance as the three I am here dealing with. Outside of the internal weaknesses of this speech, as I dealt with them above, Virgil is attempting little beyond a gloss on a phrase of Guido's which has puzzled the pilgrim.

9. That Dante—or at least Marco—holds to the doctrine of stellar influence may seem odd to us, but let us not dismiss the question with a careless thought about the dark ages. For one thing we must realize that Dante succeeded much better than Shakespeare in reconciling a belief in stellar influence with Christian doctrine.

In order to satisfy your request that I should write on the lawfulness of coming to decisions from reading the stars, I have been at pains to give you the patristic position.

You should know, to begin with, that the powers of heavenly bodies influence lower bodily processes. Augustine recognizes no absurdity in allowing for the part they play in bodily changes. Consequently, there is nothing wrong in consulting the stars in order to foretell bodily effects, for instance, the weather, health and sickness, the harvest and so forth, all of which depend on bodily and physical causes. To observe the heavens is general practice: farmers sow and reap at times determined by solar movement, sailors navigate by the moon, doctors choose critical periods settled by the heavens. There is no impropriety, then, in taking more occult phases of the stars into account when dealing with physical processes.

This, however, should be held unwaveringly—man's will is not determined by the stars. Otherwise his freedom would go by the board, and with it any merit for his good deeds, and censure on his evil ones. Every Christian is bound to hold that acts which issue from a man's own will, namely all his human acts properly so called, are not subject to determinism: *be not dismayed at the signs of heaven, as the heathens are dismayed at them.* In order to lead people into error, the devil occupies himself in the business of those who calculate human events by the stars. . . . Therefore to decide by the stars those issues which depend on man's freewill is certainly gravely wrong.—Aquinas, *Letter* to Reginald of Piperno (Gilby).

Finally we may look at a comment by Gilson:

'. . . what retarded mediaeval progress in science was no backwardness in believing in universal determinism. Quite the contrary; putting man's free will on one side, philosophers and theologians all agreed in a universal determinism of an astrological kind. St. Thomas considers that the movements of lower bodies are caused by those of the heavenly bodies, and that all the phenomena of the sublunary world are ruled by the movements of the stars. Albert the Great and Roger Bacon went still further; in fact, the latter did not hesitate to cast the horoscope of religions, not even excluding the Christian religion. . . .

When St. Thomas is asked whether astrological determinism imposes an absolute necessity on terrestrial phenomena he replies in the negative on the ground that besides all that is determined by the movements of the stars there exists a vast field for chance.'—Gilson, *The Spirit of Mediaeval Philosophy*, pp. 366-7.

10. Even Beatrice's account of free will, at *Par.* 5.17 sqq., must be understood in the light of the relation between free will and the vows of the inconstant, in whose circle of heaven her account is recited.

R. Altrocchi finds here one of his 'Three Coincidences in *The Divine Comedy*' (Annual Reports Dante Soc., Cambridge, 1934, pp. 31-5).

Virgil here tells the pilgrim that Beatrice will address him on free will; she does so in the heaven of the moon. Virgil makes his statement at *Purg.* 18.73-5. The very next lines read:

> *The moon, retarded almost to midnight,*
> *made the stars appear more thin to us.*

This coincidence may mean, at most, only that Dante already knew while writing *Purgatory* where in *Paradise* this speech of Beatrice would be placed; or it may set up some involved connections among free will, inconstancy, greater and lesser lights.

11. Perhaps a parallel is suggested by Dante's use of a contemporary theory of light, as in 15.67-70: this light of inspiration comes down to meet an already bright mind, and the amount of light coming down is directly proportional to the amount of brightness already there.

12. The bubble is based on the opening image of seeing through a mist, as a mole through the skin over his eyes; in this image the return to consciousness after the second bubble has broken (at 15.40-1) is to be likened to the light of the sun seen once more at 15.7-8.

13. Ideas of blindness, of temporary blindness, of light, of blinding light have come in heightened succession ever since the appearance of the Angel of Fraternal Love at the opening of canto 15.

14. The terms Virgil uses for the two kinds of love are *o naturale o d'animo. Naturale* here may also be translated 'natural,' or 'instinctive'; love *d'animo* may be translated 'rational' or 'intellectual.' Possibly the terms 'involuntary' and 'voluntary' might make the clearest distinction between them—especially as used by the anatomist in speaking of involuntary muscles (such as those that effectuate breathing and heartbeat) and voluntary muscles such as are used to run or to manipulate a typewriter.

15. Virgil disagrees here somewhat with Aquinas, who treats this threefold definition of sin at *Summa Theol.*, I-II, 72, 4. Here, in the reply to objection 1, Aquinas says: 'To sin against God is common to all sins, insofar as the order to God includes every human order; but insofar as order to God surpasses the other two orders, sin against God is a special kind of sin.'

16. Virgil's reply to the later question is immediately followed at 18.40-2 by the same combination of thankful courtesy and unsatisfied curiosity. The combination occurred earlier, in a somewhat primitive form, at the beginning of the great logical chain we have been follow-

ing. At 15.82 the pilgrim's 'Thou dost satisfy me' remains unuttered because the travelers have arrived at the next circuit. Is there any doubt, though, that here too it would have been a 'Thou dost satisfy me, but . . .'? Perhaps the most subtle instance is here at 18.10-3 where the pilgrim says, in effect: You have made me understand everything dealt with in your discourse—therefore (*però*) explain to me the one term, love, on which depended everything you said.

17. The finality of this explanation recalls the similar tone of Virgil's *quia* statement (*Purg.* 3.28)—if it were not impolite to remind Virgil of the time when he was content with a considerably lower level of knowledge than he now presumes to have.

18. Wicksteed (*Dante and Aquinas,* p. 138) points out that this tercet (18.55-7) depends on Aquinas' distinction among affections, appetite, and intellect:

'Intellect starts from axioms or other ascertained truth and then builds up the edifice of knowledge; action is determined by goal: i.e., we start, not from where we are but from where we wish to be. The desire for blessedness, according to Dante, is implanted in every human soul as surely and inevitably as the honey-making instinct in the bee.'

19. As mentioned earlier, Beatrice's discourse on free will comes in the heaven of the inconstant, at *Par.* 5.46 sqq. Some words that she utters just before this (*Par.* 5.7-12) may throw some light on the merits and deficiencies of Virgil's concept of love. She says:

'I note well how already the eternal light
reglows in your intellect,
the light which when only seen always kindles love;

and if something else should seduce your love,
it is only some vestige of this light,
ill understood, as it shines through therein.'

20. Some other comments by Aquinas on this sin testify to the variety as well as the frequency of his interest in it. In speaking of minor, miscellaneous sins, Aquinas says:

. . . we might say that all the sins which are due to ignorance can be reduced to sloth, to which pertains the negligence by which a man refuses to acquire spiritual goods because of the attendant labor . . . (*Summa Theol.,* I-II, 84, 4, *ad* 5).

Say a man voluntarily undertakes a duty of obedience, but groans at the boredom and burden. He has not fallen into *accidie,* for his sadness is about an outward temporal evil, not an inward eternal good.—Disputations, xi *de Malo,* 1, *ad* 4 (Gilby).

Accidie is a shrinking of mind, not from any spiritual good, but from that to which it should cleave as in duty bound, namely the goodness of God. —Disputations, xi *de Malo,* 3, *ad* 4 (Gilby).

Aquinas (*Summa Theol.,* I, 35, 8) quotes a saying of Gregory of Nyssa: '*acedia est tristitia vocem amputans*'—sloth is a sadness cutting off the voice.

CHAPTER NINE

1. Those commentators (e.g., Rossetti, Valli) who endeavor to reduce all figures in the poem to symbols, say, of Church and Empire, are likely to solve this question by saying Lucia = Eagle = Symbol of Empire. This is convenient but antipoetic. The ways in which Lucia differs from the Eagle are probably more important than her resemblances or equivalences to it. Dante could have had Lucia enact the carrying in the first dream as easily as he has her function in the second (if this *is* Lucia here).

Sayers (*Purgatory,* 220-1) says that the Lady here is not

Beatrice, Lucy, or any other of the poem's *dramatis personae.* It will be noticed that she acts more promptly than Virgil (reason); but she cannot ['does not' might be safer to say] herself unmask the Siren; she calls upon Virgil to do so. She symbolizes something immediate, instinctive, and almost automatic: one might call her an intuition, or perhaps the reflex action of a virtuous habit, whose instant warning puts the soul on the alert and prompts it to think rationally about what it is doing.

Or the Lady may be Lucia, with economy of intervention, using Virgil because he is all that is needed for this job.

2. Carroll (*op. cit.,* p. 249):

Virgil's words later on show that the Siren stands for the complete round of fleshly sin on the three remaining terraces—Avarice, Gluttony, Sensuality. Dante on waking is bowed down with misgiving by the memory of the dream, and Virgil says to him:

'Sawest thou that ancient witch,
Who alone above us henceforth is bewept?'

This is very misleading if it does not mean all three of the upper Terraces. . . . The Siren represents that Excessive Love to which Virgil has already traced the three sins of the flesh—that inordinate desire after lower natural goods, which proves to be a mere phantasm of happiness, and, by its very excess, ends in a positive disgust and loathing, which wakes us from the dream.

Two of the many discussions of the Siren will serve as examples of old and recent interpretations of the *Comedy.* Dante's son, Pietro, gives us a good example of fourteenth-century allegorizing in his discussion of the Siren (as paraphrased by John Paul Bowden in *An Analysis,* etc., p. 58):

Pietro explains that the word 'siren' means 'attraction,' specifically the attraction of avarice, gluttony and lust. That is why Dante comes upon the Siren after having considered the other principal vices of pride, envy, wrath and sloth. The former vices, Pietro says, come from a deceiving attractiveness, while the latter arise out of malice. Dante describes these three attractions in the person of the woman, whose stuttering denotes gluttony, her side-glances, lust, her crooked hands and feet, avarice. By her deceiving delight the Siren would submerge us in the three vices in the middle of the sea, i.e., midway through life's course, if the honorable lady, who represents our intellectual power, did not come to our assistance.

This is a good demonstration of the commentator's obligation to handle the literal sense of the poem with care. The pilgrim does not simply 'come upon' the Siren: he dreams her and very nearly calls her into existence.

John Ruskin discusses the Siren in *Munera Pulveris* (quoted by George P. Huntington in *Comments of John Ruskin on the Divina Commedia,* pp. 152-7):

[The Siren,] the Idol of riches, made doubly phantasmal by Dante's seeing her in a dream. She is lovely to look upon, and enchants by her sweet singing, but her womb is loathsome. Now Dante does not call her one of the Sirens carelessly, any more than he speaks of Charybdis carelessly; and though he had got at the meaning of the Homeric fable only through Virgil's obscure tradition of it, the clue he has given us is quite enough. Bacon's interpretation 'the Sirens, *or pleasures,*' which has become universal since his time, is opposed alike to Plato's meaning and Homer's. The Sirens are not pleasures, but *desires:* in the Odyssey they are the phantoms of vain desires; but in Plato's Vision of Destiny, phantoms of divine desire; singing each a different note on the circles of the distaff of Necessity, but forming one harmony, to which the three great Fates put words. Dante, however, adopted the Homeric conception of them, which was that they were demons of the Imagination, not carnal; desire of the eyes, not lust of the flesh; therefore said to be daughters of the Muses. Yet not of the Muses, heavenly or historical, but of the Muse of pleasure; and they are at first winged, because even vain hope excites and helps when first formed; but afterwards, contending for the possession of the imagination with the Muses themselves, they are deprived of their wings. . . .

It is, then, one of these Sirens whom Dante takes as the phantasm or deceitfulness of riches; but note further, that she says it was her song that deceived Ulysses. Look back to Dante's account of Ulysses' death, and we find it was not the love of money, but pride of knowledge, that betrayed him; whence we get the clue to Dante's complete meaning: that the souls whose love of wealth is pardonable have been first deceived into pursuit of it by a dream of its higher uses, or by ambition. His Siren is therefore the Philotime of Spenser, daughter of Mammon—

Whom all that folk with such contention
Do flock about, my deare, my daughter is—
Honour and dignitie from her alone
Derived are.

By comparing Spenser's entire account of this Philotime with Dante's of the Wealth-Siren, we shall get at the full meaning of both poets; but that of Homer lies hidden much more deeply . . .—*Munera Pulveris,* ch. III, sec. 88-93.

3. It is possible that, to emphasize the concupiscent qualities of his Siren, Dante has synthesized in her Homer's Siren, Circe, and Calypso. This is not probable; if it were so, she would still in a sense be lying.

The Siren is not a real object of love (see 18.22-6), but rather an egotistical fantasy which reduces the personality itself to a mere illusion. It is not the thing, the object, which undergoes the transformation in the dream, but rather that the pilgrim's senses have changed—from message-bearers to deceivers.

Aquinas again throws light on this question, in a statement bearing on fantasy, imagination, and the senses:

. . . although the first immutation of the imagination is through the agency of the sensible, since *the phantasm is a movement produced in accordance with sensation,* nevertheless, it may be said that there is in man an operation which by division and composition forms images of various things, even of things not perceived by the senses.—*Summa Theol.,* I, 6, *ad* 2 (Pegis).

4. Carroll, *op. cit.*, pp. 257-9:

The penalty here is the recoil of Avarice upon the moral nature. The Sin consists essentially in the cleaving of the soul to the dust, a deliberate preference and choice of the earth before God. It is this contrast between God and the dust which constitutes its peculiar baseness. As Aquinas says (*Summa,* ii-ii. 9.cxviii.a.5):

'We may rank sins in order of the good on which the human heart is inordinately fixed; and the less that is, the more unseemly is the sin: for it is baser to bow to an inferior good than to a higher and better one. But the good of exterior things is the lowest of human goods: for it is less than the good of the body, and that is less than the good of the soul, and that is less than the good that is for men in God. And in this way the sin of covetousness, whereby the human heart is subjected even to exterior things, has in some sense a greater deformity than the rest. . . .'

Along with this earthliness of soul goes a second punishment,—the binding of the hands and feet, that is, the paralysis for a time of the active powers in the direction of good. The hands that were never reached out in generous giving, and the feet that never moved on any errand of mercy, are now powerless in the bonds of the old selfish habit. . . . This too is why they lie so near the edge of the Terrace that Dante and Virgil have to walk at the foot of the cliff on the inner side, 'as one goes along a wall close to the battlements.' The meaning is that they are set as near as possible to the edge of the precipice which falls down to the Terrace of Sloth, to indicate the power of that sin still within them.

5. While the canto endings in the *Commedia* do not necessarily clinch an idea or an episode, these last lines seem especially inconclusive. Perhaps they thus support the belief that Alagia (Malaspina) was Dante's hostess in 1306. This, being known to Dante's readers, would provide sufficient point for a canto-ending in the ironic understatement of the generous niece in an avaricious family.

6. Carroll, *op. cit.*, p. 273:

The night brings on 'a contrary sound.' The idea is, perhaps, that the nightfall recalls the memory of their own schemes of Avarice over which they once brooded in the darkness, and which must now be fought by resolute contemplation of men and women who perished in their greed. Seven examples are given, as if to show the entire gamut of this vice. As Dr. Moore points out, they are arranged in three groups, parallel to the three examples of the virtue: '(1) two instances from profane history or legend; (2) three instances from Scripture; and (3) again two instances from profane history.'

They seem to be chosen to show how 'the love of money is a root of all kinds of evil,' (1 Tim. vi. 10 R.V.)—sins against kindred and self, against God and His Church, against the sacred laws of hospitality, against the human race.

and, p. 275:

As Scartazzini points out, these seven examples correspond to the seven 'daughters of Avarice' according to Aquinas, Pygmalion representing Treachery; Midas, Restlessness; Achan, Fraud; Ananias and Sapphira, Perjury; Heliodorus, Deceit; Polymnestor, Inhumanity; and Crassus, Violence (*Summa,* ii-ii. q. cxviii. a. 8).

7. This is, of course, *mutatis mutandis,* the reverse of the movement in the *Inferno,* where the progress from the least intellectual to the most (socially) intellectual perversions of reason provides the steady increase of power in that canticle. Similarly, the *Paradise* moves towards greater and greater encompassings of intellect.

CHAPTER TEN

1. Moore (1st series, p. 33) says: '. . . If Virgil (as is generally admitted) represents Human Reason, and Beatrice Revelation or Theology, we may perhaps suppose that Statius typifies something intermediate; such as Human Reason, generally enlightened by Christianity, but not specially instructed or interested therein.'

At the close of the preceding chapter we noted the paradox of the 'intellectuality' of the sins of the flesh. The joining with Statius may require a slight rephrasing of this notion. Statius is Christian (at least in Dante's belief); as such his enlightenment (intellectual as well as moral) must be added to the qualities possessed by Virgil in order that the problems and obstacles of the cornices of the flesh may be overcome.

2. Vernon notes on this passage: 'Statius begins by answering Virgil's first question as to who he was, and he does so in much the same fashion as Virgil in the first canto of the *Inferno* had answered a like question from Dante. Virgil answered Dante: Nacqui sub Julio, and only ten lines later is the name of Virgil mentioned. Here Statius first says he lived in the reign of Titus, and tells his name ten lines later.'

There are other parallels that may be noted between these two speeches: both are constructed with elaborate, almost artificial rhetoric.

3. Even the details that might in another poet (or another time) be treated as mechanically factual: 'I wrote two poems and died before finishing the second,' in Dante come in the shape of ornamental puzzles: 'but I fell by the way with the second burden.' A second thought, however, shows that this is not mere ornament: 'fell,' 'way,' and 'burden' are images essentially connected with Dante's concept of the nature of life and poetry.

4. The meeting with Statius has called forth many glowing tributes from critics. A characteristic one is that of F. Flora in *Storia delle letteratura italiana* (Milano, 1940): 'The meeting between Statius and Virgil . . . is one of Dante's most original lyrics, and, though clothed in medieval mode, is the earliest poetry of Humanism.'

Vittorio Capetti (*Illustrazioni al poema di Dante*), in a warm and touching account of this meeting, says (p. 39): '. . . the three poets, representatives of three worlds, spirits capable of feeling all the poetry of the time that moved them.'

5. On this tree Carroll comments that the later one (of *Purg.* 24.103-17) is clearly the Tree of the Knowledge of Good and Evil (of which Eve ate). And so the present tree must be something else, although it is a scion of the other. This, he says, is the Tree of Life—representing Temperance and the life which Temperance nourishes.

6. Probably . . . what Dante is really censured for is the wasting of his time in a vain curiosity which was akin to that which led Eve to the first sin. . . . Curiosity, which may be regarded as an intemperance of the mind, is held by Aquinas to be a vice when, as in the case of Dante, it draws aside from some duty and pries into some truth beyond human ken. (*Summa* ii-ii, q. clxvii. a. 1.)—Carroll, *op. cit.*, p. 313.

7. Carroll says of these poems (p. 320, n. 1): 'It would certainly be a relief to believe that Dante never wrote those attributed to him.'

8. The blinding red-furnace color of the Angel is in part an anticipation of the fires which burn in the next terrace. Also, the angelic furnace, far from sending out a blast of consuming fire, breathed the sweet life-giving breeze of a May morning (24.145-50)—Carroll, *op. cit.*, p. 321.

CHAPTER ELEVEN

1. Another instance of the bow-imagery. Note that here the bow is arched to its limit—ready to shoot.

2. Here again we have a passage that may throw some light on the question of the literal sense of the *Comedy:* is the literal sense of Dante's journey through the realms of the afterlife, lighted by an increasing closeness to God, to be limited to the things knowable in this life?

3. Cf. Aquinas (*Summa Theol.,* I-II, 81, 3, *ad* 2): 'Original sin is taken away by baptism as to the guilt, in so far as the soul recovers grace as regards the mind. Nevertheless original sin remains in its effect as regards the "fomes," which is the disorder of the lower parts of the soul and of the body itself (in respect of which, and not of the mind, man exercises his power of generation).' (Pegis.)

4. Aquinas (*Summa Theol.,* I-II, 81, 5, *ad* 1): 'The child pre-exists in its father as in its active principle, and in its mother as in its material and passive principle . . .' (Pegis.)

5. This part of Statius' exposition goes back to the Aristotelian theory of the soul as the form (or form-giver) of the human body: *anima est forma corporis.* It was a theory which provided an invaluable link between psychology and physics. Below, at 25.88-108, we see the otherworldly fulfillment of this Aristotelian theory. (Also see footnote, p. 221.)

6. Aquinas' article on this point (*Summa Theol.,* I, 118, art. 2) is highly complex and interesting. His argument may be condensed as follows:

> It is impossible for an active power existing in matter to extend its action to the production of an immaterial effect. Now it is manifest that the intellectual principle in man transcends matter, for it has an operation in which the body takes no part whatever. It is therefore impossible for the seminal power to produce the intellectual principle.
>
> . . . Since [the intellectual soul] is an immaterial substance it cannot be caused through generation, but only through creation by God. Therefore to hold that the intellectual soul is caused by the begetter is nothing else than to hold the soul to be non-subsistent, and consequently to perish with the body. It is therefore heretical to say that the intellectual soul is transmitted with the semen.
>
> . . . We conclude therefore that the intellectual soul is created by God at the end of human generation, and this soul is at the same time sensitive and nutritive, for the pre-existing forms have been corrupted [or, almost, absorbed]. (Pegis.)

7. The wordless kiss used by these spirits was the greeting used in early Christianity; it later was prohibited.

8. The apple is used in another connection by Dante that almost makes the apple of Eden a temptation for children—it is the first object of a child's desire (*Conv.* 4.12):

. . . so our soul, on entering the new and untraveled way of life, looks to the highest good as to its goal, but mistakes for its final goal each thing that bears any semblance of good; . . . the smallest good appears great and attracts at first the soul's desire. Thus we see children fix their hearts, first on an apple, then, as they grow, on a little bird. . . .

9. This entire question—of free will, free choice, predestination, determinism, etc.,—is often complicated by the use of the same phrase—either 'free will' or 'free choice'—to translate the medieval *liberum arbitrium* (free judgment) and *libera voluntas* (free will).

The following discussions may help clarify the question.

Thomas Lyle Collins, in an article 'Freedom and Necessity in the *Divine Comedy*' (in the *Personalist,* XXIII, 62-70), treats the lines at 16.79-81 which state the dependence of human free will upon God. His argument may be outlined as follows: Freedom is of two kinds. The first is freedom of choice between natural necessity and moral necessity; the second is freedom that is identical with moral necessity. Under the first condition—as we see its operation on the terraces of Purgatory—the will is able to free the soul from the Seven Deadly Sins and to free it for the love of God. Under the second condition, there is no dilemma when one submits to the necessity of loving God.

Somewhat fuller is the statement by Gratia Eaton Baldwin, in *The New Beatrice; or, The Virtue that Counsels* (Columbia University Press, 1928), p. 43:

[My study thus far has shown that] free-will is not a choice based on counsel, but a choice submitted to counsel. The agent is not a will preferring good to evil. The agent is an intellect, illuminated and actualized by truth, instilling its power into the will. It is the giving up of a false freedom for a true. It is the joyful surrender of a faculty which may lead to death to a vision which leads to truth and life. Man's freedom is not in knowing that, although he embraced the good, he could have followed evil. His freedom is rather in knowing that in that power of choice is his bondage. Man cannot establish his own righteousness, for his righteousness is in being subject to God. If there is an alternative, there must be doubt. If there is opposition, then is he twain. Man is free only when he is one.

In a related connection Aquinas points out that: 'The practical reason and the speculative reason are not different powers' (*Summa Theol.,* I, 79, 11).

Finally, a verbal echo in the text may set us on this same path. In the first tercet of the poem we met the image of the horror of the dark wood 'where the straight way was lost'—*che la diritta via era smarrita.* Here, just after the three poets have passed through the fires which are the last stage of purgation, we read (27.64): *Dritta salia la via* . . . 'the way mounted straight . . .' The way is, finally, straight—with no confusion, and ascending as well.

10. St. Bernard on action and contemplation (quoted by Carroll, *op. cit.,* pp. 464-5):

> The breasts from which you nourish the children you bring forth are better—that is, more necessary, than the wine of contemplation. The one is that which maketh glad the heart of one man alone; but the other that which edifies many. For, although Rachel be the fairer, Leah is the more fruitful. Do not, therefore, linger too much over the sweetness of contemplation, for the fruits of preaching are better.—*Cantica Canticorum,* sermon 38.

Hettinger (*Dante's Divina Commedia,* trans. H. S. Bowden, p. 305) connects choice of Leah and Rachel with figural interpretation:

> The life of Christian virtue is twofold—contemplative and active. The former, typified by Rachel, is engaged in the contemplation of Divine truth, the latter by Lia, in external action.
>
> These two appear to the poet in the night, as representing the comparatively defective virtue of the Old Covenant. Matelda and Beatrice, on the other hand, come to him by day, for they express the perfection of the active and contemplative life in the New Covenant. Dante preferred these characters to Martha and Mary, the patristic types of the two lives.

This adds further complication. Why did Dante *not* use Martha and Mary? Why at this point in the journey did he want a 'defective' presentation of the active and contemplative life?

Charles Williams, *The Figure of Beatrice* (London, 1943), p. 174:

> Dante, for the last time, dreams: of Leah gathering flowers—what else is all action? and of Rachel looking in her glass—what else is all contemplation? for now the soul may justly take joy in herself and in love and beauty.

11. Dante's purpose in the third dream is, seemingly, to assimilate Leah and Rachel as much as possible to each other without destroying the individuality of either. Thus we are not to look upon them as

tokens of counterparts to come—Matelda = Leah and Beatrice = Rachel (or the other way about) but rather as the continuation of that convergence of choice, of parallel lines, getting ready to meet at infinity (see above, note 9). They indicate an arrow which will become first Matelda, then Beatrice, and ultimately (at *Par.* 31.108) Mary. It is an arrow which has been waveringly adumbrated in the deceptions of the flight to Heaven in the first dream, and in the essence of the false-woman of the second dream.

In the sequence of the three dreams there is a certain similarity to the three kinds of vision described by Augustine (*De Genesi ad Litt.*, XII; 6; 7; 24): corporeal, which is an action of the sense; spiritual, which is an action of the imagination or fantasy; and intellectual, which is an action of the intellect. Aquinas, in citing this definition (*Summa Theol.*, I, 78, 4) comments that (*ad* 6): 'Augustine calls that vision spiritual which is effected by the images of bodies in the absence of bodies. Whence it is clear that it is common to all interior apprehensions.'

Aquinas' comment, that in some sense the term spiritual covers all three kinds of vision, does not invalidate Augustine's distinction—in a passage that Dante may well have read and decided to apply to his three dreams. All three are of course 'spiritual' (which in this sense is very nearly equal to 'an action of the imagination or fantasy'), yet they show a progress of emphasis: the first dream is a fantastic enactment of the sense-response to being carried (or to the condition of being soon to be carried—we cannot be sure of the relation between Lucia's action and the pilgrim's dream). The second dream we have already discussed as an example par excellence of the medieval concept of the *immaginazione*. The third dream, as I have discussed it, seems to fit well into Aquinas' definition of the agent intellect—almost equivalent to 'reason' —as given in *Summa Theol.*, I, 79: the intellect, freed, is an activity of the soul about sense and more accurate than imagination.

12. In the line, 'you can sit or walk among them,' referring to the flowers and shrubs, Virgil explicitly recalls the conditions of Rachel and Leah.

13. Carroll, *op. cit.*, p. 368, points out that the 'crown and mitre' may refer not to two authorities but to the secular alone. 'The words *mitratus et coronatus* were used in the Roman ritual for the coronation of the Emperor . . .'

This is unlikely and, at best, removes only part of the difficulty of this line.

14. Professor Singleton, in his *Essay on the Vita Nuova,* describes this function, relation, of the woman to the poet. He is here speaking of this relation as shown in the *Vita Nuova;* while I agree that her function in the *Comedy* is a somewhat different thing, I question his statement that there 'she unquestionably becomes an allegory.' He says (p. 77):

This scheme by which Beatrice holds a medial position, not only in the downward path of Love from God to man but in the upward and returning path of love from man to God as well, is the solution which Dante has brought to the conflict between love of woman and love of God. Love of Beatrice is charity, which means that love of her begins in God and ends in God. This love's upward way does not come to a stop at *domina* as did the love of the troubadours. It goes beyond to God, whence it came.

And again, at p. 111:

Neither in the poems of the others [Guinizelli, Cavalcanti, *et al.*] nor in Dante's early poems is the *donna angelicata* an allegorical figure. Nor is Beatrice made to be such a figure in the *Vita Nuova*. Like the ladies of those other poets, Beatrice is a creature, a wondrously beautiful individual of flesh and blood who lived once in time. In the *Vita Nuova* we see her die. Beatrice will not happen again. Let us for the moment forget the allegories of the *Convivio,* and let us forget Beatrice as she is in the *Comedy*. For there Beatrice unquestionably becomes an allegory, though she does not, for that cease to be the person she was in the *Vita Nuova*. But in the *Vita Nuova,* Beatrice has no *other* name which may be spelled with a capital initial.

CHAPTER TWELVE

1. For the first time on the Mountain—or in the pilgrim's journey —he comes onto a plain, where ups and downs, ledges and boulders, crevasses and clefts are not there to interfere with quiet walking and enjoyment of the scene.

Federico Olivero (*op. cit.,* p. 10) in his chapter on the 'Gradual Appearing of the Image,' discusses the technique of description in the Earthly Paradise.

. . . in the symbolic vision in the Earthly Paradise we notice that light, sound and form become more and more distinct with a parallel growth.

First a sudden lustre appears through the forest and a melody flows through the luminous air (*Purg.* 29.16-22); then the atmosphere under the green boughs becomes like fire and the vague harmony is perceived to be a chanting (34). And now we discern in the splendour the outline of golden trees (43) which turn out to be huge candlesticks of gold (50) while the word 'Hosanna' is distinctly heard in the singing.

This technique is perhaps less of unfolding images than of processes of growth and metamorphosis. A similar process is used in the gradual unveiling of Beatrice—eyes, lips, smile . . . —a process that continues into Paradise: cf. *Purg.* 30.22; 31.119, 136; 32.5; then *Par.* 27.105; 31.71; and 33.38.

2. Is Matelda, like Cato, a permanent dweller on the Mountain? Or is she part of Beatrice's train, come down to prepare the pilgrim for the coming of the greater lady? The poem provides no direct answer to this question; to a great extent the answer is involved with the matter of Matelda's identification. If she is the Duchess of Tuscany (or some similar great person) she is more likely to be a fixed inhabitant of the Garden. If she is one of Beatrice's friends or acquaintances—perhaps the *pargoletta* herself—then she is more likely to be temporarily here. Some slight clue might come from the fact that she *is* one of the pilgrim's guides: the guides, typically, are temporarily away from their eternal positions (Virgil and Beatrice) or not yet possessed of a fixed abode (Statius). (But note Beatrice's final speech, esp. 33.128.)

In chapter 1 (p. 76) we noted some of the symbolic identifications of Matelda. Here we may note the ingenious and attractive hypothesis of Gerald G. Walsh, S.J. (*Dante Alighieri—Citizen of Christendom,* Milwaukee 1946). Father Walsh says of Matelda, p. 92: 'Something about her reminded Dante of the *mother* of Proserpine and of the *mother* of Cupid. She was more like a parent than a teacher or priest.' The change of only two letters turns *Matelda* into *Materna.*

3. Original sin is a sin of nature. It came to Adam through his actual fault, in other words, his personal sin. Here person corrupted nature. Through this corruption the sin of our first parents descends on their progeny. Here nature corrupts person. Grace, however, comes to us from Christ, not through human nature, but solely through his personal action. Consequently, there is no need to extend the parallel between Christ's grace and Adam's actual and original sin. Christ's personal sanctifying grace and his grace as Head of the Church are essentially the same; they differ merely as different topics for study.—*Summa Theol.,* 3a. viii. 5, c. & *ad* 1. (Gilby.)

Although by his death Christ sufficiently merited salvation for the whole human race, each of us must there seek his own cure. Christ's death is like the universal cause of deliverance, as the sin of our first parents was like the universal cause of perdition. Nevertheless even a universal cause must be applied to be effective. The effects of original sin come to us through bodily birth; the effects of Christ's death through the spiritual rebirth whereby we are incorporated in Christ.—iv *Contra Gentes,* 55. (Gilby.)

4. 'Man was happy in [Earthly] Paradise, but not with that perfect happiness to which he was destined, which consists in the vision of the divine essence.'—*Summa Theol.,* I, 94, *ad* 1.

Aquinas thus augments Aristotle:

Man is by nature a social animal. Hence in the state of innocence (if there had been no Fall) men would have lived in society. But a common social life of many individuals could not exist unless there were someone in control to attend to the common good.—*Summa Theol.,* I, 96, 4. *Now in the place where he was crucified there was a garden.* Christ was captured in a garden, he suffered his agony in a garden, and he was buried in a garden. These facts are symbols. The virtue of his Passion frees us from the sin Adam committed in the garden of Eden, and consecrates the Church which is a garden enclosed.—Aquinas, Commentary, St. John, xix, lect. 6 (Gilby).

Wicksteed (*Dante and Aquinas,* p. 215 sqq.) discusses Dante's relation to Aquinas on this matter of the nature of man before the Fall and his hopes of happiness on earth after the Fall:

Before the Fall, says Aquinas, man had all the physical appetites that he has now, and, moreover, the delight of the senses was much keener yet than it now is. But the desires and appetites were all in perfect harmony, because subject to reason. . . .

[Before the Fall] the ideal earthly life was in due course to have been superseded by the heavenly life, in which man would pass from the perfect balance and fulfillment of his human nature, as created by God, to the perfect fruition of faculties raised above themselves and above their nature by illuminating grace. Then he would see God in his essence.

This being so, the ordinary conception of the course of human history was that when man fell, the state of earthly blessedness, being once lost became absolutely and eternally unattainable; but through the grace of God and in virtue of the atoning death of Christ, by faith and the sacraments, man, though he could not regain the experience of full earthly blessedness, might pass from the storms and trials of this life into that higher life, to which Eden was to have been the prelude. According to this, the Fall permanently cut out of the programme of man what had been an essential part of the first conception of the Deity.

Dante apparently could not accept this divine failure, and believed that if not here, then hereafter, not only must the Heavenly Paradise be gained, but the Earthly Paradise also must become an actual experience (and not a mere tradition) for each one of the redeemed; that so the divine plan for humanity should be realised in its integrity, and man should know the earth not only as a place of exile, but as a home, not only as the scene of temptation and trial, but as the garden of delight, in which he should experience the frank and full fruition of his nature, as God first made it.

How far this beautiful conception was a positive objective belief with Dante it would be hard to say; but as a symbol it interprets and crowns all that we have insisted on previously in reference to the steady trend of his mind in the direction of linking up the secular and temporal order with the spiritual and eternal, and raising it into worthy partnership with it.

For in spite of what we may call Dante's official pessimism, he was not really content to abandon this life to the powers of darkness. If men did live in a tangled forest they might live, even on this side the grave, on the sunlit hill of a well-ordered state on earth, of which Eden is the symbol; and it was the specific function of Roman Law to restrain or banish the brutal passions that bar the way to such an earthly state; and who could say when the political Messiah might arise to drive the wolf of greed back to hell and make earth like Eden?

5. Dante's son Pietro set the tone for much of the subsequent symbolic interpretation of the *Comedy*. The following (adapted from Bowden, *An Analysis*, etc., pp. 91-2) will exemplify his method.

Before coming to speak of Beatrice Pietro Alighieri explains that *gratia operans* (operant grace) prepares man's will to wish what is good; *gratia cooperans* (coöperant grace) helps him not to wish in vain. In canto 2 of *Inferno* we were told that a noble Lady (*gratia operans*) moved Lucia (*gratia cooperans*), who in turn moved Beatrice (Theology), who sent Virgil (Reason) to rescue the pilgrim from the dark wood. Virgil's function was to demonstrate the truth of Hell to Dante to persuade him to renounce his vices: such is the spiritual interpretation of these agents.

The situation may also be considered allegorically. The noble Lady then represents natural philosophy; Lucia, mathematics; Beatrice, theology; Virgil, rational philosophy; and Statius, moral philosophy. By the power of natural philosophy, then, Dante is directed by mathematics toward the truth.

When the travelers come to the Earthly Paradise (which represents man's active moral state), Virgil hands the pilgrim over to Statius and to Matelda (the active life). Beatrice appears to the pilgrim amidst the words of the theologians; the cloud of flowers represents the books of the theologians; her veil symbolizes the discerning use of theology. Dante, says his son, wished to show that he had loved theology, had stopped, and now wishes to begin again. Dante turned to Virgil, but he was gone—because reason fails in such a situation.

Dorothy Sayers (*Purgatory,* pp. 302-3) has this to say of the pageants of the Earthly Paradise:

. . . the great focal point of the *Commedia*—the reunion of Dante with Beatrice—is deliberately set, as though upon a stage, between two great pageants or masques, in which the characters are not *symbolic personages* but *allegorical personifications* in the traditional manner, embodying abstract ideas. . . .

Between them, the two Masques display the history of the Church (1) up to and including the Incarnation, and (2) from the days of the Apostles to the time of writing. The first is primarily doctrinal; the second, historical and political.

Then, p. 304, on the first masque:

The form in which the Masque is presented is, in general outline, that of a Corpus Christi procession. . . . The seven processional torches were widely used in the West at the Bishop's Mass (now, only at a Papal Mass), their number being no doubt connected with the seven golden candlesticks of *Rev.* i. 12-13, and signifying the seven gifts of the Spirit (wisdom, understanding, counsel, might, knowledge, piety and the fear of the Lord).

6. Isidore of Seville (*Etymol.* 8.2) defines the symbolic nature of Christ as a griffon:

Christ is a lion for his regality and fortitude . . . an eagle because after his resurrection he mounted to the stars.

7. Remarking that four of seven Gifts of the Holy Ghost, namely Wisdom, Knowledge, Understanding, and Counsel, pertain to the reason, while the remaining three, namely Fortitude, Piety, and the Fear of the Lord, pertain to the appetitive powers, some writers have explained that as a faculty of reason our free will is endowed with the Gifts, whereas as a faculty of will it is endowed with the virtues—for but two of the virtues, namely faith and prudence, reside in the reason, while the remainder reside in the affective parts of the soul. This would be a strict division only supposing that all the Gifts were cognitive and all the virtues affective or appetitive.—Aquinas, *Summa Th.,* 1a-2ae. lxviii. 1 (Gilby).

8. They are the virtues which make us well adjusted to our last end, which is God himself: hence they are called theological, for they not only go out to God but also reach him. To be well adjusted to an end we must know and desire it; the desire demands that we are in love with this end and are confident we can attain it. The theological virtues are therefore three—*faith,* which makes us know God; *hope,* which makes us look forward to joining him; *charity,* which makes us his friends.—Aquinas, Disputations, *de Virtutibus in communi,* 12 (Gilby).

9. Commenting on the words, *Blessed be ye poor,* Ambrose says that four cardinal virtues are recognized, namely, prudence, justice, fortitude, and temperance. Cardinal comes from *cardo,* a hinge on which a gate turns, *as the door turneth upon his hinges, so does the slothful man turn upon his bed.* The cardinal virtues support the portals that open into a properly human way of life. The life of the senses we share with animals, the life of the mind we share, though imperfectly, with angels; the life of practical reasonableness is our appointed level. The life of a voluptuary is that of a beast, the life of a contemplative is more than human. The active life, exercised through moral virtue, that is proper to man; the cardinal virtues are those on which the other reasonable virtues are based and revolve.

Of these four, prudence is in the reason, justice in the will, temperance in the sense-appetites which seek pleasure, fortitude in the sense-appetites which meet emergencies. The sense-appetites, the seats of our emotional life, can be entered by reason and will, and therefore can be regarded as abilities for acting voluntarily and in a human manner. Hence the fourfold division of the cardinal virtues matches the essential elements of virtue, the situations with which virtues deal, and the faculties in which they reside.—Aquinas, Disputations, *de Virtutibus Cardinalibus,* 1 (Gilby).

10. In the *Summa Contra Gentiles,* while interpreting *Job* 26.14, Aquinas speaks of thunder as symbolic of the drawing aside of the veils which hide any truth of revelation—to enable man to see it as it is in itself.

11. Lizette Andrews Fisher (*The Mystic Vision in the Grail Legend and in the Divine Comedy,* New York, 1917), p. viii:

The point of departure [for this study] was the cry of greeting to Beatrice as she appears in the Earthly Paradise, *Benedictus qui venis,* words which not only hailed the entry of Christ into Jerusalem but which day by day in the mass herald the expected coming of Christ to the altar at the moment of consecration. Dante, fully aware of the eucharistic association with the words, must have been conscious that by their use at this point he was suggesting an allegorical connection between the coming of Beatrice and the sacramental coming of Christ. Such an allegory, in all its ceremonial detail, is not only consistent with the belief and worship familiar to Dante, but leads also to a genuinely organic interpretation of the whole episode. Just as the eucharistic presence of Christ vouchsafed to the church is foretaste and pledge of the final vision of God, so the revelation of Beatrice in the Earthly Paradise is the foreshadowing of the revelation of God with which the *Divine Comedy* closes.

Carroll, *op. cit.*, p. 433: 'The gender of Benedictus is, of course, a difficulty; but it would have sounded unnatural to change words so familiar. On the other hand, it is scarcely conceivable that Dante, as some think, would be guilty of the irreverence of applying them to himself . . .'

The masculine termination of this word remains a problem. Professor Singleton uses it as the clinching argument in his case that by this point in the poem Beatrice = Christ.

Dorothy Sayers (*Purgatory,* p. 32) indirectly suggests another solution.

. . . Dante was nurtured upon the poetic doctrine of Courtly Love. That doctrine . . . was a devotion—part amorous and part worshipful—to a particular lady who in rank and culture was your acknowledged superior, and who was addressed normally as "madonna," but frequently also, among those Provençal poets with whom the cult started, by the masculine title "midons—my liege."

In her notes on this passage (*op. cit.*, pp. 311-2), Miss Sayers identifies Beatrice, in the allegory of the pageant, with the 'Image of the Holy Host,' and then with Christ.

12. We have just had, at 30.2 and 30.48, quotations from the *Aeneid,* as though to emphasize the poetic guidance of Virgil which is so soon to end.

Even in the deep grief of Virgil's departure there is clear vision of poetic relationships: in the 'dew' and 'dark' and 'tears' there is a reminder not so much of *Purg.* 1 as of the remnants of Hell with which the pilgrim had entered Purgatory.

From a student's paper: at the disappearance of Virgil—'But the thought of abandoning a dear friend is much harder to withstand than the mere exchange of Reason for Revelation.'

CHAPTER THIRTEEN

1. We learn in the *Paradiso* that memory of sins has not completely faded from the souls in a state of bliss: in Augustine's distinction sin is remembered intellectually but forgotten as experience. See *Par.* 9.103-8.

2. It is hard to believe that Dante, in this section of his poem, did not have in mind the reproach delivered by Boethius' Lady Philosophy. This is a reproach for having deserted philosophy for poetry, while Beatrice's reproach is (probably) for having forsaken a higher kind of poetry for a lower, but there are striking parallels in the two episodes.

In fact, Dante may well have meant his readers, who would surely know the passage from the *Consolation,* to set the two works together to arrive at an induction: there is a kind of poetry that, as a man matures, must be set aside in favor of philosophy; beyond this, however, is another kind of poetry that embraces and transcends philosophy itself. This is the course of Dante's development as we have followed it in this canticle.

Boethius in Book One of the *Consolation of Philosophy* (translated by W. V. Cooper), first describes the Lady Philosophy as she appears to him, alone and sick, in prison:

> There appeared standing over my head a woman's form, whose countenance was full of majesty, whose eyes shone as with fire and in power of insight surpassed the eyes of men, whose colour was full of life, whose strength was yet intact though she was so full of years that none would ever think that she was subject to such age as ours.

Then the reproach:

> When she saw that the Muses of poetry were present by my couch giving words to my lamenting, she was stirred a while; her eyes flashed fiercely, and said she, 'Who has suffered these seducing mummers to approach this sick man? Never do they support those in sorrow by any healing remedies, but rather do ever foster the sorrow by poisonous sweets. These are they who stifle the fruit-bearing harvest of reason with the barren briars of the passions: they free not the minds of men from disease, but accustom them thereto. I would think it less grievous if your allurements drew away from me some uninitiated man, as happens in the vulgar herd. In such an one my labours would be naught harmed, but this man has been nourished in the lore of

Eleatics and Academics; and to him have ye reached? Away with you, Sirens, seductive unto destruction! leave him to my Muses to be cared for and to be healed.'

Another passage from the *Consolation* is worth quoting as indicating a possible source for the concept and plan of the *Commedia.* Both the desperate situation of Boethius and the method of his redemption as outlined by the Lady seem strikingly parallel with the pilgrim in the dark wood and the means devised by the noble Lady to bring about his salvation. This is at the end of Book One; the first speaker is the Lady:

'. . . tell me, do you remember what is the aim and end of all things? What the object to which all nature tends?'

'I have heard indeed, but grief has blunted my memory.'

'But do you not somehow know whence all things have their source?'

'Yes,' I said; 'that source is God.

'Is it possible that you, who know the beginning of all things, should not know their end? But such are the ways of these distractions, such is their power, that though they can move a man's position, they cannot pluck him from himself or wrench him from his roots. But this question would I have you answer: do you remember that you are a man?'

'How can I but remember that?'

'Can you then say what is a man?'

'Need you ask? I know that he is an animal, reasoning and mortal; that I know, and that I confess myself to be.'

'Know you naught else that you are?' asked Philosophy.

'Naught,' said I.

'Now,' said she, 'I know the cause, or the chief cause, of your sickness. You have forgotten what you are. Now therefore I have found out to the full the manner of your sickness, and how to attempt the restoring of your health. You are overwhelmed by this forgetfulness of yourself: hence you have been thus sorrowing that you are exiled and robbed of all your possessions. You do not know the aim and end of all things; hence you think that if men are worthless and wicked, they are powerful and fortunate. You have forgotten by what methods the universe is guided; hence you think that the chances of good and bad fortune are tossed about with no ruling hand. These things may lead not to disease only, but even to death as well. But let us thank the Giver of all health, that your nature has not altogether left you. We have yet the chief spark for your health's fire, for you have a true knowledge of the hand that guides the universe: you do believe that its government is not subject to random chance, but to divine reason. Therefore have no fear. From this tiny spark the fire of life shall forthwith shine upon you.'

3. Miss Sayers (*Purg.*, p. 36) picks up this point of the pilgrim's education:

But if we pursue our researches into the *Paradiso* we find that Beatrice shows no desire to possess Dante: she takes him with one hand only to give him away with the other. . . . When she has completed her work for her lover, she quietly hands him over to St. Bernard, herself returning to her own joy in everlasting contemplation of the 'Eternal Fountain.' She is not the heavenly mother, nor even the heavenly mistress, so much as—and this figure also is Dante's [*Par.* 25.64]—the heavenly schoolmistress, who having seen her pupil safely through his examination, goes on her way rejoicing. She looses him into freedom—even from herself—and he is willing to be set free.

Father Walsh, *op. cit.*, p. 95, discusses the theology of Dante's confession:

Thereupon with symbols that may or may not have any personal applications to the historical Dante's moral failings, 'Dante' makes an act of perfect contrition, a full confession of sins, and a sincere purpose of amendment.

The confession is too drawn out for lyrical poetry. If this were a meeting of the real Dante and the real Beatrice the scene would be slightly ridiculous. But the psychology of repentance is admirably analyzed; and the theology of the *contritio cordis,* the *confessio oris,* the *satisfactio operis* is equal to the psychology.

4. Carroll, *op. cit.*, pp. 452-5, summarizes the problem of Dante's fall:

We come now to one of the most hotly disputed questions in the *Commedia,* the exact nature of Dante's unfaithfulness. Setting aside minor variations, the theories reduce themselves to two—devotion to Philosophy to the neglect of Theology and a fall into an immoral course of life. There is really no reason why these should be pitted against each other as if they were mutually exclusive. It seems to me quite certain that Dante meant to confess both, when he speaks of 'the present things,' and 'false pleasures,' and 'things deceptive.' . . .

The advocates of the philosophical theory are usually indignant with those who see in this passage the confession of a moral lapse. The reason is that far too much emphasis is laid by both sides on the 'pargoletta,' the 'little girl,' of line 59. All sorts of identifications have gathered round her: Beatrice herself, Gemma Donati, the poet's wife, the Gentucca of Canto XXIV, the Donna Pietosa of the *Vita Nuova,* the Pietra of the Canzoni commonly known by that name. . . .

The conclusion, then, to which his own statements lead us, is that his unfaithfulness to Beatrice was twofold—intellectual and moral. . . . His confession here on the Mountaintop is not a new one, distinct and separate from that of the various Terraces; it is simply the clear recognition of his memory, as it reviews the course of his life, that the fountain-head of all his errors, intellectual and moral alike, had been unfaithfulness to Beatrice and to the ideal of which she was the Divine Revelation.

Denton J. Snider, in *Dante's Purgatorio and Paradiso,* p. 368, thus comments on Dante's offense against Beatrice:

Now Dante has sinned against this idea of Beatrice in two ways: in thought and in deed. He followed a new school, he probably leaned toward Averrhoism which denied the infinite nature of man—individual immortality—and so denied the whole foundation of man's redemption and purification. Thus he undermined the basis of this Purgatory, and we see that the sin against Beatrice is the universal sin, not a special one here punished, but the sin against Purgatory itself as a whole, as a process. Man's infinite nature denied and there is no purgation.

Such is the sin in thought, the sin in deed is the sensuous life corresponding.

5. The word translated 'splendor'—*isplendor*—is used by Dante in a specific sense, as he explains it at *Convivio* III, 14:

The custom of the philosophers is to call Heaven *light* insofar as it exists in its primal fountain; to call it a *ray* insofar as it exists in the medium between its source and the first body by which it is caught; and to call it a *splendor* insofar as it is thrown back on some other object which it illuminates.

'Splendor,' then, is not direct light from God but light reflected by a prime receiver of God's light.

6. In the course of the journey through Paradise the pilgrim becomes able to sustain the glory of Beatrice's smile. In the brilliant passage in which this episode is narrated (*Par.* 23.46-75) there is a notable assemblage of the various images of poetry that we have been pursuing: the 'book that records the past' (recalling the book of the beginning of the *Vita Nuova*); the idea of figure (line 61); the intercepted pathway (line 63); the little boat on its voyage (line 67); and the fair garden (line 72). We are also told that the sacred poem, in order to figure forth Paradise, must make a leap—*saltar,* as in the saltatory development we have spoken about.

CHAPTER FOURTEEN

1. Perhaps a collateral source of Dante's bow-and-arrow imagery is in Aquinas' use of this image to denote the good control exerted by a higher over a lower being:

Now if a thing cannot attain to something by the power of its nature, it must be directed thereto by another; thus, an arrow is directed by an archer towards a mark. Hence, properly speaking, a rational creature, capable of eternal life, is led towards it, directed, as it were, by God.—*Summa Theol.*, I, 23, 1. (Pegis.)

2. The imagery in the tercet preceding the arrow-flights and the murmur of 'Adam' supports this notion of the rolling-back of time; 32.31-3:

> *So in our pacing the high woods, empty*
> *by the fault of her who believed the serpent,*
> *a song of angels kept time with our steps.*

The woods (*selva*), Eve and the serpent, the song of angels, the pacing —here are Inferno, Purgatory, and Paradise, with the movement kept in order by the angel's song.

3. Kenelm Foster (in '*God's Tree*') says, p. 29: 'For while the Empire, like the Church, presupposes Original Sin, the tree does not. Dante's tree, at least under one aspect, means something older than sin.'

And, p. 32:

I take [the tree] then as a symbol, primarily, of the moral order of the cosmos viewed in relation to man, and especially to the two chief and, so to say, typical sins of man: the sins of Adam and of Christendom, of man pre-Christian and post-Christian. The first sin is only recalled here as a memory; the second is enacted allegorically in the horrors of canto XXXII, culminating in the frightful kissing and conflict of the harlot and her *drudo*.

It is obviously a social breakdown that is enacted, a breakdown therefore of justice. It is less obvious that the first sin, the sin of Adam, was injustice precisely. . . . But how precisely was Adam unjust?

. . . Adam's sin was at once an act of disobedience, as a flouting of the divine will, and an act of injustice as a violation of the order which derives as *jus* from the divine unity.

4. This episode too arouses some questions which, in the terms I have been using, might be thus phrased: assuming that this may be the Cru-

cifixion and Ascension which even primal, pre-sinful man finds too awesome and too mysterious to witness; assuming that Dante may now be completely himself, no longer separated into pilgrim and poet—

1. What has Dante become after seeing the dual nature of the griffon?
2. Who is now watching the pageant? Can he be asleep and watch it at the same time?
3. Why is the Crucifixion not to be seen by him?
4. Why is it Matelda who tends him?
5. What, in short, is the nature and what is the history of the Dante who is being readied to see, understand, and inscribe the pageant of the Church?

5. 32.127-9:

And, as coming from a heart that sorrows,
such a voice came from heaven, and spoke thus:
'O my little boat, how ill art thou laden.'

This is a car, a chariot, but still—when its burden is to be spoken of—it can become a *navicella,* a 'little boat,' and carry us back to the beginning of *Purgatory,* to the 'little vessel of my mind' and to the angel's boat—both better laden than this one.

6. In *Inferno* 19 among the simoniacs, Pope Nicholas III mistakes the pilgrim for his own successor, Boniface VIII, and says:

'Are you so quickly sated with that wealth
for which you did not fear to seize by deceit
the beautiful lady, and then make an affront of her?'

This transformation of the 'beautiful lady' (the Church) probably accounts for the harlot in the chariot; the confusion—however it is to be explained—between Boniface and the pilgrim may cast some light on the harlot's roving eye flirting with the pilgrim.

This beast of *Revelation* is presented in a peculiarly altered fashion in this same scene (at *Inf.* 19.106-11), as *Revelation* is heavily drawn from in the entire episode of the pageant in the Earthly Paradise.

Some aspects of Dante's relation to the Church (a relation other than that to the beliefs of the Church) may be mentioned. The significant passages in *Purgatory* are at 3.141, 4.129, 5.70, 8.71, and 13.117.

The article by Lilli Sertorius, 'Dante und die Kirche' (*Romanische*

Forschungen 60.500-35), is a good summary of the question. She points out, for example, that in his writings Dante 'calls the Church by all the names used by the orthodox: *Ecclesia militans, milizia santa, Mater Ecclesia, Mater et Virgo, Sposa e Secretaria, Sponsa Christi, Sposa de Dio,* and *Sposa di Cristo.*'

She thus interprets the dragging-off of the chariot (pp. 532-3):

> What happens at the end of the fission in the earthly paradise . . . does not mean that the Church of Christ is immediately coming to its end; it must mean something else. And that is connected with the fact that the cart represents the Church but not the whole Church; it symbolises only the eternal institution—otherwise the expression *currus sponsae* in the Letter to the Cardinals has no meaning. This expression *currus sponsae* stands next to another—*sedes sponsae: sede sponsae, quae Roma est* (*Ep.* VIII, 11). The Bride, the Church in her innermost essence, has a seat, Rome, and a chariot, her external form. This chariot can err, as the Letter puts it, can be drawn from its right path.

Finally, one interpretation of the ten steps of 33.17 is that they represent the ten years after the beginning of the Papacy at Avignon, the Babylonian Captivity—when Dante was to write the *Commedia.*

Bibliography

This bibliography is a selection from the works I have found useful in writing this book. Those marked with an asterisk have been especially useful.

Allegherus, Petrus. *Super Dantis ipsius genitoris Comoediam Commentarium*. Firenze, 1845.

Anglade, Joseph. *Les Troubadours de Toulouse*. Paris, 1928.

Aquinas, St. Thomas. *Basic Writings of St. Thomas Aquinas,* ed. Anton C. Pegis. 2 vols. New York, 1945.*

——*St. Thomas Aquinas: Philosophical Texts,* trans. Thomas Gilby. London, 1951.*

——*St. Thomas Aquinas: Theological Texts,* trans. Thomas Gilby. London, 1955.* These two works by Father Gilby are perhaps the best direct introduction to the style and thought of Aquinas.

——*The Political Ideas of St. Thomas Aquinas,* ed. with introduction by Dino Bigongiari. New York, 1953.

Aroux, E. *Dante hérétique, révolutionnaire et socialiste.* Paris, 1853 (reprinted 1939).

Auerbach, Erich. *Dante als Dichter der irdischen Welt.* Berlin, 1929.*

——*Neue Dantesstudien: Sacrae Scripturae Sermo Humilis; Figura; Franz von Assisi in der Komödie.* Istanbul, 1944.

——*Mimesis: The Representation of Reality in Western Literature,* trans. Willard R. Trask. Princeton, 1953.

Augustine. *The Confessions of St. Augustine,* Books I-X, trans. F. J. Sheed. New York, 1942.

Barbi, Michele. *Della fortuna di Dante nel secolo XVI.* Pisa, 1890.

——*Problemi di critica dantesca.* Prima serie (1893-1918). Firenze, 1934. Seconda serie (1920-37). Firenze, 1941.*

——*Life of Dante,* trans. Paul G. Ruggiers. Berkeley, 1954.

Belperron, Pierre. *La "joie d'amour"; contribution à l'étude des troubadours et de l'amour courtois.* Paris, 1948.*

Biondolillo, Francesco. *Dante Creatore del Dolce Stil Nuovo.* Palermo, 1937.
——— *Poetica e Poesia di Dante.* Messina, 1948.
Bird, Otto. 'The Canzone d'Amore of Cavalcanti According to the Commentary of Dino del Garbo,' in *Med. Studies* II, 150-203; and III, 117-60.*
Botticelli, Sandro. *Drawings for Dante's Divina Commedia.* Intro. and comm. by F. Lippmann. London, 1896.
Bowden, John Paul. *An Analysis of Pietro Alighieri's Commentary on the Divine Comedy.* New York, 1951.
Busnelli, Giovanni. *La Concezione del Purgatorio dantesco.* Roma, 1906.
Butler, A. J. *Dante, His Times and His Work.* London, 1895.
Calcaterra, C. 'I drammi dottrinali nella figurazioni della Divina Commedia,' *Convivium* X, 610 sqq.
Capellanus, Andreas. *De arte honeste amandi,* ed. Trojel. Hauniae, 1892.
——— *The Art of Courtly Love,* trans. John Jay Parry. New York, 1941.
Capetti, Vittorio. *Illustrazioni al poema di Dante.* Città di Castello, 1913.
Caplan, Harry. 'The Four Senses of Scriptural Interpretation and the Medieval Theory of Preaching,' *Speculum* IV, 282-90.
Carducci, Giosuè. *Dante's Work,* trans. Gina D. Frati. Lucca, 1923.
Carlini, Armando. *Del Sistema Filosofico Dantesco nella Divina Commedia.* Bologna, 1902.
Carroll, John S. *Prisoners of Hope: An Exposition of Dante's Purgatorio.* London, 1906.*
Carter, B. B. 'Dante's Political Ideas,' *Review of Politics* V, 339-55.
Chaytor, H. J. *The Troubadours.* Cambridge, 1912.
Chioccioni, P. Pietro. *L'Agostinismo nella Divina Commedia.* Firenze, 1952.*
Church, R. W. *Dante and Other Essays.* London, 1897.
Ciafardini, Emanuele. *Problemi di Critica dantesca.* Napoli, 1948.
Coli, Edoardo. *Il paradiso terrestre dantesco.* Firenze, 1897.*

Cosmo, Umberto. *A Handbook to Dante Studies,* trans. David Moore. Oxford, 1950.

——— *Con Dante attraverso il Seicento*. Bari, 1946.

Cossio, Aluigi. *Teoria dell'arte e della bellezza in Dante*. Ravenna, 1921.

Cross, Tom Peete and William A. Nitze. *Lancelot and Guenevere: A Study on the Origins of Courtly Love*. Chicago, 1930.

Curtius, Ernst Robert. *European Literature and the Latin Middle Ages,* trans. Willard R. Trask. New York, 1953.*

Curto, Carlo. *Le Tre Donne Benedette nella Commedia di Dante*. Bologna, 1925.

Dante. *Tutte le opere di Dante Alighieri*—the Oxford Dante, ed. E. Moore. Oxford, 1904.

——— *The Works of Dante Alighieri*. Temple Classics Edition, 5 vols. London, 1900—. Perhaps the most useful text-with-translation.*

——— *The Divine Comedy,* trans. H. R. Huse. New York, 1954.

de Choiseul, Comtesse Horace. *Dante—Le Purgatoire*. Paris, 1911.

del Lungo, Isidoro. *La figurazione storica del medio evo italiano nel poema di Dante*. Firenze, 1891.*

del Monte, Alberto. *La Poesia Popolare nel Tempo e nella Coscienza di Dante*. Bari, 1949.

Denomy, Alexander Joseph. *The Heresy of Courtly Love*. New York, 1947.*

——— 'Courtly Love and Courtliness,' *Speculum* XXVIII, 44-63.*

——— 'An Inquiry into the Origins of Courtly Love,' in *Med. Studies* VI, 175-260.*

——— 'The De Amore of Andreas Capellanus and the Condemnation of 1277,' in *Med. Studies* VIII, 107-49.*

——— 'Concerning the Accessibility of Arabic Influences to the Earliest Provençal Troubadours,' in *Med. Studies* XV, 147-58.

De Salvio, Alfonso. *Dante and Heresy*. Boston, 1936.

de Sanctis, G. B. *Dante*. Perugia, 1950.

de Wulf, Maurice. *Philosophy and Civilization in the Middle Ages*. New York, 1953.*

Dinsmore, C. A. *The Teachings of Dante*. Boston, 1901.

Dinsmore, C. A. *Aids to the Study of Dante*. Boston, 1903.*
di Pino, Guido. *La Figurazioni della Luce nella Divina Commedia*. Firenze, 1952.
d'Ovidio, Francesco. *Dante e la filosofia de linguaggio*. Naples, 1892.
——*Nuovi Studii Danteschi; Il Purgatorio e il suo Preludio*. Milano, 1906.*
Duhem, Pierre. *Le Système du Monde,* 5 vols. Paris, 1913-7.
Dunbar, H. Flanders. *Symbolism in Medieval Thought and its Consummation in the Divine Comedy*. New Haven, 1929.*
Dupin, Henri. *La Courtoisie au moyen âge*. Paris, 1931.
Eliot, T. S. *Selected Essays*. New York, 1950.
Faithfull, R. Glynn. 'The Esoteric Interpretation of Dante,' *Italica* XXVII, 82-7.
Farnell, Ida. *The Lives of the Troubadours*. London, 1896.
Fauriel, Claude Charles. *Dante et les origines de la langue et de la littérature italiennes,* 2 vols. Paris, 1854.
——*History of Provençal Poetry,* trans. G. J. Adler. New York, 1860.
Federn, Karl. *Dante und seine Zeit*. Stuttgart, 1921.*
Fergusson, Francis. *Dante's Drama of the Mind*. Princeton, 1953.
Ferretti, Giovanni. *I Due Tempi delle Composizione delle Divina Commedia*. Bari, 1935.
Filomusi-Guelfi, Lorenzo. *Studii su Dante*. Citta di Castello, 1908.*
Fisher, Lizette Andrews. *The Mystic Vision in the Grail Legend and in the Divine Comedy*. New York, 1917.
Flamini, Francesco. *Introduction to the Study of the Divine Comedy*. Boston, 1910.
Fletcher, Jefferson Butler. *Dante*. New York, 1916.
——*Symbolism of the Divine Comedy*. New York, 1921.
Foster, Kenelm. 'God's Tree' (Purgatorio XXXII-XXXIII), *Italian Studies* VII, 24-35.
Friederich, Werner P. *Dante's Fame Abroad, 1350-1850*. Rome, 1950.
Gardner, Edmund G. *Dante's Ten Heavens*. London, 1904.
——*Dante and the Mystics*. London, 1913.*
——*Dante*. New York, 1923.*

Gere, Robert Harlan. "The Troubadours, Heresy, and the Albigensian Crusade." Unpublished thesis, Columbia University, 1955.
Gilbert, Allan H. *Dante's Conception of Justice*. Durham, N.C., 1925.
Gilson, Étienne. *The Mystical Theology of Saint Bernard*, trans. A. H. C. Downes. New York, 1940.
——— *Dante the Philosopher*, trans. David Moore. London, 1948.*
——— *History of Christian Philosophy in the Middle Ages*. New York, 1955.*
Gorra, Egidio. *Delle Origini della Poesia del Medio Evo*. Torino, 1895.
——— *Il soggettivismo di Dante*. Bologna, 1899.
Graf, Arturo. *Miti, leggende e superstizioni del medio evo*, 2 vols. Torino, 1892-3.*
Grandgent, Charles H. *Dante Alighieri—La Divina Commedia*—text, edited and annotated. Boston, 1913.*
——— *The Power of Dante*. Boston, 1918.
——— *Dante*. New York, 1921.*
——— *Discourses on Dante*. Cambridge, 1924.
Griffin, A. K. *Aristotle's Psychology of Conduct*. London, 1931.
Gunn, Alan M. F. *The Mirror of Love—A Reinterpretation of 'The Romance of the Rose.'* Lubbock, Texas, 1952.
Haller, Johannes. *Dichter und Mensch*. Basel, 1954.
Harris, W. T. *The Spiritual Sense of the Divine Comedy*. New York, 1889.
Haskins, Charles Homer. *Studies in the History of Medieval Science*. Cambridge, 1927.
Hatzfeld, Helmut. *Dante, seine Weltanschauung*. München, 1921.*
——— 'The Art of Dante's Purgatorio,' *Studies in Philology* XLIX, 25-47.*
Hauvette, H. *Études sur la Divine Comédie*. Paris, 1922.*
Hawkins, D. J. B. *A Sketch of Mediaeval Philosophy*. New York, 1949.
Henderson, Henry F. *With Dante on the Mountain—A Guide through the Circles of the Purgatorio*. Cincinnati, 1910.

Hettinger, Franz. *Dante's Divina Commedia; Its Scope and Value,* trans. Henry Sebastian Bowden. London, 1887.*

Hill, Raymond Thompson and Thomas Goddard Bergin. *Anthology of the Provençal Troubadours.* New Haven, 1941.

Hopper, Vincent F. *Medieval Number Symbolism; Its Sources, Meaning, and Influence on Thought and Expression.* New York, 1938.

Jeanroy, Alfred. *La Poésie lyrique des Troubadours.* Toulouse, 1934.*

——*Les origines de la poésie lyrique en France au moyen âge.* Paris, 1926.

Jourdain, E. F. *Le symbolisme dans la Divine Comédie.* Oxford, 1904.

Kuhns, L. Oscar. *The Treatment of Nature in Dante's Divine Comedy.* London, 1897.

Laistner, M. L. W. *Thought and Letters in Western Europe, A.D. 500 to 900.* London, 1931.

La Piana, Angelina. *Dante's American Pilgrimage.* New York, 1948.*

La Piana, George. 'Joachim of Flora: A Critical Study,' *Speculum* VII, 257-82.

Leclerc, Joseph. *The Two Sovereignties.* London, 1952.

Leclère, Albert. *Le mysticisme catholique et l'âme de Dante.* Paris, 1906.

Leigh, Gertrude. *A Study in the Heterodoxy of Dante.* London, 1932.

Lenkeith, Nancy. *Dante and the Legend of Rome.* London, 1952

Leo, Ulrich. 'Dante's Way through Earthly Paradise,' *Italica* XXIV, 277-303.

——'The Unfinished Convivio and Dante's Rereading of the Aeneid,' in *Med. Studies* XIII, 41-64.

Lewis, C. S. *The Allegory of Love.* London, 1953.

Leynardi, Luigi. *La Psicologia dell'Arte nella Divina Commedia.* Torino, 1894.

Lind, L. R. *Lyric Poetry of the Italian Renaissance.* An anthology with verse translations. New Haven, 1954.

Lipari, Angelo. *The Dolce Stil Nuovo, according to Lorenzo de'Medici.* New Haven, 1936.
Lowell, James Russell. *Among My Books,* second series. Boston, 1876.
MacCulloch, J. A. *Medieval Faith and Fable.* London, 1931.
Maggini, Francesco. *Introduzione allo Studio di Dante.* Bari, 1948.
Mandonnet, Pierre. *Siger de Brabant et l'Averroisme.* Louvain, 1911.
——— *Dante le théologien; Introduction à l'intelligence de la vie, des œuvres et de l'art de Dante Alighieri.* Paris, 1935.
Masseron, Alexandre. *Dante—La Divine Comédie—Purgatoire.* (Traduction, Introduction et Notes.) Paris, 1945.*
——— *Dante et Saint Bernard.* Paris, 1953.*
Mattalìa, Daniele. *La Critica Dantesca.* Firenze, 1950.
Méautis, Georges. *Dante—L'Antepurgatoire—Essai d'une explication.* Genève, 1944.
Mellone, Sydney Herbert. *Western Christian Thought in the Middle Ages.* Edinburgh, 1935.*
Misciatelli, Piero. *Dante poeta d'amore.* Milano, 1922.
Momigliano, Attilio. *Dante, Manzoni, Verga.* Messina, 1944.
Monahan, M. Grace. 'Dante's perception of the soul's purgation,' *Ursuline Tradition and Progress* IV, 23-40.*
Moore, Edward. *Studies in Dante.* First, Second, Third, and Fourth Series—4 vols. Oxford, 1896-1917.
——— *Dante and His Early Biographers.* London, 1890.
Mott, Lewis Freeman. *The system of Courtly Love studied as an introduction to the Vita Nuova of Dante.* Boston, 1896.
Nardi, Bruno. *Dante et la cultura medievale.* Bari, 1949.
Naumann, Walter. 'Hunger und Durst als Metaphern bei Dante,' *Romanische Forschungen* LIV, 13-36.
Oliviero, Federico. *The Representation of the Image in Dante.* Torino, 1936.
Olschki, Leonardo. *The Genius of Italy.* Ithaca, New York, 1954.*
Orr, M. A. *Dante and the Early Astronomers.* London, 1913.*
Ozanam, Fredéric. *Dante and Catholic Philosophy in the 13th Century,* trans. Lucia D. Pychowska. New York, 1897.

Pacheu, Jules. *De Dante à Verlaine (études d'idéalistes et mystiques)*. Paris, 1897.
——— *Psychologie des mystiques Chrétiens; les faits; le poème de la conscience; Dante et les mystiques*. Paris, 1909.
Palgen, Rudolf. *Das mittelalterliche Gesicht der Göttlichen Komödie*. Heidelberg, 1935.
——— *Ursprung und Aufbau der Komödie Dantes*. Graz, 1953.
Pascoli, Giovanni. *La Mirabile Visione*. Messina, 1902.*
Passerin d'Entreves, Alessandro. *Dante as a Political Thinker*. Oxford, 1952.
Patch, H. R. *The Tradition of Boethius*. A Study of His Importance in Medieval Culture. New York, 1935.
Perez, Francesco. *La Beatrice Svelata*. Palermo, 1897.
Piccioli, Giuseppe. *Matelda—studio dantesco*. Bologna, 1902.
Pietrobono, L. *Il poema sacro. Saggio d'una interpretazione generale della Divina Commedia,* 2 vols. Bologna, 1915.*
——— *Dal Centro al Cerchio—La Struttura Morale delle Divina Commedia*. Torino, 1923.
——— 'Virgilio, L'Impero e il di là,' *Studi su Dante* VII, 73-108.
Ragusa, T. *Studio critico sul Catone Dantesco*. Prato, 1898.
Rajna, Pio. 'La genesi della Divina Commedia,' *Vita italiana nel trecento* II, 225-68.
Renaudet, Augustin. *Dante, humaniste*. Paris, 1952.
Resta de Robertis, Raffaele. *Dante e la filosofia dell'amore*. Bologna, 1935.
Rizzi, Fortunato. *Un Personaggio Singolare nella "Divina Commedia." (Dante discepolo)*. Milano, 1947.
Rolbiecki, John Joseph. *The Political Philosophy of Dante Alighieri*. Washington, D.C., 1921.
Rossetti, Dante Gabriel. *Poems and Translations, including Dante's "Vita Nuova" and "The Early Italian Poets."* London (Everyman's Library), n.d.
Rossetti, Gabriele. *La Beatrice di Dante*. Imola, 1935.
Rossetti, Maria Francesca. *A Shadow of Dante*. London, 1901.
Rossi, Mario. *Gusto Filologico e Gusto Poetico—Questioni di Critica Dantesca*. Bari, 1942.

Rowbotham, John Frederick. *The Troubadours and Courts of Love.* London, 1895.
Ruskin, John. *Comments of John Ruskin on the Divine Comedy,* compiled by George P. Huntington. Boston, 1903.
Sacchetto, Aleardo. *Il Gioco delle Imagini in Dante.* Firenze, 1947.
St. Clair, George. *Dante Viewed Through His Imagery.* Albuquerque, N.M., 1935.
Sainte-Palaye, Jean Baptiste de Curne de. *Histoire litteraire des troubadours,* 3 vols. Paris, 1774.
Sannia, Enrico. *Il comico, l'umorismo e la satira nella Divina Commedia.* 2 vols. Milano, 1909.
Santangelo, Salvatore. *Dante e i trovatori provenzali.* Catania, 1921.*
Santi, Antonio. *L'ordinamento morale e l'allegoria della Divina Commedia,* 2 vols. Milano, 1923-24.
Sayers, Dorothy L. *The Comedy of Dante Alighieri The Florentine* —Cantica I: Hell. (1949.) Cantica II: Purgatory. (1955.) Harmondsworth (Penguin Classics).
——— *Introductory Papers on Dante.* London, 1954.
Scartazzini, G. A. *Dantologia—Vita ed Opere di Dante Alighieri.* Milano, 1894.
——— *Enciclopedia Dantesca,* 2 vols. Milano, 1896-8.*
——— *Concordanza della Divina Commedia di Dante Alighieri.* Leipzig, 1901.
——— *La Divina Commedia, Testo Critico Riveduto, col Commento Scartazziniano,* Rifato de Giuseppe Vandelli. Milano, 1938.
Schneider, Friedrich. *Dante: Sein Leben und sein Werk.* Weimar, 1947.
Shaw, J. E. 'Dante and Bonagiunta,' *Annual Rep. Dante Soc.* (1936), pp. 1-18.
——— *Essays on the Vita Nuova.* Princeton, 1929.
Silverstein, H. Theodore. *Dante and Virgil the Mystic.* Cambridge, 1932.
Singleton, Charles S. *An Essay on the Vita Nuova.* Cambridge, 1949.*
——— *Commedia—Elements of Structure.* Cambridge, 1954.*

Smith, James Robinson. *The Earliest Lives of Dante,* trans. from the Italian of Giovanni Boccaccio and Lionardo Bruni Aretino. New York, 1901.

Smith, Justin H. *The Troubadours at Home: Their Lives and Personalities, Their Songs and Their World,* 2 vols. New York, 1899.

Snider, D. J. *Dante's Purgatorio and Paradiso.* A commentary. St. Louis, Mo., 1893.

Spitzer, Leo. 'The Addresses to the Reader in the "Commedia,"' *Italica* XXXII, 143-65.

Spoerri, Theophil. *Einführung in die Göttliche Komödie.* Zürich, 1946.

Symonds, John Addington. *An Introduction to the Study of Dante.* Edinburgh, 1890.

Thayer, William R. *Italica: Studies in Italian Life and Literature.* Boston, 1908.

Thorndike, Lynn. *A History of Magic and Experimental Science,* 6 vols. New York, 1923-41.

Tomlinson, Charles. *Dante, Beatrice, and the Divine Comedy.* London, 1894.

Tondelli, L. *Il Libro delle Figure dell'abate Giocchino de Fiore,* 2 vols. Torino, 1940.

Toynbee, Paget Jackson. *Dante Alighieri, His Life and Works.* New York, 1910.

——— *Concise Dictionary of Proper Names and Notable Matters in the Works of Dante.* Oxford, 1914.*

——— *Dante Studies.* Oxford, 1921.

Tozer, H. F. *An English Commentary on Dante's Divina Commedia.* Oxford, 1901.

Tròccoli, Giuseppe. *Il Purgatorio Dantesco.* Firenze, 1951.*

Valli, Luigi. *L'allegoria di Dante secondo G. Pascoli.* Bologna, 1922.

——— 'Il simbolo centrale della "Divina Commedia": La Croce e l'Aquila,' *Il Giornale dantesco* XXIV, 11-30.

——— *La Chiave della Divina Commedia. Sintesi del Simbolismo della Croce e dell'aquila.* Bologna, 1925.

——— *La struttura morale dell'universo dantesco.* Roma, 1935.

Vallone, Aldo. *La Critica Dantesca Contemporanea.* Pisa, 1953.

van Heel, Wilhelm Heilermann. 'Der Bergsteiger Dante,' *Stud. Dant.* XIV, 82-99.

Vento, Sebastiano. *La prima allegoria del poema dantesco.* Palermo, 1926.

Vernon, W. W. *Readings on the Purgatorio,* 2 vols. New York, 1907.

Viscardi, Antonio. 'Il Catone dantesco e l'idea imperiale della "Commedia,"' *Il Giornale dantesco* XXVII, 271-4.

Vittorini, Domenico. 'Dante e il concetto d'amore,' *Symposium* V, 22-37.*

von Falkenhausen, Friedrich F. *Dante.* Berlin, 1951.

Vossler, Karl. *Die Göttliche Komödie,* trans. as *Medieval Culture —An Introduction to Dante and his Times,* trans. William C. Lawton, 2 vols. London, 1929.

——— *Die philosophischen Grundlagen zum "süssen neuen stil," des Guido Guinicelli, Guido Cavalcanti, und Dante Alighieri.* Heidelberg, 1904.

Walsh, Gerald G. *Dante Alighieri, Citizen of Christendom.* Milwaukee, Wis., 1946.

——— 'Dante's Matelda,' *Thought* XII, 78-101.

Wicksteed, Philip H. *Dante and Aquinas,* London, 1913.*

——— *From Vita Nuova to Paradiso.* Manchester, 1922.*

Wilkins, Ernest H. 'The Prologue of the Divine Comedy,' *Annual Rep. Dant. Soc.* (1926), pp. 1-7.

Williams, Charles. *The Figure of Beatrice.* London, 1943.

Witte, Karl. *Essays on Dante.* Selected, trans. and ed. by C. Mabel Lawrence and Philip H. Wicksteed. London, 1898.

Zingarelli, Nicolo. *La Vita, i Tempi e le Opere di Dante,* 2 vols. Milano, 1931.

Index

Proper names and selected subjects are here indexed. References to Dante, *Commedia,* and Purgatory have not been included; references to Virgil in chapters 2 through 14 have not been included.